The Last Great Strike

The Last Great Strike

LITTLE STEEL, THE CIO, AND
THE STRUGGLE FOR LABOR RIGHTS
IN NEW DEAL AMERICA

Ahmed White

UNIVERSITY OF CALIFORNIA PRESS

University of California Press, one of the most distinguished university presses in the United States, enriches lives around the world by advancing scholarship in the humanities, social sciences, and natural sciences. Its activities are supported by the UC Press Foundation and by philanthropic contributions from individuals and institutions. For more information, visit www.ucpress.edu.

University of California Press
Oakland, California

Library of Congress Cataloging-in-Publication Data

White, Ahmed, 1970–.
    The last great strike : Little Steel, the CIO, and the struggle for labor rights in New Deal America / Ahmed White.
        p.   cm.
    Includes bibliographical references and index.
    ISBN 978–0-520–28560–6 (cloth : alk. paper)
    ISBN 978–0-520–28561–3 (pbk. : alk. paper)
    ISBN 978–0-520–96101–2 (ebook)
    1. Little Steel Strike, U.S., 1937.   2. Iron and steel workers—Labor unions—United States—History—20th century.   3. United States—History—1933–1945.   4. New Deal, 1933–1939.   I. Title.
    HD5384.I521937 W45   2016
    331.892'86910973090043—dc23

                                                            2015018714

Manufactured in the United States of America

24   23   22   21   20   19   18   17   16
10   9   8   7   6   5   4   3   2   1

In keeping with a commitment to support environmentally responsible and sustainable printing practices, UC Press has printed this book on Natures Natural, a fiber that contains 30% post-consumer waste and meets the minimum requirements of ANSI/NISO z39.48–1992 (R 1997) (*Permanence of Paper*).

To my parents, Marion Overton and Doris Morein White,
who taught me so much about the meaning of struggle;
and to the steel workers, whose story of struggle
I am so honored to tell

CONTENTS

ACKNOWLEDGMENTS

I was first enthralled by the story of Little Steel and the CIO seven years ago, while researching other episodes of labor conflict in the New Deal era. Soon convinced that the strike had not received nearly the attention from researchers that it deserved, I set out to write this book. As I suppose is often the case with first-time authors of books like this one, my enthusiasm for the project may have led me to underestimate the challenges that lay ahead. But I was also fortunate, for a number of people and institutions helped me along. It is my pleasure to acknowledge their support in bringing this story to print.

I must stress at the outset how grateful I am to my editor at the University of California Press, Neils Hooper, and his assistant, Bradley Depew, for their faith in this project and their labors in helping to produce a publishable work. I am equally indebted to Kate Hoffman and Julie Van Pelt for their help in editing the manuscript for publication and to the reviewers of this book, most of them still anonymous, who found merit in the manuscript and provided me with useful recommendations and advice. And I am beholden to Cecelia Cancellero for the excellent work she did in preparing the manuscript for review and shepherding it through the process.

Quite a few librarians and archivists aided me in negotiating archival sources and putting together the research on which this book is based. This book would have been impossible without Penn State University's Historical Collections and Labor Archives, an outstanding institution that houses the records of the United Steelworkers of America and its predecessor, the Steel Workers Organizing Committee. My efforts there benefited tremendously from the generosity and expertise of librarians James Quigel Jr. and Barry Kernfeld. Equally important were the collections of government, union, and company records at the Ohio Historical Society, in Columbus, and the Youngstown Historical Center of Industry and Labor. There, too, the librarians and archivists were models of professionalism and patience. I am compelled to give special thanks to Martha Bishop at the Youngstown Historical Center, who very generously accommodated my frenzied schedule at the expense of her own time and convenience. I was similarly favored at the Western Reserve Historical Society in Cleveland, where I was granted access to the records of the Republic Steel Corporation, and at the Chicago Historical Society, home to significant regional union records and important documents pertaining to the strike's deadliest incident. And I received vital, last-minute assistance from the staff of the American Catholic History Research Center and University Archives at Catholic University in Washington, DC.

A number of friends and colleagues, including Emily Calhoun, Kenneth Casebeer, David Hill, Alan Hyde, James Pope, and Pierre Schlag, generously read the entire manuscript and provided me with valuable commentary and constructive criticisms. Ellen Dannin closely and critically reviewed an early introductory section of the manuscript, and Michael Goldfield listened patiently and responded incisively to my descriptions of the project. Jane Thompson, librarian at the University of Colorado School of Law, and her assistant, Matt Zafiratos, gave me crucial research support, especially with respect to securing obscure secondary sources. Nefertari Kirkman-Bey, Marissa McGarrah, Liana Orshan, Hunter Swain, and Tarn Udall, all former students of mine, provided valuable research assistance. Along with my faculty assistants, Nicole Drane and Charlie Bowers, whose unfailingly courteous efforts advanced many aspects of this project, Tarn also exceeded all reasonable expectations in working to secure copyright permissions for the images that illustrate the book.

I wrote this book entirely during my service on the faculty of the University of Colorado School of Law, where, I am happy to say, I found the standard resources more than adequate to cover the costs of research and travel, as well as my own upkeep. Among other advantages, this privileged circumstance spared me the trouble—and, dare I say, contradiction—of seeking financial assistance from corporate entities, or from the foundations, fellowships, and prizes they fund, in order to write this book about class struggle and the dangers of corporate power. For this, I am most grateful to the students and the people of the state of Colorado.

I presented aspects of the research that comprises this book on several occasions over the years. The strike was the topic of the 2009 Austin Scott

Lecture at my own institution, as well as of presentations at Loyola Law School, Los Angeles, the Boyd School of Law at the University of Nevada–Las Vegas, the 2010 How Class Works Conference at SUNY–Stony Brook, the 2012 ClassCrits Conference at the University of Wisconsin–Madison, and the 2013 Cleveland Laborfest and Forum. At each of these gatherings, I received a host of helpful suggestions, criticisms, and encouragements from scholars, community activists, and, perhaps most notably, former steel workers and their children.

I am bound to give special thanks to other friends, including the late Don Wright. A veteran of more recent struggles in steel and a thoroughly remarkable individual, Don shared stories of that period in his life during a holiday party in Aurora, Colorado, on a frigid night in 2008, which did much to motivate me to write about Little Steel. Unfortunately, Don never realized this. I also owe a debt of gratitude to Jim Hayden, a former neighbor of mine and one-time steel worker himself, and Tom Sodders, retired union man and activist in northeast Ohio. Both passionate intellectuals, Jim and Tom gave me numerous insights about this project and showed an enthusiasm for it that helped sustain my own labors. Indeed, it is impossible for me to name all of the friends and colleagues who provided me with advice on some part of this project or another or otherwise inspired me to see it through. But at least a few others warrant special mention, including Aya Gruber, Lakshman Guruswamy, Jane Hill, George Priest, Todd Stafford, Mark Squillace, Niles Utlaut, and Tilman Wuerschmidt.

I would be terribly remiss if I did not also mention the support I received from my family, including my siblings, John White, Lia White-Allen, and Ismail White, and their spouses, Joycelyn Cortez, Troy Allen, and Corrine McConnaughy. Educators and intellectuals all, they helped me think through many aspects of this project while also providing me with more practical forms of assistance, including, in the case of Ismail and Corrine, accommodating me during two lengthy research trips to Ohio. Finally, I must thank my partner, Teresa Bruce, whose many inspired suggestions, steadfast conviction that this project would eventually succeed, and loving support were all, in the end, essential. Of course, any shortcomings in the book are entirely my own.

FIGURE 1. The Memorial Day Massacre: Chicago police assault strikers and supporters attempting to picket Republic Steel's South Chicago Works, May 30, 1937. © 1937, Associated Press/ Carl Linde.

Introduction

"I'd never seen police beat women, not white women," Jesse Reese marveled as he crawled through the grass under the afternoon sun on a desolate field in the southernmost reaches of the city of Chicago. It was Memorial Day— Sunday, May 30, 1937. All around Reese, scores of club-wielding police were beating people, men and women, black as well as white, and firing gas weapons and firearms, striking down dozens. Reese, a black man and a fugitive from a Mississippi chain gang years earlier, was no stranger to brutality and injustice. And yet he was stunned as he beheld victims of this onslaught, running and stumbling and crying out in shock and pain.[1]

Moments earlier Reese had been firmly on his feet, one of at least fifteen hundred demonstrators who had marched to within a couple hundred yards of the gate of a steel mill owned by the Republic Steel Corporation. The demonstrators' cause was industrial unionism. Earlier that afternoon they had rallied at an old tavern that served as local headquarters for the union that had called a strike against Republic. Reese himself, a union organizer in a nearby steel plant, had arrived with truckloads of other strikers. From the tavern he and the other demonstrators had walked down the street five or six blocks and then marched across an open field toward the mill's gate. It was just after 4:00 P.M. Along with strikers from Republic and their families, the demonstrators' ranks included workers from other steel companies as well as an assortment of sympathizers who supported the union's cause. Ethnically and racially diverse, the demonstrators were mostly men. But there were many women, too, and also a few children, brought along by some who anticipated a festive outing.

As they made their way across the field, the throng of demonstrators fanned out into a ragged column. Led by two strikers bearing American flags, the crowd chanted slogans, the main refrain an affirmation of the labor federation that sponsored their efforts: "CIO! CIO!" The demonstrators' aim that afternoon was certain, at least to themselves. They intended to assert their right under federal law, as they saw it, to establish a large picket line at Republic's gate. Some held signs denouncing the steel company or proclaiming their right to picket. A handful carried sticks and rocks, and many must have expected some kind of fracas with the police, at least when the crowd closely approached the steel plant. But few could have anticipated what awaited.

Stationed between the approaching throng and the mill gate were about 250 uniformed members of the Chicago Police Department, armed with revolvers, nightsticks, hatchet handles, and various gas weapons. Beyond the police, at the gate and behind the barbwire-topped fence bounding the mill, were dozens of Republic's own police armed with gas weapons, billy clubs, and firearms. About one thousand workers at the mill had defied the call to strike and remained inside the plant. At least one hundred, and maybe many hundreds, of these men were stationed behind the company police, some wielding clubs and pipes.

When the demonstrators reached the police position, representatives on each side faced off while many others, police and demonstrators, bunched up behind, forming thick, ragged lines. Arguments erupted as the demonstrators demanded their right to picket the gate, and the police refused them passage, insisting that they disperse. After a few minutes, the standoff exploded in the flash of violence that left Reese crawling in the grass. With little provocation, the police fired their revolvers and gas weapons into the gathering of strikers and supporters, mortally wounding ten men and inflicting nonlethal gunshot wounds on some thirty men, women, and children.

The demonstrators fell like wheat before a scythe, one victim recalled. Films and the testimony of numerous witnesses document a horrific scene as the demonstrators' raucous shouting, smiling faces, and relaxed, upright demeanors were reduced in an instant to overwhelming expressions of shock and fear and contortions of panic and agony. Those who could, ran for their lives. But many were unable because they had been seriously injured or, like Reese, had been knocked to the ground. Others, showing great courage, went to the aid of shocked or wounded comrades. Still others from the broken crowd simply stood in place.

The police rushed forth into this mass of people, firing more shots from their revolvers, beating the demonstrators, men and women, wounded and able-bodied, and manhandling dozens, wounded included, into waiting patrol wagons. Some of the police exulted as they attacked the helpless and compliant unionists, or were consumed by rage. Some went about this business in a workman-like fashion. A small few were themselves shocked by the mayhem. When after several minutes the violence waned, about two hundred gunshots had been fired, all by the police, and approximately one hundred demonstrators had been hurt, including those fatally shot. The police suffered only about thirty injuries, none very serious.

LITTLE STEEL, THE CIO, AND THE NEW DEAL

A signal moment in the history of labor and class conflict in America, the "Memorial Day Massacre," as it came to be called, was but one of many violent chapters in a bitter and prolonged strike during the summer of 1937. The "Little Steel" Strike pitted steel workers aligned with the Steel Workers Organizing Committee (SWOC) of the Committee for Industrial Organization (CIO; later renamed the Congress of Industrial Organizations) against a group of powerful steel companies. The companies—Republic Steel Corporation, Bethlehem Steel Corporation, Youngstown Sheet & Tube Company, and Inland Steel Company—were dubbed "Little Steel" only to distinguish them from the enormous U.S. Steel Corporation, or "Big Steel," as every one of them ranked among the hundred largest firms in America. Acting in concert, they were also interlinked with other capitalist interests, including powerful trade groups and business organizations. This coalition of capitalists was intent on using the strike to mount what one commentator went so far as to call an "armed rebellion" against the movements for economic reform and industrial unionism that surged with such strength in that era.[2]

The SWOC launched the strike against Little Steel on May 26, 1937, after a year's struggle to organize the companies' workers. The striking steel workers asserted the right to build an independent union, to provoke meaningful collective bargaining, and to protest by striking and picketing. Although for decades denied most American workers, these rights had been enacted into federal law two years earlier, via the Wagner Act, a legislative centerpiece of the Roosevelt administration's "Second" New Deal that was held constitutional by the U.S. Supreme Court only weeks before the strike began in the landmark decision *NLRB v. Jones & Laughlin Steel*.[3] But as the men who ran the steel companies saw things, the letter of the law could not trump their prerogatives as industrial capitalists. True to the industry's tradition of violent and effective opposition to organized labor, Little Steel aggressively resisted the SWOC's organizing efforts and refused the union's demands. The companies defied the Wagner Act and the authority of the agency charged with enforcing it, the National Labor Relations Board (NLRB). And they bucked a trend among other large industrial employers during that same period, including U.S. Steel, which had begun to retreat from decades of absolute opposition to basic labor rights.

The Little Steel Strike played out across seven states and involved around thirty mills. At its height in June 1937, over eighty thousand steel workers, along with at least ten thousand CIO miners and other sympathy strikers, were off the job. Although many steel workers were passive participants and thousands opposed the strike, tens of thousands embraced the union's cause. Aided by sympathizers, these men picketed plant gates for weeks and even months in the face of widespread threats, provocations, and assaults. They tried desperately to inflict economic damage on the companies and to sustain support for their cause among fellow workers, with the broader public, and among politicians and other elites. And they took the offensive against the companies and their allies, organizing sympathy strikes as well as acts of sabotage and violence and intimidating picket lines.

By the end of that summer, at least sixteen people, all unionists, had lost their lives; hundreds of people had been badly injured; and as many as two thousand had been arrested in confrontations between union people, on the one hand, and public and company police, National Guardsmen, and loyal employees, on the other. But the mills reopened and the strike was crushed. Afterward, the companies effectively fired upward of eight thousand strikers, and the SWOC and CIO stood in disarray. It would take years of litigation as well as changes in political economy wrought by the Second World War before the companies acceded to the rights the workers had demanded.

THE STRIKE AND THE MEASURE OF LABOR RIGHTS

The Little Steel Strike has the distinction of being the deadliest strike, not only of the 1930s, but probably of the whole period from the early 1920s through the present time. The strike embodied class conflict on a scale and with a raw intensity seldom surpassed in American history. Nevertheless, the strike has not been well studied, or even much remembered. Although professional historians, labor law scholars, and popular writers mention the conflict in nearly every history of labor relations or the New Deal era, the strike has garnered little focused attention outside of a few accounts of the Memorial Day Massacre, a couple of other localized studies in journals, and brief narratives in broader histories of the New Deal.[4] The best book about the conflict, a 2010 volume by Michael Dennis, focuses on the Memorial Day Massacre and tends to condense the far-ranging and drawn-out conflict into this one incident.[5] The closest thing to a comprehensive history of the strike remains an unpublished 1961 doctoral dissertation by Donald Sofchalk.[6] No one has marshaled the available sources, including scattered archival collections, examined the whole of the strike in its larger historical context, or shown how the strike was affected by and in turn shaped labor law and policy and labor relations. Seventy-eight years later, fundamental questions about this, the last great strike of an era defined by spectacular upheaval, have remained unresolved and the strike's significance unappreciated.

When the strike is discussed, it is common for its events to be misunderstood and its meaning and legacy miscast. Scholars and other commentators often describe the companies' eventual concession to union recognition as a symbol of the final victory of the CIO, New Deal labor law, and the NLRB over a deeply entrenched tradition of unqualified employer opposition to labor rights that had long presided in steel and other important industries.[7] The struggle with Little Steel is thereby folded into a larger, dominant narrative about the triumph of industrial unionism, becoming a dramatic but temporary setback on a march to sweeping victory. In the same vein, some historians have argued that the strike even "boomeranged" to the overall benefit of labor and the labor law, its specters of open class warfare supposedly warming the public and elites alike to the need for a functional regime of labor rights.[8]

Elsewhere the strike is dismissed, even by those who profess to honor its martyrs, as a poorly timed and badly executed gambit by the SWOC and the CIO that played into the companies' strengths and revealed more about the need for "mature" tactics and preparation by industrial unionists than it did anything ominous about the state of labor rights in New Deal America. Reflecting back on the strike from the late 1960s, when both the industry and the SWOC's successor, the United Steelworkers of America (USW), were at their peak of wealth and stability, David McDonald, secretary-treasurer of the SWOC during the strike and, later, president of the USW, declared the strike a lesson in poor planning that was nonetheless vindicated, along with the labor law, by the companies' eventual agreement. While Little Steel may have prevailed in the short term, and while the unionists' defeat "hurt like hell when it happened," said McDonald, "the processes and those of us who stood by them proved too strong in the end. The victory of Little Steel was short-lived."[9] McDonald's emphasis on those who remained committed to "the processes"—by this he meant the workings of the NLRB and other government-sponsored institutions—is significant, as it reflects another claim often heard from the union's leadership and their allies: that the union's defeat could be blamed on irresponsible militants and radical leftists, who played a prominent role in the conflict but were later purged by the union's leadership. Even today, with its position in steel much weakened, the USW continues to describe the strike as a prelude to organizing success and a validation of the New Deal.[10]

There is something to say for this notion that the Little Steel Strike was a tragedy remediated, eventually, by triumph. Little Steel's belated surrender was an important and hard-won victory for labor rights, one that rested on the sacrifices of many workers and union organizers and the diligent efforts of NLRB staff. The companies' eventual capitulation rightly symbolizes the last gasp of organized, violent resistance to labor rights and the advent of a new age in labor relations, defined by unprecedented reliance on collective bargaining, relatively peaceful conduct of labor disputes, and greater fidelity to the law. There is also considerable room to criticize the way the strike was conducted by unionists, radicals and moderates alike. Nevertheless, it is a grave mistake to see the strike simply as a delayed victory, as a mere tactical failure, or as evidence of the superiority of responsible unionism and practical industrial relations over opposing concepts of class extremism. For entangled in and often obscured by these conventional accounts of the strike is a complex and sobering story, untold, that speaks important truths about the New Deal and the place of unions and labor rights in modern America.

Above all, the Little Steel Strike was a crucial episode in a larger struggle between industrial workers and industrial capitalists to determine what sort of America would emerge from the political and legal ferment of the New Deal and the unprecedented outbreak of economic crisis, class conflict, and political struggle that characterized that era. In this regard, the Little Steel Strike was, for labor, not merely a brief setback in a journey from defeat to victory or tragedy to triumph, but a clear revelation of the contradictory course that labor rights, class politics, and political economy would take through a key period in American history. As the first major test of the NLRB and the Wagner Act after the *Jones & Laughlin* decision, the strike revealed both the promises and shortcomings of the agency and the new labor law. The NLRB's diligent prosecutions of the Little Steel companies for their manifold violations of the Wagner Act in provoking the strike, and for their conduct during and after the strike, helped compel the companies to finally recognize and bargain with the SWOC. The agency's success made clear that the new legal regime would have real value as an institution of reform. And yet, anticipating problems that endure to this day, this process took years and featured remedies that were generally inadequate, even as the agency pushed the limits of the Wagner Act and the patience of its supporters. In this way, the strike confirmed that the NLRB and the Wagner Act would neither fundamentally alter the overall contours of industrial relations nor uproot capitalist hegemony in the workplace.

On a broader plane, the Little Steel Strike also took the measure of the New Deal. It probably does not go too far to say, as one authority does, that the strike "signaled the beginning of the end of the New Deal."[11] The strike certainly revealed, and in some ways shaped, the limits of the New Deal and the rightward trajectory of social policy in the late 1930s. Little Steel's victory over the SWOC confirmed how much power industrial capitalists retained despite the economic crisis, the New Deal's regulatory undertakings, and the spectacular growth of the CIO. The strike encouraged capitalists to redouble their resistance to reform, even as the violent methods that defined it faded from practice. Moreover, at the same time that it inspired the CIO's increased dependence on political favors and legal processes, the strike strained the alliance between the CIO and the Roosevelt administration. In all these respects, the strike can be seen as an important moment in the process, maybe best described by historian Alan Brinkley, by which the New Deal of the late 1930s accommodated itself to unbroken corporate power.[12]

The Little Steel Strike also took the measure of the CIO and its radical allies at a critical moment in their epic drive to organize the industrial working class. At the same time that it highlighted some impressive successes in organizing a fractured and much-persecuted workforce, the strike also exposed the weakness of the CIO and the deficiencies of its leadership. In particular, the strike revealed how much CIO leaders had overestimated the strength of their alliance with liberal New Dealers and also showed how unprepared the CIO was for dealing with the kind of resistance that Little Steel offered. Riding a tide of victories anchored on the General Motors sit-down strikes of the previous winter, but now faced with company obstinacy backed by thousands of armed men and massive stores of political and economic power, CIO and SWOC leaders appeared inept and often confused about how to sustain the strike's effectiveness. Defeat, when it arrived, not only destroyed the drive in steel; it broke the CIO's momentum, diminished its leaders' appetite for organizing by means of strikes, and drove the CIO and the SWOC to rely on the problematic workings of the NLRB and other government agencies to achieve what had not been won on the picket lines.

Radical organizers, many of them connected to the Communist Party, joined with rank-and-file workers in spearheading some of the most resolute, courageous, and promising opposition to Little Steel, only to have their efforts disavowed by the SWOC's leadership. But while the strike did much to confirm the virtues of radicalism and the limitations of the leadership's program, it also revealed how little these radicals and militants offered in the way of an effective strategy for overcoming Little Steel's resistance or rolling back the power of industrial capitalists more generally. Indeed, more clearly than in any strike during the 1930s or since, the Little Steel Strike exposed the dilemma inherent in the very concept of labor militancy that they embraced. Tactics like mass picketing and sabotage provided unionists a way of countering the steel companies' inherent advantages in raw economic power, overcoming the limitations of the Wagner Act, and realizing an effective right to strike. But these very tactics played directly into the companies' advantages in access to law enforcement and courts and in their capacity to manufacture disapproval of the strike. For militancy begat confrontations like the clash on Memorial Day, which the companies cynically forged into a potent narrative about strike violence that cast unionists as enemies of public order, weakened support for the strike among elites and the public, and justified the wave of intervention by state police and Guardsmen that ultimately finished the strike. In the decade following the strike, this same disingenuous story about violence and labor rights became the centerpiece of a sustained attack on the NLRB and the Wagner Act, led in part by steel companies and culminating in the Taft-Hartley Act of 1947, which cast the agency and the law as too indulgent of unions and in need of dramatic reforms.

In all these ways, the Little Steel Strike was a pivotal moment in American history. The story of the strike is a study in the realities of class struggle and labor conflict that emphasizes the formative role that violence played in shaping the contours of labor rights. Replete with drama and tragedy as well as troubling insights about the true history of the New Deal, it is neither a happy narrative nor an unrelenting dirge so much as a cautionary tale about class conflict and the limits of labor rights and social reform in liberal society.

The chapters that follow unfold in three main parts. Part 1 examines the forces that gave rise to the Little Steel Strike and shaped its course, including the conflict's roots in a decades-long contest between workers and capitalists over working conditions and labor rights. Part 2 tells the story of the strike itself, from its chaotic beginnings in the late spring of 1937, through the sequence of dramatic clashes and political intrigues that punctuated the grinding struggle on the picket lines, to its eventual collapse later that summer. After considering why the strike failed, part 3 then describes the aftermath of the conflict, including efforts to prosecute the companies under the new labor law; the forces that led to the companies' eventual capitulation; and the strike's legacies in law, policy, and labor relations. The book then concludes with a reflection on the strike's enduring relevance in our world.

PART I

The Open Shop

Steel barb-wire around The Works.
Steel guns in the holsters of the guards at the gates of The Works.

CARL SANDBURG
Smoke and Steel (1920)

Like a Penitentiary

STEEL AND THE ORIGINS OF THE OPEN SHOP

In the course of making steel, companies like Republic also manufactured a potent system of labor repression. This is the essential metaphor in *Smoke and Steel,* Carl Sandburg's epic poem about the contradictions and tragedies of steel labor in the early twentieth century: "Steel barb-wire around the Works . . . ."[1] In the decades preceding the Little Steel Strike, this burgeoning capacity to control labor, which the steel companies embraced as a mandate of industrial production, converged with the increasing obsolescence of traditional patterns of craft unionism to almost eliminate union representation from the entire industry. The industry flaunted this condition, which it described, misleadingly, as if it really meant a benign indifference to unionism, as an "open shop" program. But the same factors that secured the open shop's reign in the first decades of the century primed a resurgence of union activism in the mid-1930s and shaped the Little Steel Strike. To understand the strike, one must therefore trace the history of the open shop, beginning with events decades earlier in Homestead, Pennsylvania.

HOMESTEAD AND THE LITTLE STEEL STRIKE

Today a monument to industrial decline, in 1892 Homestead was a bustling company town and the scene of one of the most important labor conflicts in American history. On July 6, 1892, three hundred heavily armed operatives of the Pinkerton National Detective Agency set out to prevent union workers there from cordoning a large mill owned by Carnegie Steel. Forewarned of the Pinkertons' arrival, armed unionists converged on the detectives as they attempted an early morning landing at the plant from two river barges.

The confrontation led to a gun battle that trapped the Pinkertons in the immobilized, decked-over barges. A siege ensued, which ended only when union leaders and local officials secured the detectives' surrender. An ugly scene then unfolded as the captured Pinkertons were repeatedly assaulted by incensed union people, some just apprised of the deaths of friends and loved ones in the day's fighting, before union leaders and local officials restored the peace.

Even before this clash, officials with Carnegie Steel were working hard to cast the unionists as vile, irresponsible enemies of public order and private property, and local authorities as derelict in their duty to keep the peace and protect the company's right to operate the plant without interference. When the newspapers got hold of the Pinkertons' humiliating rout, such charges flowed freely, accompanied by demands that the militia be dispatched. State authorities agreed, and on July 12 the first of some eighty-five hundred troops arrived, guns at the ready. They forced aside the picketers and allowed Carnegie Steel to fully reopen the mill with scabs. When after weeks of further conflict things finally settled down, around a dozen people had been killed, most of them unionists; and dozens of people, all unionists, had been charged with murder and treason.

The dispute at Homestead primarily involved workers aligned with the Amalgamated Association of Iron, Steel, and Tin Workers (AA). Although the unionists routed the Pinkertons that July day at the river, they lost their bid to defend favorable working conditions and effective union representation. In fact, the struggle at Homestead was a crucial battle in a campaign by the steel industry to establish an open shop throughout the industry. Even as the fighting raged on the banks of the Monongahela River, workers, including many far from the scene, understood that defeat at Homestead would undercut any claim that their interests could rival those of property and capital.[2]

At the time of the Homestead affair, unionism was relatively well established in the iron and steel industry. In 1858, following their defeat in a strike, "iron puddlers" in the Pittsburgh area founded an organization called the Sons of Vulcan. The puddlers proceeded in great secrecy, as even then unionists risked being tarred as radicals, fired, and blacklisted. Not until 1862 did the Sons of Vulcan make public its existence. Membership gains were slow but methodical. In the mid-1870s the organization entailed over eighty separate "lodges," as its locals were called, and "was regarded as one of the strongest unions in the United States."[3] A craft union, the Sons of Vulcan embodied a model of unionism—by which unions only admitted workers possessed of particular skills and organized them strictly on this basis—that would predominate into the 1930s.

In 1876 the Sons of Vulcan "amalgamated" with two other craft unions built around skills on the "finishing" side of the trade to form the AA. The birth of the AA was accompanied by the creation of other, smaller unions at locations and skill levels scattered elsewhere in the industry. In the years leading up to Homestead, these organizations were involved in numerous strikes and lockouts and managed to secure favorable agreements on wages and substantial control over working conditions.[4] They also built impressive membership rolls. By 1892 perhaps half of the industry's workers were organized to some extent, either by the AA or one of the independent unions. On the eve of the Homestead dispute, the AA counted nearly twenty-five thousand fully fledged members. It was among the most powerful unions in the country and its health measured that of the entire labor movement. Yet within just over ten years, the AA was in crisis and unionism in the industry had been almost completely destroyed.[5]

The most immediate reason for this dramatic shift in labor's fortunes was the campaign that began at Homestead. The Homestead dispute was engineered by the company's director, chairman, and part owner, Henry Clay Frick, to break the AA's hold within the plant. Frick provoked the unionists by insisting on retrograde contractual terms he knew union workers would not accept without a struggle. Frick then locked out key contingents of workers as his deadline for agreement to the contract expired. Although insidious, this stratagem was hardly a secret, as Frick publicly announced his intention to break the AA. While the company's founder and principal owner, Andrew Carnegie, cavorted in Scotland and worried over his public image, Frick stockpiled guns and ammunition and had "Fort Frick" buttressed with barbed wire, searchlights, fencing with loopholes for riflemen, and water cannon.[6]

The hemorrhage of AA members began soon after the union's defeat at Homestead, as Carnegie Steel, which dominated the industry, systematically withdrew recognition of the union at all of its other plants. Other steel producers followed suit. Mill by mill, they renounced their union contracts or insisted upon unacceptable terms; they refused to negotiate new agreements to replace expired contracts; or they simply opened new mills on a nonunion basis. By 1894 the AA's membership had already been reduced by more than half, to about ten thousand. And greater losses were to come.[7]

Nine years after Homestead, a merger centered on Carnegie Steel created U.S. Steel. A watershed moment in the evolution of modern capitalism, the birth of this colossal new firm held in store another blow to steel unionism, as the new corporation was founded with an explicit commitment to holding the line against any extension of union representation anywhere in its domain. Later, "the Corporation," as it was often known, took an even more aggressive approach, reconstituting nearly all of its many subsidiaries as open shops.[8] In fact, extending the open shop in steel was part of the reason U.S. Steel was created in the first place, for this aligned with the company's congenital commitment, inherited from Carnegie himself, to employ rationalized management and production techniques, gigantic scale, and raw power in a relentless drive for efficiency and profits. "He always wanted to know the cost," said one of Carnegie's business partners. "The pressure is always on to make all the economies you can."[9] Achieving these economies required longer hours, faster paces of work, lower wages, and no unions.

In the first two decades of the new century, the open shop emerged as both an ideal or ideology and a concrete set of practices for ridding firms of unions and preventing their resurgence. Ideologically, the open shop appealed to fanciful notions of negotiated individual contracts and the "right to work" in defiance of union contracts and bargaining demands. Practically, it rested on coercive and sophisticated means of union repression, including blacklists; espionage; "yellow-dog" contracts, by which workers foreswore union affiliation; dependency-creating company welfare programs; intimidation and outright violence; and schemes for ensuring the companies' domination of civil life and public authority in the communities surrounding their mills. With these measures, companies decimated union support and crushed the strikes and organizing campaigns that occurred in the early part of the 1900s.

THE ASCENDANCE OF STEEL AND THE CHANGING GROUND OF CLASS CONFLICT

The growth of the open shop was deeply rooted in the industry's transition from iron to steel production, even though the two metals are really but different categories of alloys of the element iron.[10] For more than two hundred years, ferrous metal production in America focused on making iron, in the conventional sense, in its two most commercially significant forms: wrought iron and cast iron. For the time being, steel was both expensive to produce and needed for few applications, and so remained a specialty product. As rising industrial demand combined with improvements in production techniques to spur increases in production, the industry spread west into regions south and southeast of Lake Erie and into the upper Ohio River valley, where producers had ready access to the necessary raw materials: iron ore, coal, limestone, and water for transportation, power, and processing. Between 1830 and 1860, annual iron production in America tripled; and by 1860, the iron industry was "large and well established."[11]

Steel began to supplant iron in ferrous metal production in the 1860s. By the 1890s, dedicated ironworks were being replaced with steel-making operations. Among the reasons for this shift were technical innovations in the manufacturing process. The most prominent of these was the advent of a remarkably efficient method of producing steel from raw iron: the Bessemer conversion process. Bessemer converters performed the most essential function in rendering steel, which is to adjust (and mainly reduce) the carbon content of the raw, or "pig," iron produced in blast furnaces, by driving superheated air through the still-molten iron, producing a flaming reaction that burned carbon and other impurities out of the iron. The result was great quantities of cheap steel. Along with the slower but higher-capacity and easier to control open hearth method, Bessemer conversion rapidly replaced the smaller-scale and much more skill-intensive "puddling" method of refining pig iron into more useful alloys (including steel), as well as the similarly cumbersome "blister" and "crucible" techniques for making steel.[12]

The shift from iron to steel had enormous implications for labor conditions. From the outset, modern steel-producing operations featured lower rates of unionization than ironworks. One reason for this was incumbency. The AA and other craft organizations had come to prominence when iron still predominated and had built their jurisdictions around skills unique to iron production. So rooted in iron were these unions that their members and leaders had difficulty even understanding the nature of their steel-making brothers' work or their grievances. At the same time, the steel-producing operations that were built in the late 1800s and early 1900s arose in an increasingly open shop environment. Union men were not established in these mills and the companies successfully resisted attempts to organize them.[13]

Steel also changed labor relations by vastly increasing the scale of plant and overall production in comparison with ironworks, which had remained relatively small through the 1800s. Unlike the older methods of refining pig iron, which could only be performed on a small scale, Bessemer production could be steadily scaled up, generating greater efficiencies and lower marginal costs while also bidding up the capital outlay required to run a competitive operation. Open hearth furnaces, too, become progressively bigger and were operated in larger and larger arrays, or batteries. By the mid-1930s, open hearth production, which produced better steel, had largely displaced the Bessemer process, a change that further increased the capital investment required for a competitive operation.[14]

A comparable development characterized the most basic stage of production: the smelting of ore to produce pig iron. Fundamentally unchanged for centuries, smelting involves burning iron ore and limestone in a blast furnace. By the mid-1800s, the use of distilled mineral coal, or coke, in lieu of wood charcoal or raw coal, to fire this process was allowing companies to erect much larger furnaces, as the coke would burn properly even when stacked very high inside the furnaces. Also in the mid-1800s, producers began to power the blowers that developed the blast with steam engines, rather than traditional waterwheels. By dispensing with the need for a gradient of falling water, this machinery permitted the plants to install multiple furnaces (and other powerful machinery) nearer to each other and also permitted the works, which still required much water, to feed on lakes and slow-moving rivers. It likewise allowed for even larger furnaces. By the 1890s, gigantic coke-fired blast furnaces, often clustered together and almost always christened with feminine names, were predominant.[15]

The mills grew in another dimension as well. Pig iron and steel production were increasingly joined together, and joined to other processing operations, in the same vertically integrated plants. A principal reason for this is that steel, if not made entirely from scrap, has to be refined from molten pig iron. A major advantage of a vertically integrated steel mill is that it allowed the pig iron from the blast furnaces to be refined while still heated, by carrying it in rail cars and ladles over to nearby steel-making furnaces. Otherwise, the raw iron had to be cast in molds, cooled, transported, and remelted, all at great expense, before being made into steel. Integration offered other technical advantages, such as the ease of using the combustible gas generated in the blast furnaces or coke-making ovens to heat the furnaces; as well as the ease of recycling scrap metal cuttings from the "finishing" mills, where steel was further alloyed and shaped into user-ready forms. These advantages were not all-determinative and not all plants were fully integrated. However by the 1930s, smelting and steel making were only rarely removed from finishing operations, or from each other.

More efficient methods for rolling, drawing, or otherwise rendering steel into useful shapes also proliferated with the turn to steel, as steel production entailed the development of refined alloys that were tailor-made for these milling processes. Often broadly described as either finishing or "rolling" mills, these actually involved a number of operations for shaping steel into consumer-ready stock besides rolling mills proper. Before it could be processed in these ways, the steel coming out of the furnaces and converters had to undergo a series of "semifinishing" operations in which it was formed into "billets," "blooms," or slabs. Though obviously distinct, for convenience of description these "primary" or "preparatory" mills were also sometimes lumped into the category of finishing mills.[16] Not only did the finishing mills—to use the term in this broad way—grow in size according to their own economies of scale; but also, as the output of the steel-making furnaces and converters increased, so did the need for larger-capacity machinery at this end of the production process.[17]

The trend toward ever-larger steel plants completed the demise of iron production and its accompanying labor relations, as steel became much cheaper than fungible forms of iron.[18] The move toward larger installations also brought with it increasingly anonymous and distant relations between workers and capitalists. Although there had always been bosses of some sort standing between workers and owners, the huge new mills further attenuated these workplace relations with multiple layers of managers and supervisors. These changes eroded traditional, craft-oriented forms of collective bargaining and union-based labor relations, which, though conflict-ridden in their own way, had put a premium on familiar and relatively informal negotiations.

The efficient production of steel mandated unprecedented controls over both machinery and workers. The resulting culture of technical rationalization subsumed larger issues of management, expressing itself in an ethos of relentless cost cutting and profit maximization, realized through advanced methods of accounting and business planning and increasingly hierarchical, top-down systems of labor control. This regime redefined ownership and management, attracting into or otherwise cultivating within those ranks an industrial aristocracy of "steel masters" who, like Carnegie and Frick, were ruthlessly calculating, unsentimental in business matters, and altogether very capable extractors of profit from earth, machines, and labor.[19] In the end, steel remade men, just as men made steel.

This new business culture converged with technical changes in production to propel a very strong trend toward concentration in the industry. Already at the time of the 1892 clash at Homestead, Carnegie Steel produced half as much steel as all the mills in Great Britain.[20] In March 1901, Carnegie merged with seven other large companies to form U.S. Steel. The new firm was capitalized at $1.4 billion—*7 percent* of the gross national product—and was by far the largest business enterprise in the world.[21] For the first three decades of its existence, U.S. Steel was less an integrated business than a holding company comprised of dozens of smaller, autonomous subsidiaries that often continued to go by their premerger names. It was to distinguish them from these subsidiaries that companies not in the fold of U.S. Steel were referred to as "independents."

These independents, including the firms that would constitute Little Steel, also moved toward concentration. First incorporated in 1860, Bethlehem *Iron* Company was reorganized as Bethlehem *Steel* Company in 1899, and reorganized again in late 1904. The firm grew considerably in the first decade of the twentieth century, such that total annual revenues increased from around $15 million in 1905 to nearly $150 million in 1915. For the company's president, Charles Schwab, the logic of expansion was clear: to realize the "undoubted advantage" of large plants over smaller ones, to reduce marginal expenses to an absolute minimum, and to leave "nothing ... to chance."[22] Republic, referred to as the "rolling mill trust" when organized in 1899 (as Republic *Iron* & Steel Company), represented an initial consolidation of some thirty-four separate steel and mining companies. Over the next decade and a half, the company more than doubled its production capacity. Youngstown Sheet & Tube (née Youngstown *Iron* Sheet & Tube), founded in 1900, and Inland, which began production in 1894, followed a similar course. Along with the two other Little Steel companies that would not directly figure in the strike, National Steel and American Rolling Mill Company (ARMCO), these companies emerged as major producers with fully integrated operations. Though never so large as U.S. Steel, they accumulated extensive "captive" mining, rail, and maritime shipping assets. Already in 1900, for example, Republic owned ten ore mines, four coal mines, three stone quarries, and two railroads, with interest in another.[23]

The reasons behind this trend toward both integration and concentration were not only technical; there was also something captured in Charles Schwab's quip about leaving "nothing ... to chance." Owners and managers embraced vertical integration in part because it promised greater control over the circumstances under which they produced and sold their products. The same quest drove the consolidation of disparate firms into larger companies in the first place.[24] Underpinning concentration, especially, was also the question of capitalization. The rapid move toward more capital-intensive operations generated efficiencies that favored still greater capitalization and were difficult to realize without ready access to cash and credit. By 1936 the investment required for the efficient operation of a plant with a blast furnace was around $100 million (about $1.5 *billion* in today's dollars, by conventional indexing); the initial cost of a new blast furnace was $3.5 million; and a new continuous rolling mill cost about $15 million.[25]

These changes in the nature of steel production unfolded in concert with a remarkable expansion in the overall size of the steel industry. U.S. Steel and the companies that became Little Steel were dominant players in an enormously powerful industry. The total value of basic steel products increased from $200 million just after the Civil War, to $800 million in 1899, to $3.4 *billion* (in 1929 dollars—about 3.4 percent of gross domestic product) at the dawn of the Great Depression. Over the same period, employment in the industry increased by equal measure, from about 78,000 wage earners in 1869, to 280,000 in 1909, to over 400,000 in 1929.[26] By the time of the Little Steel Strike, American companies ruled the industry internationally, accounting for nearly half of world steel production.[27] In 1937, U.S. Steel produced nearly as much steel as the Soviet Union, the world's second-largest producer. And Republic could boast that its production exceeded that of Belgium and Japan combined, and that its Corrigan-McKinney plant in Cleveland made more steel than all of Sweden.[28]

THE LOGIC OF CONTROL, THE DEGRADATION OF LABOR, AND THE OBSOLESCENCE OF CRAFT UNIONISM

The methods of production that prevailed when iron reigned supreme could only be performed by a workforce populated with many experienced and highly skilled workers. Their essential role in producing the metal allowed these workers great control over the production process and over their own conditions of employment. This control formed the foundation of craft unionism, which organized and safeguarded workers' sovereignty. Steel, though, had much less need for these craftsmen. Many of the processes used in making it could be performed by largely untrained operators applying methods devised from afar by university-educated chemists and metallurgists.[29] With steel, too, shop-floor authority could be devolved from craftsmen to foremen, the latter chosen more for their ability to drive other men and faithfully execute orders from on high than for any particular expertise in making the product. At higher levels of management, formal education increasingly certified men as trustworthy representatives of ownership interests while also investing them with the necessary knowledge to comprehend the new processes of making steel.[30] While Carnegie never attended college and Frick left after a year, in the mid-1930s both Republic's president, Tom Girdler, and Bethlehem's president, Eugene Grace, were college-trained engineers.

Actually, the move to steel production was as much the product of a conscious effort to bring ferrous metal production, including its labor relations, in line with the emerging ethos of efficiency and rational management as it was a determinant of that reorganization. The truth of this point is evident in the history of Carnegie Steel, whose owners envisaged Bessemer converters, open hearth furnaces, and newer finishing mills not simply as wonderfully productive technologies but as effective means of displacing older, worker-controlled methods.[31] Steel was more than a name for various alloys of iron. It was a device for liberating production from the control of workers.

The resulting conflict between craft unionism and the new management approach defined the industry's labor relations from the late nineteenth century right through the Great Depression. Researcher John Andrews Fitch, author of a classic study of the social conditions of steel production in Allegheny County, Pennsylvania, in the early 1900s, recounted that a "prominent official" with Carnegie Steel told him after Homestead how that dispute grew out of the fact that "the union was firmly entrenched" at the mill; "the men ran the mill and the foreman had little authority. There were numerous vexations." The official claimed that this situation made it difficult to get rid of "incompetent men" and frustrated the company's quest for control over the production process.[32] William Jones, who ran Carnegie's Edgar Thomson Works in the 1870s, said that he felt as though he were entering a "penitentiary" when he ventured into some parts of the plant, so palpable was the conflict between workers and managers.[33]

Of course, industrial capitalism is as much an ideology as it is a collection of workers and machines, or a set of business practices and production techniques. In steel, the effort to wrest control of the production process from workers and replace their autonomous authority with rules and procedures authored and enforced by industrialists and their managers became a goal unto itself. Grounded intellectually in a fetishization of the norms of efficiency, control, and deskilling, this program aimed to reduce labor to a factor of production that would surrender to the same quantifiable economics as had coal and ore. In this respect, it was entwined with the larger ideology of scientific management, a set of innovations associated with (though by no means exclusively developed by) Frederick Winslow Taylor. It is no coincidence that Taylor, who abhorred unions, formulated his system while working as a foreman, manager, and technical innovator in the steel and metalworking industries.[34]

Scientific management intellectualized the effort to reorganize work. In steel, it was realized by a shift in production techniques aimed at diminishing human interface with the means and processes of production, including both mechanization and machine-age forms of automation. The collateral effects of mechanization and automation on labor relations were, in turn, important but notably uneven. Their tendency to eliminate skilled labor was counterbalanced somewhat by increased employment in newer, more capable finishing mills, whose complicated mechanisms required the attendance of workers possessed of an array of new skills. At the "hot end" of the plants—the coke works and the iron- and steel-making furnaces—the tendency was more toward replacing workers with machines or reducing them to attendants of those machines. And this was the net effect of mechanization and automation. Through the late 1800s and early 1900s, the ratio of skilled to unskilled workers in the steel industry decreased dramatically as the total number of workers increased.[35] By the early decades of the twentieth century, no more than one-third of employees in the big plants were skilled workers, with the remainder equally divided between unskilled and semiskilled jobs.[36]

The disparate effect of these processes at the hot end of the plants versus the "cold end" had another important consequence. Mechanization and automation gradually established the finishing mills as home to the largest contingents of workers in the industry. Moreover, the concentration of skilled workers in the finishing mills heightened their influence and status relative to other workers in the industry. The men who operated these mills were usually paid more than workers elsewhere in the plants.[37] In general the finishing mills became in the early twentieth-century redoubts of relative status and privilege. And yet, the same factors that favored these workers identified them as the ripest targets for the continued extension of the mandates of scientific management. The workers were often aware of this and proved keen to defend their interests, which would make the finishing mills and other specialty operations important battlegrounds in the 1930s.

Rationalization also undermined the stable and relatively intimate social groupings—and the accompanying norms—around which iron making had been organized. With their skills less integral, workers found that their identities were being reshaped around an ability to sell their capacity to be ordered around in often crude and highly alienating ways. Nowhere was this degradation more salient than in the identification of workers by accounting numbers and in the requirement that all workers, regardless of skill, be identified by "check number" badges bearing these numbers. A participant in the Little Steel Strike recalled how the numbers affirmed the reduction of the workers to objects of authoritarian control. "We were nothing but a number," he said. "We weren't even addressed by our full name or our first name; we were called either 'You dago' or 'You Hunkie' or 'You black so and so.' My check number was 11940 and they used to refer to me, 'Check Number 11940' or 'You Italian so and so we want this done or that done.'"[38]

The reshaping of the workplace was part of a larger contest encompassing disputes over pay and working hours, as well as politics and ideology. In this struggle the steel companies would prevail, although never quite completely. The Taylorist goal of preempting workers' autonomy and individuality was impossible to fully realize in steel, as even the most advanced machine-age devices depended on significant levels of human control, which the workers sought to retain. One means of resistance was the conscious effort by workers to monopolize critical knowledge about and influence over the intricacies of the production process, including inevitable idiosyncrasies in the operation of the machinery. Other means of resistance to the new management regime were more intimate and direct: innumerable acts of disobedience, soldiering, minor sabotage, and theft of company property and time. Although lacking much organizational structure, these tactics nonetheless were often ritualized, symbolic, and consciously retaliatory.

Throughout the rise of steel, unions represented the most direct challenge to employers' push to install autocratic and alienating management practices. For steel capitalists, unions not only threatened higher costs and inefficiencies; they also impeded the effort to assert managerial control over the production process, which the capitalists viewed as a prerogative of ownership. This attitude was evident to John Andrews Fitch, who summed up the companies' labor policy as "a determination to control, in pursuance of which object the employers inflexibly exclude the men from any voice in the conditions of employment."[39] As historian David Brody puts it, as early as Homestead, the steel companies had resolved that maximum efficiency required "complete freedom from union interference."[40] Here can also be found the immediate impetus of a number of bitter strikes. Already by 1885, a conflict involving work assignments caused a major strike in the Wheeling, West Virginia, area.[41] The Homestead affair was also a contest over control—it was explicitly conceived by Frick and Carnegie as a bid to break the AA in order to make way for a reorganization of production. Indeed, conflicts over control would at least partially define every major strike up to and including the Little Steel Strike, constituting the overriding rationale of a struggle that otherwise could seem irrational.

Besides completely eliminating some jobs, the turn to steel reduced many jobs to rote functions. Of course this rendered workers in these positions increasingly vulnerable to replacement if not by machines then by other workers, which further discouraged attempts to organize and bargain effectively.[42] Steel also fragmented the workplace via a proliferation of separate departments within the plants. Indeed, the big mills were incredibly elaborate institutions, composed of scores of departments and dozens of structures and buildings. An integrated mill combined the furnaces necessary for the production of iron and steel with blooming, casting, and rolling mills, as well as a vast array of other operations: batteries of coke ovens; by-products reclamation installations; electrical and steam power plants; masonry, blacksmith, and metal working departments; dock and rail facilities; motor pools; metallurgical laboratories; fire, police, and medical services (even hospitals); and so forth. These many ancillary operations also created toeholds in the mills for about twenty other craft unions besides the AA, including organizations of bricklayers, electricians, plumbers, and so on.[43] Even the more prominent of these, for instance, the International Association of Machinists, claimed jurisdictions nowhere near as extensive as the AA's. But their existence further complicated labor relations in the mills.

The byzantine organization of the plants supported the notion, so central to craft unionism, that there existed a functional hierarchy of jobs that both labor and management were bound to respect. However, this structure did nothing to prevent the degradation of skills in the plants and consequent erosion of unionism. Deskilling reduced the relevance of the AA and other craft unions, along with the autonomy, relative numbers, and overall importance of the craftsmen themselves. Increasingly, even when a significant number of skilled workers with crucial skills withheld their labor, they could be outlasted by companies armed with huge reserves of capacity spread among redundant plants and increasingly potent means of labor repression.[44]

The size of the new mills alone altered labor relations in still other ways. Already in the 1910s, steel plants were among the country's largest factories, with the bigger integrated mills employing over ten thousand people working around the clock in either two or three shifts, or "turns."[45] Such concentrations of workers presented unionists with real challenges. One obvious difficulty was the scale of organizing and the complicated logistics required to successfully organize such large factories, particularly if the aim was to build an industrial union that encompassed the plants' many departments. Another difficulty flowed out of the power that the huge factories projected over the workers. Typically well-fenced, with their gates guarded by armed company police, the largest mills stretched for miles along rivers and lakefronts. Merely to enter these enormous complexes, on which one was so dependent, could be a daily exercise in supplication.

THE POLITICAL AND CULTURAL LANDSCAPE
OF LABOR CONTROL

The large steel companies often wielded extraordinary influence at local and state levels. Some plants loomed over company towns, some of which were constructed by the companies from the ground up; others were located in sprawling urban areas, amid fairly diversified economies. But everywhere steel was produced, several factors worked to align companies' interests with those of public authorities and civic groups, including political campaign contributions, tax payments, direct purchases of land and services, and the employment of middle-class professionals and managers into relatively high-paying and secure jobs. And of course there were the payrolls. In 1936, the industry claimed a nationwide monthly payroll of $45 million.[46] Often, this made for a lot of money in relatively small places. By the time of the Little Steel Strike, Bethlehem's Cambria Works in Johnstown, Pennsylvania, disbursed a weekly payroll of $500,000 spread among about 13,000 workers, in a city of only around 70,000 people.[47] Even whole regions could be dominated in this way. In 1937, Republic Steel was the largest industrial firm in Ohio and the dominant employer in northeast Ohio, with over 30,000 production workers in Cuyahoga, Mahoning, Stark, and Trumbull Counties.[48]

Occasionally, the steel companies' power amounted to nearly totalitarian control. The communities in Hancock County that eventually became Weirton, West Virginia, were ruled by Weirton Steel, which controlled the police department, the administration of municipal services, the banks, and the *Weirton Daily Times*.[49]

From such a position, the companies could threaten communities of workers and civic officials alike with the prospect of relocating or downsizing operations if faced with labor conflict. The same store of political and economic power gave the companies inordinate influence over elected officials as well as police and the courts. Even voting rights were manipulated. Well into the 1930s, the companies not only encouraged workers to vote a certain way; they operated political machines, ordering workers to vote for particular candidates (usually Republicans) under the threat of firings or collective loss of work.[50]

Although there were conflicts, the companies were generally successful in cultivating controlling, often paternalistic relations with local business groups and commercial associations. This was aided by large donations. From the beginning of 1933 through the end of 1937, Youngstown Sheet & Tube—"Sheet & Tube," as it was generally known—donated over $85,000 to local business associations and chambers of commerce.[51] In 1937, payments from Republic Steel accounted for around 10 percent of the budget of the Warren (Ohio) Chamber of Commerce. Republic paid that organization five times as much in dues as the next nearest firm and occupied a perennial position on its board; and it was the lead sponsor of the Trumbull County Manufacturers' Association.[52]

The companies secured their dominance of the mills and mill towns by employing networks of informants whose ranks included professional labor spies, attentive foremen and managers, and everyday workers. Besides sniffing out union organizing efforts, these agents cultivated a climate of fear and intimidation, built on the pervasive suspicion that the companies were privy to everything, including casual talk about unions or politics. John Andrews Fitch saw this in the steel towns of Allegheny County, Pennsylvania, in 1907, where men went to great lengths to avoid speaking with him at all, for fear that he was a company agent or would make imprudent use of their words. He found the workers equally reticent to speak with each other about unions or politics, for the same reasons. Fitch knew there to be many Socialists in these towns, and yet he could find no party establishments. He knew there to be unionists, but they too were elusive. The wisdom behind the workers' cautious attitude was not lost on Fitch, who observed numerous instances where the steel companies managed to identify those who had attended union meetings and then fired and blacklisted them.[53]

These suspicions played out on an intricate social landscape. By the early twentieth century, the workforce in steel consisted not only of native-born white "Americans" of mostly northern European origin and African Americans, often newly arrived from the South, but also Hispanics, both native and immigrants; Italians, Greeks, and Hungarians; various Slavic peoples from southern and eastern Europe; as well as people from the Baltics. Indeed, in the early twentieth century, American steel workers hailed from almost every place on earth. In the first decade of the twentieth century, over half were foreign-born; the remainder were native-born, although often to foreign-born parents.[54] In Chicago in 1920, only 15.6 percent of white steel workers (and whites were then 95 percent of that population of workers) were born to native parents.[55] Although the number of immigrants later fell dramatically, first because of the Great War and later because of Congress's enactment of stringent quotas, even by the 1930 U.S. Census, about one-third of steel workers were foreign-born whites. Another 10 percent were black, 2 percent were Mexican, and the remainder were native-born whites.[56]

These many races and ethnicities often formed communities with distinct spatial, ethnic, and class boundaries. Long celebrated for defying the homogenizing influences of industrial capitalism and the emergence of a common American identity, and by definition exclusionary, the prominence of such "enclaves" in the lives of the workers raises crucial questions about how ethnicity and place affected labor relations. The enclaves isolated workers in their domestic and civic lives from the diversity that prevailed around them, reinforced differences among workers, and likely diminished the social resonance of class. Language barriers aside, racial and ethnic identities were accompanied by considerable chauvinism in a society in which social privileges and opportunities were very much defined by race and ethnicity. The period between Homestead and the Little Steel Strike was, after all, the era of Jim Crow, race riots, and lynching and the height of anti-immigrant reaction. For their part, the steel companies were quite adept at cultivating chauvinism among their workers in order to frustrate organizing efforts or otherwise undermine solidarity.[57] To this end, as much as for the stated reasons that workers preferred it that way, the companies imposed racial and ethnic segregation in company-controlled neighborhoods in towns like Aliquippa, Pennsylvania; Gary, Indiana; and Youngstown, Ohio.[58] In essence, the companies created the enclaves right along with the plants they bordered. Whatever their origins, these neighborhoods bred bigotry, mistrust, and regular outbursts of ethnic and racial violence, not least among gangs of young males on the verge of beginning work in the mills.[59]

Within the mills themselves, workers were often segregated by a process that preemptively identified skill levels with ethnicity and race. American-born workers of northern European ancestry dominated the more lucrative, higher-skilled positions, such as operating cranes and rolling mill machinery; an array of eastern and southern European ethnicities populated jobs of intermediate quality, including many positions around the furnaces; and Hispanics, blacks, and very low-status Europeans generally held the worst jobs, like common labor or service in the coke works.[60] In part because many racial and ethnic groups embraced such practices to benefit their own members, and in part because the organization of work along such lines was convenient to the companies, these patterns were commonplace.[61]

To some degree, this situation certainly frustrated the development of solidarity and heightened suspicions and resentments among groups of workers.[62] Such was evident to a Communist labor organizer at a small steel plant in 1933 who discovered that all he could sign up were "Italian workers, [and] a couple of South Slavs." Most workers "will speak to people of their own nationality. They won't approach anyone else. And for this reason it is very hard to get contacts."[63] The system afforded employers yet another advantage. When skill mapped along ethnic or racial lines, a protest by skilled workers could be presented to other workers as the machinations of a greedy and privileged aristocracy against the interests of less privileged groups.

These difficulties were exacerbated by the AA's long-standing hostility to blacks and low-status ethnic groups. Well into the New Deal period, many AA lodges either refused to admit these workers or blatantly discriminated against them regarding job assignments and grievances. Such practices combined with company-sponsored discrimination to prevent most blacks and many immigrants from ever obtaining the skilled positions that were the mainstay of the AA and other craft organizations. The result was a vicious cycle, as systematic exclusion primed many in these groups to serve as strikebreakers. This led to the charge that immigrants and especially blacks were inveterate scabs, which in turn was used to justify the discrimination inflicted on them by the AA and other craft unions. Eventually many blacks and low-status ethnics embraced the open shop as a prerequisite to their own collective uplift.[64]

At the same time, native-born, "American" workers of European ancestry (who also dominated the ranks of owners, managers, and foremen) were often deeply invested in such employment patterns. For these workers—and often for the AA and other craft unions that represented them—"whiteness" and American-ness were both currency and markers of class standing, social privilege, and relative economic security. For "Americans," the mere presence in the mills of racially or ethnically downcast workers threatened these interests, especially if accompanied by any suggestion that these people intended to test the existing alignments of race and ethnicity with workplace status.

Even for workers of modest standing, it often made sense to defer to these hierarchies because doing so affirmed the possibility, at least, of future upward mobility. This was surely true for many European immigrants on their way to achieving the status of generic whiteness. But for many more workers in this situation, deference to the status quo was informed by the fear of losing ground. Only the especially enlightened and courageous would unhesitatingly challenge company-sponsored segregation—or the open shop—when doing so could easily result in alienation from one's ethnic peers and consignment to a worse position, if not discharge.[65]

Clearly, the geographic and demographic realities of steel labor impeded the organization of effective unions. Nevertheless, as a number of scholars have recently highlighted, ethnic and racial identities and the chauvinism that accompanied them were neither all-determinative nor inevitably antithetical to class consciousness.[66] Besides demonstrating the remarkable degree to which class identity successfully competed with identities of ethnicity and place, this work shows how class was often entwined with, and sometimes supported by, these other identities. In the mill towns, loyalty to ethnicity, race, and place could become a mandate for class solidarity, just as class solidarity could reinforce these other identities. The strength of this logic manifests in the answer an Italian American worker from Youngstown gave his wife when she asked him why he joined the Little Steel Strike. Everyone else from the village back in Italy struck, he said, so "we had to strike."[67]

As much as racial and ethnic hierarchies might have safeguarded existing privileges and promised future ascendance, they also generated anxieties and resentments. Workers could well perceive the ways they were being manipulated and turned one against the other to the benefit of people whose own social and economic standing was at no risk whatsoever. Although this could be evident to anyone, the less white a worker was, the less privileged he was, the more acutely he perceived these pains of discrimination and manipulation. Notwithstanding their position on unionism, ethnically or racially downcast workers were often more likely than "Americans" to harbor resentments of the companies and their managers. As the new century unfolded, these workers proved increasingly receptive of the idea that employment practices in the mills needed to be radically restructured.

Moreover, although many workers did indeed inhabit insular enclaves, there were integrated worker neighborhoods. And the enclaves were not all-encompassing. Rather, they were porous, penetrated by political parties and other social groups and by individuals who preached the gospels of universal rights, common grievances, and collective values. Moreover, many steel workers simultaneously inhabited larger communities that were very cosmopolitan, bringing together a far greater variety of peoples, cultures, and political ideas than the mill owners and managers experienced in their own lives.[68]

There was also the considerable mixing of races and ethnicities within the mills, notwithstanding company stratagems. An unusual witness to this was a man named Charles Rumford Walker. The son of a New Hampshire physician, a graduate of Phillips Exeter and a "Bonesman" at Yale, Walker signed on to Jones & Laughlin's Aliquippa Works in 1919 after a serving in France as an officer in the Allied Expeditionary Force. But Walker was no "lost generation" dilettante. His purpose at Jones & Laughlin was to learn how steel was made, a base of knowledge on which he later built successful careers as a journalist and expert on industrial relations. While working at "J&L," Walker was eventually able to see far enough past his own rather bigoted views to appreciate the humanity of the men he labored alongside. Walker's accounts of the men's lives highlight a level of camaraderie and sense of common struggle that transcended the workers' many different cultures and backgrounds.[69] Decades later, many of the men who participated in the Little Steel Strike recalled how conflict and mistrust across racial and ethnic lines coexisted with a growing sense of common interests and identity.[70]

In a world defined by shared hardships, workers' identities were eroded and reshaped around universal values as much as they were preserved and contained within more narrow cultural frameworks. Ironically, this was an important part of what it meant for immigrants to become Americans. And if the mills and mill towns could remake immigrants into Americans, they also made them into industrial workers with a common perspective defined around a shared identity, which would eventually comprise a foundation of the CIO's challenge to the companies' hegemony. In the tense arena of social conflict formed around the mills and mill towns, workers and capitalists would find themselves struggling, not only to contend with the realities of race and ethnicity, but also to contest and reshape their meaning and bearing on the class struggles that increasingly enveloped all.

They Should Honor Us

WORK AND CONFLICT IN THE OPEN SHOP ERA

In the steel plants, men worked around, upon, beneath, and within incredibly powerful machinery and towering installations. Plunged into this world on his first real day of work, Charles Walker was nearly overcome: "The mill noises broke on me: a moan and rattle of cranes overhead, fifty-ton ones; the jarring of the train-loads of charge-boxes stopping suddenly in the front of Number 4; and minor sounds like chains jangling on being dropped, or gravel swishing out of a box." Walker found himself "conscious of muscles growing tense in the face of this violent environment, a somewhat artificial and eager calm. I walked with excessive firmness, and felt my personality contracting itself into the mere sense of sight and sound."[1]

Walker's reaction was hardly unique. Writing in 1920, journalist Mary Heaton Vorse decided that the steady movement of huge machines gave "the illusion of ritual" and that she "would rather see steel poured than hear a great orchestra."[2] The social scientist John Andrews Fitch opened his study of steel workers with an ode to the awesome and implacable potency of the mills: "The very size of things—the immensity of the tools, the scale of production—grips the mind with an overwhelming sense of power. . . . The display of power on every hand, majestic and illimitable, is overwhelming."[3]

LIFE, DEATH, AND RESENTMENT AMONG THE FURNACES

For Vorse and Fitch, the incredible physical impressions of steel making could distract the observer from a more fundamental fact. Into the mills, said Fitch, "you must go again and yet again before it is borne in upon you that there is a *human* problem in steel production."[4] For Vorse, the

FIGURE 2. A worker at Republic Steel's Warren, Ohio, plant oversees the pouring of molten metal, date unknown. Courtesy of the Ohio History Connection.

realization that men were in the mills working among the mighty machines could easily come as "an after-thought."[5] It was men who made steel by a process whose majesty belied its tribulations and dangers. Despite the reduction of manual labor brought about by mechanization and automation, steel work was "hot and heavy," with at least half the wage-paying jobs in the 1930s requiring "great physical exertion" and the other half requiring promotion from these difficult jobs as a precondition of higher employment.[6] This was definitely a "human problem." For measures to make the mills cleaner, less punishing, and safer slowed the pace of work, loomed inefficient, and ate into profits.

As Fitch perceived, the introduction of more capable machinery exacted another price besides sweat and physical exertion: "In some cases physical toil has been lightened by the new devices, but in almost every case where this is true responsibility has become heavier. The hot strain on back and muscles has been eased only to make way, often, for increased nervous strain."[7] In terms reminiscent of Karl Marx's classic discourses on workplace alienation, Fitch sees in this the subordination of the workers to the machines. Mechanization and automation not only facilitated the intensification of work; increasingly, they required this. As the companies replaced labor with machinery, they were compelled by the very reasons they had adopted the machines to extract from them the greatest possible value. And so the machines drove the men.

To be sure, both mechanization and automation spared workers some hazardous and difficult tasks. For example, few complained when the mechanical skip hoist eliminated the exceedingly dangerous and physically demanding job of charging blast furnaces by manually dumping tons of ore, coke, and limestone into them from precarious structures eighty or one hundred feet above the ground, amid waves of searing heat and clouds of toxic gasses. But automation, especially, eliminated jobs that workers depended on and robbed workers of control in the jobs that remained, while mechanization did not always make work easier or safer.

Well into the Depression era, workers complained of being driven to the limits of endurance, sometimes till they dropped. Some departments, like the coke works, had to be overstaffed at the outset of the shifts to account for those who would collapse from heat and exhaustion.[8] Nevertheless, cost-conscious managers often increased output by denying workers rest and meal breaks, offering performance bonuses, or imposing exploitative piece rates. Indeed, a culture of shop-floor violence and intimidation reigned at many mills, characteristic of what radical economist Richard Edwards calls the combination of "simple" and "technical" forms of management control that proliferated in industrial America in this period.[9] Pressured by plant superintendents, foremen and supervisors bullied workers to pick up the pace. Those who faltered or protested were frequently threatened or summarily fired.[10]

Work schedules were also geared to maximum exploitation. Unlike iron making, which was structured around "heats" whose timing the workers themselves controlled, steel was more efficiently produced on a round-the-clock basis, broken into definite and regular shifts. The steel-making furnaces and coke ovens were susceptible to catastrophic damage if they were too quickly shut down; and doing so was especially dangerous. Moreover, the heat lost in shutting down and restarting the furnaces was quite literally money burned. Then, too, there was the drive to exploit expensive capital investment to the fullest. For all these reasons, the mills ran continuously—day and night, all year round, and with regular stoppages only for repair and renovation of equipment and occasional holidays.[11]

One of Fitch's informants told him that "home is just the place where I eat and sleep. I live in the mills."[12] Until at least the 1920s, most plants ran their key departments on twelve-hour shifts. When the men switched shifts at two-week intervals, they were regularly required to work back-to-back shifts—the twenty-four-hour "long turn." Also, workers were often expected to labor every day of the week.[13] A very common target of worker complaints, the effects of these practices are vividly described in Thomas Bell's autobiographical novel, *Out of This Furnace*. A native of Braddock, Pennsylvania, and one-time worker at U.S. Steel's venerable Edgar Thomson Works in that community, Bell paints his characters in relentlessly realistic tones. One of them complains, "Here the work never stops. The furnaces are going day and night, seven days a week, all the year around. I work, eat, sleep, work, eat, sleep, until there are times when I couldn't tell you my own name." Later, Bell describes the long turn. Halfway through, a worker "became a mere appendage of the furnace, a lost, damned creature. 'At three o'clock in the morning of a long turn a man could die without knowing it.'"[14] A man could well die working like this, whether he knew it or not. For such fatiguing practices prevailed in an industry that could not have been more hazardous to begin with.

The most obvious danger in making steel was to be burned—scalded, flash burned, splattered by molten metal, even incinerated in the metal itself. Precisely because it essentialized the many other ways that workers could come to grief in the plants, the last of these risks preoccupied steel workers—so that ghastly stories about someone falling into an open furnace or a ladle full of molten metal prevailed in many mills, regardless of whether such a thing had actually occurred there. The scenario forms the principal allegory in several of the period's literary critiques of steel, including Sandburg's *Smoke and Steel*.[15] "Five men swim in a pot of red steel / Their bones are kneaded into the bread of steel," writes Sandburg, amid verses that evoke the extraordinary repression and exploitation that workers in the industry experienced and the deceits of a dominant ideology that subrogated these injustices to fables of individual opportunity, corporate paternalism, and the right to work.[16] For Sandburg, the image of men immolated in steel, and later forged into the artifacts of industrial society, underscores how much of the workers' lives and selves was appropriated by the industry, whether they were burned alive or not.

Work around the furnaces, where temperatures could exceed three thousand degrees Fahrenheit, was like "constantly sticking your head into a fire place," said Charles Walker.[17] Walker's *Diary of a Furnace Worker* chronicles a constant struggle to escape being burned amid the confusing movements, deafening cacophony, and blinding shadows and glare around the furnaces. And there were many ways to be burned. A small amount of water introduced to hot machinery or a vessel of molten metal could generate a tremendous burst of scalding steam and globs of searing, molten metal. So could the failure of some equipment or the clumsy execution of a routine task. Nor were the furnaces and ovens the only places a worker might be burned. At the "soaking pits," where steel was prepared for milling, and in the rolling mills themselves, the workers often manipulated massive ingots and blooms, some only barely congealed, that emitted intense heat and could inflict terrible burns on a worker who came too close. Everywhere hot metal imparted terrific heat to the machinery, presenting the unwary or unlucky with countless other opportunities to be burned.[18]

The risk of being burned was a "human problem," too. After the president and chairman of U.S. Steel assured a U.S. Senate committee that open hearth workers were often "at leisure" during their twelve-hour shifts and worked only half the time for which they were paid, a liberal organization called the Interchurch World Movement investigated labor conditions in steel and published a raft of contrary testimony from workers. That group's 1920 report includes the testimony of a man who described having to run with a sack of coal on his shoulder "toward the white-hot steel in a 100-ton ladle." The challenge was to "get close enough without burning your face off," hurling the sack "using every ounce of strength, into the ladle," and running away "as flames leap to [the] roof and the heat blasts everything to the roof." And yet the man emphasized that this "was not the worst of his daily grind."[19]

Even with marginal safety improvements, steel workers in the 1930s still suffered from the heat. Drawing on interviews, Joseph Turrini describes the dreadful conditions at a Republic plant at the time of the Little Steel Strike. Men could only work twenty or thirty minutes at a time. "Despite taking salt tablets, it was not uncommon for the workers to pass out because of the heat exhaustion." One man recalled that "you could tell who worked in the hot-mill because their cheek bones were bleached out red—carried like rouge all the time from the terrible heat."[20] Heat-scarred faces were so common that John Andrews Fitch learned to recognize the men who worked the hottest jobs merely by noting the condition of their skin.[21]

The mills offered other perils besides fire and heat, including being crushed, broken in falls, sickened by dusts, blinded by objects in the eye or exposure to excessive radiant heat, deafened by the constant din, torn by explosions, electrocuted, asphyxiated, or even drowned. The rolling mills were especially dangerous, as their moving parts, driven at high speed and by the enormous forces required to shape the metal, and often left unguarded, could easily crush or shred an unfortunate worker. Also very dangerous were the ubiquitous overhead cranes. The men themselves often fell from heights or were crushed or electrocuted while working with and around these essential devices.[22]

In 1906, a *New York Times* headline exclaimed that in the previous year, the industry's "casualties near Pittsburgh exceed those of some big battles." The writer's proof: insurance company data from Alleghany County showing some 9,000 injuries and deaths in the steel mills in that year alone.[23] A year later, another journalist documented 46 deaths and as many as 2,000 injuries at U.S. Steel's South Works in Chicago.[24] The papers regularly reported on catastrophic accidents in the steel mills. In one notable incident, the local coroner found that in the days preceding a 1907 explosion of the blast furnace at Jones & Laughlin's Pittsburgh plant, which killed 13 men, other workers had quit the furnace gang in fear for their lives.[25] In 1926, 22 members of a blast furnace crew at the Woodward Coal and Iron Company near Birmingham, Alabama, were killed when the furnace exploded and 400 tons of molten metal poured onto them.[26] That same year, a coke oven explosion at a U.S. Steel subsidiary in Gary, Indiana, killed upward of 20 workers and wrecked the mill's by-products plant.[27]

Prompted to examine conditions at Bethlehem Steel's South Bethlehem Works by a bloody strike there in 1910, federal investigators determined that in the course of a year, the plant's daily workforce of 8,000 had suffered 838 injuries.[28] Other studies by the U.S. Department of Labor confirmed that such conditions were widespread.[29] Nationwide, between 1910 and 1914 some 1,500 workers died in the mills, nearly 5,100 were permanently disabled, and more than 225,000 were temporarily disabled. Over the next five years, the number of injuries fell somewhat, while the number of workers killed actually increased to over 1,700.[30] Although the 1920s saw some improvement, in 1928 alone the Labor Department counted 229 deaths and 993 permanently disabling injuries in the mills; and in 1934, with production and employment numbers reduced by the Depression, there were still 109 deaths and 900 permanently disabling injuries.[31]

The dangers of work in the mills impressed the men involved in the SWOC organizing drive. Interviewed decades later, workers from Youngstown recalled how much they worried about safety, some recalling gruesome accidents. John Occhipinti, who started on at Republic Steel's Youngstown Works in 1936, remembered how the effort to avoid injury would "make you a nervous wreck."[32] Joe Kerrigan, who worked at U.S. Steel's nearby Ohio Works, had scars to prove where he had been burned by splashing hot metal. Kerrigan saw "a man being crushed. And I saw people burned"; he "saw people engulfed in flame," too, including when a charging machine operator dumped moisture-contaminated metal into a furnace.[33]

Until the 1950s, safety equipment was negligible and protocols were widely ignored if they interfered with production. Nor were the risks of injury or death much compensated by high wages—if ever such things can be. Steel had a reputation for paying better wages than other mass production industries. The companies boasted of this and some workers believed it to be true.[34] But wages in steel in the early twentieth century were not much different than in other major industries. In the words of an investigative journalist in the 1930s, "The popular impression that steel is a high-wage industry is a triumph of the propagandists' art," achieved in part by cynically including management officials' salaries in the wage calculations.[35] Although wages increased in the first part of the century, compensation remained altogether low.[36] The Interchurch World Movement contended in its 1920 report that many steel workers, particularly the unskilled, struggled to satisfy their most basic needs.[37] U.S. Department of Labor data show that in 1924, a good year for wages, the average rate for unskilled workers was only around 40 cents per hour. Wages for other steel workers were not much higher. That year, overall wages averaged between 50 and 80 cents per hour, or about $7 to $10 per hour nowadays, by conventional indexing.[38]

The Interchurch World Movement's report also confirmed that the shop floors were ruled by caprice and arbitrariness, aggravated by the absence of functional grievance apparatuses.[39] Workers complained bitterly of facing discharge for the most insignificant or contrived reasons; of cronyism, nepotism, and rigid ethnic and racial job hierarchies; of arbitrary and discriminatory pay; and of compulsory kickback and other job-buying schemes run by foremen and supervisors.[40] These practices dogged workers into the New Deal period. John Sargent, who was hired on at Inland in 1936, later recalled how "the worst thing—the thing that made you most disgusted—was the fact that if you came to work and the boss didn't like the way you looked, you went home; and if he did like the way you looked, you got a promotion."[41] Carl Beck, a worker from Youngstown who was active in the 1937 strike, credited his embrace of socialism and unionism to his time in Republic's mills in the 1920s, where he and his fellow workers suffered through exceedingly dangerous conditions, persistently irregular employment, and inscrutable rules governing wages.[42]

These harsh conditions generated enormous profits, which fed vast private fortunes, derived from ownership as well as managerial salaries and bonuses.[43] The Mellons, Mestas, Morgans, Phipps, Rockefellers—all these families built their fortunes on steel and steel labor. In 1915, Bethlehem Steel confronted a minor scandal when the newspapers revealed that it had paid its recently appointed president, Eugene Grace, a bonus of $1 million. Undeterred, the following year Bethlehem paid its officers and heads of departments nearly $5 million in bonuses.[44] Between 1918 and 1941, Grace would draw an *average* annual compensation of $600,000.[45]

But neither terrible working conditions nor blatant exploitation translated easily into support for union organizing. In fact, oppressive conditions often worked hand in hand with other company tactics to undermine labor organizing. The risk of being discharged haunted workers already consigned, by the very conditions that might spur them to action, to poverty and insecurity. Low wages left workers with scant reserves to see them through a strike or blacklisting. Often, their situation was made more tenuous by their dependency on company-owned housing or credit at company stores. Nor was job loss the only threat. The prospect of retaliatory demotion within a workplace that featured so many arduous, dangerous, and low-paying jobs could be a very effective deterrent. Nevertheless, if conditions in and around the mills could deter strikes and union organizing, they hardly reconciled workers to their fate. As the Yale man, Charles Walker, found, work in the mills generated a "deep-seated hatred . . . against the whole system of steel."[46]

Such anger and resentment fed a well-formed current of class consciousness that ran deep within these workers right through the end of the twentieth century. But it was not just resentment that underlay workers' consciousness, and resentment did not evolve in a vacuum. Even as the might of the industrial machinery alienated, oppressed, and sometimes killed the men who worked in the mills, the fact that it was *they,* the workers, who mastered these powerful and dangerous devices validated their social importance and their essential potency. Exploited and deskilled though these men were, they fed the furnaces, caressed the fires, and made the steel. The workers' mighty toils left Walker dreaming of the pyramid builders.[47] The men who made steel "seemed like heroes" to one of Bell's characters, and the thought that "men built that" made him "proud I'm a man." He continued: "If they let me I could love that mill like something of my own. It's a terrible and beautiful thing to make iron. It's honest work, too, work the world needs. They should honor us."[48]

With some workers, pride and resentments displaced fear and impelled union membership. Labor scholar Jack Metzgar recalled his father's decision to sign up with the SWOC in 1936 despite threats by his employer, U.S. Steel, and doubts that joining would yield any practical benefits. The older Metzgar "hated" his job and was tired of living "with the fear." "I knew the company hated the union, so I joined."[49] Other workers developed a fully formed political consciousness that challenged the companies' hegemony and exploitative policies, if not the very concepts of private property and wage labor. For a significant minority, radicalism expressed itself overtly, despite company repression of active involvement in leftist parties. Indeed, many immigrant workers arrived in the country already steeped in radical traditions, or came from families that were.[50] Nor was actual membership in such parties a full measure of the overall level of workers' appetite for radicalism, as workers often quietly embraced radical notions even if they declined to join or actively support a leftist party. As one worker explained to John Andrews Fitch, "Ninety-nine per cent of the men are socialists, if by that you mean one who hates a capitalist."[51]

These refractory tendencies conflicted with more conservative impulses, including aspirations of economic security, material acquisition, and social and political acceptance; ethnic or neighborhood loyalties; and even, among some workers, a basic faith in the tenets of industrial capitalism. Indeed, neither radicalism nor conservatism nor, least of all, an affinity for political moderation, can be said to capture the essential orientation of steel workers in the early twentieth century. The workers lived in a world buffeted by crosscurrents: deep and transparent exploitation, uncertain but sometimes real promises of upward mobility, formidable means of repression and ideological justification of corporate rule, and very powerful obligations to family and community—to name only the most salient. In this world, individual workers, no less than entire communities, might react very differently over time to otherwise similar events, like an organizing drive or a strike. And they might have similarly inconsistent, even contradictory views regarding unionism. Ultimately, in the domain of steel, ideas and ideology would be as contestable as basic policy.[52]

Three years after the 1892 clash, workers at Carnegie's Homestead Works heard that the company was preparing to impose another cut in wages, and so one thousand of them met together to discuss a response. The next day, the company began firing men "by fives and tens" for having dared to attend the meeting. The workers responded by meeting in secret, in much smaller groups, to plan a response. The company answered by firing the remaining leaders of the movement, AA men whose identities were uncovered by company spies. In 1899, Homestead workers yet again tried to organize in secret; again the company fired them—this time several hundred. This was the reality of the open shop: corporate sovereignty, founded in immense power and an extraordinary capacity for repression.[53]

The first two decades of the 1900s followed a similar pattern. The first major steel strike in the post-Homestead era occurred in 1901 at newly formed U.S. Steel. U.S. Steel's directors initially tolerated a few pockets of union representation, provided the unions exercised almost no authority and made no demands. But the company was ultimately committed to rooting out unionism completely.[54] The 1901 dispute began with a disagreement over union representation of skilled workers and the payment of union-scale wages in the company's subsidiaries on the finishing side of the trade. After a number of strike threats and smaller job actions around these issues, and failure to reach a compromise, the strike began in July with walkouts at the finishing mills. When further efforts at compromise also failed, the AA called for a general walkout at U.S. Steel's plants, beginning in August.[55]

The result was an unmitigated disaster that proved how much the union's position had weakened since Homestead—and how much power the world's largest corporation wielded. Many workers, including some skilled AA members, simply did not heed the strike call.[56] Only weeks into the strike, the company reopened the struck mills with workers who crossed the picket lines, green replacements (many of them blacks imported from the South), and professional strikebreakers brought in to provoke and intimidate the strikers. When the company threatened to permanently close some of the struck mills, the union folded. It avoided complete destruction only by signing agreements with terms less favorable than those that had prompted the strike, including a promise *not* to organize nonunion mills.[57]

At least eighteen mills that were unionized before the strike were nonunion when it ended. In the decade that followed, the company set about eliminating union representation from the remaining plants, often by provoking strikes that were then broken decisively and then either refusing to deal with the local lodges at all or forcing them to renounce their function as bargaining representatives. Alternatively, the company simply selected union mills to be closed for good as it consolidated the vast array of plants that it inherited when it formed. In executing this strategy, U.S. Steel avoided excessive tumult, which was easy, as it faced little resistance.

On June 1, 1909, U.S. Steel announced to workers at its American Sheet and Tin Plate subsidiary that the company would no longer recognize any unions and would unilaterally cut wages. This provoked a series of desultory strikes and other protests from the AA. But at mill after mill, the union was crushed. In some places, strikers were routed by police or vigilantes. Elsewhere, the corporation broke the strikes by transferring, or threatening to transfer, production from union to nonunion mills. A combination of economic exhaustion, organizational impotency, and depletion of strike funds sealed the fate of the walkouts. With other companies following in lockstep with Big Steel, the industry's victory over craft unionism was essentially complete.[58]

As they consolidated the open shop, the steel companies invoked the concept's pretense, professing not to discriminate against union members and claiming that they merely declined, in their workers' interests, to deal directly with unions. This position was cleverly conceived. For it cast the companies' authoritarian opposition to unions in progressive, libertarian terms and unions, by contrast, as tyrannical, inefficient, and outmoded. By the time of the Little Steel Strike, such rhetoric had become the mainspring of the steel companies' ideological war on unionism.

Then there was the practical side of paternalistic control. As early as 1883, Carnegie Steel provided some workers with coal for their homes and offered company-subsidized home loans. By the 1910s, such programs were commonplace at the large steel producers and included options to buy or rent subsidized, company-owned property; "loyalty" bonuses and seniority schemes; stock options; and the array of life, health, and accident insurance programs that would form the most enduring legacy of "welfare capitalism." Though sometimes of genuine value, every one of these programs cultivated dependence on the companies and left workers with more to lose if they were fired for organizing or striking, not least because the programs' value was often contingent on continued employment in good standing.[59] As Upton Sinclair put it in his 1938 novel about steel labor, the programs' logic could be reduced to this: "Figure up the cost of a strike, and give a tenth part of that."[60]

Despite all this, there were sporadic but important strikes in the period following U.S. Steel's move against unions, including a 1909 walkout by workers at Pressed Steel Car Company in McKees Rocks, just outside of Pittsburgh; a 1910 strike at Bethlehem Steel in South Bethlehem, Pennsylvania; and a strike in the winter of 1915–16 at Sheet & Tube and Republic in East Youngstown. All of these were tumultuous and deadly affairs in which workers faced off against heavily armed company police and public authorities. Although none achieved lasting gains for the workers, the strikes revealed the persistence and depth of workers' opposition to the open shop. They also highlighted a willingness of workers to challenge the most parochial aspects of the craft union system, whose obsolescence, impotence, and irrelevance to less skilled workers were increasingly exposing it as an accomplice of the open shop. Notably, the strikes at McKees Rocks and East Youngstown were spontaneous affairs, launched by unskilled workers without the sanction of incumbent craft unions; and though initiated by skilled machinists, the Bethlehem strike featured the aggressive recruitment of unskilled workers.[61]

The open shop's hold was also weakened somewhat by the First World War, which increased demand for steel and labor, made uninterrupted production imperative, and introduced the industry to an unprecedented level of government contracting. In this context, the federal government began to experiment with the use of administrative agencies to regulate industrial production and labor relations. In April 1918, it created a National War Labor Board, empowered to dictate basic employment conditions, including the right of workers to organize unions free of employer restraint. The board adopted an earlier Labor Department recommendation that stipulated, "The right of workers to organize in trade-unions and to bargain collectively through chosen representatives is recognized and affirmed. This right shall not be denied, abridged, or interfered with by employers in any manner whatsoever."[62] Although this bold pronouncement never evolved into any functional rights, its existence signaled the possibility that labor rights might enjoy the affirmative protection of the law.[63]

In a bid to alleviate war-related shortages, the steel companies imported large numbers of black workers from the South, further increasing the racial diversity within the mills. To better exploit available labor, the companies also extended work schedules and increased the pace of production, while increasing wages only modestly. These measures heightened conflict in the mills but also reduced workers' vulnerability to discipline and discharge. Organizing became easier and the AA was able to more than double its membership and increase its number of lodges by about 40 percent.[64] More importantly, it seemed that an offensive against the open shop was at last feasible.

Among those who perceived this was William Z. Foster, a veteran of the radical union, the Industrial Workers of the World (IWW), future Communist Party leader, and, in 1918, an organizer with the American Federation of Labor's (AFL's) Brotherhood of Railway Carmen. Working with fellow unionist John Fitzpatrick, Foster had led a remarkably successful campaign in 1917 to organize the ethnically diverse and terribly exploited workers of Chicago's sprawling stockyards and meatpacking plants.[65] With Fitzpatrick, Foster proposed in April 1918 that the AFL, parent federation to the AA and most other craft unions, mount a serious, industry-wide drive in steel. They requested over $200,000 from the AFL to finance the effort. Although a reasonable amount, given the magnitude of the task and relative ease with which the funds could be raised during the war, the federation initially provided the organizing front, the National Committee for Organizing Iron and Steel Workers, with only a few thousand dollars.[66] But the AFL did authorize the drive, which was by no means foreordained. The resulting campaign culminated in the largest strike in American history to date and constituted a crucial prelude to the Little Steel Strike.

THE OPEN SHOP TESTED: THE GREAT STEEL STRIKE OF 1919

One of a number of big strikes in a year of upheaval, the "Great Steel Strike" began to unfold on September 21, 1919, when the steel companies, led by U.S. Steel, categorically rejected a set of demands centered on an eight-hour day, abolition of the long turn, better wages, a seniority system, standardization of work rules, and the reinstatement of men who had been fired for union activities.[67] The next day, September 22, workers began walking off the job in huge numbers.

The conflict is a study in the effective use of labor repression. In the lead-up to the walkout, pro-union workers were blacklisted and fired by the hundreds.

Hundreds, perhaps thousands, of spies were employed to defeat the drive and the strike.[68] And in the Calumet region along the southern shores of Lake Michigan, thousands of state militiamen and regular army troops armed with rifles, machine guns, and field artillery barred strikers from meeting, picketing, or congregating on the streets and drove many back into the mills. Similar conditions prevailed in western Pennsylvania and bordering districts of New York, Ohio, and West Virginia. Foster estimated that during the strike, along the Monongahela River around Pittsburgh, the steel companies had some twenty-five thousand armed men in their "service." And by the time the strike was broken the following January, at a minimum twenty people, at least eighteen of them unionists, had been killed and hundreds injured in clashes concentrated in western Pennsylvania, eastern Ohio, and the Calumet.[69]

Throughout the region, police and company vigilantes disguised as "citizens groups" and "back-to-work" advocates assaulted strikers by the thousands, accosting them on picket lines and in their homes. Strikers were arrested, sometimes more than one hundred at a time, and offered release if they renounced the union or agreed to return to work. Union leaders, including Foster, were repeatedly harassed, arrested, and threatened with physical violence. And the companies and their agents relentlessly suppressed union meetings, to the point of banning them altogether in many locations.[70] In the end, the strikers were simply unable to picket in key strike zones, let alone ensure that their lines would not be run through by police, strikebreakers, and scabs.

Aided by allies in Congress, the companies invoked Foster's radical background to tar the strike as a Bolshevik, IWW, or anarchist conspiracy, aimed at fomenting a general uprising of the working class. The unearthing of an obscure, out-of-print IWW pamphlet that Foster had coauthored in 1911, titled *Syndicalism* and redolent with anticapitalist rhetoric and militant exhortations, anchored these efforts. Although the pamphlet was never found to have influenced the workers' campaign, it was reprinted and widely distributed by the steel companies to create such impressions.[71] Foster and other union people were grilled at length by the U.S. Senate Committee on Education and Labor, where they were charged with using the strike to strangle the economy and topple the industrial order in pursuit of revolutionary aims.[72]

Although certainly a radical, Foster harbored no illusions about what the strike might realistically accomplish and seemed focused on organizing the workers and realizing the demands communicated to the companies. Nor did Foster enjoy nearly as much control over the campaign as the charges against him implied, as the National Committee, controlled by the AFL, was ultimately in charge. Nevertheless, the ideological and political assault on the strikers and their leaders was unrelenting and led many elites, and likely many other Americans besides, to see the strike as a genuine threat to their social values and material investments.[73]

The strike also highlighted the liabilities of labor's commitment to craft unionism. The National Committee adopted a federated model of union organizing, hoping thereby to temper the craft model's parochialism and facilitate an industry-wide drive without impinging on the jurisdictions of existing craft organizations.[74] But while this approach did little to prioritize the interests of unskilled workers, it departed from the craft model enough to inflame the insecurities of skilled workers. Jurisdictional conflicts among the twenty-three AFL-affiliated unions besides the AA that had toeholds in the industry also impeded organizing and strike activities. Many AA members honored their contracts and continued to work in the struck mills.[75] Nor did the National Committee organize effective sympathy actions by other workers. Several attempts to expand the strike to other industries, or mount localized general strikes, met with indifference of the AFL leadership.[76]

Under Foster's leadership, organizers aggressively recruited blacks and immigrants.[77] Among the 100 to 125 organizers sent to the mills were some twenty-five foreign-born operatives (and a few women). By translating literature into the workers' native languages and approaching them in their own communities, organizers make commendable inroads with many immigrants, whose support for the strike eventually proved stronger than that of "American" workers.[78] However, primed by the AA's and AFL's legacies of discrimination and derision, many blacks and low-status ethnics resisted the drive and thousands served as scabs.[79] For their part, the companies fomented ethnic and racial conflicts during the strike, publicly dubbing the dispute a "Hunky" affair and directing their agents to incite conflict among the various groups—something that in at least one instance almost caused a race riot.[80] Tragically, the National Committee's effort to recruit black and ethnic workers actually led many Americans and craft unionists to eschew the campaign as a threat to the job control and access to wage premiums they still enjoyed.[81]

Although the reign of the War Labor Board ended in August 1919, the strike was taken up by an Industrial Conference that President Woodrow Wilson convened to address postwar labor issues. But its efforts to settle the conflict foundered in the face of the companies' intransigence and the conference's lack of authority. The chance that this body—or any other federal initiative—might have settled the strike suffered, too, from the president's obvious indifference. The Interchurch World Movement investigated the strike—this is what prompted its investigation of labor conditions in steel—and also attempted to broker a settlement. Its representatives met with U.S. Steel's chairman, Elbert Gary, in early December but got nowhere.[82]

The strike failed for another, more basic reason. Despite a well-organized relief campaign, strikers suffered greatly, and many exhausted their slender savings. Even strikers not yet in the grips of privation had to reckon with deteriorating postwar labor conditions and the possibility that, once the strike was lost, they would be blacklisted and find few prospects for work elsewhere. The strike visited no hardships on the men who led the companies. And the losses incurred by the companies were easily offset by the accumulated wealth of several years of wartime prosperity. In the end, the companies proved too powerful.[83]

There were still things to appreciate in what Foster and the National Committee accomplished. Despite everything, organizers managed to enroll about 100,000 workers prior to the strike and eventually brought out at least 250,000 workers—a majority of the industry's workforce. A large part of the industry was shuttered, with entire production complexes and whole regions shut down entirely. When the strike was called off in early January, as many as 100,000 workers were still out. Although the power of the companies had been affirmed, the strike suggested what the rank-and-file might accomplish if aided by a more ambitious, better-funded program of industry-wide organizing.[84]

THE OPEN SHOP DECADE

When Foster and his colleagues called off the Great Steel Strike, they dispatched a telegram to strike centers that concluded with the words, "All steel strikers are now at liberty to return to work pending preparations for the next big organization movement."[85] A couple of isolated and desultory efforts notwithstanding, the "next big organization movement" would not come until the 1930s.[86] Indeed, there were fewer steel strikes between 1922 and 1932 combined than in any one of the four years prior to 1920—and no big strikes.[87] The AA's wartime gains evaporated, such that by the early

1930s, the union could count among its members fewer than 2 percent of the industry's workforce.[88]

For the millionaires in charge of the steel companies, the dearth of overt conflict in the 1920s was a ratification of working conditions and a workers' referendum against union representation.[89] The "New Era," as the triumphant business class called it, was truly a decade of peace and prosperity for capitalists and highly placed professionals. But for steel workers, as for most of the industrial working class, the decade brought rising prices, stagnant wages, and regular bouts of unemployment.[90] Long hours, physical toil and risks, and all manner of tyrannies continued to define work in the mills.[91]

On the rare occasions when steel workers attempted to organize or strike, the companies crushed them. Often they welcomed a strike as an opportunity to further rid themselves of unions.[92] Although firings, espionage, and physical threats remained commonplace, a more insidious method of control also came into prominence: company-dominated unions, or employee representation plans, as they were more blithely called. The industry's first "ERP" was likely established by ARMCO in 1904 at its mill in Middletown, Ohio, but steel companies widely embraced these organizations during the war.[93] This move drew inspiration and legitimacy from the policies of the War Labor Board, which had casually affirmed the right of workers to form unions without anticipating how this endorsement might be perverted. In fact, many liberal reformers regarded the ERPs as legitimate forms of worker representation. For instance, Sheet & Tube's ERPs hewed to the formulations of the prominent Canadian politician MacKenzie King, a liberal political economist whose popularization of such organizations was sponsored by the Rockefellers.[94]

Nevertheless, the companies' main purpose in adopting these organizations was simply to preempt effective union representation—something that nearly 42 percent of employers with ERPs admitted to in 1935.[95] Often, the ERPs were total shams, empty shells that served no purposes beyond the needs of company propaganda. In some instances—particularly at U.S. Steel's and Bethlehem's plants—the plans endeavored to operate like unions and actually addressed some employee grievances. But even then, the ERPs did nothing to alter the fundamental balance of power and control in the mills. The ERPs remained under the companies' dominion and safeguarded their interests.[96] Well into the 1930s, the ERPs were the centerpiece of a system of welfare capitalism marked by dependency and steep hierarchy, which contemporary critic and former steel worker Horace Davis called the "feudal domain of steel."[97]

The AA was very poorly positioned to counter this program. The punishing defeats of the preceding decades had driven many of the union's best organizers and shop-floor leaders out of the industry.[98] Moreover, in the immediate aftermath of the Great Steel Strike, amid a nationwide Red scare, the union's top leadership purged Foster and other radicals, never mind their generally capable performance during the drive and the strike.[99] If the leadership's own conservatism and general ineptitude were not fully captured in the writer Louis Adamic's reflection on how many of its previous presidents ended up either as officials in the steel industry or as Republican politicians, these traits were certainly personified in its venerable president, Michael Tighe, a dull and reactionary man who was, in the words of historian Irving Bernstein, "barely above the level of literacy."[100]

Steel unionists' main achievement in the 1920s is simply that they were not entirely eliminated from the plants and maintained some semblance of a national organization. A few lodges survived, albeit with little hope of actually bargaining contracts or effectively prosecuting workers' grievances. And workers doggedly adhered to their unionist ambitions, often defiantly carrying AA cards. Unsurprisingly, many of these men openly expressed their frustrations with the AA's conservative program and inept leadership. For these dissidents, the course ahead was fraught. Although its dysfunctions seemed increasingly insoluble, the AA maintained a national bureaucracy that could prove essential to any revival of steel unionism. Moreover, the idea of forming an alternative to the AA ran up against a resistance to dual unionism that had long suppressed workers' interest in industrial unionism.

THE GREAT DEPRESSION AND STEEL

Although saddled with excess production capacity, the increasing buying power of industrial consumers, and the breakdown of efforts to rationalize pricing and restrain competition, the steel companies were able to overcome a period of postwar recession and realize another decade of growth and concentration.[101] Bethlehem Steel, which was highly profitable in the late 1920s, acquired several major producers during the decade. One of these, Cambria Steel, gave Bethlehem ownership of a large integrated mill in Johnstown, Pennsylvania, which would be a key arena in the Little Steel Strike. Republic, which realized nearly $40 million in profits in the 1920s, reorganized itself in 1929 from the Republic Iron & Steel Company into the Republic Steel Corporation. The restructuring involved the acquisition of several firms whose mills would also play integral roles in the 1937 strike. These included Union Drawn Steel, with plants in Massillon, Ohio, and Beaver Falls, Pennsylvania; Central Alloy Steel, with a complex in Canton, Ohio, and a plant in nearby Massillon, and another plant in the Chicago area; Interstate Iron and Steel, which provided the company with its South Chicago Works; and Trumbull Steel Company and Trumbull-Cliffs Furnace Company, which comprised a large plant in Warren, Ohio. Although they underwent less dramatic changes, the other big independent producers, including Sheet & Tube, Inland, ARMCO, and National (founded in 1929 by a merger entailing Weirton Steel), evolved similarly.[102]

By the end of the decade, U.S. Steel, Jones & Laughlin, and the Little Steel firms dominated so-called basic steel production, accounting for more than three-quarters of total output, and towering over a handful of specialty firms and smaller producers.[103] However, U.S. Steel, which controlled two-thirds of the industry when it formed in 1901, accounted for only about 40 percent of production by 1930, with the balance of the market largely in the hands of the Little Steel companies.[104] This shift, which accompanied growing discomfort among the independent producers with U.S. Steel's domineering reign over their oligopoly, would eventually lend the Little Steel group an autonomy that shaped the 1937 strike.

The arrival of the Depression plunged the steel industry into crisis. Demand for durable goods contracted dramatically. Purchases of automobiles, the manufacture of which accounted for the single-largest share of steel production, fell by nearly half in the first years of the Depression. Blast furnace, steel making, and finishing mill operations were all radically curtailed. By 1932, steel-making furnaces were operating at only 20 percent of capacity; and steel production that year was about one-third the level of 1930. Between 1929 and 1932, overall production of steel fell from sixty-three million tons to fifteen million tons—the latter figure being half of total production in 1910.[105]

The major steel companies nearly collapsed. In their worse year, 1932, the top companies ran a combined deficit of $135 million. Although a substantial share of these losses was borne by U.S. Steel, the Little Steel companies suffered too. From 1932 through 1934, Bethlehem lost about $30 million. The smaller Republic fared relatively worse, running operating deficits from

1930 through 1934 also equal to about $30 million; and so did Sheet & Tube, which likewise lost about $30 million between 1931 and 1935. With the exception of National Steel, all of the Little Steel companies incurred substantial losses during this period. With demand and revenues so low, the companies found themselves burdened with huge stocks of idle capital that could only be sold, if at all, to rival firms.[106]

Initially, the companies adhered to a so-called wage-maintenance program—a voluntary scheme that business interests promoted as a way to sustain consumer demand and arrest the economic slide without resort to government interventions. However, as sales and production continued to plummet, wage maintenance inevitably led to substantial reductions in payrolls. Overall employment in steel in 1932 was about half of what it was in 1929.[107] The layoffs and discharges that underlay this were made especially difficult by the fact that, from the workers' standpoint, they were often imposed arbitrarily and discriminatorily, in a context in which full-time work had disappeared. By April 1933, U.S. Steel had half the employees it did in 1929, of whom almost none worked full-time.[108] Although the loss of work fell most heavily on the less skilled, it reached every category of workers. As one worker recalled, "Even the engineers were laid off, the plant guards were laid off. There was no work. They were down completely. And the plant guards' positions were taken over by the supervision."[109] Significantly, "the distinction between skilled and unskilled" labor was "seriously eroded," as skilled workers were demoted or found their bargaining position drastically undermined.[110] In the meantime, the wage-maintenance plan proved ineffective and unsustainable. Beginning in the fall of 1931, the major steel producers (and companies in other industries as well) followed U.S. Steel and Bethlehem by imposing the first substantial cuts in wage rates.[111]

The industrial working class responded to the Depression with remarkable stoicism and grace. Nevertheless, as is so strikingly documented by writers like Louis Adamic and photographers like Arthur Rothstein, who both had much to say about steel, times were desperate indeed.[112] Many steel workers, including some who were quite skilled, were reduced to "shaping up" in a "bull pen," and sometimes even fighting each other at the mill gates, for the chance to be picked to work a shift. According to Augustine Izzo, who worked at Sheet & Tube's Brier Hill plant, a man would find out when he might work "from day to day"; there was no schedule, no seniority system, just a shape-up at the beginning of each shift.[113] Johnstown worker Johnny Metzgar recalled having to show up at the plant gates three hundred days in

1932, to be chosen to work only fifty-two days. Metzgar remembered how even a certain man with a good reputation in the plant was reduced to mowing his foreman's grass, shoveling snow at his residence, and bringing him home-cooked dishes, all to keep his job. The worker drew the line—and lost his job—when he refused to arrange a date with his daughter.[114]

Industry-wide, wage rates declined by about 20 percent between 1929 and 1932 before beginning to rebound somewhat.[115] Actual earnings fell much more, as workers put in fewer hours, sometimes working only one or two days per pay period, and lost more of their wages to job-buying schemes. Using data from the federal government and Chicago relief agencies, journalist Harvey O'Connor, a former IWW member active in the 1919 steel strike, determined that, in 1934, the average annual earnings of a steel worker amounted to $950, while the "minimum health and decency budget for a family of five" was $1,550. A number of workers related their struggles to O'Connor. For example: "Five in my family. I work for years, buy home, lost it—everything. Food—I must pay $200. Get $42 in wages last year." And another: "They take back my furniture. I paid $200 and had $180 more to pay. Relief sent up two beds for five people. I owe $80 for groceries, $300 for rent. Five in my family. I make $355 last year."[116] Even with improved economic conditions, union researchers found that on the eve of the Little Steel Strike workers at Republic's South Chicago Works averaged only about 50 cents per hour in wages, typically worked only four days a week, and made $750 a year in wages; they were not allowed overtime, but were forbidden to do any work outside the mill—"even an odd job house painting." They received no pension or health benefits, were hard-driven, and "quit as soon as they can get another job."[117]

George Patterson, who worked at U.S. Steel's South Works in Chicago and later became a SWOC organizer when the company fired him, described his experience in the Depression quite bluntly: "I almost starved to death." Part of Patterson's problem was that his earlier investment in company stock, undertaken to put his money in a safe place, had become worthless.[118] Although it is not clear how many steel workers or their families were affected, "starvation was a fact of life" during the Depression.[119] Amid occasional food riots and acts of expropriation, hordes of working people were malnourished and hundreds died of hunger.[120] In one notorious episode in 1931, steel workers recalled to their jobs in Pittsburgh were too weakened by hunger to do the work.[121]

Many steel workers reeled at the loss of company housing and the modest insurance and pensions that some firms provided, while others worried that the companies would fire them just before their insurance or pensions vested. The companies did attempt to spread what work there was among a larger number of people, which is one reason that so few workers experienced full-time employment. They likewise provided direct cash payments, in-kind aid allowances, and credit on company account, albeit more often to skilled workers than the lower ranks. But in the end this aid was both inadequate and also integrated with broader efforts to maintain control. In some instances workers were forbidden to accept public relief; and some recalled receiving "donations," only later to learn that the companies had logged these as loans.[122]

Inevitably, work became more dangerous, too, as heightened performance pressures led to a perilous tendency to neglect staffing requirements and safety measures. Workers labored under the constant threat of being thrown out of work, if not because their department or mill was shut down, then perhaps because they did not work hard enough, refused a risky or arduous task, or failed to stay in the good graces of a foreman. Management also took advantage of workers' desperation, using performance incentive programs that further encouraged difficult and dangerous approaches to work. The Depression may have devastated the steel companies' bottom line, but it enhanced the advantages they enjoyed over their workers. At least initially, this also entailed a greater ability to deter union organizing within the mills.[123] Under these circumstances, conditions in the mills degenerated to what one worker called "a mean jungle of animals and wild savages."[124]

Sure, We Have Guns

THE OPEN SHOP IN THE DEPRESSION ERA

"Sure, we have guns in our plants," said Tom Girdler, president and chairman of Republic Steel, as the Little Steel Strike reached its violent climax.[1] Girdler's public boast referred to a massive arsenal of firearms and gas weapons that Republic had placed in the hands of its company police. Even had he said it well before the strike began, Girdler's assertion would have surprised few people. For in the years prior to the strike, the major steel companies had evolved potent systems of labor repression that included political and legal resources as well as extensive police forces and stockpiles of armaments. And Girdler himself headed the group of industrialists who spearheaded this effort. As workers in the New Deal period began to challenge the open shop, the steel companies continued to develop these assets, deploying them in skirmishes that anticipated the course of the 1937 strike, while using their political resources to contest the New Deal itself.

THE DEPRESSION AND THE STATE OF LABOR REPRESSION

In the late 1930s, a subcommittee of the U.S. Senate Committee on Education and Labor—known as the La Follette Committee after its chair, Wisconsin's Robert La Follette Jr.—undertook a broad-ranging investigation of employers' systematic interference with the rights of workers, one that examined the conflict at Little Steel. The La Follette Committee recognized that the means of labor repression it brought to light had been in regular use for over a half century. In line with previous official investigations of the subject, the committee found that company-sponsored violence, typically perpetrated by detectives, private police, and professional strikebreakers, was not a by-product of labor struggles, but a tool used by employers to deny workers basic labor rights. It also determined that even union-sponsored violence was often the product of employer provocations that were calculated to prompt intervention by courts and police to the same effect.[2]

The 1930s provided the La Follette Committee with plenty of evidence to support these judgments, especially in the antiunion strongholds of mass production, mining, and agriculture. The decade opened with an escalation of fighting in eastern coal country and widespread violence against agricultural workers and organizers in California and the South before unrest spread into the industrial cities. In March 1932, twenty-three workers and their supporters were shot and four killed when police and company guards confronted a Communist Party–led protest against hunger and unemployment at the main gate of Ford's River Rouge plant in Dearborn, Michigan.[3] The year 1934 alone featured several spectacular labor battles: a massive waterfront strike in San Francisco; a strike by workers at a Toledo automobile parts factory; and a general strike in Minneapolis in which a twenty-three-year-old activist named Gus Hall played a role he would reprise in the Little Steel Strike. Each of these left several people dead and scores injured. Bloodier still was an enormous textile strike that year, which extended through Appalachia and into New England, involved over four hundred thousand workers, and left more than a dozen people dead.[4] Nationwide, between the summer of 1933 and the end of 1934, at least one hundred unionists were killed in labor disputes; in 1935 and 1936, perhaps another fifty lost their lives.[5]

The La Follette Committee's investigations of labor repression, like the NLRB's early cases, implicated a veritable who's who of American industry. But one company, the Remington Rand Corporation, which manufactured office equipment, stands out for the systematic way that it deployed its antilabor resources. The company's labor repression scheme was dubbed by its president, James H. Rand Jr., the "Mohawk Valley Formula" after the location of one of its important plants in upstate New York. On June 12, 1936, just as his company was breaking a strike at several of its plants, Rand gave a speech in which he bragged how he had discovered a potent method for defeating unions and urged other employers to embrace it. The National Association of Manufacturers (NAM) then published a summary of the formula in its *Labor Relations Bulletin*.[6] The scheme figured in the Little Steel Strike, as several authorities would accuse the steel companies of patterning their response to the steel strike after Rand's formula.

Rand's formula consisted of no fewer than nine steps, all oriented to employing threatening armed forces, spies and provocateurs, company-sponsored back-to-work movements, and staged reopenings to terrorize and demoralize strikers, provoke them to violence, and discredit them; then using the specter of violence and pretense of a "state of emergency" to mobilize opposition to the strike on the part of local police and courts; and finally announcing that the strike has been broken and that any remaining resistance was the work of an intractable minority hostile to community values and the "right to work."[7] The central insight behind the formula was that violence and the threat of violence could be used, not only to drive workers off picket lines and paralyze them with fear, but also to turn both the law and political sentiments against unionists while justifying the employer's own conduct and excusing its contempt for labor rights.[8] By these means, a clever employer could create conditions under which strikers might be routed and labor rights flouted in the name of peace and American values.

THE BERGER STRIKE

Two years before the Little Steel Strike, Republic Steel faced a strike at one of its subsidiaries, Berger Manufacturing, which employed about 450 workers in making steel office equipment in Canton, Ohio. The Berger plant was near five other Republic plants in Canton. At the time, the union at Berger was an AFL affiliate named the Loyalty Lodge. Independent of the AA, the Loyalty Lodge was one a number of "federal" unions that the AFL experimented with during this period as a means of avoiding the dysfunctions of traditional craft unions without embracing true industrial unionism. It had formed in 1933 amid a general upsurge in union organizing that accompanied the enactment of Section 7(a), the labor rights provision of the National Industrial Recovery Act (NIRA), which was the First New Deal's statutory centerpiece. The Loyalty Lodge was legally certified as the bargaining agent of Berger's employees in early May 1935, by a labor board established to enforce Section 7(a). But the company simply refused to recognize the union, even though it represented a clear majority of the workers. Instead, Berger, or Republic, secured an injunction against the labor board. This intransigence prompted the Loyalty Lodge to launch a strike on May 27, 1935—the very day the Supreme Court declared the relevant provisions of the NIRA unconstitutional.[9]

Well before the strike began, Republic purchased thousands of dollars' worth of "gas munitions" to augment a local company arsenal already well stocked with firearms and armored trucks; and it dispatched dozens of men to Canton to reinforce Berger's police force and serve as strikebreakers. Soon after the union set up pickets, company police began confronting the picketers and driving trucks through the picket lines at breakneck speeds. These actions were meant to provoke and demoralize the strikers, as picketers were not interfering with company operations.[10]

Republic's campaign against the strikers culminated in a "planned attack" by heavily armed company police on hundreds of strikers and sympathizers that left over a dozen people seriously injured.[11] Days later, about forty company police in armored trucks drove out of the plant and into surrounding neighborhoods, where they indiscriminately gassed, beat, and shot at everyone in their path, including people entirely unconnected to the strike. One of the victims, a homebound invalid who was struck in the head by a gas projectile, later died; another was a pregnant woman, struck twice in the legs with buckshot. For some time after the attack, gas fired by the company police was so thick in the neighborhoods that firemen responding to a call had to don gas masks.[12]

The next day, company personnel even gassed the city police, who finally threatened to machine-gun Republic's men and arrested some of them. The raids "plunged [Canton] into a state of terror and disorder" that only lifted when the strike itself ended after a coercive, company-sponsored election among workers at the plant, which excluded the strikers, showed widespread support to return to work.[13] Besides the one fatality, the attacks seriously injured dozens and later resulted in Republic and its insurer paying tens of thousands of dollars to settle claims from over one hundred victims. As the La Follette Committee recognized, the violence that Republic perpetrated during the Berger strike was part of a premeditated program for breaking the strike, which also featured the mobilization of "citizens groups" and a back-to-work movement, propaganda, and the deployment of spies and provocateurs.[14] And it worked.

LITTLE STEEL'S ARSENALS OF LABOR REPRESSION

By the time of the Berger strike, the steel companies' capacity to deploy massive resources in defense of the open shop was buoyed by improving economic performance. In 1936, Bethlehem's total revenues were near $300 million and its net income, $14 million; the next year, its revenues reached $425 million and its net income, $32 million. Republic turned a net profit of about $4.5 million in 1935 (after five years of losses) and made over $9 million in each of the next two years. Inland "prospered," earning sizable profits and roughly doubling employment and production in the years separating the onset of the Depression and the Little Steel Strike. ARMCO and National managed improvements; and Sheet & Tube turned around as well, earning significant profits, rebuilding its workforce, building up its fixed capital, and paying out substantial dividends.[15]

By 1937, the total number of employees in steel exceeded the figure for 1929.[16] Over 200,000 worked at Little Steel: roughly 85,000 at Bethlehem; 50,000 at Republic; 29,000 at Sheet & Tube; and 14,000 at Inland.[17] ARMCO and National employed 12,000 and 20,000, respectively.[18] These workers were strewn across a vast array of facilities that were often managed by a tangle of subsidiaries and subdivisions.[19] In 1937, Republic operated fourteen steel plants, twenty-one manufacturing plants, eleven ore mines, and ten coal mines. Consisting of some thirty-six subsidiaries, it maintained substantial operations in thirteen states and one Canadian province; and its gross assets (less depreciation) were valued at $365 million.[20] Sheet & Tube had assets totaling around $220 million.[21] Among these were "580 by-product coke ovens, 4 coke by-products recovery plants, a sintering plant, 12 blast furnaces, 4 Bessemer converters, 31 open hearth furnaces," and a host of preparatory and finishing mills. The company also owned ore and coal properties in Michigan, Minnesota, Pennsylvania, and West Virginia; interests in a limestone quarry in Ohio; and interests in three lake shipping companies.[22] Although similar in structure, Bethlehem's empire was quite a bit larger, without counting its substantial ship-building and dry dock operations.[23] And even the smallish Inland fed its big plant at Indiana Harbor with captive ore mines in Michigan and Minnesota, captive coal mines in Kentucky, a wholly owned subsidiary limestone quarry in Michigan, and a fleet of ore freighters on the Great Lakes.[24] In 1935, every one of the Little Steel companies ranked among the top one hundred American industrial firms by value of total assets. Bethlehem, in the seventh position, was the largest and Inland, in the seventy-first position, was the smallest.[25]

A cornerstone of the companies' defense of the open shop, illustrated in every major strike, was their ability to mobilize armed forces. In early 1936, Republic maintained a permanent police force of about 270 men spread among its plants; in response to the SWOC's organizing efforts, it would expand this force to about 350 in early 1937 and nearly 400 by August of that year. The men on this force were often dubious characters, conspicuously inexperienced and untrained in conventional policing or plant security work. They oversaw efforts to spy on, harass, and assault organizers and picketers and synchronized the company's antiunion efforts with those of the other Little Steel firms.[26] But these men represented only a fraction of the armed forces that Republic—or the other firms—had at its disposal. For in the past, all the companies hired men on a temporary basis to deal with outbreaks of labor trouble. And they would do just that during the Little Steel Strike. The companies could also be expected to respond to union trouble by securing more armed men through strikebreaking firms; and they could expect the support of local public police and National Guardsmen.[27] The La Follette Committee determined that during the strike, the Little Steel companies in Ohio and Michigan were backed by 3,600 armed men (not counting the National Guard), of which nearly 2,000 were under their direct control.[28]

The companies did not lack for weapons, either. Republic admitted to the La Follette Committee that at the time of the Little Steel Strike its company arsenal comprised 861 firearms, including 64 rifles, 552 handguns, and 245 shotguns, with over 77,000 rounds of ammunition; and 204 gas guns of all types, for which it had over 6,000 rounds of ammunition. Sheet & Tube's stock of weapons was even more impressive: 369 rifles, 453 handguns, 190 shotguns, and 8 machine guns, for a total of 1,020 firearms, with over 76,000 rounds of ammunition; and 109 gas guns of all types, with 3,000 rounds of ammunition. Just before the strike, Sheet & Tube also acquired 25 "gas machine guns." Nor were Sheet & Tube's conventional machine guns, which were Colt and Lewis models, the only weapons of a military character stocked by these companies. Many of their rifles were as well. And much of the gas the companies stockpiled was potentially lethal—an important fact so soon after poison gas had bathed the killing fields of Europe. On top of this, both companies also possessed impressive stores of blunt-force weapons, flares, bandoliers, and other military and police accessories.[29]

These figures likely undercount the weapons these companies actually owned, as they largely reflect divulgences by companies that went to considerable lengths to foil the La Follette Committee's investigations. The committee's staff had to resort frequently to subpoenas to conduct their work and on several occasions secured key documents just before company personnel could destroy them. Although the committee focused its efforts on cataloguing arsenals at Republic and Sheet & Tube, it mustered evidence of similar stockpiling at Bethlehem, Inland, ARMCO, and National, as well as U.S. Steel and Jones & Laughlin.[30] In fact, the La Follette Committee found that "munitioning" was pervasive among employers across a range of open shop industries. But it uncovered the most impressive arsenals and purchasing practices in the steel industry. The nation's four top purchasers of gas in the five years before the Little Steel Strike—governments included— were steel companies: Republic, U.S. Steel, Bethlehem, and Sheet & Tube, in that order, just ahead of General Motors and the Ohio National Guard. A committee map that used dots to plot the destination of each sale of gas munitions resulted in a "huge black blur" completely covering the steel-making region of western Pennsylvania and most of Ohio.[31]

Records collected by the La Follette Committee show that the companies augmented their stocks of firearms and gas in anticipation of labor trouble. Faced with organizing activity in 1933 and 1934, Weirton Steel purchased 71 Smith & Wesson revolvers as well as $12,000 worth of gas munitions.[32] Confronting the same upsurge, in 1934 alone, Republic purchased 166 .38 revolvers, 26 riot guns, and 412 gas munitions. That year, Sheet & Tube spent over $10,000 on ammunition and gas weapons.[33] Between October 1933 and June 1937, Bethlehem purchased over $36,000 worth of gas munitions, most of it actually during the Little Steel Strike. Despite a more benign reputation, Inland also had gas munitions and purchased several rifles on the very day the Little Steel Strike began.[34]

The companies, whose police went about well armed, made no effort to conceal the existence of these weapons from the workers, which suited their purpose as instruments of intimidation.[35] The La Follette Committee dismissed the companies' claims that the arsenals were for the legitimate purposes of defending life and property. Not only were these contentions contradicted by the timing of the purchases. In the committee's view, they were refuted by the historical record and the way that weapons were used in labor disputes like the 1935 Berger strike. There was also the size and nature of the stockpiles (for instance, Sheet & Tube's carriage-mounted machine guns and the Thompson submachine guns that at least three steel companies possessed), as well as the way the armaments were marketed, purchased, and maintained.[36] In truth, the weapons *were* for the purpose of defending property, albeit a notion of property rights incompatible with a functional system of labor rights.

The Little Steel companies also used their stockpiles to arm public police forces that allied with them—the better to cultivate congenial relations. In fact, Republic and Sheet & Tube maintained a kind of revolving door of employment between company police and local, public police. One-third of the nearly 150 "special police" hired during the Little Steel Strike by the city of Youngstown, Ohio, were employees of Sheet & Tube or Republic.[37] Evident throughout the strike zone, these practices would play a hand in several episodes of deadly violence during the conflict.

BRASS HATS, TOM GIRDLER, AND GIRDLERISM

In the spring of 1937, the principal Little Steel companies were all publicly traded corporations. However, besides Inland, which was controlled by the Block family, each was headed by a powerful individual: Eugene Grace at Bethlehem, Tom Girdler at Republic, Frank Purnell at Sheet & Tube, Charles Hook at ARMCO, and Ernest T. Weir at National. Although not absolute dictators of their corporate domains, these men exerted a level of influence that contradicted the companies' formal commitment to diffuse structures of corporate governance. "Brass hat" industrialists all, the leaders of Little Steel vehemently opposed the New Deal and abhorred the labor rights being asserted in that era; and they saw it as their special mission to stop the SWOC and the CIO. As Irving Bernstein puts it, these "steel masters" imagined the contest as an epic struggle on which depended not only their own interests but the future of American industry and the fate of fundamental American values.[38]

The leadership of Little Steel was not entirely monolithic. Although certainly not progressive on labor relations and not above defending its interests aggressively, the Block family did seem to be less intransigent and more reticent to use force than the leaders at the other companies. Another iconoclastic figure in Little Steel was ARMCO's Charles Hook, who instituted at that secretive company a management program that combined innovative production methods with a deeply paternalistic—and apparently effective—system of company-dominated labor relations.[39] More visible and considerably less benign, though, were Grace, Purnell, and Weir. By the mid-1930s, Weir was a particularly prominent enemy of the New Deal and one of the most outspoken members of the profoundly reactionary American Liberty League.[40]

FIGURE 3. Tom Girdler, chairman of the board, Republic Steel, and leader of the Little Steel group, testifies before the U.S. Senate Committee on Post Offices and Post Roads, June 24, 1937. Library of Congress, Prints and Photographs Division, photograph by Harris & Ewing, LC-H22-D-1744.

At the head of this group was Tom Girdler, whose character and social vision are key to understanding the strike. For Girdler was not only the main author of the policies that would lead to so much violence that summer; more than any of these men, he personified Little Steel's ideological commitments and practical interests. Writing in the *Nation* magazine in 1937, journalist Benjamin Stolberg described Girdler as "the big industrialist and the congenital small-time vigilante in one and the same person."[41] Irving Bernstein summed up Girdler's worldview in the notion that "every man has a price and any man can be shaken by fear."[42] Although forbidding, these descriptions are inadequate testaments to a man singularly committed to the most grimly reactionary social and political views and willing to resort to extremes to realize them. Not for nothing did "Girdlerism" come for a time to describe the very concept of violent antiunionism.[43]

In 1943, Girdler, with a coauthor, published an autobiography titled *Boot Straps*. The book makes no pretense of self-criticism. And yet it is a remarkably confessional document. Its many homilies bespeak Girdler's social vision: "There is still squalor in America but it is my considered opinion that much of the squalor is made by those who live in it." Or: "Father had a lot of voice, as befitted the boss of a family; in my opinion, unless there is a boss, you don't really have a family."[44] Girdler was married four times, the last time to his much younger secretary, facts that do nothing to impede his veneration of traditional family. His book rarely mentions his own family (he also had four children) and usually only to segue into a point about Girdler's own character or professional achievements. Girdler boasts about how as a child he exploited his younger siblings, "subcontracting" them to do chores for which he had been paid. For Girdler, even the family is an incubator of capitalist norms, just as industrial capitalism is the realization of patriarchal values.[45]

Tom (not Thomas) Mercer Girdler was born in southern Indiana in 1877 on the inner periphery of an industrial family. As a youth, he worked in his uncle's cement quarry and mill, where he claims to have learned that the well-being of the nation depended on a paternal relationship between management and workers unfettered by government regulations or unions. For Girdler, the open shop steel mills embodied a just and natural order, legitimately defended by force. Thus he revels in the barbaric modes of authority that ruled the mills, describing the typical mill as somewhere "you kept your place only if you were good enough to lick anybody who disputed your authority." The "boss of a steel mill was traditionally a big man physically"; the foremen were "as tough as pig iron and a general superintendent was never a man to be crossed if you valued your good opinion of yourself."[46] Girdler would have readers see him (a stout but not particularly large man) as a specimen of this type, too. He regales with a tale of how, while a foreman at Oliver Iron & Steel in the early 1900s, he brutally beat a worker who tried to knock off a few minutes early.[47]

These ruminations and boasts are among many in *Boot Straps* that reveal Girdler's obsession with authority and control in the workplace, which explains much about the nature of his opposition to unionism. Unions, he said, were a "terribly *disorganizing* force"; they rendered the "boss . . . no longer the boss." And it was this, more than greed, that "made so many employers the bitter opponents of the labor union movement in the old days. They foresaw what now eats at us."[48] While other industrialists might be readily moved by the changing economic realities and opportunities of the new order arising out the New Deal, not Girdler, whose problem with unions could not be so easily muted by the promise of greater financial reward.[49]

Girdler's time at Oliver was his first real job in steel. He did managerial stints at Colorado Fuel & Iron and Atlantic Steel before serving sixteen years at Jones & Laughlin in Aliquippa, Pennsylvania. Girdler eventually ran the Aliquippa Works, where he refined a most effective system for defending the open shop. In 1930, amid rumors that he was feeding proprietary information from Jones & Laughlin to Republic, Girdler was tapped by Cyrus Eaton, the industrialist who reorganized Republic, to help run that corporation. When the SWOC began organizing in the summer of 1936, Girdler was the company's president, chairman of the board, and director. By the time the strike began in May 1937, he had conceded the presidency and directorship, but not his leadership of the company; and his annual salary was a healthy, though by industry standards not extraordinary, $175,000.[50]

Girdler contortedly depicts Aliquippa under his rule as a "benevolent dictatorship," run not by himself or the company but rather "the citizens."[51] For Girdler, the segregated company town was a place of social harmony where police preoccupied themselves defending the honor of women. The police only bothered "outside" agitators, not loyal employees seeking membership in legitimate, responsible unions. However, Girdler could not resist describing how roughly those whose interests fell outside this definition were actually treated.[52] On Girdler's watch, company lawyers arranged a private prosecution of five Croatian immigrants for holding a union meeting in 1926. The men were "convicted" of sedition and confined for five years in the county workhouse.[53]

The La Follette Committee saw Girdler's work at Jones & Laughlin as highly relevant to his role in the Little Steel Strike and probed this subject. Although it was difficult to get the cagey steel man to confess anything, Robert La Follette compelled Girdler to admit that his service in Aliquippa significantly influenced his management of labor relations at Republic. Girdler brought over from Jones & Laughlin a number of company policemen and labor relations officials. And he used the Jones & Laughlin police as a template in reorganizing the force at Republic, putting the latter for the first time in proper uniforms (patterned after the Pennsylvania State Police) and equipping them with standard sidearms.[54]

In 1934, Girdler delivered an address at the annual meeting of the Iron and Steel Institute in which he vowed, "I have a little farm with a few apple trees, and before spending the rest of my life dealing with John Lewis [then with the AFL, later principal founder of the CIO] I am going to raise apples and potatoes."[55] Girdler certainly had a penchant for bluster. However, his opposition to the CIO, the Wagner Act, and the New Deal was real enough, and it was fully shared with the other leaders of Little Steel. Through both example and collusive advice, Girdler definitely influenced those companies. But whether Girdlerism ever truly constituted an even more popular program is a different question. Though surely significant, his contacts with other industrialists are difficult to trace; and unlike James Rand, Girdler never publicly promoted his methods as a formula—not least, one imagines, because doing so would have made Republic more vulnerable to prosecution, which is what happened to Remington Rand. In any event, once the 1937 strike was under way, Girdler's strategy was evident for all to see.

LITTLE STEEL VERSUS THE NEW DEAL

Girdler's leadership of Little Steel overlaid the common interests that bonded the companies together. Underlying these linkages was what the La Follette Committee called a "community of interests" among top shareholders. Each company's ownership tended to be dominated by a small number of powerful families and corporate investors. For instance, among the largest owners of common stock at Bethlehem were representatives of the Mellon, Morgan, and Rockefeller families. And prominent investors like these often owned considerable stock in more than one of the other companies. The fifty largest common-stock holders at Bethlehem included thirteen concerns that were also among the twenty largest shareholders at Republic and four that were among the largest shareholders at Sheet & Tube.[56] A similar pattern was evident with the Cliffs Corporation and the Cleveland-Cliffs Iron Company. With primary interests in mining and Great Lakes shipping, these sister companies in 1937 owned the largest share of common stock in both Republic and Sheet & Tube, as well as a significant interest in Inland. In fact, the Cliffs companies were two of more than twenty major businesses that, either by stock ownership or by interlocking directorates and top management personnel, further tied the Little Steel companies together.[57] In February 1935, the U.S. Department of Justice unsuccessfully sued Republic and nine other companies on grounds that these interlocking directorates violated antitrust laws.[58]

These ties were bolstered by common membership in the NAM as well as the American Iron and Steel Institute. By the mid-1930s, both organizations were influenced by Little Steel far in excess of the companies' share of production or their nominal voting power. Between 1933 and the end of 1937, Girdler, Weir, and Hook each served at different times as vice president or director of the NAM; and Girdler and Purnell also served as president of the Iron and Steel Institute. During that five-year period, the six Little Steel companies contributed over $140,000 in dues to the NAM and were among the organization's most prominent financial backers.[59]

The companies' participation in the NAM and the Iron and Steel Institute organizations points to an aspect of Little Steel's common ideology that belied the companies' more familiar and more loudly voiced commitments to the free market and similar ideals. For the steel masters, there was nothing fundamentally wrong with collective bargaining, if this meant the prerogative to band together for their own purposes. Nor was economic planning intolerable, so long as it remained the province of businesses and business leaders. In these respects, the leaders of Little Steel shared a perspective common among many business leaders of the day and reflected in the business community's initial support for the NIRA.[60]

But this support for the NIRA, which the steel industry with its own history of self-regulation rejected anyway, never extended to its program of labor reform.[61] Led by the U.S. Chamber of Commerce, the NAM, the American Liberty League, and an array of ad hoc groups and trade associations, capitalist interests centered in mass production had vigorously opposed the NIRA's tepid attempts at labor reform. They took this position even though many of their constituents had sworn to abide by that statute when they earlier signed "codes of fair competition" promulgated under the NIRA, and even though some of them (albeit not in steel) initially favored the corporatism of the new regime. After helping to finance the legal attack on the NIRA that culminated in the Supreme Court declaring it unconstitutional, the members of this coalition aggressively resisted the enactment and enforcement of the Wagner Act.[62]

Opposition to the Wagner Act was fronted by a "Lawyers Vigilance Committee" and later a "National Lawyers Committee." Stacked with top corporate lawyers, these lawyers groups operated under the auspices of the Liberty League and were headed by Raoul Desvernine, president of specialty steel producer Crucible Steel. Other top lawyers involved with these groups included Earl Reed, who litigated the *Jones & Laughlin* case to the Supreme Court, and John W. Davis, conservative Democratic nominee for president in 1924, namesake of the venerable law firm now known as Davis Polk & Wardell, and defender of racial segregation before the Supreme Court. These lawyers led the attack on the Wagner Act's constitutionality. While the lawyers publicly couched their position in the belief that the act would be found unconstitutional, the industrialists' campaign was hardly a dispassionate concession to an inviolate jurisprudential truth. They opposed the act because it impinged on their interests and ideology. And they believed that if the act were never effectively enforced, it would more likely be found unconstitutional.[63]

In the end, it seems that Mary Heaton Vorse was quite right when, writing in 1938, she said that "every evidence points to Girdler's offensive having been a planned attack on the Administration by big business of which the independent steel companies were the spearhead. Behind them was the force of the U.S. Chamber of Commerce, buttressed by the other powerful anti-Administration forces in Congress."[64] As the La Follette Committee and other commentators also understood, by 1937 a broad coalition of American capitalists was pushing Little Steel to fight the CIO in a bid to check the advances of organized labor, nullify the Supreme Court's decision in the *Jones & Laughlin* case, and roll back the New Deal.[65]

4

I Never Gave That Guy Nothin'

THE NEW DEAL AND THE CHANGING LANDSCAPE
OF LABOR RELATIONS

It is difficult to overstate the depth of economic catastrophe in the 1930s or the changes that the crisis helped bring about in American society, especially those mediated by organized labor. Staggering job losses and a weakening of workers' bargaining power initially drove overall union membership well below the dismal levels to which it had already sunk in the 1920s. Between 1929 and 1933, union membership receded by 20 percent, or nearly one million.[1] But unlike many economic downturns, the Great Depression soon featured a dramatic upsurge in organizing efforts and worker militancy and the rise of unionism in open shop strongholds like steel.

The roots of this movement can be found, in part, in the impoverishment of the working class. The efficacy of company repression faltered, ironically, as workers found themselves embittered and with so very little to lose. For many, union representation appealed as a way of challenging intolerable working conditions. Typical was the experience of a worker who recalled discovering in 1936 that his new job at a steel plant required him to pay his foreman three-quarters of his salary as a condition of employment. "When I heard that, I says, 'I'm gonna go out for the union.' And I did. I never gave that guy nothin.'"[2] But poverty and resentments alone did not undermine the open shop. The surge of unionization was influenced by the arrival from above of a new political economy premised on greater regulation of industrial production by the federal government, and the emergence from below of a coalition of workers and activists determined to harness workers' discontent and government reforms to an effort to unionize the industrial workforce.

SECTION 7(A) AND THE RATIFICATION
OF BASIC LABOR RIGHTS

The economic and social crisis of the Depression spurred a realignment of the relationship between the state and private capital. This was the essential nature of the New Deal. Although rooted in a widespread "belief that the misuse of business power was responsible for the economic breakdown and the persistence of depression conditions," this agenda was contingent and ambiguous, as powerful constituencies battled over how the reconfiguration of the country's political economy would play out.[3] Nevertheless, the New Deal's legislative agenda purported to redraw the role of government and law vis-à-vis basic labor rights. The first positive incarnation of this shift on labor rights was the enactment of Section 7(a), included amid the far-ranging provisions of the First New Deal's most important legislation: the NIRA.

It is debatable whether Section 7(a) was merely a dismissive "restatement of progressive homilies" added to the bill in a cynical attempt to deflect demands for more meaningful labor reforms, or a genuine concession to workers extracted from the president and Congress by government progressives and labor leaders as the price of their support for the NIRA.[4] But what is clear is that the labor rights provision was not a priority in the NIRA's overall scheme, which focused instead on instituting corporatist controls over the economy to the ultimate benefit of the business community.[5] Moreover, even before Title I of the NIRA, which contained Section 7(a), was declared unconstitutional by the Supreme Court in May 1935, Section 7(a) had shown itself to be a thoroughly inadequate means of legislating labor rights.

By its literal terms, Section 7(a) purported to guarantee workers the right to form unions, provoke meaningful collective bargaining, and, by implication, to strike. But nowhere was the provision really effective in thwarting run-of-the mill antiunion practices, including discriminatory discharges. Workers who took the lead in organizing were often simply fired, a tactic redolent with reminders of the companies' prerogative to throw workers into destitution during a time of widespread unemployment. A worker named Ruben Farr witnessed this when he and other workers, encouraged by the apparent shift in national labor politics, attempted to organize a U.S. Steel mill in Alabama during the NIRA period: "We went ahead and set up a local and elected a president and vice president. The next day, when the president and vice-president went to work, they found them-selves fired." That was the end of their drive.[6]

Section 7(a)'s endorsement of labor rights was supposed to be integrated verbatim into industry-specific "fair competition codes." The codes were promulgated through a collaboration of representatives of government, business, and labor, and bore primary responsibility for effectuating the NIRA's labor provisions and its overall scheme for stabilizing the economy. However, the inclusion of Section 7(a) amounted to little, as there were no effective penalties for noncompliance. The worst that might happen to a company if it violated the tenets of Section 7(a) was that it would be excluded from the NIRA's various competition-controlling and price-fixing pro-grams.[7] In theory, a company so excluded would forfeit economic benefits. But these benefits were neither direct nor substantial, and no major com-pany was ever effectively penalized anyway. Equally problematic was that in drafting the industry codes, industry representatives, including those in steel, successfully flouted the spirit of Section 7(a).[8]

The labor boards that were charged with enforcing Section 7(a)—the National Labor Board (NLB) and its successor, the (first) National Labor Relations Board—held questionable legal authority and wielded little power. The NLB could hear cases alleging violations of Section 7(a) but had no authority to enforce its own decisions. Intended to mediate between parties, it was comprised of representatives from industry and labor serving under a government chairman. Neither subsequent reforms to that board, nor the creation of the first NLRB, nor any of the industry-specific and regional labor boards erected in the meantime, rectified these shortcomings.[9]

The NLB did resolve several important strikes in its first few months.[10] But the regime's weaknesses were completely exposed by a conflict at Weirton Steel. In late September 1933, workers struck the company, in part in sympa-thy with United Mine Workers (UMW) miners who had walked out of the captive mines of several other companies, and in part over a dispute at Weirton's plant in Weirton, West Virginia. Within days, the strike entailed ten thousand steel workers, including men at other plants who joined in demanding that the company recognize and bargain with their AA lodges. After several weeks, the steel workers returned to work under an NLB-brokered agreement that stipulated settling their claim for recognition by means of an election. However, as soon as the workers were back on the job, Ernest T. Weir, chairman of Weirton's parent company, declared that a company-sponsored referendum on workers' support for the company union (which the company union "won" by a twenty-to-one margin amid all manner of company bribes) satisfied Weirton's obligations under Section 7(a). Weir then defied the NLB and barred its officials from company property. Attempts by Justice Department lawyers to enjoin this contemptuous behavior foundered before a judge who thought the NIRA unconstitutional.[11]

The dysfunctions of the Section 7(a) regime reflected the degree to which the NIRA and the lead agency for administering it, the National Recovery Administration (NRA), were more concerned with implementing a system of government-sponsored industrial planning and cartelization than with vindicating labor rights. Steel workers recognized the new regime's limitations and soon joined others in denouncing the NRA as the "National Run Around." But Section 7(a) was perhaps not entirely useless, as its text plainly purported to protect the right of workers to organize and engage in collective bargaining free of employer interference. Even if this endorsement paid few benefits before the labor boards, it did put the companies in the unfamiliar position of having to justify themselves, and it legitimated workers' efforts to seize these rights for themselves and realize the statute's promise.[12]

But as Weir's gambit showed, Section 7(a) also encouraged the formation of company unions, or ERPs. Although the steel companies tried and failed to encode the legitimacy of ERPs in the industry's fair competition code, these barriers to genuine union representation could still be interpreted to satisfy the requirements of the statute, at least if they were presented as the product of a "free expression" of the workers' will. Taking advantage of rulings to this effect by the NRA, open shop employers claimed exactly this. Under the NIRA, Republic and National established fully fledged ERPs in their plants for the first time.[13] Other steel companies revived moribund ERPs that had been set up in the 1910s and 1920s. The overall number of company unions in steel increased during the NIRA period from nine to ninety-three; and the fraction of workers nominally represented by ERPs leaped from 20 percent in 1932 to over 90 percent in 1934.[14]

With the advent of the New Deal, the NAM and the Iron and Steel Institute took the lead in a nationwide campaign to encourage the formation of ERPs. To ensure the ERPs' antiunion function, the companies vested leadership in pliant workers, especially older, married, native-born whites from the higher skill positions. The ERPs were closely monitored by company men, who participated in their day-to-day operations. And membership was often made a condition of continued employment. Structured in these ways, the ERPs mostly did nothing but preempt genuine unions, particularly at Republic, Sheet & Tube, and National.[15] However, at other companies, including U.S. Steel and Bethlehem, the company unions exercised a measure of independence and to some extent actually addressed workers' day-to-day grievances.[16] Where they functioned in these ways, the ERPs were still effective antiunion foils. But they could also provide important cover for covert organizing by the same independent unionists whose organizations they were supposed to preempt.[17]

THE WAGNER ACT

More than a year before the Supreme Court invalidated the NIRA, a coalition of progressives in Congress led by Senator Robert Wagner of New York moved to enact a more effective labor rights statute. The sponsors of what would become the Wagner Act cobbled together an alliance of liberal and loyal Democrats and some liberal Republicans. Among the motivations behind the act was to redress the New Deal's continuing failure to establish a functional means of redistributing income and sustaining wages and effective consumer demand. Wagner and other progressives also genuinely supported the idea of labor rights for workers' sake. But there was also the matter of stanching militancy. By 1935, New Dealers from President Roosevelt downward confronted a swell of disaffection with the entire New Deal, emanating from the working class as well as key elements of the political left and aggravated by the failure of Section 7(a). The Wagner Act represented, in part, an effort to shore up support from these quarters and diminish the appeal of more radical responses.[18]

Aided by the calculation of some in Congress who opposed the law but predicted that the Supreme Court would strike it down, supporters of the Wagner Act overcame resistance from both the business community and congressional conservatives. The statute passed the Senate by a wide margin, cleared the House by a voice vote, and was signed into law by Roosevelt on July 5, 1935. Notwithstanding his popular reputation as a class traitor and friend to labor, Roosevelt was ambivalent about the legislation and waited until it was destined to be enacted before featuring it in his agenda. But characteristically, he allowed the act's politics to sort themselves out.[19]

The new labor law differed markedly from the old NIRA scheme.[20] The Wagner Act created a new NLRB which, unlike the Section 7(a) boards, was established by the statute as an independent administrative agency, staffed by three members appointed by the president, and expressly empowered to interpret and enforce the law. Unlike the NIRA, too, the Wagner Act itself was independent of any larger corporatist program (even if elements of such a program might be read into its provisions). The new statute was also clearer in setting forth basic labor rights. Section 7 of the Wagner Act closely resembled Section 7(a) in the way it accorded workers the right to organize unions and provoke collective bargaining. Sections 7 and 7(a) were also nearly identical in how they encased the right to strike in a broad prerogative of workers "to engage in other concerted activities for the purpose of collective bargaining or other mutual aid or protection." However, the Wagner Act recognized the right to strike more explicitly in another provision, Section 13, which held that nothing in the labor law "shall be construed so as either to interfere with or impede or diminish in any way the right to strike." Even more important was Section 8, which established a number of "unfair labor practices" that advanced the rights in Sections 7 and 13 by proscribing a range of employer practices, including the following: coercing, discriminating against, or otherwise unjustifiably interfering with workers in the exercise of their Section 7 rights (§8[1] and [3]); establishing a company union or interfering unduly with an independent union (§8[2]); and refusing to bargain "in good faith" (§8[5]). Other key provisions of the new law were Section 9, which set forth procedures for determining that a union enjoyed the right to represent a group of workers, and Section 10, which defined the remedies available to the NLRB for sanctioning unfair labor practices and effectuating the aims of the law. Section 1 of the act memorialized the convergence of Keynesian-like economic norms, a program of industrial peace, and progressive reformism that defined the new law's purposes.

The Wagner Act stands as the strongest expression of government support for labor rights in American history, and its general thrust was clear enough from its text and legislative history. Nevertheless, the statute left a number of questions unanswered, including, Which among its several purposes would predominate? How far would the new board's remedial powers extend? What would the right to strike and picket entail? And what would satisfy the mandate to bargain in good faith? Even more immediate than these ambiguities was uncertainty as to whether the statute would survive review by the Supreme Court, which invalidated the NIRA just as the Wagner Act was moving toward passage. This issue of constitutionality was intertwined with whether employers would successfully flout the law. If they did, an already hostile Supreme Court would likely feel a greater license to declare it unconstitutional.

The Supreme Court in *NLRB v. Jones & Laughlin Steel* did uphold the statute, but only after almost two years of legal uncertainty—and as James Pope has argued, only after a massive wave of worker militancy, punctuated by the spectacular six-week sit-down strike at General Motors' plants in Flint, Michigan, demonstrated what might happened if the court decided the case differently.[21] Moreover, the Supreme Court extracted a price in upholding the act, one that played off the statute's ambiguities. On its face, the Wagner Act was certainly concerned with limiting violence, achieving labor peace, and protecting the flow of interstate commerce. But these were not necessarily its exclusive or even predominant aims. They appeared in the statute's text and legislative history alongside other important goals, including equalizing bargaining power between workers and capitalists and securing workers' rights for workers' sake. Although these latter aims were central to the aspirations of activists whose pressures ultimately brought the statute into existence, *Jones & Laughlin* declined to prioritize them or even hold them on par with the more conservative ones. Instead, the decision emphasized Congress's power to govern the flow of interstate commerce and intimated that this constitutional purpose disfavored violence and strikes—notwithstanding that some unrest and disorder might prove essential to advancing the very labor rights the statute endorsed.[22]

Nevertheless, even more so than Section 7(a), as enacted the Wagner Act embodied the view that labor rights were central to the New Deal's effort to rebuild the economy and, perhaps, reorder society in a more just way. Seeing the political value of this, workers and union organizers lost no time describing their efforts as now consonant with the president's and the federal government's wishes. With a greater confidence than was ever before possible—and with an equally clear understanding of how vulnerable the new legal regime was—unionists countered employer resistance armed with the argument that it was *they* who now represented legal right and an official vision of the commonweal.

THE BIRTH OF THE CIO

The union upsurge that accompanied the enactment of Section 7(a) had declined in late 1934 and early 1935. But it rebounded after the passage of the

Wagner Act, evolving into a massive campaign to expand unionization in previously nonunionized parts of the economy. The institutional basis of this campaign was a dissident movement that emerged out of the AFL in 1935. Composed at the top by representatives of the AFL's few established industrial unions, including the UMW, and in the lower ranks by a diversity of upstart industrial unionists from industries like rubber and radio equipment production, this faction challenged the federation's ineptitude and congenital antipathy to industrial organizing. Led by the UMW's John L. Lewis, in the fall of 1935, the dissidents pressed the AFL leadership at the federation's convention to commit to a new organizing model. Rebuffed, they founded the Committee for Industrial Organization, or CIO (later renamed the Congress of Industrial Organizations). Lewis and his allies understood that the rank-and-file militancy that peaked in 1934 could be harnessed by an organization better suited to engage with these workers' aspirations and grievances. And for Lewis, a man of great personal ambition and ruthless determination, no less than for the CIO itself, there was also the possibility of dominating the entire labor movement. At its inception, the CIO maintained a titular relationship to the AFL—it purported to serve only an "educational and advisory" role. However, from the beginning the CIO was actually a bitter rival to the older federation. In September 1936, the AFL expelled the constituent unions of the CIO and the CIO became an independent labor federation.[23]

The CIO was never a radical organization. Its top leadership consisted of mainstream trade unionists with left-liberal or social democratic views and not a few genuine conservatives. However, the CIO was also staffed with radical organizers associated with the Socialist Party, the IWW, and especially the Communist Party. Despite their modest numbers, these radicals endowed the CIO with some its most experienced, courageous, and altogether gifted organizers—men and women willing to risk life and limb and infiltrate dangerous open shop redoubts to press the organization's cause. Ironically, given their characteristic dogmatism, among the advantages that Communists brought to the table were insights they had derived through relentless self-criticism of the party's earlier efforts to independently organize open shop industries like steel.[24] Party organizers played a pivotal role in the CIO's campaign to challenge the open shop in automobiles, machinery, textiles and clothing, lumber, rubber, glass, agriculture, maritime transportation, and mining.[25]

The strength of the rank-and-file forces that gave rise to the CIO and ensured its vitality in its early years can be seen in basic strike statistics, which show a dramatic increase in organizational strikes between 1932 and 1936. By 1936, around half of these strikes were successful.[26] In some industries, most notably agriculture, the CIO was checked by organizational shortcomings and employer-sponsored repression. But elsewhere CIO unionists achieved considerable success, even without yet receiving any direct, effective assistance from the Wagner Act or the NLRB. Before *Jones & Laughlin* was decided, CIO unions were already negotiating and signing collective bargaining agreements. As a result of the CIO's industrial organizing model, some of the contracts were huge in scope, covering one hundred thousand or more workers, as was the case at General Motors and Chrysler. Although obvious challenges loomed, by early 1937 it seemed that the CIO might soon eclipse the AFL as the dominant labor federation and organize nearly the entire industrial workforce.[27]

The CIO could not thrive without tackling steel, however. The ambition to organize steel was a motivating factor in John L. Lewis's move to create the CIO in the first place. As UMW president, Lewis had offered little support to the outbreak of rank-and-file steel militancy that expressed itself in the 1933 Weirton strike, believing the workers' efforts doomed to fail and destined to frustrate UMW dealings with the companies regarding their mining interests. However, by 1936 Lewis's attitude toward steel had changed. The heaviest of heavy industries and the most basic of basic industries, steel had long exemplified the crippling shortcomings of traditional craft unionism. The industry was also positioned between the CIO's homeland in coal mining and its other primary target when formed, the automobile industry. Moreover, a number of major mining operations were controlled by the steel companies, which could influence wages and prices even at independent coal companies. For all these reasons, Lewis committed the CIO to organizing steel.[28]

THE RANK-AND-FILE UPSURGE AND
THE DEMISE OF THE AA

The appearance of Section 7(a) and the Wagner Act occasioned, in each instance, an increase in support for unionism among steel workers. But conventional narratives notwithstanding, it is not at all clear that the enactment of these statutes was the principal cause of these upsurges in labor militancy. Other factors played a part. Among these were influences brought to light by Lizabeth Cohen in her study of industrial workers in Chicago in the open shop and New Deal periods. Cohen's central thesis is that the proliferation of ERPs and other implements of welfare capitalism whetted workers' appetite for security and shop-floor justice even as they served as bulwarks of the open shop system. When the Depression rendered these schemes dysfunctional, she argues, workers turned with renewed interest to unions and government programs as means of satisfying their desires for benefits, job security, and a measure of control of their work.[29]

The flourishing of militant industrial unionism was also catalyzed by (and in turn gave impetus to) a broader cultural shift. As historian Robert McElvaine has shown, the Depression years engendered a culture of cooperation and mutuality, accompanied by an intense suspicion of the power and privilege of big business and the wealthy. Amid desperation and conflict, Americans became more inclined to identify downward, with working people and the poor, and to embrace ideas and policies that were imposed on wealth and property in order to serve the common good. Those who were working class or poor came to see themselves less as deviant and dysfunctional and more as victims of an unfair and defective social system, even as handmaidens of a new, more just society. Although by no means universal or uncontested, these changes formed a pillar of the New Deal, as they altered the way working people and elites alike viewed the role of the state vis-à-vis the conflict between workers and capitalists, and the role of unions in society.[30]

Amid these broader developments, and in the context of growing immiseration and doubts about the legitimacy and viability of the existing economic order, steel workers took the initiative in challenging the open shop. By 1931 there was unrest among the industry's workers. By the following year there were also increasing efforts by militants and radicals to build from this a coordinated challenge to the open shop. That year, the Communist Party, operating though its labor organization, the Trade Union Unity League (then under the leadership of William Z. Foster), established the Steel and Metal Workers Industrial Union (SMWIU). The SMWIU had little success achieving contracts or even building stable membership rolls. However, the union offered ideological substance to the rank and file's appetite for industrial unionism while also honing the skills of future organizers. Joe Weber, an important figure in the Little Steel Strike, organized for the SMWIU in a Chicago mill, where he and his fellow unionists devised a cellular organization structure to foil the efforts of company spies.[31] And the SMWIU did successfully organize a few individual departments in mills scattered throughout the Ohio Valley and Great Lakes regions. It also led a few strikes, including a messy but prominent stoppage in 1932 at Republic Steel in Warren, Ohio.[32] At its peak in 1934, the union had probably fifteen thousand members.[33]

In 1934, in part because of a string of defeats in strikes like the one in Warren, the Communist Party abandoned its "Third Period" strategy of attempting to organize the working class by forming separate, party-controlled industrial unions.[34] In line with a new charge to "bore from within," the party disbanded the SMWIU in late 1934 and sent its activists to join the AA and some of the ERPs. Many soon found a home in the broader rank-and-file movement that increasingly challenged the AA's inept leadership and stubborn commitment to the values and structures of craft unionism. For party activists, this undertaking remained an act of infiltration, as they and their agenda were not at all welcomed by the AA's leadership. However, a working relationship evolved between party members and AA reformers among the rank and file.[35]

Although the Communist presence became significant, the majority of the men who composed this rank-and-file movement were never party members. There were other partisan factions, including non-Communist radicals. And there was also an important and well-defined centrist element, headed by a young college man named Harold Ruttenberg.[36] But most of all, the rank-and-file activists were always just that: men who labored in the mills, formed their own grievances, and attained leadership by strength of action and personality. Against all the odds, these men were able for a time to harness worker discontent and frustration with the old AA, the inspirational effect of the New Deal, and broader changes in worker sentiment and culture to organize new lodges and achieve real increases in membership.[37]

With an innate opportunism rooted in years of concessionary dealings and ideological ambivalence, the AA's leadership initially viewed the new organizing efforts as an occasion to collect more fees and dues, but it quickly came to oppose the movement as a threat. Especially obstructive was President Michael Tighe himself, who in the summer of 1933 responded impassively to pleas from the AFL leadership that the AA meet the growth of ERPs with an organizing campaign of its own.[38] Tighe had been forced by the strength of the rank-and-file movement to endorse a more coordinated campaign. However, when it became clear that the movement might threaten his authority, Tighe again changed course and moved to expel its leaders.[39]

Initially, Tighe and his allies were unable to restrain the dissidents. Over 110 new AA lodges were formed, and total membership increased from less than 5,000 in early 1933 to over 50,000 (and maybe as many as 100,000) a year later.[40] But successful recruitment did not translate into effective representation. Few company representatives would even acknowledge the new lodges' existence, let alone bargain with the union or discuss shop-floor grievances.[41] Rather, the companies set out to undermine the resurgent lodges. Typical of their efforts were events at Republic's plant in Warren, where organizers formed three new lodges only to have attendance at meetings plummet from huge crowds to handfuls of diehards. As local leader John Grajciar remembered, support collapsed when the company bribed some supporters and fired twenty-five or thirty others. All but one of the lodges at Warren passed out of existence.[42]

These countermeasures inflamed an already volatile situation in steel. As early as 1931, there had been significant, though localized, strikes in protest of wage cuts.[43] The 1933 walkout at Weirton and the one at Warren the year before were among a number conflicts that further underscored this state of unrest. After the passage of the NIRA, the strikes increased in frequency and their purpose shifted from merely defending against company demands for concessions, attempts to withdraw recognition, or other reprisals, to genuine organizing. The U.S. Department of Labor counted eighteen strikes in basic steel from 1927 through 1932 (involving around 8,000 workers), of which only four were organizational; but it counted thirty-nine strikes from 1933 through 1936 (involving over 45,000 workers), including twenty organizational strikes.[44]

In the words of leftist journalist Harvey O'Connor, by early 1934 the AA faced the same choice William Z. Foster had in 1919. It could launch "a national strike to force recognition from the hostile magnates, or an inch by inch retreat under the steady drumfire of company unions, discrimination, propaganda and espionage until its demoralized members abandoned the union."[45] Over two hundred delegates from some fifty upstart lodges conferred prior to the AA's 1934 convention in Pittsburgh and determined to launch an industry-wide strike. When the convention opened, this program met with the full opposition of Tighe and his old guard, who declared it unworthy of discussion. Tighe eventually ruled the strike agenda out of order. When delegates objected and threatened to walk out, Tighe relented, allowing approval of the strike agenda while reverting to behind-the-scenes manipulations to undermine it.[46]

Planned for mid-June, the big strike never happened. The companies remained adamant in their refusal to recognize the AA lodges and probably would have welcomed a strike as an opportunity to crush the insurgency. Aided by the erratic maneuvers of the NRA's administrator, Hugh Johnson, they also frustrated efforts by the rank and filers to bring the administrative machinery of the NIRA to bear on the dispute. Meantime, Tighe and his lieutenants successfully thwarted planning for the strike at the convention. Outmaneuvered, the leadership of the rank-and-file group tabled the strike threat for good when Roosevelt and his congressional allies, eager for compromise, moved to reform the procedures for enforcing the NIRA. By executive order and congressional resolution, they created the (first) National Labor Relations Board and the National Steel Labor Relations Board, and charged the former with enforcing Section 7(a) and the latter with administering labor rights in steel. These moves dissipated workers' enthusiasm while doing nothing to roll back the open shop.[47]

In the last days of 1934, after the debacle of the strike threat had passed, rank-and-file delegates from western Pennsylvania met again and again proposed, over Tighe's opposition, an attempt to organize steel, by means of a strike if necessary. Although its immediate effect was mainly to further anger Tighe, this conference was followed in February 1935 by yet another, larger meeting, this one attended by four hundred delegates. This time Tighe purged the lodges that supported these dissident moves, casting out three-quarters of the AA's membership in steel. While the purge solidified Tighe's control of the AA, membership reverted to 1920s levels.[48]

New Left activist and scholar Staughton Lynd has suggested that the rank-and-file movement could have made substantial, lasting progress in organizing steel had the organizers been better supported by the AA, the AFL, and the Communist Party. Lynd argues that the leadership of each of these organizations squandered a golden opportunity, not only to successfully organize steel years before this was actually achieved, but to build a powerful, independent, and progressive union. He contends that the decision of the Communist Party to disband the SMWIU was especially destructive in this regard, as it deprived the steel workers of independent leftist leadership at a crucial juncture and, perhaps most importantly, positioned John L. Lewis and his acolytes to dominate subsequent efforts to organize steel.[49] Although Lynd's point about deficient leadership of the rank and file is entirely consistent with the chaotic, sometimes reckless, and often transparently self-interested maneuvers by all the major parties during the mid-1930s, it is difficult to say whether his conjecture that things could have turned out differently is also correct. It does seem true that the rank-and-file movement was more substantial and promising than SWOC and CIO leaders were later inclined to admit. The movement was also, in contrast to the SWOC that succeeded it, a genuine uprising among the workers themselves, led by shop-floor activists, and thus inherently more vital. But as historian James Rose argues, and as Lynd himself admits, it is unclear that the rank and file was strong enough to effectively challenge the open shop, even if better led or supported.[50] After all, the steel companies had not played their strongest hand either.

THE FORMATION OF THE SWOC

If it was to organize steel, the CIO could not do so by simply beefing up the AA. The new federation would have to either reform the older union or, alternatively, displace it entirely. But both approaches presented serious challenges. In early 1936, the CIO was still nominally a creature of the AFL, and the AA held a charter from the AFL giving it the exclusive right to represent the workers in basic steel. If the CIO founded a rival alongside the AA, the older organization would raise the damaging charge of dual unionism. And despite having been battered, AA lodges maintained a presence in many mills and could be useful to a renewed drive. But if the AA could not be cast aside, its recent history certified that it could not be easily reformed either.

Faced with this conundrum, John L. Lewis felt about for a viable course. In February 1936, Lewis proposed that the UMW, enriched by a surge in membership in its own ranks, fund an AFL-sponsored drive to organize steel on an industrial basis. When the AFL refused, Lewis and company turned directly to the AA. Although opposed to the CIO's program of industrial unionism and to the militants and radicals it would bring along, the AA's leadership had to reckon with the prospect of circumvention by the CIO if they resisted these entreaties. The leadership convened in Canonsburg, Pennsylvania, in late April 1936, to consider what to do. Wooed by the CIO's promise of energetic organizing efforts and $500,000 to foot the bill, but jealous of their own authority and concerned by the prospect of disloyalty to the AFL, AA leaders stretched the convention to the edge of summer, hoping the AFL might somehow match the CIO's offer. But no such offer emerged, and Tighe and his old guard reluctantly accepted the CIO's bid. On June 3, the

AA's leadership entered into a memorandum of understanding with the CIO whereby the AA would affiliate with the CIO and the two organizations would create the Steel Workers Organizing Committee—the SWOC.[51]

The SWOC was not a conventional union but rather, as its name suggests, an ad hoc organizing institution dedicated to establishing a framework for union representation in steel. Like the National Organizing Committee that led the 1918–19 drive, CIO leaders attempted to negotiate a jurisdictional accord with the AA's leadership by which the SWOC could organize in mills with an AA presence without supplanting existing AA lodges. Those AA lodges that had no collective bargaining agreements were to be taken over directly by the SWOC. All others would be issued new charters. Technically, new members would join the AA but their dues would go to the SWOC. In fact, the terms of the accord were quite confusing. But unlike in 1918, this agreement pushed aside the AFL leadership and subordinated that of the AA to SWOC leaders chosen by Lewis himself.[52] Even before the SWOC was established, some AA lodges had petitioned the CIO to allow them to reaffiliate with it, or to launch a CIO drive in steel.[53] What occurred was essentially a takeover by the CIO, which was a major reason for the deepening of the rift between the AFL and the CIO in the summer and fall of 1936.[54]

Organizing through existing AA lodges and building its new organization around AA stalwarts, the SWOC was notably faithful to elements of the AA's craft heritage. But the new organization was an industrial union, dedicated to organizing under one tent the production and maintenance workers, not only throughout basic steel, but also in steel fabrication and ore mining. Independence from the AFL did not make the SWOC autonomous, though. From the time of its founding through its eventual transformation into the USW, the SWOC remained under the control of the CIO—not the AA and not its own lodges, either. So complete was CIO control that for its entire existence, the SWOC did not have its own constitution. This dependency would have important implications for the course of the Little Steel Strike and for steel unionism generally. As for the AA, its gamble with the CIO failed; in all but name it essentially "passed out of existence."[55]

Just days after the agreement between the CIO and the AA, a SWOC governing board was established, dominated by Lewis's people. Four of the board's eight members were UMW men: Philip Murray, vice-president of Lewis's UMW; David McDonald, who had been Murray's personal assistant at the UMW; and Van Bittner and Patrick Fagan, both with long standing in the miners' union. Two other members of the board hailed from other CIO unions and also had close ties to Lewis. And the remaining two were officers in the AA whose presence served obvious political purposes. McDonald was named the SWOC's secretary-treasurer. Bittner was appointed one of the SWOC's three regional directors, along with William Mitch, another UMW man, and Clinton "Clint" Golden, one of the few important SWOC officials not tied to Lewis or the UMW. Lewis handpicked Philip Murray to chair the SWOC.[56]

Murray's presence would prove important. Born in Scotland to Irish Catholic parents, he had immigrated to the United States in 1902, when he was sixteen years old, and began working in the Pennsylvania coal fields. Intelligent, ambitious, and a committed unionist, Murray rose rapidly through the UMW ranks. In 1920 he was elected vice president of the UMW on Lewis's ticket. In that role, he proved a competent servant of Lewis's vision and interests, as well as Lewis's often reactionary and dictatorial excesses. Like Lewis, Murray was no radical—years after the Little Steel Strike he famously proclaimed that "we have no classes in this country."[57] And he was not overly captive to the ideals of union democracy. Unlike Lewis, though, who was intuitive, impulsive, and often intemperate, Murray's demeanor was calm and polite; and his politics were rooted in the corporatist teachings of the Vatican. While he was no shill for business interests, this orientation disposed Murray to negotiate and compromise and to trust that the law and the state could serve as effective supports for workers' rights.[58]

Murray convened the SWOC in Pittsburgh on June 17, 1936, and the organization launched its drive just a few days later, on Sunday, June 21. The kickoff event was a rally on the banks of the Youghiogheny River, near the city dump in McKeesport, Pennsylvania, well in sight of several large U.S. Steel plants. The SWOC used an initial disbursement of $25,000 from the UMW to secure space for its headquarters on the thirty-sixth floor of the Grant Building in downtown Pittsburgh—eight floors above the offices of National Steel. As more money came in, the SWOC also made arrangements to begin publishing a free newspaper, *Steel Labor*, edited by an experienced newspaper man named Vincent Sweeney. And it set its organizers to work. Initially, the UMW provided thirty-five to forty organizers. Within weeks, the SWOC had over one hundred organizers working the mills and steel towns. By the end of the summer there were two hundred, with more to come.[59]

To Banish Fear

For Philip Murray, the collapse of the rank-and-file uprising left the SWOC with a defining challenge: "Our first problem was to banish fear from the steel workers' minds."[1] But although the debacle allayed few workers' concerns about the extent of the companies' power, such fear was neither universal nor the only impediment to successful organizing. Moreover, what Murray did not acknowledge was that many workers' fears were also rooted in their recollections of how much the leadership of the AA had undermined the rank and file during that heady period.[2] Ironically, memories of this betrayal likely inclined workers to cede control of the drive to the SWOC and its people, to let them prove their commitment, even though this meant a surrender of local sovereignty and laid the groundwork for a culture of authoritarian leadership that would define the future of steel unionism. Such were the underpinnings of one of the most remarkable organizing drives of the 1930s.

THE SWOC'S PROGRAM FOR ORGANIZING STEEL

From the outset, the SWOC's drive embraced groups unwelcomed by the AA, including Communists. Perhaps eighty of the two hundred SWOC organizers working by the end of that first summer were Communists.[3] As the SMWIU's efforts underscored, Communists had long maintained an important presence in steel. Even through the open shop era, a vanguard of party members and sympathizers remained in and around the mills. By the 1930s, they were increasingly asserting themselves and their program, sometimes very overtly and at great expense in personal security. On Memorial

Day, 1931, several hundred Communists and supporters congregated in Youngstown to agitate for better redress of the dire economic conditions in the region. The protest devolved into a riotous confrontation with local officials and self-appointed patriots that ended with the police arresting some two hundred protesters.[4] In the larger steel cities like Cleveland and Chicago, Communist-led protests like these, typically aimed at preventing residential evictions or agitating for the unemployed, and often ending in disorder, were commonplace in the early Depression years.[5]

The decision by the SWOC leadership to include Communists in the drive was both opportunistic and sagacious. As one organizer later suggested, the Communists' presence represented a practical decision by the CIO's anti-Communist leadership to ally with "tireless builders" who could be "counted on" to "provide a link to the great mass of foreign-born, largely Eastern Europeans, as well as blacks in steel."[6] This judgment was confirmed by other SWOC organizers, including one who abjured that in the thick of the struggle, few people were overly concerned with party affiliation: "the job was to do the organizing."[7] Because the Communists were capable and well positioned in and around the mills, they were enlisted. John Williamson, at the time of the strike the party's leader in Ohio, recalled that the CIO eagerly recruited Communists: "Lewis and Murray made every effort to enlist Communists." Williamson claimed that "in Ohio our entire party and Young Communist League staffs in the steel area" were thrown into the drive.[8]

John Grajciar, a non-Communist organizer who worked alongside Communist organizer Gus Hall in the Youngstown area, described working well with Communists when their aims converged, while moving quickly to discharge those whose party commitments clashed with SWOC interests.[9] Grajciar was also clear "that if it hadn't been for the communists in the early stages of this organization we would have had no union," as so many other workers were too fearful to take on the job.[10] Another Youngstown organizer, James Gallagher, a staunch anti-Communist, was quick to concede "that they were good organizers."[11] Canton-area organizer John Johns confessed his respect for Communists and ventured that they "had guts" and were "darn good organizers."[12]

Although its members were involved from the outset, the Communist Party formalized its commitment to the drive later in the summer of 1936.[13] The party's motives in joining the drive are rather obvious. As in other cases where it allied with the CIO, the decision to throw in with the SWOC accorded with the party's Popular Front program of ingratiating itself to the CIO and enhancing its standing in liberal and progressive circles. But the motives of individual Communists were less straightforward and are harder to chronicle. Beyond simple allegiance to the party's agenda, many Communist organizers may have believed, optimistically, that the drive represented a real step toward social revolution. However, most were likely impelled, at least in part, by more immediate and realistic goals, including politicizing the workers they organized and, perhaps most importantly, joining in a fight against real enemies of the industrial proletariat.[14]

Communist involvement in the SWOC's campaign would be particularly pronounced in northeast Ohio and especially in the greater Youngstown area—Youngstown, Warren, and Niles, Ohio.[15] Not coincidentally, the struggle would be especially hard fought there, with the strong and well-coordinated support of the rank and file, complicated by racial conflict, running up against powerful resistance on the part of the steel companies and their allies. Chicago, the cradle of American Communism, was another center of party activity. The party was exceptionally strong in South Chicago, in and around the Calumet's big steel mills, and Communists would play a key role organizing in the region.[16]

Although often prominent at the grassroots level, Communists certainly did not control the SWOC, whose overall aims were defined by Lewis, Murray, and others in the UMW contingent. The ranks of lower-level organizers were also fairly dominated by UMW people, many of them with close ties to Murray. Veterans of bitter conflicts in the coal fields, many UMW organizers were steeped in a tradition of militancy and acquainted with the challenges of organizing in the face of repression.[17] At the same time, their aspirations were definitely to the right of the SWOC's Communist elements, as they opposed the Communists' social vision and were wary of the party's implicit infusion of radicalism into the union's program. If Communist support for the drive reflected an amalgam of reformist and radical themes, the political motivations of the CIO leadership and its organizers were moderate, with a strong corporatist, social democratic flavor.[18]

The SWOC eventually deployed over four hundred paid organizers in the drive, a majority on full-time pay. These professional organizers worked alongside perhaps five thousand informal, volunteer organizers.[19] In testament to both the spirit of the times and the CIO's standing as one of the truly great social movements in American history, hundreds of these volunteers were radicals or reform-minded activists with few direct connections to the industry. But the majority of volunteer organizers were rank-and-file steel workers, some of whom had been laid off, some already fired for union activity, and others still on the job; many, too, were AA stalwarts and veterans of the upsurge, eager to renew the struggle. As Inland worker John Sargent remembered, the most important organizers "were essentially workers in the mill who were so disgusted with their conditions and so ready for a change that they took the union into their own hands."[20] Sargent's sense that these volunteer organizers were often more important than the professional ones is certainly correct, as the SWOC's force of professional organizers was spread thinly across a workforce more than a thousand times larger.

Volunteer or professional, Communist or UMW, these organizers' efforts were hierarchically structured by the SWOC's leadership around departments at the regional, subregional, and district levels and, finally, around the local lodges, which were based on individual plants, clusters of smaller plants, or divisions within the really huge plants.[21] They were dedicated to a program built around three avowed strategies, each a conspicuous response to the perceived lessons of previous years: overcoming racial and ethnic differences among the workers; cloaking the campaign in the authority of the Wagner Act and the federal government and making use of whatever practical influence the newly created NLRB might have; and infiltrating and usurping the company unions.[22]

The first of these goals was uniquely important, not least because of the position of black workers in the plants. Their reputation as interlopers notwithstanding, blacks were at home in ferrous metal production before there was a steel industry. In colonial and antebellum times, free blacks and slaves proliferated among the skilled workers in ironworks. However, the proportion of black workers diminished as the industry consolidated after the Civil War amid a tide of foreign immigration and Jim Crow discrimination.[23] By 1910, blacks were a "negligible" presence in the mills—certainly fewer than 5 percent nationwide, with most concentrated in the South.[24] These patterns began to change as a result of both the importation of blacks as strikebreakers and the "First Great Migration," when more than a million southern blacks moved into the industrial regions of the Northeast and Midwest. The number of blacks in the northern mills increased, approaching 10 percent of workers before falling off a bit in the face of discriminatory hiring practices and Depression layoffs. By 1930, large numbers of blacks worked in the mills in the bigger cities and towns of the North, especially Cleveland, the Pittsburgh area, and the Calumet.[25]

Meanwhile, having comprised a majority of all steel workers in 1910, foreign-born workers were less than one-third of the industry's employees in 1930. The same shift was evident in the demographics of the mill towns. Between 1910 and 1930, the foreign-born population in Youngstown fell from over 31 percent to around 19 percent, while the percentage of black residents over the same period increased from 2.4 to 8.7.[26] More critically, although distinct ethnic identities and the neighborhood enclaves they constituted often persisted for generations, by the mid-1920s the trend for immigrants and their children was toward assimilation. Even in the mills themselves, ethnic employment patterns began to break down as language barriers and residency patterns eroded, intermarriage increased, and a greater diversity of Europeans achieved generic whiteness.

For black workers, though, the experience of the 1920s and 1930s was very different. Nationwide in 1930, black steel workers made up 16.5 percent of common laborers but only 6.5 percent of skilled and semiskilled operatives and only 4 percent of rolling mill workers. In that year, nearly three-quarters of all black steel workers were common laborers who performed the roughest work and bore the brunt of capricious hiring policies and shop-floor authoritarianism.[27] Indeed, whatever their job classification, blacks were nearly always concentrated in the hottest, dirtiest, and most dangerous departments, especially the coking operations and the iron- and steel-making furnaces—a practice many whites justified with the ridiculous theory that blacks were inherently more resistant to heat.[28] With bad jobs came poor pay and more frequent and lengthier periods of unemployment. By the advent of the Depression, many black workers and their families were descending into concentrated isolation in squalid ghettos, frequently in the grimy approaches to the plants. In addition to being routinely discriminated against by relief agencies, blacks bore the brunt of layoffs and downward reassignments. Although partially a consequence of possessing less seniority and fewer important skills—both accumulated products of discrimination—their fate was often a result of simply being ousted from long-held positions in order to open up jobs for whites.[29]

In this context, the attitudes of black workers toward unionism were ambiguous and their position in the organizing drive difficult to predict. Black workers were justifiably skeptical of unionism. The AFL's overall record with black steel workers was abysmal, characterized by rank discrimination and outright exclusion. So was the AA's. As one authority put it, "In its fifty-three years of existence, from 1880 to 1933, the Amalgamated

Association had not made a single serious effort to include Negroes in its ranks in a position of full equality with White members."[30] To be sure, the influence of rank-and-file reformers, some of them black, led some AA lodges in the NIRA period to modify their more racist policies. Boosted by the concentration of resentments among blacks and low-status ethnics, these efforts led to these groups being *overrepresented* in many of the lodges during this period. But the AA's reputation on race remained very poor. When SWOC organizers showed their keenness to recruit them, many black workers reacted with suspicion, believing they were being lied to or might be used as "cat's paws" by treacherous white unionists.[31] And even if fully convinced of the organizers' sincerity, black workers had other reasons to be cautious. As sociologist Horace Cayton Jr. pointed out in his 1939 study of black workers in the SWOC's campaign, if blacks rejected the union they risked the ire of white unionists; but if they joined, they had every reason to think they would be the first fired, denied relief, or evicted from their homes.[32]

Decades after the strike, Oliver Montgomery, a black official with the USW, recalled how his father, an activist in the 1930s, avowed that no one "even needed a union but the foreigners and the niggers."[33] The elder Montgomery exaggerated. But he was right that unrelenting discrimination and deteriorating working conditions had disposed many blacks to be especially receptive to the program of rationalizing employment policies that was central to the CIO's agenda.[34] Black journalist Claude Bennett's "Gary Report," based on interviews in 1936 and 1937 of black steel workers in the Calumet, found that black workers blamed workplace discrimination in substantial part on the racist policies and manipulations of plant superintendents and foremen and that surprisingly high levels of support for the SWOC among blacks were grounded in cautious optimism that the new union movement would redress racial inequities.[35] The position overlaying these views was well expressed in a 1936 commentary by activist Eleanor Rye, published in the nation's premier black newspaper, the *Chicago Defender.* Seeking to cultivate support among the wives of steel workers, Rye, who was black, insisted that only through the CIO "will their husbands and relatives have the opportunity of advancement to higher paid jobs, be freed from the evil of 'dead work,' unsanitary working conditions, jobs full of hazards to life and limb, with little or no safety and precautionary measures being used."[36] Nor were better opportunities the only motivation for black workers. By the mid-1930s a substantial minority of blacks (including Rye) had come to understand their social plight in terms of a deep, perhaps inextricable convergence of class and race domination. For these radicals, the CIO's program was, if anything, too modest.

For many progressives and radicals in the CIO, building an integrated union was an imperative in its own right. Black or white, they understood that black steel workers *deserved* to be part of the new union and that an industrial union that excluded them did not warrant the name. But there were practical reasons, too, that mandated that the SWOC make inroads with black workers. While there were not enough blacks to run the mills during a strike, as scabs or replacement workers blacks could be used to antagonize and discredit the strikers. A recurrence of the racial conflict that characterized the 1919 strike would deal a serious blow to the CIO's reputation. Moreover, a functional system of plant-wide collective bargaining was inconceivable except on an integrated basis. At the same time, the successful organization of black workers offered a tactical advantage, as the frequent consignment of blacks to the hardest jobs on the "hot end" of the plants placed them in critical departments.[37]

Though crucial on its face, the aspiration to wrap the drive in the mantle of the newly enacted labor law was perhaps the least important of the three strategies. Certainly, this was true when the drive began in the summer of 1936, when most informed observers felt that the Supreme Court would eventually invalidate the Wagner Act. In this light, the success of the SWOC's effort to organize steel was possibly less dependent on the act than the act's survival was dependent on the success of this and other big CIO drives. Still, until such time that the Supreme Court might throw it out, the statute gave political sanction to the organizers' efforts. And if the Wagner Act was destined to be upheld, it was important to begin building cases against the steel companies and invoking whatever authority it and the Roosevelt administration might convey. Likely, it would have paid little for the SWOC and its leaders to ignore the law and remain at a distance from the New Deal, for this would have given ambivalent New Dealers the opportunity to write them out of the reform agenda.

Only days into the drive, the SWOC's lead legal counsel, Lee Pressman, dispatched a memorandum advising organizers to document every instance in which workers' rights under the labor law had been violated.[38] During the drive and the strike, union leaders, local and national, lost no opportunity to invoke the Wagner Act, to couch their demands as consistent with the New Deal and the wishes of the president himself, and to present the effective mediation of the state as an essential prerequisite to labor peace and industrial prosperity. Indeed, a number of SWOC lodges, like New Deal Lodge No. 1124 at Republic in Massillon and Blue Eagle Lodge No. 1033 in South Chicago, wrapped themselves in the language of the New Deal.[39] (Maybe more prescient in name was Rubicon Lodge No. 1014, at U.S. Steel's South Works in Chicago.) And during the strike, union picket signs regularly featured slogans like "Who Is Bigger, Purnell or Roosevelt?" or "Roosevelt Gave It! Company Is Trying to Take It Away."

On July 5, 1936, the anniversary of the signing of the Wagner Act, CIO organizers held a meeting of miners and steel workers in Homestead, Pennsylvania. The men running U.S. Steel showed how much the New Deal impressed them when their company police prevented Secretary of Labor Frances Perkins and Pennsylvania lieutenant governor (and UMW secretary-treasurer) Thomas Kennedy from speaking in a public park. The meeting had to be held at the U.S. Post Office. The change of venue should have given workers occasion to rethink the value of Kennedy's promise that they would receive protection and aid from the government in the event of a strike.[40]

The SWOC's third strategy, to infiltrate the ERPs, mimicked an approach adopted by Communists and rank-and-file activists in the NIRA era. As we saw earlier, even before the SWOC's drive got under way, the ERPs had probably already undermined their founding purpose by legitimating the idea of collective demands and negotiations between workers and employers.[41] Mindful of this, organizers figured that once they had established influence within the ERPs—either by winning over their officers or infusing their ranks with SWOC people—they could use the ERPs to press the demands the SWOC intended to make its own. The company unions were also a practical place to organize for the simple fact that they already existed, at company expense no less. And if the ERPs could be captured, even partially, the SWOC insurgents could press for concessions and then claim that any made were the product of their agitation. If the companies yielded nothing, the organizers could present this as evidence of the need for independent union representation. Subverting the company unions would also go a long way toward accomplishing the goal that Murray and others saw as essential to a union victory: dispelling the notion that the companies were simply too powerful to defeat.[42] For if they could not control their own unions, were they really that invulnerable?

Not everywhere was this strategy feasible. Organizers first evaluated the viability of penetrating particular ERPs by assessing the degree of management control over their functions.[43] Where there was no prospect of capturing them, or where they effectively blocked independent unionism, the only option was to outmaneuver or destroy them. This would be the SWOC's approach, for example, at Inland's big mill at Indiana Harbor. Nor was the capture strategy always successful. In practice, penetrating the company unions, influencing their leadership, and using them to press for better conditions of employment and more favorable disposition of grievances was neither simple nor easy. A danger for the SWOC was that this effort might backfire by boosting the legitimacy of the ERPs without undermining their antiunion function. Moreover, anyone engaged in these gambits could still be fired, as happened on some occasions.[44] It all had to be done carefully. In a memorandum to subregional directors, dated September 11, 1936, Murray urged organizers to approach company union officials "in a friendly and courteous manner, gaining their confidence and good will, explaining our purpose and objectives intelligently."[45] Elsewhere, Murray advised organizers to be cautious in distinguishing those company union men who took the interests of their fellow workers seriously from those "who enjoy basking in the favor of the bosses" and those "who are definitely of the stool pigeon variety."[46] Union records document extraordinary efforts to adhere to these sensible principles.[47]

RESISTANCE AND THE CHALLENGE OF RACE

By the mid-1930s, large corporations had learned that favorable narratives about labor disputes were best developed in the same professional, rationalized, even scientific way that the companies made radios, automobiles, or steel.[48] When the SWOC's drive began, the steel companies set out to undermine the union's effort in just this way. In July 1936, the Iron and Steel Institute spent nearly $500,000—as much as the CIO's total initial outlay to fund the drive—on a full-page advertisement in 382 newspapers in which it sought to explain its constituents' refusal to deal with the CIO. The advertisement billed the unionists as outsiders who would employ "coercion and intimidation" and "foment strikes"; it contrasted the "closed shop" to the right-to-work principle that "no employee in the steel industry has to join any organization to get or hold a job"; it touted the companies' ERPs as effective vehicles for "collective bargaining"; and it warned of the risks that unionism posed to the industry's viability. It closed with a promise that the industry would strongly resist the organizing drive.[49]

The NAM joined in this public relations crusade. Recently reorganized and reinvigorated under the leadership of Ernest T. Weir, Charles Hook, and Tom Girdler, and with a membership of three thousand manufacturing firms and relationships with thirty thousand other companies, the NAM was powerful and wealthy, and it was virulently opposed to the New Deal, the Wagner Act, and the CIO. Through its National Industrial Council and National Industrial Information Committee, the NAM sponsored a massive advertising campaign centered on a series of "harmony ads" that ran for a number of weeks in 1936 and 1937 in local newspapers in nearly two hundred cities and towns. Designed to undermine union organizing drives, the advertisements sought to rehabilitate the reputation of industrial capitalism by underscoring the communities' dependence on big business and touting the virtues of American capitalism. These were part of a broader newspaper-based campaign that contrasted images of irresponsible industrial unionists, dangerous radicals, and misinformed New Deal progressives to a reassuring mosaic of conservative homilies highlighted with captions like "No Classes Here" and "Put *Yourself* in his [the boss's] place"; disarming non sequiturs (like how to remove skunk scent from clothes); folksy, commonsense defenses of industrial capitalism (many authored by conservative academics); and appealing caricatures of middle-class prosperity. The NAM also generated leaflets and pamphlets, billboard posters, motion pictures, canned letters for company shareholders, prewritten editorials and newspaper columns, and "fact sheets" for foremen, which were distributed in virtually all the steel towns.[50]

Despite these efforts, SWOC organizers had success cultivating support among the many ethnic groups represented in the mills.[51] The union actively solicited the support of ethnic social clubs, churches, and small businesses; it enlisted organizers from these groups, deployed public speakers fluent in the workers' native languages, and published organizing materials in these many languages. Translators were provided by the International Workers Order, a collection of local Communist Party–affiliated fraternal and mutual benefit organizations. The union also plied ethnic workers with evidence of the CIO's commitments to social tolerance, the relative diversity of the union's staff, and the CIO's opposition to discrimination. This last vow had to be played delicately, as some workers were more interested in maintaining their relatively privileged positions in the mills than in realizing the higher principle of equality. Nevertheless, the SWOC's appeal to ethnics was quite successful. By late winter 1937, organizers were reporting significant progress, even in enclaves that had earlier resisted the drive.[52]

Recruiting black workers proved more challenging. In a circular dated November 8, 1936, Philip Murray stressed that "our policy" is "one of absolute racial equality in Union membership" and flaunted union efforts to work with black organizations. But Murray also held that "it is our conviction, however, that the organization of the negro steel worker will follow, rather than precede, the organization of the white mill workers."[53] The SWOC's record with blacks was, in line with Murray's circular, rather contradictory.

The SWOC did indeed reach out to black steel workers, promising them equal and fair representation as well as improved working conditions.[54] And it matched this rhetoric with concrete actions. The union established branch offices in black workers' neighborhoods. In early 1937, it also formed the National Conference of Negro Organizations to Support the Steel Drive, which coordinated SWOC efforts with those of black community groups and churches, the National Association for the Advancement of Colored People (NAACP), the National Urban League, and the National Negro Congress. These groups joined with prominent black politicians in supporting the drive.[55] Linked to the Communist Party and with a strong presence in steel producing areas, the National Negro Congress was especially important, as it provided the SWOC with most of its black organizers.[56] The drive also drew the support of A. Philip Randolph's Brotherhood of Sleeping Car Porters, the most prominent black union of the time.[57]

The effort to recruit blacks benefited from the fact that many SWOC organizers were closely tied to either the Communist Party or the UMW. Organizers trumpeted the progressive racial politics of both organizations, and they bore their affiliation as proof of their commitment to racially just unionism. Though hardly free of racist tendencies, the UMW had long enrolled black miners, even at the height of Jim Crow, when few civic organizations were integrated at all.[58] The Communist Party's reputation among blacks was even more favorable. Under William Z. Foster's leadership, the party had made recruitment of black members and opposition to racial inequality major points of agitation. The party lost no opportunity to assail racial injustice and undertake symbolic acts that challenged the racial order, including choosing a black man as its candidate for vice president of the United States in 1932 and 1936. It also played a prominent role through much of the 1930s, organizing legal representation for and agitating on behalf of the "Scottsboro Boys"—the nine black youths who repeatedly faced execution or life imprisonment on dubious charges that they had raped two white women in Alabama. Several Communist organizers, including John Steuben, a leading figure in Youngstown, and black organizer Ben Careathers, who worked the area around Pittsburgh, were personally endowed with the credibility that came from advancing this well-known cause.[59]

Also impressive to black workers was the party's earlier organizing in steel. In the early 1930s, the SMWIU had aggressively recruited blacks and explicitly advocated racial equality in the mills; and it was not uncommon for local party organizations to be fairly dominated by black members.[60] Later, party members played a prominent role in recruiting blacks during the rank-and-file upsurge. There was also the party's unparalleled record in attempting to integrate blacks into its social functions.[61] Nowhere was the party's appeal to blacks more resonant than in Chicago, which in the early 1930s had a higher percentage of black members than any other branch.[62] There and in nearby parts of northwest Indiana, the party had a strong presence among black steel workers well before the SWOC came into existence.

Although the SWOC's leadership and professional organizing corps were largely composed of "Americans," many of its full-time organizers were ethnics and at least fifteen were blacks.[63] In choosing some of these organizers, the SWOC sought out the recommendations of black political organizations and even vowed to deploy the organizers on an integrated basis.[64] Several black organizers were either members or fellow travelers of the Communist Party. Jesse Reese, whose recollections of the Memorial Day Massacre open this book, was frank and unabashed about his communism. At the start of the drive, Reese was president of the AA lodge at one of Sheet & Tube's plants, having earned great respect from the integrated workforce.[65] Other black Communist organizers included Ben Careathers, a veteran of the SMWIU; Henry Johnson, the college-educated son of an IWW member who had experience organizing packinghouse workers; Hosea Hudson, an Alabama steel worker later renowned as a civil rights pioneer; Eleanor Rye, a fearless character who was one of a handful of black women with the SWOC, an important liaison to the National Negro Congress, and an affiliate of both the Brotherhood of Sleeping Car Porters and the Furriers Union; and Leondies McDonald, a one-time follower of the black nationalist Marcus Garvey and representative of the Chicago Federation of Labor.[66]

The SWOC proclaimed the organization's support for civil rights initiatives and even sent black delegates to regional civil rights conferences.[67] The union consciously installed blacks as officers in its lodges, often arranging for lodges to be led by a white president and a black vice president. This fueled charges that the SWOC had consciously deployed the so-called

UMW formula for racial diversity. SWOC people tended to deny this, perhaps rightly so. For similar practices were already in place at some AA lodges during the rank-and-file upsurge and had been employed by the Communist Party as well. And staffing the lodges in this way was an obvious and convenient way for the SWOC to court black members without alienating too many whites. Regardless, by enlisting blacks as organizers and leaders, the SWOC signaled the seriousness of the CIO's vow to challenge exclusive quotas, job segregation, and other racist policies within the mills.[68] Nor was this the only advantage of placing blacks in leadership positions. Frequently lauded for their public-speaking ability, command of the English language, and ability to articulate a compelling, rights-based concept of labor reform, blacks often proved especially capable organizers—to the point that some whites were surprised to find themselves preferring black leadership at the local level.[69]

The recruitment of blacks was aided by favorable coverage of the drive in the *Pittsburgh Courier*. One of the country's largest black newspapers, the *Courier* was exceptional for its prolabor views, and it was published in the heart of steel country.[70] The *Courier's* editor, Robert L. Vann, strongly endorsed the SWOC's effort to organize steel workers.[71] So did other writers, including the radical Ernest Rice McKinney, who participated in the organizing drive. At the outset of the drive, McKinney penned a piece in the *Courier* in which he challenged "Negro steel workers" to embrace the drive as an opportunity to overthrow the "dominating weakness of the race." McKinney acknowledged the fraught history of the relationship between blacks and organized labor but urged black workers to take seriously the CIO's promise of racial justice and to support industrial unionism as the ideal means of advancing their interests in an age of mass production.[72] Nearly as significant as the *Courier's* coverage was the surprisingly favorable treatment the drive received in two prominent but traditionally antilabor outlets: the Associated Negro Press, a service with over fifty newspapers on its rolls, and the nation's largest black newspaper, the *Chicago Defender*.[73]

In many places, organizers enlisted significant numbers of black workers. In and around the major urban centers of the Calumet, Cleveland, and Pittsburgh, black support for the drive and the strike that followed was strong.[74] In some locations, organizers even reported stronger support from blacks than from whites. The SWOC's success in these areas reflected a general upsurge in favorable views of unionism—and of the CIO especially—among black workers as well as the urban black middle class.[75] But it also reflected the success of the SWOC's own organizers, both black and white, in challenging the antipathy and mistrust that had so long defined the relationship between blacks and unions.

A sense of how this was achieved emerges from organizers' records from the Calumet region. Rather than revealing dramatic breakthroughs, they document the gradual inroads that organizers, including Johnson, McDonald, and Rye, were able to make among wary black workers. There are nearly weekly notations of "steady progress" or "good progress," with the occasional descriptions of "splendid progress" and accounts of truly large and enthusiastic meetings of black workers, as well as of disappointing turnouts and other setbacks. The records likewise evidence painstaking efforts to win over black preachers, professionals, and community leaders, culminating in occasional declarations of building confidence, for instance, "Negro ministers have pledged 100% cooperation," a note from late January 1937, about one of the plants at Indiana Harbor; or, with reference to the same mill, "leading Negro professionals are cooperating."[76] The records also document strenuous efforts to counter company efforts to build antiunion groups among blacks and to check anxieties generated by rumors of racial violence in other labor disputes.

Nevertheless, as historian Bruce Nelson points out, to some extent the SWOC's leadership did seem content to see the SWOC make an initial push among blacks and then pull back in anticipation of revisiting the issue after sufficient whites had been enlisted.[77] And it was partially because of this that support for the union among black workers remained weak in some places. This was certainly true where overall union support was low, including mills on the periphery of the steel-making regions that were not a priority for organizers, as well as mills in the South.[78] But it was also true in more critical regions, like the greater Youngstown and Canton-Massillon areas, where organizing was otherwise aggressive and successful. In such places, sometimes inadequate outreach to blacks was compounded by entrenched apprehension of union racism and radicalism.[79] Ironically, another difficulty concerned the CIO-led automobile sit-down strikes. Even though the strikes electrified many steel workers and were not racist affairs, some blacks saw in their spectacular militancy the worrying specter of racist vigilantism.[80]

Although some blacks put their faith in the open shop, the union's difficulties with black workers did not always reflect deep-seated opposition. Many blacks were favorably disposed to the SWOC but content not to take the lead in organizing an industry in which whites predominated and monopolized the better jobs. And so they waited. For example, in early November 1936, a group of black workers in the Chicago area told Henry Johnson "they feel they can't sign up till whites do." Characteristically, Johnson responded by inviting them to attend an interracial meeting and by approaching "officers of their social club."[81] Nor was the SWOC easily deterred by the difficulties it encountered recruiting blacks in certain areas. Despite persistent problems in mills of the Youngstown area, the union dispatched black organizers there and continued its efforts right through the end of the strike. Amid these struggles, a consensus took hold that while black workers might be more difficult to organize, once enrolled they proved particularly loyal.[82]

U.S. STEEL AND J&L

Initially, the SWOC's main target was U.S. Steel, and for good reasons. In 1936, Big Steel was still roughly as large as all the big independents combined and employed roughly half of the employees in basic steel.[83] Although the company's leadership role had diminished, it still influenced industry labor policy and functioned as a price leader. If the SWOC could succeed at U.S. Steel, it would conquer nearly half the industry in one stroke and might reasonably expect the other major independents to fall in line. On the other hand, if U.S. Steel remained un-unionized, there was little chance the other companies would give way.[84]

The campaign at U.S. Steel seemed to unfold surprisingly well, despite company resistance. Organizers and workers who supported the union ran the usual gauntlet of espionage, harassment, and provocation at the hands of company police, foremen, and spies. Often, union people were menaced by company men and their allies, as for example in late November, when a group of organizers led by George Patterson was harassed and had their literature confiscated by police near U.S. Steel's South Works in South Chicago.[85] Then, in January, police armed with blackjacks attempted to move organizers away from one of the mill's gates.[86] There were also quite a few firings at the South Works. Eleven union men were discharged and several others "had the law layed [sic] down to them" by company managers, all on the same day in early February.[87] Despite these tactics, organizers working at U.S. Steel were able to hold union meetings and rallies; build the support of community groups, including churches, social clubs, and, crucially, "saloon keepers"; distribute union literature; and, most importantly, meet with the workers in intimate settings where they might make a compelling case for union representation.[88]

The SWOC's bid to capture the ERPs at U.S. Steel also appeared to pay off as unionists repeatedly won over the leaders of the ERPs or maneuvered their own people into leadership positions.[89] When U.S. Steel offered workers better terms, the union promptly claimed these were the product of SWOC agitation. When the company proposed targeted increases in wages and benefits via a members-only "contract" with its ERPs, the union vowed to have the NLRB declare them illegal company unions, which compelled the company to accord the benefits to all employees. As early as August 1936, the SWOC's newspaper, *Steel Labor,* openly boasted of its success using these methods to capture the ERPs.[90] Remarkably, by fall of 1936, the SWOC claimed effective control of U.S. Steel's company unions, alleging that ERPs at over forty plants had defected.[91]

SWOC organizers also claimed impressive gains in signing up U.S. Steel's employees. At the outset of the drive, the SWOC counted about 16,000 members; this increased to 86,000 in November 1936 and 125,000 by the first day of 1937, disproportionately from U.S. Steel's plants.[92] These figures were exaggerated, but they did reflect at least a core of support at the company's mills that could, if properly handled, rally many more workers to the union's cause. And these numbers likely worried company officials, who saw bad news piling up. In 1936 the CIO and the SWOC went all out to support New Deal candidates, donating over $500,000 and, in the case of the SWOC, mounting an intensive get-out-the-vote campaign in the mill towns.[93] These efforts helped achieve dramatic increases in support for the president and other Democratic candidates in Ohio, Pennsylvania, and Indiana.[94] Unionists celebrated the election as another step toward a CIO victory, taunting the "bosses" and propagandizing the results as a mandate for the CIO.[95]

The New Year brought another worry for Big Steel: the six-week-long wave of sit-down strikes against General Motors, which compelled that company to abandon its categorical opposition to union representation and enter a contract with the CIO's United Automobile Workers. GM was every bit as powerful as U.S. Steel and its capacity for labor repression at least as great; yet it was nearly shut down by the strikes. Seeing this, officials at U.S. Steel could not but wonder what costs their company would incur if they opted to defend the open shop to the last.

On January 9, 1937, U.S. Steel's chairman and director, Myron Taylor, initiated a brief conversation with John L. Lewis after a chance encounter in the dining room of the Mayflower Hotel in Washington, DC. Further conversations followed, initially unknown to other company and union officials. In these meetings, Taylor surrendered to notions he had begun to embrace months earlier: that unions were an unavoidable reality in the future of steel production and that continued resistance would only delay the inevitable while exposing the company to considerable political and economic risks. Unlike Girdler and the other leaders of Little Steel, Taylor was an industry outsider, a corporate lawyer and financier; he fancied himself an "industrial statesman" who could deal with a union without sacrificing the company's critical interests.[96] Taylor had long-standing contacts, through the Business Advisory Council, with New Deal politicians; and in his brief tenure at the company he had brought in many younger executives who shared his pragmatic perspectives on politics and labor relations.[97] Taylor had also worked with Lewis and Murray to settle the coal strike that catalyzed the 1933 walkout at Weirton Steel, and he knew that Lewis was hardly a radical when it came down to it. From this vantage, Taylor was able to see collective bargaining as a low-risk opportunity to rationalize production at a company increasingly burdened with instability and anarchical labor policies.[98]

Clearly *not* an important factor in the company's retreat from the open shop was the level of confirmed support for the union at U.S. Steel. In 1937 David McDonald was the SWOC's secretary-treasurer. Years later, he confessed that the union had actually signed up only 7 percent of U.S. Steel's workers when Taylor's negotiations with Lewis unfolded—not the hundred thousand or more suggested in public statements. McDonald admitted that the image of huge numbers of workers flooding into the SWOC was an artifact of union propaganda that he "helped to write." He mused that, while the "rest of the steel industry was outraged" at news of U.S. Steel's capitulation, "they would have been apoplectic had they known how little we had to bargain with at the time Taylor capitulated."[99] It is difficult to assess the accuracy of the egotistical McDonald's comments or the overall level of support for the SWOC at U.S. Steel that spring, and it is difficult to judge what Taylor and others at U.S. Steel knew about the extent of union support or how this might have influenced them. In fact, for reasons we will examine shortly, *no one* could really know where the drive stood at U.S. Steel—or anywhere else, for that matter. But in early 1937 the SWOC had not signed up a clear majority at U.S. Steel.[100] Yet the company yielded. In a move that astonished observers, in March 1937 U.S. Steel signed a collective bargaining agreement with the SWOC, covering over a dozen major plants of its main steel-producing subsidiary, Carnegie-Illinois Steel.[101] Legend has it that company men removed a portrait of Henry Frick from the room where the agreement was signed because they "did not think he could stand it."[102] In truth, the contract was a brief document that called for tangible, but undramatic, improvements in wages and benefits. Moreover, it was a "members only" agreement that covered only SWOC enrollees—exclusive representation would come later, along with contracts at other U.S. Steel subsidiaries.[103]

Still, the agreement was momentous, and the SWOC and the CIO held it up as a harbinger of industry-wide success.[104] The Communist Party's *Daily Worker* declared the steel companies and their "stooges" in crisis, exulted that workers elsewhere had been inspired and were signing up in droves, and predicted that the SWOC was on the verge of an overwhelming, industry-wide triumph.[105] And so it might have seemed. For only a few weeks later, on April 12, the Supreme Court upheld the constitutionality of the Wagner Act. A landmark decision that essentially validated the constitutionality of the entire New Deal, the case also accelerated a contest with the captioned party, Jones & Laughlin Steel, in which the SWOC would prevail decisively.

Not in U.S. Steel's league in size and influence, J&L also seemed increasingly reticent to join the common position emerging among the Little Steel group. The nation's fourth-largest producer, the company operated two large plants: one in Aliquippa, Pennsylvania, the other on the south end of Pittsburgh. Its labor policy was virulently antiunion, particularly in its company town of Aliquippa—home to Tom Girdler's self-described "benevolent dictatorship" in the 1920s, where in 1933 and 1934 company police dealt with AA organizers by tracking them down, beating them, and ejecting them from town. In 1934, the wife of Pennsylvania's governor was able to address a union meeting in Aliquippa only with state police protection, and perhaps with company machine guns trained on the crowd. SWOC organizers working in Aliquippa also faced intense repression. Their rooms and persons were searched without warrant and their union material confiscated and destroyed. Unionists were arrested "by the dozen" and charged with disorderly conduct, with the resulting fines deducted directly from their pay, if they worked for the company. And if they worked in the mill they likewise faced demotion or discharge.[106]

Nevertheless, organizers penetrated J&L's ERPs.[107] In a brazen challenge to company hegemony, in 1936 they organized a Labor Day march in Aliquippa. And when Roosevelt trounced Alf Landon in the November elections, unionists claimed his victory as one for the workers over the "steel barons" and lost no opportunity to point out that Landon's uncle was an official at Jones & Laughlin. When J&L granted a 10 percent wage increase, the organizers claimed it as the result of their efforts. Most importantly, they continued to recruit new members, although company pressure was so intense that organizers made no attempt to set up local lodges but rather sent newly signed union authorization cards directly to headquarters.[108]

By spring, J&L's resistance began to crumble. The signing of the U.S. Steel agreement was an important blow, as was the Supreme Court's ruling. Unlike the other major producers, J&L also had not made a profit in years and feared the consequences of a drawn-out strike.[109] Facing these facts, company management reluctantly proposed terms to the SWOC similar to the U.S. Steel contract, with a provision allowing the company to continue dealing separately with dissidents. But the SWOC, buoyed by its string of successes, scorned the company's entreaties. Instead it launched a massive walkout.

The strike at Aliquippa was a telling display of how successfully organizers had battled the company on the ground. Beginning on May 12, huge numbers of picketers besieged the mill, taking advantage of the plant's geography to place a cordon sanitaire around it. Armed with bats, clubs, and pipes, they routed the company police. J&L was forced to close the mill as well as its Pittsburgh plant.[110] Fearing for the company's financial viability and bowing to the fact that J&L could not foresee ousting the picketers anytime soon, after three days company officials capitulated. They agreed to grant the SWOC exclusive representation if it won a NLRB-sponsored election. Little over a week later, on May 25, the union prevailed decisively and entered its first exclusive contract with a major steel producer.[111]

Amid these developments, a growing number of smaller basic steel producers and fabricating firms also agreed to SWOC representation without a strike and, in most cases, without forcing litigation before the NLRB. In March, the union claimed contracts with around twenty-five companies; in April, 51; in May, over 100; and by early June, 142, covering upward of 300,000 employees.[112] Even as the SWOC counted these victories, however, a showdown loomed with Little Steel. Already in mid-January, anticipating the breakthrough at U.S. Steel but a tough fight at Little Steel, Philip Murray ordered SWOC organizers to refocus their efforts at the latter.[113]

FIGURE 4. SWOC leaders pose at the union's Pittsburgh office after the signing of a momentous collective bargaining agreement with U.S. Steel, March 13, 1937. Left to right, seated, are Philip Murray and David McDonald; standing are William Mitch, Clinton Golden, Van Bittner, and Lee Pressman. © 1937, Associated Press.

ORGANIZING LITTLE STEEL

Among the first organizers to arrive in Little Steel's stronghold of Youngstown was Frank Shiffka. In August 1936, Shiffka reported to headquarters how he and the people who met with him in and around Youngstown were "rough shadowed" by Republic's police and spies through June and July. One of the men Shiffka had union dealings with was followed to a picnic by company men who told him "not to be afraid, that their chief had not given orders to shoot yet."[114] It later emerged that Republic's police had placed a man in a hotel room near Shiffka's to monitor the organizer's actions.[115]

Another organizer, a young man named Robert Burke, filed a report with the union that described a week in mid-August spent dodging city and company police at Republic, Sheet & Tube, and U.S. Steel mill gates in and around Youngstown. Burke's report records both the workaday efforts involved in organizing and the perils that organizers faced. It recounts a several-day period in mid-August of near-continuous struggle to distribute leaflets at various plant gates, obtain signatures on authorization cards, manage the volunteers who were helping him, and most of all talk to the men themselves—all "without the cop's [sic] seeing me."[116] Burke's attempt to elude police in Campbell, Ohio, failed on the afternoon of August 19, when he and his men were arrested, thrown in jail, and fined. When released that night, they got right back to work handbilling the plant gates.

Several days later, on August 22, Burke and his men were in Youngstown when city police seized their literature and a belligerent man brandishing a gun and a blackjack told Burke to "mind your own business while you're still in one piece." When the organizers reported the threat to other city police and asked that their materials be returned, they were told that the papers had been destroyed and that the man who had threatened them was a deputy and the police did not care to do anything about it. A little later, Burke took up the matter with the chief of police, who contended that the organizers had no right to distribute literature on the streets anyway, never mind that other groups freely did so.[117]

Burke's travails continued into the fall. In mid-November, he and an organizer named Jack McKeowan, an old AA man, were distributing literature outside Republic's plant in nearby Warren when someone slashed all the tires on Burke's car. He got them fixed and returned to join McKeowan distributing handbills at the main gate during the late-night shift change. Burke recalled looking over at McKeowan when, "Suddenly I found myself flat on my face, not quite cold, but I looked up and saw the boots coming and more blackjacks sort of raining down, and I gathered myself up in a ball and rolled away." Burke got up in time to see three men assault McKeowan before they ran off.[118] The attacks occurred in full view of workers entering and leaving the mill as well as uniformed company police, who merely laughed. Both men were cut and bruised but vowed to resume organizing at the plant. The attackers got away.[119]

Burke's path to the SWOC is a revealing commentary on the nature of the drive and the motivations of those who spearheaded it at the ground level. Born in the Youngstown area in 1914, Burke worked for a year in the city's steel mills and drove a truck for two years to save enough money to enroll at Columbia University. There he did odd jobs to pay his way, including washing dogs for wealthy people and teaching boxing. The young man quickly established himself as an excellent student and well-known

FIGURE 5. SWOC organizer Robert Burke in Youngstown, Ohio, June or July 1937. An area native who joined the drive after being expelled from Columbia University for antifascist activism, Burke was one of approximately eighty Communists who served as full-time organizers. Courtesy of Penn State University Special Collections Library, Historical Collections and Labor Archives, Meyer Bernstein Papers.

activist. He organized protests in favor of striking university employees and was elected president of his junior class. In May 1936, Burke led several protests against Columbia's hosting of Nazi officials from Germany, which included picketing the president's home. This put Burke in deep trouble with the university's administration, which expelled him. Before it became certain that neither a lawsuit, nor vigorous student protests, nor the efforts of prominent liberals would compel the university to reverse its decision, Burke had returned to Youngstown intending to work with his father building houses.[120] Burke explained that he and his father soon decided he should work for the SWOC, since that is what he really wanted to do. He was told to see Frank Shiffka, who had just begun organizing in the area.[121]

If he was not a Communist when he left Youngstown, Burke surely was when he returned. Youngstown-area leader Thomas White had this to say about Burke's blunt and aggressive style: "On pay day he would go to a beer garden and tell the guy to shut off the drinks. He would give a speech and I'd go out and sign them up. He was rambunctious, boy, I'm telling you." Burke was different from fellow Communist Gus Hall, whom he worked alongside. While Hall "had to persuade you that what he was saying was correct ... Bob figured he could thump it into you." Nevertheless, White insisted that Burke was convincing, and White was among many unionists, radical and otherwise, who appreciated Burke's gumption and general effectiveness.[122]

Burke's story is rather unique. But what he experienced around Youngstown was not. Union fieldworker notes from the Calumet district abound with references to organizers being arrested or "having trouble" with police near the mills.[123] Both company and public police regularly seized organizers' literature or prevented them from distributing it on the streets and sidewalks. As in the incidents reported by Burke, this often involved public police claiming the authority to ban this activity. On many occasions, too, organizers attempting to distribute literature around mill gates were attacked, sometimes quite viciously, by company men.[124] In Cleveland in January 1937, an organizer named Gerald Breads was shadowed all day by Republic's men before being kidnapped while distributing litera- ture at a mill gate; he was severely beaten with blackjacks and the butt of a gun.[125] In April, an organizer named Paul Castman was also assaulted while distributing literature and collecting authorization cards at a Republic gate in Cleveland. A company policeman beat Castman so severely with a black- jack that he remained hospitalized for sixteen days.[126]

Nothing better illustrates the physical courage required of SWOC organ- izers than the experiences of two men, Kenneth Koch and Steve Barron, who were attempting to organize Weirton Steel at its complex in Weirton, West Virginia, and nearby Steubenville, Ohio. Koch and Barron spent August 31, 1936, distributing *Steel Labor* on the streets of Weirton, only to be accosted by "special watchmen" who threatened to kill them if they persisted in their efforts and then smashed Koch's car with bricks and clubs. On September 11, after securing an empty promise of police protection, Koch and Barron resumed distributing the paper, taking up a position several hundred yards from the plant gate to avoid exposing workers who accepted copies. At around three o'clock that afternoon, the two men were attacked by special watchmen and had to be hospitalized. On October 14, Koch and Barron were menaced several times by large groups of armed men as they attempted to distribute union material door-to-door. Unable to secure effective police protection, they were able to carry on their work only by assembling a guard of eighty-five or ninety friends and allies. On the evening of October 16, Koch and two of Barron's sisters set out to pick up another sister so that they all might attend a union function. Before they could rendezvous, Koch and the two women were surrounded in their car by special watchmen who dragged them out and beat them. Koch and one of the sisters were knocked unconscious and all three victims required medical treatment.[127]

Organizers everywhere faced intense espionage by company agents.[128] In Massillon, Ohio, SWOC supporters met in darkened fields and parks to avoid notice by company agents.[129] John Steuben, another Communist organizer in Youngstown, changed his name, moved his family, and arranged emergency accommodations in a bid to escape threatening surveillance by company police, but he was only partially successful.[130] Steuben's difficulty highlights the very real problems organizers faced merely trying to tend to life's everyday necessities. Another organizer, a recent Cornell graduate named Meyer Bernstein, who had hitchhiked from upstate New York to join the drive, experienced similar difficulties in the Pittsburgh area. In February 1937, Bernstein wrote a friend, "I was kicked out of another house yesterday."[131] Bernstein was lucky to be single. George Kimbley, the first full-time black person on staff with the SWOC, recalled being chosen for the position over several others because he did not have a family to worry about.[132]

The La Follette Committee and NLRB confirmed that a number of supposed SWOC organizers were actually company spies. Several company agents testified to the committee how they managed to infiltrate the SWOC's lower ranks with workers they recruited to the company's cause and people they planted for that purpose. These stratagems were sometimes enhanced by the companies' contriving to "discharge" these spies from their jobs for their apparent support for the union. Among the planted spies were men with criminal records, several who went under multiple aliases, and some who performed their work on a professional or semiprofessional basis. The spies gathered the names of people who signed up with SWOC organizers and reported on the overall structure and progress of the organizing drive. Early in the drive, Youngstown organizers uncovered a spy who turned in "the first sixteen men who joined."[133] Another Youngstown spy, a man named Harold Vargo—alias Richard Brooks, alias Ira Albert, alias Ira Alberts—managed to become financial secretary of a lodge being organized at Republic's plant, where he had access to the names of nearly two thousand SWOC members. A company agent in at least six other strikes, Vargo arrived in Youngstown outfitted with a fake wife.[134]

The La Follette Committee determined that Republic formed the center of a "labor-spy ring among the steel companies." Using Federal Bureau of Investigation forensic tests of the typeface of documents, the committee established that the National Metal Trades Association functioned as a clearinghouse for sharing espionage reports among the companies.[135] The committee's findings confirmed the feelings of many unionists that they faced a conspiracy of company opposition that dated at least from the time of the Great Steel Strike.[136] Although the extent remains unclear, some expressions of company collusion during the drive are apparent. With the consent of Jones & Laughlin officials, Republic sent around two dozen men, including company police captains, to Aliquippa to "observe," Republic said, the events surrounding the SWOC election in May.[137] In Youngstown, Republic and Sheet & Tube pledged to coordinate both espionage and overall police functions during the strike.[138] Although Republic and Sheet & Tube relied primarily on their own police to conduct and coordinate their spying programs, both Inland and Bethlehem employed the services of the Pinkerton Agency, which conspicuously stopped providing Bethlehem with written reports shortly after the organizing drive got under way. Weirton contracted with a company called Central Industrial Services; and ARMCO used Corporations Auxiliary, an agency that had played a prominent role in the Great Steel Strike.[139]

Quite often, union supporters and organizers identified by company spies were summarily discharged.[140] Thomas White, who worked and organized at Republic's Youngstown plant recalled, "I was elected president [of the union] on the Friday of that month and when I went to work the following day, which was Saturday, I was told I was discharged and no longer employed at Republic Steel for three years and two months. That was the penalty I had to pay." White soon discovered he was one of the people exposed by "a guy by the name of Ira Alberts."[141] If not discharged, organizers identified by means of espionage were subjected to harassment or more intensive espionage, the better to learn the scope of the drive and identities of other union supporters.

A revealing picture of how the companies used discharges, sometimes justified by pretexts, to undermine the drive can be found in the records that union lawyers prepared after the strike to support legal cases against the companies. For instance, Gus Ritchie, who worked at Republic's plant in Buffalo, New York, recalled the trouble he experienced after passing out union cards and wearing a CIO button to work. Following months of harassment, Ritchie was told that he could not continue working at the plant, ostensibly because he had "incurred the displeasure of the men he worked with."[142] On April 20, 1937, a Sheet & Tube worker from Youngstown named Joe Ramun wore a CIO button to work and was "sent home." Walter Halatek, another Sheet & Tube employee and volunteer organizer, was discharged December 21, 1936, for "bad work" after distributing union cards. Halatek's foreman told him he "shouldn't have gotten into the C.I.O." A month later, Halatek got his job back, only to be fired again two months later. "Before I was fired," he said, "Superintendent Jones warned me to lay off the C.I.O. and offered me an Assistant Foreman's job if I would tell him the names of the C.I.O. members and other union information."[143]

To overcome all of this, as well as the torrent of propaganda directed against them, organizers needed not only to pass out literature and make speeches but to meet with workers one-on-one and in small groups, where they could press the virtues of unionism and assuage workers' fears. To this end, organizers met with workers in churches, in saloons, at specially convened meetings, on the streets and at the mill gates, and in workers' homes. While there were risks in all of these places, no place was a more difficult—or more important—ground for organizing than within the mills themselves. The mills' size and labyrinthine structures could make the jobs of foremen, company police, and spies more difficult. However, company agents were vigilant; and within even the biggest mills, the usual practice of organizing departments into smaller work crews created an intimacy that could aid the efforts of company agents. Similarly, the proliferation of departments isolated workers, impeding plant-wide and industry-wide solidarity.[144] But the level of intimacy within the departments could work to the advantage of organizers. Work crews were often bound by ethnic and neighborhood ties, and the performance of dangerous work cultivated trust among the men, which could lend itself to considerable solidarity—and secrecy.[145]

John Johns, who worked in one of Republic's Canton mills, recalled the craftiness and aplomb required to organize there. Johns took advantage of the array of different jobs he performed to sign up new members. His work as a

FIGURE 6. Unidentified SWOC organizer distributes *Steel Labor,* probably in the Pittsburgh area in late 1936. Note the apprehension on both men's faces. Courtesy of Penn State University Special Collections Library, Historical Collections and Labor Archives, Meyer Bernstein Papers.

chainman and stoker "took me all over the plant," he said; and he used this mobility to approach potential recruits. But evenings, Johns also did first-aid work. "So almost every time anyone came into that first-aid room," he recalled, "I'd talk to them about signing up. I used the approach on most of them[:] 'Gee, haven't you signed up yet. Boy, you must be one of the very few remaining.'"[146]

Only active employees could organize inside the well-guarded mills. If they were found out, not only might they be fired, and perhaps assaulted, but so might the men they recruited. At the same time, the ability of organizers to operate successfully inside the mills challenged traditional notions regarding the sovereignty of private property, notions central to the steel companies' ideological and juridical opposition to unions and their collective resistance to the Wagner Act. Like nothing else the organizers might do short of winning recognition, roaming company property in order to recruit new members portended that the steel companies' absolutist vision of industrial relations might be nearing its end.

As a rule, SWOC organizers divided the mills by departments and then cautiously recruited members in those departments until they had built up a critical mass of support. As Ohio Communist leader, John Williamson, recalled, "The task was to establish a core of secret union members in one department after another, without the company's knowledge." This often required first approaching workers covertly, sometimes at their homes, perhaps after dark to avoid arousing the suspicions of neighbors.[147] Williamson's description of organizing is consistent with a memorandum developed by Clint Golden in June 1936, which directed local organizers to abstain from seeking formal charters from the union office until a "sufficiently large" number of members had been enrolled.[148] In September 1936, Philip Murray admonished the union's subregional directors to "take no uncalled for and unnecessary chances," particularly those that might get organizers fired.[149]

In August, Steuben, the Communist organizer in the Youngstown area, reported that while "sixteen of our people" had been "uncovered," only one organizer had yet been fired; the others were "warned but not yet fired."[150] Steuben's observations on the progress of the drive come from a report he dispatched to the party's trade union secretary. Giving further confirmation to the union's cautious and flexible approach, it describes a policy, learned from William Z. Foster's experiences in steel and practiced by Communists during the 1933–34 upsurge, of not holding public meetings unless Steuben could count on several thousand people to attend; of focusing on organizing smaller departments one at a time, rather than "spread[ing] out too much";

and of organizing workers in "chains"—that is, by securing from those who signed up the names of two or three others who might also be approached. Using such methods in 1936, Steuben noted that he had already recruited two hundred workers and that he and "other comrades" would soon reach five hundred each, at which time he could turn his attention to more strategic concerns.[151] Nor were these tactics employed only by Communists. For black organizers in the Calumet, organizing in chains was a natural application of their experience in community organizing.[152]

A striking account of the resistance organizers faced inside the mills can be found in the NLRB's main case against Republic for what occurred at its Ohio plants. Foremen at Republic's two Massillon plants quashed "all talk of organization in the shop" by threatening to fire union supporters. Those workers who did not desist were simply identified and discharged. In Canton, where the CIO and the SWOC were relatively strong, unionists were able to convene large public meetings in the weeks preceding the strike. But this did not stop Republic from insisting on workers' "duty of loyalty to the Company" and proclaiming the right to immediately "disrupt" the employment relationship of disloyal workers. During the drive, the company fired at least three "disloyal" organizers there. And it shut one of its Canton mills just prior to the strike after failing to root out all the organizers. In Youngstown, Republic closed a foundry because the workforce harbored two organizers and union activity had become too extensive. Elsewhere in Republic's Youngstown Works, employees were systematically interrogated about SWOC affiliation. The pattern repeated itself at the company's mill in Warren, where, in a move that likely communicated how much the company knew about union efforts, company managers gave union supporters a map showing where they were allowed to go within the plant. In Cleveland, the NLRB established eleven cases of men being fired for organizing activity.[153]

Antiunion repression was clearly extensive and undoubtedly deterred organizing efforts. But it is impossible to know exactly how effective these tactics were, not least because it remains unclear how much progress organizers were making. Union records are scattered to begin with. And only months into the drive, faced with disappointing recruitment numbers, the SWOC leadership allowed organizers to begin gathering authorization cards from enlistees without requiring payment of dues. By April, organizers had ostensibly signed up strong majorities at quite a number of plants, including at Little Steel's mills in the Calumet. And yet the same records reveal that only somewhere between two-thirds and one-half of enlistees (and at some mills, fewer than half) were paying their dues.[154] Nevertheless, these records and subsequent NLRB investigations indicate that by late spring, SWOC organizers had made considerable progress at Inland's and Sheet & Tube's mills and had probably built majorities there. By the same measures, the organizers were less successful at Republic's plants. They had built genuine majorities at some mills and were on their way to doing so at others. But particularly at Republic's more isolated operations, organizers' efforts were checked by strong resistance, or they had barely begun to organize at all.[155]

SWOC organizers were not faring so well at Bethlehem, ARMCO, and Weirton, either. As we shall see, the exact situation at Bethlehem was confused even for SWOC insiders by the company's size and geographical dispersion, the prominence and resilience of its ERPs, and the union's decision to focus its efforts on capturing these. But it is clear that the SWOC was not building overwhelming majorities at Bethlehem's mills. The situation at National and ARMCO is even clearer. At ARMCO, organizers were unable to make inroads against an array of semifunctional ERPs and other paternalistic controls, backed by run-of-the-mill repression.[156] At National, resistance was more aggressive and at least as effective. The *Nation*'s Benjamin Stolberg expressed a common sentiment when he called the company's base in Weirton, where Koch and Barron were hunted by special watchmen, a "little fascist principality, patrolled by notorious killers" and concluded that it was "too dangerous [there] to ask the men to strike for their rights."[157] As the conflict came to a head in early May and workers throughout Little Steel began to prepare for a strike, a "hatchet gang" structured around the company-supported "Employee Security League" descended on union men at Weirton, beating them and, in a series of episodes leading into June, physically evicting more than two dozen from the company's mill.[158]

STALEMATE

By midspring, it was increasingly evident that Little Steel was not willing to yield to the SWOC. Still, the union had reasons to be optimistic about its chances for wresting an agreement from the companies either by a strike or threat of a strike. The political situation seemed favorable. The previous fall had given something of a mandate to Roosevelt's New Deal, partially paid for by CIO funds and voters. Congress was controlled by Roosevelt loyalists, and governors of the states that were home to Little Steel's most important installations—Indiana, Ohio, and Pennsylvania—were all New Deal Democrats. Moreover, the months since that election had witnessed dramatic improvements in the overall economic situation in steel, and in employment numbers.[159] Although the first signs of the "Roosevelt Recession" were manifest in a decline in orders for steel in May, the steel companies had yet to curtail production and the economic outlook seemed largely positive.[160] The CIO had prevailed over U.S. Steel and many smaller companies, and the SWOC was on its way to signing a contract with Jones & Laughlin. And then there were the CIO's spectacular triumphs over General Motors and Chrysler, which accounted for a majority of production in an industry that had become the leading consumer of steel products. With the automobile companies making cars under CIO contracts, and U.S. Steel and the smaller independents also making steel under contract, if a strike at Little Steel proved necessary, it might well subject the companies to significant competitive and political pressures. The UMW was likewise established at dozens of coal companies, including some captive mines. CIO organizers were at work at the vital ore mines in the Upper Great Lakes and were attempting to organize seamen on the ore boats. And a number of railroads servicing the mills were also unionized. If a strike came, these workers might help the SWOC to starve Little Steel's plants.

SWOC organizers had achieved some success penetrating Little Steel's ERPs, even if not so much as in U.S. Steel's mills. They had also signed up thousands of workers into SWOC lodges. Although membership was unevenly distributed among companies and mills, there were stalwarts in all the plants; and as the struggle at Jones & Laughlin suggested, a strike could activate a well of latent support. Moreover, if there was a strike and the companies resorted to violence and provocation on the picket lines, these moves might be countered by the ongoing investigations of the La Follette Committee and by what seemed to be considerable sympathy for the CIO in liberal and progressive circles. And the *Jones & Laughlin* decision suggested that the authority of the Wagner Act might finally be brought to bear as well.[161]

Despite all of this, there were reasons to worry that should a strike prove necessary, it might fail. According to an internal SWOC memorandum, far from signaling imminent success, the signing of the Carnegie-Illinois agreement had "brought the SWOC face to face with several problems that affect seriously the future welfare of the Union." Among these was growing impatience among the rank and file at the companies not under contract, as well as continued organizational shortcomings.[162] There were early signs of dissention in the ranks between Communist and UMW organizers, who had begun to argue over organizing tactics as the struggle descended into stalemate.[163] Moreover, uncertainties about how the workers might react to a strike cut both ways. The SWOC could not be too sure of its support even in the mills that seemed well organized, especially after passing out membership cards to almost anyone who would take one. Nor could it be certain that support for a strike would prove enduring anywhere. The brief recovery notwithstanding, few steel workers had the resources to easily weather a long work stoppage, let alone the firings and blacklisting that would likely follow a failed strike.

The SWOC had other worries, too. Far from sitting on a healthy strike fund, it was heavily in debt. The organizing drive had already cost as much as $2 million, most of which the UMW had fronted in loans. The UMW's coffers were not inexhaustible; and SWOC's membership rolls were not healthy enough to generate a substantial and reliable flow of money from dues.[164] It was one thing to sign people up but quite another to collect $1 dues every month. While the SWOC claimed over eight thousand members at Bethlehem's Cambria Works in Johnstown, it collected only $883 from them in April and $2,071 in May.[165] In the entire Calumet region, where the SWOC claimed 52,295 members in April, it collected only $30,755 in dues that month and $25,891 in May.[166]

The national political situation was yet another area where positive signs belied reasons for concern. By late spring, a prescient judge of politics might have seen beyond the 1936 elections and concluded that the currents of anti-unionism and antiradicalism were beginning to flow more strongly against the CIO, not least because of the wave of sit-down strikes that winter. Their concerns no longer preempted by whether the Supreme Court would uphold the New Deal, prominent liberal editorialists were beginning to express misgivings about the CIO's tactics and social vision. And there was, too, the lurking issue of Communist involvement in the CIO.

Most ominous of all was the companies' unwillingness to concede. They seemed increasingly inclined to welcome a strike as an opportunity to test the SWOC and the CIO, even the whole New Deal. And they might well meet a strike with intense repression, including lethal violence, confident they could turn this to their advantage, as they had done in previous strikes. The steel workers who knew their history also understood that despite the La Follette Committee and the NLRB, they, the workers, might easily bear the blame for violence inflicted on them. And yet, few steel unionists could have appreciated the many injuries that lay in store.

PART II

The Strike

We want a union contract
Signed on the dotted line.
We'll march until we get it
On the union picket line.

CIO steel workers' song, South Chicago,
Illinois (1937)

The Spirit of Unrest

FROM STALEMATE TO WALKOUT

On March 30, 1937, the SWOC's director for its northeast region, Clint Golden, dispatched a letter to the Little Steel companies, as well as several other firms, containing a proposed collective bargaining agreement similar to the Carnegie-Illinois agreement. A members-only contract, it provided for an eight-hour workday and forty-hour work week, time and a half for overtime, a $5 per day minimum wage, and paid vacations; it also provided for health and safety standards, seniority, and adjustments of grievances.[1] After receiving the contract, the heads of the companies, minus ARMCO, conferred on a response. Several days later, company directors met in New York following a regular meeting there of the Iron and Steel Institute, where "a promiscuous talk" was had about the contract proposal. According to Frank Purnell, a consensus emerged to reject the contract and fight the SWOC. The only dissenters were Pittsburgh Crucible Steel and Jones & Laughlin, which also opposed dealing with the SWOC, but prevaricated, concerned that a strike might ruin them. The Little Steel companies were firm in their opposition.[2]

For another month, the Little Steel companies refused any conference with the SWOC. Tom Girdler convened a meeting at which Republic officials reviewed and rejected the contract. This decision was relayed to local company officials, but not the union. Republic did not communicate with the SWOC at all until May 5, when company representatives made clear that they would not sign a written agreement but were ostensibly open to meeting with "anyone to bargain … concerning whomsoever he represents." This prompted a telegram from Golden to Joseph Voss, Republic's director of industrial relations, in which Golden asked sarcastically whether the company proposed "that contracting parties commit provisions verbally agreed upon to memory."[3] Nevertheless, Republic reaffirmed its refusal to sign a written contract at a May 11 meeting between company and union representatives. Republic underscored its position by locking out workers at its heavily organized plate mill in Canton and later, on May 20, at its Massillon Works.[4]

Sheet & Tube met with SWOC representatives on April 28. At that three-hour conference, company representatives were amiable and claimed to be willing to bargain with the CIO, but only with respect to SWOC members. This seemed to open the door to negotiating toward the Carnegie-Illinois contract. However, company representatives scotched any prospect of this by also refusing to enter into a written agreement. They dismissed warnings that the union leadership would be unable to keep the workers from striking and that a strike would be costly to all sides; and they declined any further meetings after initially promising otherwise. According to Sheet & Tube's record of the meeting, Philip Murray "boasted considerably" about the SWOC's success in undermining U.S. Steel's ERPs and also "boasted" of another company, unnamed, whose chairman wanted to sign but felt constrained by the company's board of directors. Sheet & Tube was unmoved. At subsequent conferences on May 5 and 10, company representatives merely reiterated their earlier stated positions.[5]

In March, lower ranking officials at Bethlehem professed their willingness to deal with the union but warned that Eugene Grace would never approve such a thing. The company stood by the results of an "election" held on March 21 at which an implausible 96.4 percent of workers expressed allegiance to the ERPs. Otherwise, Bethlehem refused to negotiate. Inland's management eventually indicated that the company would probably not enter into a written agreement but deferred a final decision until May 25, when it presented SWOC negotiators with a "statement of policy" that asserted the company's tolerance of union membership, and even its willingness to hear grievances through AA representatives. However, the document expressed a refusal to recognize the CIO, negotiate from the Carnegie-Illinois agreement, or sign a contract.[6]

In his popular history of New Deal labor, Irving Bernstein asserts a common view, shared by the La Follette Committee, that the companies saw in the SWOC's proposal a chance to "force the union into a premature strike" and that "Girdler . . . picked the moment to trigger the Little Steel strike."[7] Certainly, the companies never intended to recognize the union and welcomed a chance to crush it. Likely, they received considerable encouragement for these positions from the NAM, the U.S. Chamber of Commerce, the Liberty League, and powerful industrial concerns, including the Du Ponts, which felt that the time had come to stop the CIO, nullify the Wagner Act, and stem the tide of New Deal reform, even if this meant provoking a costly strike.[8] But what is not so clear is whether Girdler and his peers knew exactly how best to effectuate these aims in the wake of U.S. Steel's signing and their own failure to fully rout the SWOC's organizers, let alone that they planned the timing of the strike. Purnell's account of the April 1937 Iron and Steel Institute meeting suggests just as much uncertainty among the company heads regarding strategy as there was consistency about the undesirability of signing. This, together with the fact that several companies at that conference—Jones & Laughlin, Pittsburgh Crucible, and Wheeling Steel—did soon sign, and the long silence that preceded final rejection of the contract, suggests real doubts among Little Steel about how to proceed.[9]

Despite intensive espionage, the companies could not know for certain the true level of SWOC support in their plants. And with no spies among the SWOC's top leadership, they could not be sure of the union's intentions, including when and where it might strike. Nor could they be certain of the political situation or the effect that the Wagner Act might have on the dispute. It was sometime after the Supreme Court decided *NLRB v. Jones & Laughlin Steel,* and in the context of this uncertainty, that the companies resolved to couch their opposition to the SWOC in the claim that the law did not require them to sign a written contract. Though dubious, this position drew a semblance of support from the fact that although the Wagner Act mandated good-faith bargaining, it did not require that the parties necessarily reach agreement on any contract at all.

In fact, this position on signed contracts allowed the companies to assert that they had already exceeded their statutory duty to bargain.[10] For in March, via the pretense of negotiations with their ERPs, they had granted wage and hour improvements that largely matched those included in the Carnegie-Illinois agreement. With these new terms in place, the companies contended that there was "no dispute" between the parties and that recognition of the SWOC was simply unnecessary.[11] In mid-May, just after its final conference with union representatives, Republic mailed a letter to all of its employees explaining its refusal to sign, claiming that the "C.I.O. made no complaints relative to wages or hours of Republic employees."[12] Sheet & Tube and Inland took a comparable stance with SWOC negotiators and later issued similar statements to their employees.[13] Well-reported in the media, these communiqués advanced the companies' arguments that the SWOC, the CIO, and their leaders were mainly interested in building up their own organizations and pushing leftist causes at the workers' expense.

The companies moved quickly to prepare for the looming strike. Frank Purnell determined in early 1937 that it might cost Sheet & Tube "several million dollars" to defend the open shop, and by May the company had already set aside $550,000 to address such "contingencies." For reasons that remain unclear, Sheet & Tube removed its machine guns from the vault where they were kept at its Campbell Works, crated them, and buried them in coke piles within the plant.[14] In May, Republic purchased $50,000 worth of munitions—mostly potent "sickening" gas—which was shipped directly to its various plants. The companies also increased their police forces and began negotiating with local police and sheriffs to deputize company men and accept donations of weapons. Between January 1, 1937, and May 5, 1937, the sheriff of Mahoning County, Ohio, where Youngstown is located, swore in 214 deputies, of whom 57 were on Republic's payroll and 114 worked for Sheet & Tube. Between May 6 and May 25, the county sheriff swore in another 168 of the companies' employees. Republic shipped directly to the Mahoning sheriff's department over $16,000 worth of munitions, mainly gas weapons; and Sheet & Tube made substantial contributions to the sheriff's store of weapons. Police officials from both companies also conferred with each other and began coordinating a strike response.[15]

Everywhere, the companies intensified espionage activities. Republic began stocking its plants with food and bedding and instructing company police, managers, and some loyal employees to prepare themselves for extended occupancy of the mills.[16] Republic equipped its South Chicago Works with provisions to support a large contingent of city police as well as loyal employees and company police. Sheet & Tube began stocking its Youngstown-area plants with supplies and installing searchlights and barbed wire.[17] Later, Bethlehem fortified its Cambria mill.[18] These preparations accompanied measures to secure expensive mill equipment, especially the furnaces and coke ovens, which would incur catastrophic damage if improperly shut down.

The companies also stepped up predictions that the strikers would sow violence and disorder at the expense of American values, that a radical plot was afoot, and that the companies might be "forced" to permanently close some mills. The letter Republic sent to employees in mid-May, in which it claimed the union had made no important demands, also accused the CIO of irresponsibility and warned that recognition of the SWOC would subject employees to union "discrimination, interference, restraint, coercion, and intimidation."[19] Company agents also distributed thousands of copies of a pamphlet titled *Join the C.I.O. and Help Build a Soviet America,* published by the right-wing Constitutional Educational League, and continued to publish the colorful "harmony ads."[20]

Preparations on the union side were not so systematic. There had been rumors of an impending strike against at least some of the major steel companies as early as January.[21] By the second week of May, it was evident that Little Steel would not seriously negotiate with the SWOC. By early May, too, rank and filers were becoming visibly agitated and had begun urging the union to call a strike.[22] In fact, many workers were convinced that the companies were implementing a program to completely destroy the union. This seemed particularly true of Republic, whose lockouts at Canton and Massillon accompanied widespread discriminatory discharges and layoffs, which gave credence to threats that Republic would permanently close some of the more heavily unionized mills in that region. In the Chicago area, too, organizers reported waves of discriminatory layoffs at Republic's plants. Philip Murray later estimated that five hundred union workers were fired during this period.[23]

As May unfolded, local leaders and rank and filers pushed a more militant stance. This was especially true in northeast Ohio, where lodges began setting up strike committees and openly threatening to strike with or without authorization from SWOC leadership.[24] Some lodges signaled their impatience by voting to authorize their local leadership to call a strike, if necessary, and transmitting this sentiment to the national leadership; and Murray himself gathered authorizations from some lodges.[25] By late May, there were scattered wildcat strikes and widespread acts of shop-floor resistance. Convinced by these developments that a major strike was imminent, local government officials, including the mayors of Youngstown and neighboring Campbell and Struthers, beseeched Secretary of Labor Perkins to broker a peaceful settlement.[26]

Although the SWOC's strength varied considerably from company to company and mill to mill, union support everywhere was contingent, with many workers waiting to see how the conflict would unfold before deciding what to do. In this context, a successful strike began to seem like a viable, possibly even essential, step in the SWOC's bid to organize the companies and a necessary defense against the persecution of union supporters.

Anchoring the latter position were the hundreds of unionists who had already been fired, as well as the locked-out workers in Canton and Massillon. Incensed by the sight of men with suitcases going into the plants and the company's increasingly explicit threat to close the mills, the men in Canton and Massillon voted to strike and, on May 25, commenced picketing without authorization from the national leadership.[27]

In the meantime, Murray himself had taken to touting the majorities the SWOC supposedly commanded across Little Steel and publicly threatening a strike if the companies continued to reject meaningful negotiations. The leadership called a meeting on May 15 in Pittsburgh, at which some one hundred organizers met to prepare further demands on the companies, backed by more pointed threats of a strike.[28] On May 25, the leadership insisted that Republic and Sheet & Tube sign the proposed contract by 2:00 P.M. on the following day. (Inland was exempted because SWOC representatives were still conferring with company officials.) The next day, May 26, the union held a "war council" in Youngstown of representatives of all the locals from Republic, Sheet & Tube, and Inland, convened just as the previous day's deadline expired without word from the companies. Murray was bombarded at the podium with demands to call a strike.[29] One delegate even swore he would get his throat cut if he tried to keep his contingent at work.[30] Bluster aside, events that evening amply support Murray's laconic comment of a few days earlier that "the spirit of unrest is quite manifest."[31]

It remains a mystery why, as a strike became inevitable, the SWOC did not target the companies separately, a strategy that may have put the targeted company at an enormous competitive disadvantage while testing its loyalty to the others. Even then, something similar seemed to be working in the SWOC's favor at Jones & Laughlin. In fact, in mid-May the union leadership suggested that it might next strike Sheet & Tube and turn to the other companies later.[32] The SWOC likely enjoyed stronger support there than at any of the companies except Inland. And despite its considerable store of munitions, Sheet & Tube's conduct during the drive suggested it was not as disposed to violence as Republic. Probably, the notion of targeting Sheet & Tube or otherwise focusing the strike was never explicitly rejected but, rather, was simply overtaken by events. Certainly, once workers in Canton and Massillon voted to strike, there could be no keeping Republic's workers out of the walkout.

But then why did the emerging strike threat not extend at all to Bethlehem? In May, some union officials claimed the support of "an overwhelming majority" of Bethlehem's workers.[33] David McDonald contended years later that he had pressed Murray to focus the strike on Bethlehem because he believed organizing efforts there had been the most successful. McDonald recalled presenting Murray with detailed statistics showing that half of Bethlehem's workers were signed up, compared to only a quarter at the other firms. "But Murray had made up his mind," said McDonald, "and he brushed me aside, saying, 'I don't pay a damn bit of attention to your figures anymore.' I tore them up in front of him."[34] It is difficult to credit McDonald's claim about this exchange, given that Murray himself was among those who boasted in May of the union's strong support at Bethlehem. Moreover, McDonald's own papers contain a report from November 1936 revealing that only 208 of the 13,000 or so workers at Bethlehem's Cambria Works in Johnstown had been enlisted, and that this was the best showing in the region where Bethlehem's plants proliferated.[35] Although by late spring the union claimed eight thousand members at that plant, even then only a few thousand were paying dues.[36] Nor is McDonald's claim that the union enjoyed more support at Bethlehem than at the other companies consistent with the course of the strike once it started. Likely Bethlehem was left out because the SWOC appreciated its weakness there.

THE STRIKE BEGINS

Before the May 26 meeting at Youngstown had even ended, a strike seemed so imminent that the *Chicago Daily News*'s Edwin Lahey announced that a general walkout at Republic, Sheet & Tube, and Inland was already underway and would commence in full that night.[37] Organizer George Patterson recalled finding out early that same morning at the South Chicago office of the SWOC that "the strike already had been started" and would begin in earnest that night.[38] However they knew it, Lahey and Patterson were right. The meeting in Youngstown ended at about 5:00 P.M. with a vote authorizing a strike at these three companies, to begin at 11:00 P.M., coinciding with the customary shift change.[39] The vote originated in a resolution from the floor by one or more representatives of a local lodge. Although few could have been surprised that a strike was called, the walkout was planned to follow the vote by only six hours, and some organizers had to hustle out of the meeting hall to get word to the men.[40]

FIGURE 7. Striking workers from Inland Steel and their supporters gather in South Chicago, May 28, 1937. © 1937, Associated Press.

In many places the strike call was spread quickly and efficiently and the walkouts were uneventful. Workers simply left at the end of the shift, burdened with personal property cleared out of lockers and changing rooms. At some mills there was more conflict, as organizers sought to increase support by loudly parading workers from the better organized departments through the more weakly organized departments.[41] Harold Williams, a union supporter in Niles, Ohio, recalled a hectic journey through Republic's plant, calling people out until confronted by company men who beat him, fracturing his skull, and pulled their guns on workers who accompanied him.[42] Other organizers in the Niles plant were accosted by armed Pennsylvania Railroad police. At Republic's South Chicago Works it was city police who confronted strike leaders and ousted them from the mill. These mills were among those that Republic kept open during the strike, suggesting that these confrontations were caused, not only by organizers' attempts to rally workers and set up pickets to meet workers arriving for the late-night shift change, but also by the company's desire to keep more workers inside.

Almost immediately, "heavy pickets" closed all the major plants operated by Sheet & Tube and Inland, as well as a number of Republic plants, including its large mills in Cleveland and Youngstown.[43] Pickets were emplaced at the plant gates, on streets and railroad tracks, and even in rowboats along lakeshores and riverfronts. Less than two days after the strike began, the SWOC claimed to have brought out all but 650 workers at the struck companies, for a total of 77,240 out on strike.[44] However, these estimates were somewhat off. Initially, the strike entailed approximately 73,000 workers, of whom about 67,000 were off the job. Although included in the strike call, various Republic mills in Chicago, Warren, Niles, Canton, and Buffalo maintained some level of production and were probably staffed by around 6,000 workers.[45]

Nor was the number of workers out on strike a referendum on actual support for the union or the strike. Many who walked out were not SWOC members. Some opposed the strike but turned out because the plants where they worked had closed, or because they were unwilling to defy the picketers. Youngstown worker George Richardson did not recall ever being recruited by the SWOC, let alone joining; he only remembered being asked to make preparations to strike, which he voluntarily did. Richardson never joined the union, but when the strike came he walked out and did not return until it was over.[46] But as SWOC people hoped, some men who were not members when the strike began not only walked out but joined the picket lines. This was the experience of John Stenthal, of Republic's Youngstown Works, who remembered walking out in defiance of a foreman who came around urging the men to stay in the mill; Stenthal later joined the picket lines.[47]

For union stalwarts, the beginning of the strike was a moment of great excitement. Even for thousands of workers not immersed in the struggle, the start of the strike brought relief from weeks of uncertainty and tension and the commencement of a momentous struggle against companies they had abundant reasons to resent. The *Youngstown Vindicator* reported masses of picketers gathering at plant gates in "exuberant" and "jocular" moods; one of the main streets leading past the mills, Poland Avenue, "looked like circus day."[48] A "holiday air" marked the advent of the strike at Indiana Harbor, according to the *Chicago Daily News's* Lahey. At a mass meeting the first evening of the strike, Lahey witnessed "a rapt assemblage" of hundreds of workers of diverse ethnicities who "roared with a happy militancy." The workers then marched through darkened streets to the plant gates and began picketing. Said Lahey, "As the pickets, shouting encouragement to each other, and carrying banners, filed in orderly circles before the entrances to the plants, the giant smokestacks of the open hearth furnaces sent licks of

flame into the night sky, in their last pyrotechnic display for an undetermined period."[49]

The strike call did not extend to Republic's mills in Birmingham and Gadsden, Alabama, nor to any of Bethlehem's operations. But two weeks into the strike, on June 10, workers on the plant railroad, the Conemaugh & Black Lick Railroad, struck Bethlehem's Cambria Works in Johnstown because the company refused to sign contracts with them. This provoked a sympathy walkout the next day by steel workers, which effectively brought these 13,000 men into the steel strike.[50] Including this stoppage at Johnstown, the strike idled over 80,000 steel workers at twenty-nine plants in seven states. The walkout was centered in two places: northeast Ohio, where roughly 40,000 workers struck; and the Calumet region around the southwest shore of Lake Michigan, from South Chicago into northern Indiana, where the strike entailed another 24,000 men.[51]

The festive atmosphere in many locations belied a combustible situation. In the words of the La Follette Committee, the "strike opened in an atmosphere charged with misapprehension and distrust."[52] Scuffles and fights between unionists and company loyalists marked its beginning almost everywhere, as did omens of more serious violence. At Sheet & Tube's Brier Hill Works in Youngstown, picketers drew gunfire from company police when they apparently prevented two crane operators from going to work in the plant. Aware of what happened there in 1916 when police had shot and killed several strikers and by-standers, Youngstown strikers brandished an abundance of sticks, clubs, and bats before being persuaded by police and SWOC leaders to put away some of these weapons.[53]

In Warren, local organizers saw men with suitcases entering Republic's property midshift before the strike began, and by 7:00 P.M. union supporters set up pickets to counter this.[54] Organizer John Grajciar was surprised to see how quickly a large crowd of union men, women, children, and spectators of all descriptions gathered near the main gate. Mindful of the tension of the moment and violent attacks on strikers in earlier conflicts, Grajciar worried that someone might stray onto company property or do something else that could give company police a pretext to attack the unionists. And so he and other organizers moved the crowd a short distance away from the mill and into town. They also set up barricades, ostensibly to keep the spectators back but soon integrated into an effort to block access to the mill.[55] On May 28, a loyal employee shot a picketer outside the plant. On the night of May 31, there was another disturbance as loyalists within the plant bombarded picketers with rocks and bricks.[56]

In Massillon, the first hours of the strike saw scattered violence as picketers beat on the cars of employees trying the enter Republic's plants.[57] In Canton, too, the strike began with scattered arrests and scuffles, as well as union accusations that men were being held at work against their will.[58] In the early hours of the morning on May 27, a Republic foreman in Canton was shot and seriously injured near a plant gate by a company policemen, who mistook him in the dark for a picketer.[59] On May 28, a Canton striker was shot and wounded by unknown parties about a mile from Republic's mills. Then, on the morning of May 30, Republic's district manager for Canton and Massillon was shot and lightly wounded at his residence by a company policeman posted there who mistook him for an invader.[60] And there were assaults by large groups of company men. On May 28, more than forty loyal employees and heavily armed company police rushed a group of Canton picketers.[61] These clashes were but harbingers of the turmoil to come.

In the Name of the People

THE INCIDENT ON MEMORIAL DAY

The Little Steel Strike included several plants in the Calumet region. Among these were Inland's mill at Indiana Harbor, in East Chicago, Indiana, which was that company's only integrated plant and one of the largest involved in the strike; Inland's much smaller plant in Chicago Heights; and Sheet & Tube mills, encompassing a large plant in East Chicago and a smaller one on the Illinois side of the border. All four of these were shut down when the strike began, but there were scattered disturbances. On the first full day of the strike, loyal employees at Sheet & Tube's East Chicago plant attempting to "crash the picket line" had their car overturned by picketers.[1] And on May 29, picketers at Inland's big mill were roused by the company's attempt to run several railcars into the plant, which they considered a violation of the union's agreement with the company that it could continue to operate some of its coke ovens (in part to maintain the gas supply for the city of East Chicago) in exchange for keeping the strikers informed of operations in the plant. The picketers' insistence that they inspect the cars prompted a fight with sixty club-wielding company police that left four picketers with head injuries requiring doctor's care.[2] Mostly, though, the situation at these mills was quiet, especially compared to events at the larger of Republic's two plants in the area, its South Chicago Works.

AN ELUSIVE RIGHT TO PICKET

Republic planned to run its South Chicago Works during the strike and stocked it with cots, food, and other supplies. The company correctly calculated that it could staff the plant with perhaps one thousand loyal employees and that their presence alone would rankle the strikers, even if they produced little steel. Republic also arranged with the Chicago police to patrol in and around the plant. The company provided the police with gas and hatchet handles and fed and billeted some of them inside; and it garrisoned the place with dozens of its own police. Republic insisted that these moves were necessary to secure the plant against criminal acts on the part of the strikers. But had the South Chicago Works actually needed defending, this could have been accomplished with minimal force, as the 274-acre plant was bounded on three sides by industrial property and the Calumet River. The other side, the east face, was separated by mostly vacant land from the nearest thoroughfare, to which it was connected by a couple of small, rough streets and a trolley line converging on one gate. The only other land entrance was via a railroad gate. The east face of the mill was also bounded by a Pennsylvania Railroad track that ran along a raised grade. Along part of this stretch of company property was a board fence topped with barbed wire; and behind this was a moat-like ditch.[3] Nevertheless, from the outset of the strike, three shifts of at least one hundred city police were posted at the plant.

This alliance between the city police and Republic was not surprising. In the 1930s, Chicago was a crucible of class conflict and its police department, long notorious for its brutality, had made quite clear which side of this conflict it was on. Staffed with an Industrial, or Red, Squad, the department was generally poorly trained but well practiced in smashing strikes and breaking up political protests. Thoroughly integrated into the city's machine politics, the department's support for industrialists was contingent only on their political support for the department.[4] Republic's standing with the police and city officials was good, and so the Chicago police stood ready to break the strike at Republic before it even started.

At around 4:00 P.M. on May 26—hours before the strike was supposed to begin, but after the union's council in Youngstown opened—a detail of forty city police tried to compel John Riffe, the SWOC's subdistrict director who was in charge of the union's efforts at the plant, to help them clear the mill of union sympathizers. The police claimed they did this because they feared the SWOC men were attempting to pull a sit-down strike. Actually, no such plan was in the works, or even feasible. Rather, the police's actions were designed to prevent unionists from rallying fence-sitters inside the plant and to stop them from setting up a strong picket to meet incoming workers arriving for the 11:00 P.M. shift. But Riffe, a seasoned UMW man from Kentucky, would not confine his appeals to union men, and so the police forced him out of the plant. One of the police captains, James Mooney, warned Riffe, "We are going to run this plant whether you like it or not."[5]

As the walkout unfolded that evening, several hundred union men assembled near the plant gate after leaving the mill, cheering other workers as they emerged. There to deal with the unionists were nearly three hundred police with four squad cars and four patrol wagons. When strike leaders tried to form the workers into a picket line, the police dispersed the crowd and arrested around two dozen, including Riffe, for unlawful assembly and disorderly conduct. Supposedly, they were threatening police and loyal employees and calling them "scabs" and "finks."[6]

Approximately twelve hundred workers at Republic's South Chicago Works joined the strike. The roughly one thousand employees who stood with Republic were mainly housed inside of the plant.[7] Their presence made the plant the focus of SWOC protests in the region and an obvious target for picketing. But over the next several days, the police severely restricted unionists' attempts to picket the mill. At first, police banned all picketing near the gate. Two days after the strike started, on Friday, a delegation of union people went down to the gate to see Captain Mooney. When they requested legal justification for the decision constraining their right to picket, Mooney referred them to the city administration. Mooney conceded the strikers' right to picket in large numbers at locations several blocks away, but not near the plant or on the roads approaching it. That day, the police also agreed to small pickets in the general area of the plant gate, but those picketers had to keep moving at all times and were prohibited from speaking or distributing literature.[8]

These limits on picketing were in apparent conflict with a statement by Chicago mayor Edward Kelly that the police would not disturb peaceful picketing. The position taken by the police also seemed to conflict with an advisory legal opinion delivered to the police commissioner two months earlier and circulated to all police captains, in which the city's corporation counsel, its chief legal officer, had concluded that the police had no authority to interfere with peaceful picketing. The police claimed that they had been prepared to embrace this policy and allow picket patrols of one hundred or more at the gate, until the unionists proved themselves unworthy of the privilege by their unruly actions on the night of May 26.[9]

More fundamentally, the policy laid out by the police conflicted with the strikers' reading of their rights under the U.S. Constitution and Wagner Act. But when strikers and their supporters tested the police on this point, they were turned back. The first time this occurred, the evening of May 27, there was a tense standoff between unionists and police, backed by armed company men. The would-be picketers eventually turned away. On May 28, the same day that Mooney conceded a very limited right to picket, an orderly column numbering between seven hundred and one thousand strikers and strike supporters marched on the plant, led by a woman, a bicyclist, and a man named Dominic Esposito bearing the American flag. A block from the mill gate, the marchers met a "force of club-swinging policemen."[10] When the unionists tried to continue to the gate, the police broke a club over Esposito's head and then laid into the other marchers, opening a brief battle that ended with the unionists in retreat. At least twenty-four people were injured, including several strikers who were hospitalized. Six strikers and supporters were arrested; and someone, almost certainly with the police, fired several gunshots.[11] As organizer George Patterson recalled, the whole affair was one-sided: "We marched, and we were determined that we were going to picket. We met the police again. This time they really took a swat at us, and they were beating the hell out of everybody in the front lines. . . . Then they fired a few shots in the air, and that scattered us. . . . We ran like hell."[12]

The police easily prevailed that Friday. Only a few officers were among the injured, including one who was "laid out" by a blow with the flagpole, which another demonstrator grabbed after Esposito went down.[13] Nevertheless, the police moved to strengthen their ranks at the mill. By Sunday, Memorial Day, a force of at least 250 city police was continuously guarding the mill. This escalation provoked a raft of fruitless complaints to the mayor by liberal and progressive groups in the city.[14]

A BLOODBATH ON THE PRAIRIE

At three o'clock on Sunday afternoon, a crowd numbering between fifteen hundred and twenty-five hundred gathered outside SWOC headquarters at a former tavern called Sam's Place, five or six blocks from the mill gate. The gathering was treated to several speeches condemning the company and the police, the fieriest being from Leo "Gene" Krzycki, a Socialist and CIO organizer who branded Mayor Edward Kelly and his staff "fascists" for their apparently duplicitous stance on the unionists' right to picket en masse.[15] The demonstrators then endorsed a proposal, which someone yelled from the crowd, that they again march to the plant and demand the right to picket. And so they set out, led by two Republic strikers bearing American flags, one named John Lotito, the other a Mexican national named Max Guzman who had been working in the United States for about twenty years. As with previous marches to picket the mill, the procession included a substantial number of women—around 15 percent, according to the estimate of a journalist on the scene; closer to 10 percent by other estimates. There were also an indeterminate number of children, including some very young. The presence of the children bespoke the peaceful intentions of the marchers. It also reflected an important element of CIO strategy, which was to strive for a festive, family air at its functions. So did the patriotic symbolism, which accorded with a conscious effort by the CIO to reshape the meaning of "Americanism," so long a foil of xenophobia and antiunion propaganda, around the values of industrial democracy.[16]

Many of the marchers were dressed in neat clothing, including jackets and ties and light dresses, and some had brought picnic lunches, even dates with them.[17] Journalist Meyer Levin, who was on the scene that day, described the crowd for the La Follette Committee as "extremely casual at that point." While the strikers among them had a more serious bearing, others "seemed to be in an almost holiday atmosphere."[18] Among the marchers were also quite a few students, artists and writers, social workers and community activists, and churchmen. In addition to Republic strikers, there were men from Inland's and Sheet & Tube's mills, workers from other steel companies and industries, and unemployed folk.[19] Every major ethnic and racial group was represented.

The demonstrators made their way southward, down South Green Bay Avenue until they reached a spot east of the point where the plant property began. Most then cut diagonally toward the plant gate, southwesterly, following dirt tracks across a large vacant field—owned by Republic but generally open to the public and known locally as a patch of "prairie"—that separated the plant's east face from South Green Bay Avenue. The plant gate lay a couple of hundred yards beyond the far corner of the prairie, at the intersection of 118th Street and the Pennsylvania Railroad. Awaiting the marchers, in the southwest corner of that field where 116th Street intersected Burley Avenue, was the bulk of the city police contingent, formed in a rough line abreast.[20]

The police were armed with .38 service revolvers, nightsticks, and blackjacks, as well as the gas and hatchet handles they had been given by Republic. Several patrol cars and other police vehicles were parked near them. A few other city police were at the mill gate. Behind the police and inside the fence surrounding the plant stood twenty or thirty company police and an uncertain number of loyal employees. The La Follette Committee suggested that around one hundred loyal employees were out near the gate.[21] But Tom Girdler asserted that "practically the entire force" of loyal employees—over one thousand men, he claimed—were "ranged along the inside of the fence," armed with "hammers, pick handles, bars of steel; any weapon."[22]

The demonstrators approached the police in an unthreatening fashion. Chanting "CIO! CIO!" they were largely unarmed, aside from a few who carried rocks or sticks. Just after 4:00 P.M., the first marchers met the police line. Stopped by the police, they too fanned out in a ragged line. A flurry of arguments erupted as the demonstrators asserted their right to picket the plant and the police demanded that they disperse. According to a worker in the crowd, the police became more agitated when some women resumed chanting—"CIO! CIO!"[23] Other marchers continued to arrive. After what was later estimated as four to ten minutes of arguing, the officers in charge, Captain Mooney and Captain Thomas Kilroy, read out an order to disperse— "in the name of the people of the State of Illinois."[24] Almost on cue, the encounter exploded in violence. The police abruptly discharged at least one tear gas canister toward the demonstrators and fired several shots in the air. Moments after this, the police let loose a fusillade of two hundred gunshots into the crowd over a period of ten or fifteen seconds, and as some were still shooting, police surged into the ranks of the marchers swinging nightsticks, hatchet handles, and blackjacks. Most of the demonstrators fled back across the prairie, stumbling and falling. Dozens though, stunned by the attack, struck by police bullets or clubs, or overcome by gas, crumpled to the ground—dead, wounded or sickened, or immobilized by shock.[25]

Those demonstrators who went down, were overtaken by the police, or were unable to run, were manhandled by the police; some were shoved, dragged, or thrown into waiting patrol wagons despite having sustained grievous wounds, and many were beaten senseless. Those who escaped the initial assault recalled a desperate flight for safety. Jesse Reese, who found himself crawling in the grass, only a few weeks earlier had been part of a SWOC contingent that met with Sheet & Tube officials in fruitless conferences. From his vantage, Reese thought, "I'm here with nothing. I should have brought my gun."[26] Another worker, Harry Harper, remembered beginning to sense danger during the standoff as he implored some of the police to let him deliver a message to his brother, whom he thought was

FIGURE 9. Opening moments of the Memorial Day Massacre, May 30, 1937. © 1937, Associated Press.

being held in the mill against his will. The next instant, the shooting erupted and Harper was struck down, driven to his knees with his left eye destroyed by the blow of a policeman's club. Harper pulled himself off the ground and ran. It was he who saw through one eye people "going down, as though they were being mowed down with a scythe."[27]

Those demonstrators who escaped across the prairie gathered themselves for a time about one hundred yards from the police. Those police not still busy abusing or arresting union people reassembled into a line facing the demonstrators. Over the next few minutes the police occasionally began to advance on the demonstrators, prompting the unionists to retreat a bit farther each time. The risk of another upsurge of violence was ended, however, when the police accidentally discharged a tear gas bomb in their own ranks—an event that managed to bring laughter from some of the shaken and angry marchers.[28]

Four demonstrators died of gunshot wounds on or near the scene; six others died over the next three weeks, also of gunshot wounds. Another thirty demonstrators were shot and sixty were otherwise injured, for a total of around one hundred significant casualties, of which around ten involved permanent disability. Among those shot was an eleven-year-old boy named Nicholas Leverich (or Leurich), hit in the ankle. A baby was wounded in the arm; and two women, Tillie Brazell and Catherine Nelson, were shot in the leg. Brazell, who worked for one of the steel companies, was also beaten and arrested. Likewise shot and beaten was John Lotito, the flag bearer.[29] Thirty-five police were injured, although none of their injuries, besides a broken arm, was serious. But while the police commanders brought in ambulances for their men, they did little to aid grievously wounded demonstrators, not even bothering to use their stretchers to carry the injured. Those they did tend to were treated roughly. One shooting victim, a man named Earl Handley, probably died because the police removed him from a union car, marked with a red cross, which was trying to take Handley to a hospital. Police slipped the tourniquet that was stopping Handley from bleeding to death and piled him, blood pouring from a severed artery in his thigh, with fifteen other people into a patrol wagon.[30]

The police arrested nearly seventy people, including Handley and the other five mortally wounded men. They were all charged with the old antilabor standby of "conspiracy to do an illegal act."[31] Dozens of injured people were seized at the scene, and at least thirty-three people were held by police for varying lengths of time at area hospitals, which were flooded with people battered and bloody. Those defendants who were ambulatory were held in jail for several days, during which time they were denied access to legal counsel or friends and family, although they were allowed to see police agents disguised as sympathetic leftist lawyers.[32] Finally, on June 2, they were hauled into court. Many were still clothed in garments covered with dirt and dried blood, some with their wounds wrapped in gauzes and plaster, visibly exhausted, wearing grim and angry looks on their faces. A few people, including George Patterson, who was in charge of picketing at the plant on Memorial Day and led the march from Sam's Place, were apprehended days later.[33]

A RIOT BECOMES A MASSACRE

The clash created an immediate sensation. Coverage dominated the major national papers that evening and the next day and continued to rule the headlines for several days to come. From the beginning, the police insisted that they were blameless and that all the fault for the carnage rested with the unionists. They claimed they had been attacked by demonstrators attempting to seize the plant; that the marchers were well-armed fanatics, under the influence of Communist agitation and marijuana; that a number of police-men had been surrounded and beaten by the demonstrators before the shoot-ing began; that the marchers had shot their own people; and that there had not even been any discussion of picketing rights before the shooting, just a brazen attack on the police. These assertions found favor in the mainstream media, not least the *Chicago Daily Tribune,* which ran overblown stories about the "bluecoats'" courageous stand against an "attack" by an "army" led by "outsiders" and radicals. The paper provided readers with a detailed sche-matic showing how the police barely managed to defend their position. In the view of the *Tribune's* editors, the leaders of the "mob" were the "murderers."[34]

In fact, it was inconceivable that even twenty-five hundred people—the uppermost estimate of how many had marched across the field—who were basically unarmed could capture a fenced plant whose only gate was guarded by four hundred heavily armed men and manned by one thousand others. Nor was there any other way to seize the plant, notwithstanding a ridiculous rumor that had the unionists planning an amphibious landing from the rear, across the Calumet River. It is also unclear how capturing the plant, which would surely have generated considerable violence and bloodshed, could have benefitted the unionists. Moreover, if the demonstrators were threatening an assault—let alone approached the police line in a manner that indicated this intention—then why had the police not made more use of gas to turn them back, or used it earlier? And why were they deployed with their flanks exposed? Nor did these accusations of an attempted inva-sion fit with the presence of children, the picnic baskets, or the well-groomed marchers.

Over the reluctance of Senator La Follette himself, who may not have appreciated how outrageous the actions of the police were, the La Follette Committee staff began to investigate the incident days after it occurred.[35] Witnesses were summoned to the hearings in Washington, DC. Hours of testimony by police officials in June and July did little to assuage growing concerns about what the police had done that day. Armed with documen-tary and photographic evidence, La Follette and his colleague, Elbert Thomas of Utah, reduced the police to increasingly implausible attempts at justification. A photograph of an officer plainly showing his firing his sidearm at demonstrators was said, instead, to depict a "black smudge" or his wielding a "rock."[36] Another, showing a man merely facing the police, somehow indicated that he was "having physical combat" with an officer.

And a photograph of people fleeing the police was said to actually depict demonstrators "running backwards," attacking the officers.[37] Most preposterous of all was one police witness's contention that evidence showing a relatively relaxed, disorganized crowd working its way toward the police line was nonetheless consistent with the claim that police faced a military formation—like the "Mexican Army," the witness said, in a nativist allusion to Max Guzman and others of Mexican descent on the field that day.[38]

The claim that the unionists, even if they did not intend to take the plant, nonetheless intended to provoke a bloody clash drew on the charge that they were led by Communists, the implication being that Communists would readily sacrifice their fellow unionists for propaganda purposes. In later years, the notion that Communists were responsible for the massacre was actually publicly endorsed by union figures, including John Riffe.[39] Indeed, there was a sizeable number of Communists in the ranks of the SWOC organizers in the Chicago area and there were definitely Communists among the demonstrators, if not so many as the police claimed. Besides Jesse Reese, Communists on the field that day included black organizer Henry Johnson and Tillie Brazell, one of the women who was shot. Joe Weber, the organizer in charge of strategy at the Republic plant, was a Communist. A veteran of the SMWIU and a former activist with the party's Unemployed Councils, Weber had just been reassigned the day before the massacre to the SWOC office with jurisdiction over Republic's South Chicago Works. Although kept from the march by an appointment elsewhere, Weber had been one of the speakers at Sam's Place. Later, he was arrested along with others who spoke at Sam's Place for "conspiring" in the riot.[40]

Nevertheless, the charge that Communists had contrived the massacre is hard to credit. While people like Weber may have been more inclined to promote militant action than other unionists, and not above viewing a confrontation with the police as a political act, it is unlikely that Weber or any other local leaders were so callous or foolish to have premeditated the deadly violence that unfolded that day. Of course, as historian Michael Dennis has pointed out, the demonstration itself was not entirely spontaneous, as evidenced by the union's preparation of first-aid stations before the meeting at Sam's Place.[41] As this and the prepositioning of ambulance cars also revealed, those promoting the march expected to provoke a confrontation with the police. After all, there was no point in marching on the plant except in hopes of either establishing a mass picket line, despite police objections, or publicizing the fact that the police would not allow such picketing; and neither of these goals, which had to be widely shared by the participants, could have been accomplished without some kind of confrontation.[42] This was essentially the conclusion of the La Follette Committee, which determined that the demonstrators' common intention was to establish a mass picket line at the mill.[43] But as the committee also appreciated, confronting the police to vindicate a legal right was a long way from contriving a massacre.

In the aftermath of the incident, the police arrested twelve "known communists," determined by them to have instigated the clash.[44] Among the supposed conspirators were dead or mortally wounded men. However, when later pressed by Senators La Follette and Thomas, the police could hardly come up with a definition that did not reduce to a Communist anyone they could blame for causing the incident. As Captain Mooney told La Follette, even the act of carrying the American flag was evidence of Communist affiliation and agitation, as Communists were "getting into that racket now."[45]

In the end, neither the police, nor the media, nor anti-Communist elements in the SWOC ever divulged any proof that the bloodbath was orchestrated by Communists.[46] But Communist intrigues were not the only thing the police tried to dig up to defend their actions. After the clash, they combed the scene for weapons, producing a bizarre collection of sticks (including tomato trestles they purloined from a local resident's garden), tree limbs, and other junk offered in support of their narrative about what had occurred. Among representative pieces of this arsenal were "2 Qt 'Hunding Dairy' milk bottles." More revealing of what really happened that afternoon were other things picked up off the field: twenty-nine hats and caps; two jackets, a jumper, and a coat; sixty picket signs; and twenty-three copies of the *Daily Worker*.[47]

The police's efforts only confirmed that the demonstrators were not even prepared to defend themselves, let alone overwhelm the police and capture the plant. There was also the inconvenient fact that of the forty people shot, only four were hit from the front; twenty-seven were hit in the back and nine in the side. When considered alongside photographs and eyewitness testimony, the pattern of gunshot wounds confirmed that most of the demonstrators had begun to flee as soon as the police discharged the first volley of shots and set off the gas, and they were shot and beaten while trying to escape. As for the demonstrators being armed, it is clear that relatively few demonstrators were armed with sticks and such, and even fewer wielded clubs and pipes. The overwhelming majority had no weapons of any kind.[48] It seems that at most one or two sticks or rocks were lobbed mortar-like at the police during the argument about picketing rights and that a rather larger salvo was thrown up or toward the police in panic or desperation, after the police began discharging gas and firing their revolvers.[49]

Among the evidence secured by the La Follette Committee was a section of Paramount newsreel footage that captured much of the fray. An extraordinary document, today designated for preservation by the National Film Registry, the film was taken by cameraman Orlando Lippert, who had been diverted from the Indianapolis 500 to cover the strike. It shows the marchers' rambling procession across the prairie; the gathering of police, visibly agitated, to meet them; some of the arguing about picketing rights; some of the shooting immediately following the initial fusillade; and much of the carnage that followed. According to the *New York Times,* the film "stunned" an audience in Times Square when screened there in early July.[50] Even today, it is perhaps the single most compelling visual depiction of class conflict in American history. So incendiary was the film that Paramount first suppressed the footage and then generated a heavily edited version clearly intended to support the police's version of events. La Follette Committee staff managed to secure the unedited film by covert means, snatching it up ahead of the Senate Committee on Post Offices and Post Roads, which was intent on producing evidence of SWOC misconduct during the strike. Once its existence became known, several cities, including Chicago, barred showing the film to the public and arrested people who violated these edicts.[51]

As historian Carol Quirke has shown, the production of the newsreel did not, as many have supposed, instantly demolish the police's story and change the way people understood the incident.[52] But eventually the film was seen to confirm much of what the strikers and their supporters had claimed. The film undermined the charge that the marchers approached the police intending to assault them, and it gave the lie to police assertions that there had been no arguments with the demonstrators about the right to picket and that the demonstrators had brazenly attacked them. The film also captured the vicious blows inflicted by the police on stunned and injured demonstrators as well as quite a few self-satisfied police gestures—smiling, dusting off their hands or jackets, in one case musing "Boy oh boy." It showed, too, their callous treatment of the wounded.[53]

The La Follette Committee was unable to determine with certainty the most immediate cause of the clash that day, in part because the Paramount film was missing seven seconds just as the shooting began, a result of Lippert changing lenses. But the committee did gather convincing evidence that the police had provoked the marchers, first bombarding them with invectives and obscenities and challenging them to try to get through the line; pushing and shoving them; and then, it seems, for no clear reason, hurling at least one tear gas grenade into their ranks. As near as the committee could tell, at that point "a stick and perhaps other isolated missles [sic]" were thrown in the direction of the police. Moments later, the police began shooting, at first into the air and then, almost immediately, directly into the crowd.[54]

The La Follette Committee's report on the incident, released in late July, also condemned the police for their actions after the initial shooting, not only for beating and dragging wounded people and cramming them into paddy wagons but also making little effort to render first aid. Several victims besides Handley might have lived had the police provided them with prompt and competent medical treatment, or allowed others to do so.[55] Others suffered needlessly. The report concluded that this outrageous conduct tended to confirm that "the use of excessive force to disperse the marchers was deliberate" in the first place.[56]

Just as damning were the committee's conclusions regarding the underlying causes of the incident. The committee noted that the police had been housed and fed at Republic's expense inside the plant, that Republic had armed them, and that they had otherwise coordinated with the company on a response to the strike.[57] Indeed, the police had appointed themselves the sole arbiters of the extent of the strikers' right to picket. For the La Follette Committee, all of this showed the police to be biased against the strikers and inclined all along to use force "far in excess of that which the occasion required."[58]

Some newspapers, including the *Washington Post,* eventually credited the La Follette Committee for exposing the misconduct of the police and Republic Steel.[59] And the intrepid reporting of Paul Anderson, with the *St. Louis Post-Dispatch,* did much to aid the committee's investigations.[60] But even after the Paramount film surfaced, others continued to follow the *Chicago Tribune* in blaming unionists for the tragedy. So did many conservative politicians, particularly a number of southern Democrats in Congress who were erstwhile supporters of the New Deal. Perhaps just as problematic for the strikers, many liberal politicians as well as much of the public seemed conspicuously indifferent toward the incident, despite the La Follette Committee's revelations and the eventual circulation of the Paramount film (which was never released as a theater newsreel, however).[61] More worryingly, the White House initially accepted the claim that police took appropriate action against a dangerous mob and never did condemn them. Besides La Follette, only a few politicians, Texas representative Maury Maverick among them, called the event what it was.[62]

Although strikers from one Little Steel company or another, along with their families, constituted the largest contingent of demonstrators, hundreds who marched that day were not so connected to the strike. For Girdler as well as the police and their allies, this was proof that the entire affair was the handiwork of agitators, including Communists.[63] The charge had little merit and did nothing to shape the La Follette Committee's conclusions. But this was probably not the point anyway. More likely Girdler and company's main purpose was to discredit something about the incident they found much more troubling: the specter of a broad-ranging solidarity that rejected the very idea that the strikers should stand alone in their struggle.

Eight of the men killed did not work at Republic. Handley, thirty-seven, who bled to death after his tourniquet slipped, and Kenneth Reed, twenty-three, were both strikers from Inland. Sam Popovich, forty-five years old, was unemployed. Joseph Rothmund, forty-eight at the time of his death, was a German immigrant and a former baker and Works Progress Administration worker with Communist ties. Rothmund was working in a SWOC strike kitchen. Hilding Anderson, twenty-seven, worked as a rigger at U.S. Steel. And although employed with a refrigerator car company at the time of the strike, Otis Jones, thirty-three, was a member of the National Maritime Union, a left-leaning CIO union whose members volunteered on SWOC picket lines in the Calumet. Leo Francisco was a boy of seventeen who according to relatives was a "volunteer picket" then working as a messenger boy, who pined to help the strikers. Lee Tisdale, a black man who was the last to expire of his wounds, on June 19, worked at Sheet & Tube.[64]

Of those killed, only Alfred Causey, age forty-three, and Anthony Tagliori, twenty-six, worked at Republic.[65] Causey had managed to get work as a carpenter at the plant after being fired for union activity at another mill.[66] Tagliori, who hung on until June 1 before the gunshot to his hip killed him, worked in the mill's open hearth department. Although happy to find a solid job after months of unemployment and service with the Civilian Conservation Corps, Tagliori joined the union because the pace of work in the mill was unbearable. According to his widow, he had declined her suggestion that they spend the holiday with their children, saying that he wanted to be with his fellow strikers.[67]

FIGURE 10. Picketers at Republic Steel's headquarters in Cleveland, Ohio, June 1, 1937. © 1937, Corbis.

The incident quickly became a rallying point for CIO unionists and gave rise to a number of episodes that underscored just how fully a "culture of unity"—to invoke Lizabeth Cohen's phrase—undergirded the rise of the CIO in the steel mills of the Calumet. The day after Memorial Day, some five thousand unionists rallied in nearby Indiana Harbor.[68] Large pickets assembled at city hall in Chicago, at Republic's headquarters in Cleveland, and at its office in New York.[69] On June 3, some seven thousand people attended a common funeral for Causey, Handley, Popovich, Reed, Rothmund, and Tagliori.[70] Even the *Tribune*'s account of the funeral exuded admiration of the throngs of working men and women of every ethnicity who arrived, some in their Sunday best, others in dusty work clothes, to honor the fallen.[71] On June 6, crowds estimated at four thousand picketed mills on the Indiana side of the Calumet.[72] A few days later, the CIO staged a rally at Chicago's Civic Opera House, attended by more than five thousand people, including A. Philip Randolph, University of Chicago professor and future U.S. senator Paul Douglas, and Carl Sandburg.[73] And on the evening of June 17, somewhere between twelve thousand and nineteen thousand CIO supporters gathered at Chicago Stadium to hear speeches by Pennsylvania lieutenant governor Thomas Kennedy and the SWOC's Van Bittner. To the disappointment of many present, John L. Lewis cancelled a planned appearance at the last minute, citing "imperative circumstances" that kept him in Washington, DC.[74] Although much smaller than these events, Lee Tisdale's funeral in early July was, in its own way, equally impressive. The *Chicago Defender* described an "imbittered group of people—family, friends, fellow-workers of both races—assembled" to hear "labor organizers rank him with the martyrs of liberty through the ages." "Tisdale was likened to Crispus Attucks ... [and] Nat Turner." As the latter "gave his life so that his people might be freed from the shackles of slavery, Tisdale, they said, will go down as one who gave his life that all workers might be freed from industrial slavery."[75] At fifty, Tisdale was the oldest person to die in the strike.

The dead men's families and close friends endured terrible grief and hardship. While the boy, Leo Francisco, lingered in the hospital for days before expiring, the Chicago police barred his overwrought mother from visiting his bedside.[76] According to the *Chicago Daily News,* about two weeks after the massacre, Sam Popovich's common-law wife, Irene, was treated in a psychiatric hospital after attempting to commit suicide.[77] Anthony Tagliori's widow, Mary, wrote the Communist Party's International Labor Defense office later in the summer regarding her financial and emotional difficulties. She had been getting milk for her two children from the organization but was in need of money for food. More than a year later, she was still receiving its assistance.[78]

In the wake of the killings, unionists showed great courage and determination on the picket lines. One of the most poignant episodes of the entire strike played out just after the massacre when three men, two black and one white, returned to picket the Republic gate. The men, whose identities are lost to history, maintained their patrol for thirty-six hours, as hundreds of police and company men milled about.[79] The three were eventually reinforced by other strikers and union supporters. Among the latter were sixteen University of Chicago students, men and women affiliated with the leftist American Students Union, who eluded police to reach the picket line.[80] Here, too, was proof of an era defined by not only bitter conflict but also a spirit of unity, compassion, and common cause

The massacre at least temporarily inspired an increase in the size of pickets and a stiffening of the strikers' resolve at other plant gates throughout the strike zone.[81] For a couple of days in early June, it appeared the union might even force an evacuation of the South Chicago mill, as union complaints about unhealthful living conditions inside convinced Mayor Kelly briefly to order the plant closed.[82] But the order had the hallmarks of a political play designed to cheaply repair the mayor's standing in working-class circles, and it was lifted before being implemented. In the meantime, loyal employees, who had to that point largely remained inside the mill, began commuting again anyway, a development that Republic invoked to defend against Kelly's closure order.[83] Republic was able to settle the matter completely by having Pullman railcars placed in the mill as temporary accommodations, which the health inspector deemed compliant.[84]

A week into June it was clear the union could not force Republic to shut the mill. Not only had Republic weathered the negative publicity surrounding the Memorial Day incident; it had partially turned the massacre against the strikers. Nor did the massacre change the disposition of the Chicago police. For days afterward, nearly one thousand police (about one-fifth of the city's entire force) guarded the approaches to the plant around the clock. Meanwhile, Girdler had the mill's land boundaries fully cordoned with barbed wire.[85]

The day after the massacre, the governor of Illinois, Henry Horner, undertook to mediate the conflict at the plant. Incredibly, Captain Mooney attended the meeting, where he openly threatened SWOC representatives. The SWOC's regional director for the Calumet and chief negotiator at the meetings, Van Bittner, summed up the meeting's value upon leaving the first session: "The conference tonight wasn't worth a thin dime."[86] With its facilities in operation and the protection of the police, Republic was gradually able to lure back a sufficient number of strikers to resume production in earnest. Horner did broker an agreement to allow a somewhat larger contingent of picketers, albeit not without continued conflicts about acceptable numbers and never in the huge numbers who marched on the plant in late May.[87] Later, a coroner's jury composed of five unemployed American Legionnaires absolved the police of any responsibility for what they had done on that warm Sunday afternoon.[88] An informal citizens' jury, composed by the National Lawyers Guild and various civil liberties groups and dubbed the Citizens Joint Commission of Inquiry, certified the views of many workers when it reached an entirely different conclusion. Reputedly, a few policemen quit their jobs in protest of the massacre; Captain Kilroy, at least, expressed some regrets about what happened.[89] But officials at Republic continued for years to blame the incident on "Communist sympathizers who wanted to create trouble."[90]

8

What Had to Be Done

THE STRUGGLE AT THE MILL GATES

Unique in intensity and notoriety, the Memorial Day Massacre nevertheless anticipated how the Little Steel Strike would unfold. The contest between the SWOC and Little Steel quickly developed into a wide-ranging struggle to determine who would control access to the mills and thus to decide whether the closed mills would stay closed and the operating ones would stay open. The fate of the strike hinged on the outcome of this struggle. Inevitably, it devolved into a grinding campaign characterized by diverse stratagems and punctuated by more episodes of extreme violence and further attempts by the parties to turn these clashes to their political advantage.

ORCHESTRATED BEDLAM AT MONROE

One place where violence flared was Monroe, Michigan, a small farming and factory town roughly midway between Toledo and Detroit and home to Newton Steel, a modest sheet mill operation that Republic acquired in early 1935 when it purchased the Corrigan-McKinney Steel Company. In April of that year, just before this deal was consummated, the plant was the scene of a strike led by the resurgent AA that involved most all of its employees.[1] At the time of the Little Steel Strike, the Newton plant was home to around fourteen hundred workers, making it the largest employer in the city.

Organizing efforts at the Newton mill had lagged, in part because Republic's small contingent of company police coordinated an active espionage campaign. The organizers' struggles may have also reflected resentments surrounding the failure of the 1935 strike and the special difficulties inherent in challenging the open shop in a small town whose civic leaders were anxious to preserve an agreeable environment for local industry. Only a couple of years earlier, town fathers had touted Monroe's supposedly placid labor relations when they begged Republic, without success, to build a new mill in Monroe. Opened with the promise of bringing prosperity to Monroe, the Newton mill had gone through several extended shutdowns in the early 1930s. Small, remote from other Republic installations, and prematurely obsolescent, the mill was not a particularly important part of Republic's operation. Ironically, this suited it as a testing ground for strikebreaking tactics.

Organizing at Monroe also suffered because the Newton mill was not a priority for SWOC leaders, who did not dispatch a full-time organizer to the area until two weeks before the strike began. Working in secret, a handful of workers at Newton, many of them AA veterans, built a nucleus of support for the SWOC and in April 1937 received a charter. However, when the nearly nationwide strike was called on May 26, the union probably enjoyed the active support of only 10 percent of the workforce. It was not till the morning of May 28 that local leaders, with the eventual approval of SWOC officials, called a strike and began picketing the single road connecting the plant to the town. The strike was conceived both to organize Newton and to express sympathy with SWOC efforts elsewhere.[2]

What started out as a few dozen picketers increased by the end of the first day to three hundred, and the union meeting that night was attended by four hundred to five hundred workers. Confronted with this outpouring of pro-SWOC sentiment, which was concentrated among employees in the plant's crucial hot mill, Republic decided that same night to close the plant. For the next two weeks, it remained closed except for maintenance and office workers who came and went unmolested. At no point during this time did the picketers forcibly block the road or, after the first day, convene in particularly large numbers. In fact, there was very little disorder during these first two weeks, and relations between the union and the local police were cordial and cooperative.

This would all change as Republic moved to break the strike at Newton and send a message to SWOC supporters elsewhere. Its plan involved building a back-to-work organization around the company union, the Steel Workers' Association. Although it originated early in the SWOC drive, the association was not fully established until about May 20, 1937. By the time the strike began, it probably enjoyed some support from maybe half the workforce, although it is impossible to say how exclusive this was of support for the SWOC. In response to the strike, the association asked local SWOC leaders to remove their pickets and allow the plant to reopen; and it dispatched delegates to meet with Michigan governor Frank Murphy, who brushed aside their request that he force an end to the strike. To greater effect, the association also solicited the support of the mayor of Monroe, Daniel Knaggs, and a number of representatives of the local business community; and it staged a series of meetings and a propaganda campaign designed to paint the strike as an irresponsible ploy by disinterested outsiders, immigrants, and radicals and to suggest that an overwhelming majority of workers opposed the strike.

The culmination of the association's efforts was an election cosponsored by the mayor and held on payday, June 7, that purported to measure workers' support for the strike and their preference for either the association or the SWOC. Some 883 votes were cast, of which the vast majority expressed opposition to the strike, support for returning to work, and support for the association. Never mind that several hundred SWOC supporters boycotted the election; it provided antiunion forces with a justification to break the picket line.[3] With the assistance of the city government, Republic set out to do just this. Mayor Knaggs recruited three hundred men to serve as special policemen, and the company provided the city with more than $1,500 worth of armaments, including over 100 gas shells and 370 clubs and baseball bats. Republic also purchased over $700 worth of gas for its own local stocks and hired another twenty-four police to augment the plant's permanent force of eight.[4] These preparations in place, the back-to-work faction announced they would forcibly reopen the mill June 10.

The appointed day began with a vicious attack on the SWOC's lead organizer in Monroe, the black radical Leondies McDonald. McDonald had been in Monroe only since mid-May—he was the first organizer sent there. But he had worked for the SWOC since the previous summer and before that in the meatpacking industry. McDonald had a good reputation in CIO circles for his ability to organize blacks and whites alike. Nevertheless, sending him to Monroe was a risky move for both the SWOC and McDonald himself. For Monroe was home to few blacks—fewer than four hundred in a population of twenty-two thousand—and was isolated from larger, more progressive urban communities. Blacks were similarly underrepresented among the workers at the Newton mill and not especially active there.

Early on the morning of June 10, word reached McDonald that company loyalists planned to either hang him or tar and feather him. McDonald was then shadowed by police and company men before being ambushed on his way out of the post office by as many as one hundred men, who severely beat him and threatened his life.[5] The mob relented and let McDonald get back into his car before pulling him out and resuming their assault. They finally dumped McDonald by the roadside, leaving him to be rescued by union people who took him to the hospital in Toledo. Uniformed officers laughed at McDonald during his ordeal and may even have participated in the attack.[6]

When news of McDonald's beating reached the picket line, the workers there knew they were next. They had recently repelled at least one attempt by a small number of loyal employees to run through their picket line.[7] Well aware that the fate of the strike in Monroe depended on whether they held their ground, they barricaded the road and armed themselves with tree limbs, iron rods, and rocks, as well as other objects taken from a nearby garbage dump. Some even donned kitchen pots as makeshift helmets. The picketers also increased their numbers to one hundred or so men and a few women, mainly strikers' wives. In the meantime, Governor Murphy, whose judicious handling of the General Motors sit-down strikes the previous winter had favored the CIO's United Automobile Workers (UAW), convened a meeting with Mayor Knaggs and delegates from Republic and the SWOC in hopes of forging an agreement to delay the reopening while efforts to settle the strike played out on the national stage. Backed by Republic's delegate, Knaggs rejected this proposal. Instead, the mayor brashly telephoned the chief of police from Murphy's office in Lansing and ordered him to proceed with plans to rout the picketers.[8]

City officials promised the governor that the back-to-work force would not gas the picketers, but this was an outright lie. Just after noon, two hundred special police were hurriedly sworn in at city hall, armed with gas and clubs, and then marched down to the picket line. Following them were hundreds of loyal employees and hundreds, maybe thousands, of spectators. A force of deputized American Legionnaires, armed with baseball bats and firearms, was left behind to patrol the city streets.[9]

As the procession made its way to the mill, the local authorities ignored Murphy's continued pleas for restraint. Brushing aside a proposal by the picketers to permit the reopening, provided the special police were also disbanded and disarmed, the motley army launched its assault. The attack opened with a flanking action by company police who sent gas behind the picket line. As the gas scattered the picketers, the back-to-work force rushed forward, beating the picketers, seizing some of them, chasing others into a swamp, and later smashing and burning their picket line installations, tearing up their automobiles, and pushing some cars into the nearby Raisin

FIGURE 11. Picketers routed by an army of loyal employees, deputies, and local police wielding gas and clubs, Monroe, Michigan, June 10, 1937. © 1937, Corbis.

River. Eleven people, six of them picketers, were treated at the hospital for injuries, mostly the effects of the gas. Amazingly, given the fury of the attack, no one was seriously injured. Some picketers were arrested that afternoon but released the following day.[10]

When news of the rout reached the automobile factories around Detroit, tens of thousands of UAW members walked off the job and prepared to march on Monroe and re-form the steel workers' picket line.[11] Back in Monroe, Republic hired an additional 426 men as police, many from the permanent workforce at Newton. The mayor and city police chief made similar moves, maintaining a force of several hundred temporary officers. Altogether, something like seven hundred men guarded the town and the plant. They chased unionists off the streets and sealed the area off from suspected CIO sympathizers. Now that the peace favored them, procompany forces began calling on Governor Murphy to help them keep it, requesting, unsuccessfully, that he declare martial law and dispatch the National Guard. Thousands of UAW members did start for Monroe. But the UAW's leadership stifled the move. Instead, they helped organize a mass meeting at a park not far from the Newton plant and under the protection of forces sent by Murphy. As tensions diminished over the next few days, the SWOC was able to negotiate the right to recommence limited picketing.[12] But by then the plant was resuming full operations and events in Monroe joined the incident

FIGURE 12. Workers assist a fellow striker overcome by gas, Monroe, Michigan, June 10, 1937. © 1937, Corbis.

in Chicago in displaying the effectiveness of company-sponsored violence in breaking the strike.

THE STOP 5 RIOT AT YOUNGSTOWN

Despite the defeats in Chicago and now Monroe, elsewhere in early June the strike was still holding fairly well. June 11 brought the workers at Bethlehem's

Cambria Works into the fray. Plans were under way to pull sympathy strikes at captive coal and ore mines. There were also signs that the governors of the key strike states or the federal government might force the companies to negotiate. And quite a number of big mills remained closed. Such was the case in Youngstown and its immediate suburbs, home to Republic's Youngstown Works and two Sheet & Tube mills, including the modestly sized Brier Hill plant and the massive Campbell Works. The city was the heart of the Ohio steel-production region and central to both companies' operations—Sheet & Tube was based there and Republic had only recently moved its headquarters from Youngstown, where they had been since 1911, to Cleveland.

The strike immediately shut the Campbell and Brier Hill works as well as Republic's Youngstown Works, located in the middle of town. At the outset of the strike, the companies announced they would close these plants, although Republic's smaller Truscon Steel subsidiary, where SWOC supporters had suffered many beatings and discharges, continued in production.[13] The first few days of the strike witnessed scattered outbreaks of violence in Youngstown, including an episode where picketers said they were shot at by company police when they prevented two crane operators from working at the Brier Hill plant. Worried that too many picketers wielded clubs and sticks, and that things could easily spiral out of control, local leaders moved to disarm them.[14] Soon, wrote organizer Meyer Bernstein, the conflict seemed to settle. Even the police were "friendly," he said, "and never interfere with the picketing."[15]

Nevertheless, the Mahoning County sheriff, Ralph Esler, continued to augment his forces. The sheriff's office added 152 special police, of whom 94 were loyal Republic and Sheet & Tube employees. Moreover, the day before the strike began, the sheriff purchased over $3,000 worth of gas weapons, and he later bought another $10,000 in gas—all in addition to supplies donated by Republic. The sheriff also obtained two large Ford trucks covered in armor plate. The city police added 144 men, of whom 59 were steel company employees, although not until some two weeks after the strike began. When the strike began, police suspended leaves and established regular patrols at the mill gates.[16] Republic and Sheet & Tube increased their own company police forces in Youngstown as well. Altogether, the La Follette Committee staff estimated that Republic and Sheet & Tube eventually controlled one thousand armed men in the Youngstown area, not counting public police and some three hundred Pennsylvania Railroad police allied with the companies.[17] Despite having closed their Youngstown plants, almost two weeks *before* the strike began Republic and Sheet & Tube signaled that they would reopen the mills as soon as pickets no longer impeded entry.[18]

Early on June 5, a large detachment of deputies, equipped with one of the armored trucks and accompanied by a number of Sheet & Tube men, rolled a boxcar into the Campbell Works. As word of this spread, a crowd of angry picketers gathered; and later, unionists clandestinely cut the tracks with a torch. Then on June 9, city police helped move a truck past picketers and into Republic's Youngstown plant. Again, strikers and sympathizers converged on the scene, this time in a steady rain and armed with clubs. As they were being addressed by Robert Burke, lead organizer at the plant, a shouting match developed between Burke and a heckler named Ralph Ross. A gunshot rang out, striking Ross in the leg. And then there were several more gunshots and a volley of gas grenades. The ensuing mêlée nearly descended into a full-scale riot before union people managed to calm the crowd. Although the gas and at least some of the gunfire surely came from the police, and although Burke himself almost certainly did not fire a weapon, he was arrested on charges that included "shooting with intent to kill or wound," disturbing the peace, and "criminal syndicalism."[19] The *Daily Worker*'s man on the scene, Adam Lapin, claimed that what Burke actually did was restrain "enraged pickets" and free "two detectives and a policeman" whom they had briefly captured after the police rushed the strikers.[20] It turns out that Ross, who had tried to contact Sheet & Tube with information about who had cut the railroad tracks at the company's mill on June 5, received a "loan" of approximately $1,000 from a law firm that represented Sheet & Tube. A year later the money had not been repaid. And although ostensibly intended to cover Ross's medical expenses, only about $400 was paid to his doctors, the remainder being given to Ross in cash.[21]

After the events of June 9, the city government accelerated the hiring of company men as special police. Sheet & Tube and Republic moved forward with plans to reopen the Youngstown mills. As at Monroe, this involved organizing back-to-work movements around company unions that had recently been revived for this role. So structured, the movements lobbied local officials, solicited the support of local business leaders, circulated back-to-work petitions among workers, and staged a number of meetings for loyal employees. Some workers testified that they were offered bribes of money and better job assignments if they supported these efforts. Other strikers were told that anyone who did not sign the back-to-work petitions would be blacklisted when the strike ended.

Until the middle of June, little came of this. The first public meeting of Sheet & Tube's back-to-work group had to be adjourned when most of those in attendance turned out to be CIO infiltrators. Nor was there evidence of any spontaneous mass movement to return to work, despite the implausible claim of those behind this effort that on June 13, nine thousand employees from Sheet & Tube alone were clamoring to get back into the mills.[22] But in less immediate ways, the antistrike efforts were bearing fruit. The mere existence of the back-to-work organizations gave credence to assertions that strike support was waning and that the strikers' intransigence was the real impediment to a settlement. Accordingly, in early June, Tom Girdler and Frank Purnell began demanding "protection" for workers who wanted to go back.[23] Besides denting the morale of strikers, who could not be sure how weak or strong the dissident movements actually were, the back-to-work campaigns also aggravated tensions on the streets, making a truly violent clash more likely to occur.

At about eight o'clock on the evening of June 19, some fifteen women were picketing off of Poland Avenue in Youngstown, near Republic's "Stop 5" gate—a narrow driveway leading from the street, underneath the New York Central Railroad track, and onto company property and known by its public-transit designation. It was "women's day" on the line and a Saturday. Organizers had planned to have a dance near the gate later that night. Tired from picketing all afternoon, some of the women were sitting on the curb and in chairs on the sidewalk when a city police captain named Charles Richmond drove up. Although the women were not obstructing anyone's passage, Richmond ordered them to remove the chairs, several of which encroached a few feet onto Republic's property, and, apparently to make their task more onerous, to get up and start patrolling. He also reproached them, as women, for picketing at all and gave them five minutes to comply. Although the women did put away the chairs, it seems they ignored Richmond's other orders, for he soon returned and angrily insisted again that they patrol. As some of the picketers recalled, what Richmond really wanted was that they stop picketing altogether. Richmond then went over to his cruiser, talked to other police, checked his watch, and approached the picketers yet again. What happened next is somewhat unclear. According to one version of events, the women cursed and laughed at Richmond. Another version has one of them slapping Richmond. Whatever the case, the conflict quickly escalated and Richmond, now incensed, said, "God damn, I['ll] make you move," and then donned a gas mask and threw several tear gas grenades at the women's feet.[24]

The gas threw the picketers into a panic and sent them running in fright, coughing and choking. Meanwhile, a dozen or so nearby union men started throwing rocks and bricks at Richmond. Amid the increasing chaos, a rumor took flight that Josephine Varone, a picketer who fled with a baby in arms, had been shot and the child killed. As the rumor quickly spread, it brought more CIO men running to the area, first from a nearby field and other hangouts, later from their homes and other more distant places. Union people began to gather near an intersection a few hundred feet down the street from the Stop 5 gate, southeast of where the initial clash occurred, and at a group of buildings across Poland Avenue from the Stop 5 gate. With the crowd of angry unionists growing, Richmond telephoned for reinforcements of men and arms. Trucks streamed in and soon the force near the gate had been augmented by 240 men from the city police, somewhere between 60 and 200 sheriff's deputies, and a few deputized Pennsylvania Railroad police. Meanwhile, Republic mobilized about 40 company police who were in and around the mill.[25]

While Robert Burke and other organizers tried desperately to disperse the crowd of union people, the police continued to lob gas grenades. As one witness recalled years later, Burke's effort to address the strikers was interrupted when "about fifteen canisters of tear gas and bullets began to flood the field from the mill."[26] In the meantime, union men continued to arrive, some armed. A worker at a nearby scrapyard thought he was hearing fireworks until a man running past corrected him: "Man, who would be shooting fireworks?" The runner was "going home to get his gun."[27] While the strikers had to fetch weapons back to the scene, the police were already prepared to use deadly force.[28] Despite the witness's recollection that bullets began to fly while Burke was speaking, it is not clear when the shooting started. Another witness claimed that the first shots came earlier, from Richmond's revolver as he fired into the pavement in anger, just after lobbing the gas grenades, perhaps as bricks and rocks rained down around him.[29]

With the help of his parents and a union truck equipped with loudspeakers, Burke managed to move most of the crowd around the corner and off of Poland Avenue and to get most of the women to positions of relative safety. The wafting gas also did its part to drive people from the streets near the Stop

FIGURE 13. Picketers mingle casually at the Stop 5 gate to Republic Steel's Youngstown Works, June 19, 1937, shortly before a confrontation between a belligerent city policeman and women picketers sparked a deadly riot. Courtesy of Penn State University Special Collections Library, Historical Collections and Labor Archives, Meyer Bernstein Papers.

5 gate, creating a no man's land on a stretch of Poland Avenue running from Stop 5, where the police were concentrated, to the intersection near where the union people had gathered. In the gloaming, the opening distance between the two sides set the stage for a wild exchange of gunfire. Several witnesses, including Burke, recalled hearing a man who had already been shot cry for help while Burke was trying to hustle the crowd to safety. When Burke returned to the street, it had become a war zone, with rifle, handgun, and shotgun fire mixing with the persistent discharge of gas shells and grenades.[30]

Called to the scene to calm things down, organizer John Steuben arrived at around 8:45 P.M., just as the light was fading. There was already a great deal of gunfire, and a number of mostly unarmed union people were pinned down at a gas station off of Poland, a few hundred feet southeast of the mill gate. While gathering these people to make a run to a safer spot, Steuben saw a man shot down just feet way. The victim was John Bogovich, a Croatian immigrant and Sheet & Tube striker. Unarmed, Bogovich was at home when he heard of the fracas at the mill and had hurried to the scene. He was pronounced dead shortly after being rushed to the hospital.[31] Around the same time, about five hundred feet away, an organizer named Charles Fagan had gotten on top of a car to urge workers near him to clear the area. "When

I got there," he said, "I thought the Great War had started over again." When a flare suddenly illuminated the scene, a man tried to pull Fagan off the car and was shot through the shoulder. According to Fagan, "Those flares kept going up at regular intervals, and as the flares would go up the firing would start again and the [gas] bombs would go around. It seemed that every time they threw [or fired] a flare, it was giving them a view of the pickets or somebody around, so that they could let go at them."[32] Fagan, whose account was corroborated by other witnesses, was certain gunfire came from a large building in the mill, across the railroad embankment that separated the mill property from Poland Avenue.[33]

Informed that Bogovich had died, Steuben again tried to disperse the strikers and was able to clear some of them from the area. Steuben then made his way down the street about a half mile to SWOC headquarters for the Republic plant, where he telephoned the sheriff and pleaded unsuccessfully for a cease-fire. In desperation, Steuben even got a state senator who happened to be on the scene to call the sheriff—who told the senator to mind his own business. Later, the senator tried to reach Governor Martin Davey to see if he would take hold of the situation, but again without success.[34]

For several hours, armed unionists, some ensconced on a hill that ran along the other side of Poland Avenue above the street and mill, continued to trade gunfire with local and company police under the occasional glare of parachute flares.[35] Other unionists, along with innocent drivers and pedestrians who were caught up in the battle, remained pinned down at the gas station, in a nearby café and barber shop, and at other spots along the street opposite the mill. Clingan Jackson, a journalist for the *Youngstown Vindicator,* who was with Steuben in the union office, down a ways on Poland, recalled that "every time you set your hand out the door, somebody shot at it." Not long after the shooting began, Jackson had to rush Ed Salt, a *Vindicator* photographer, to the hospital after Salt was shot in both legs and his right arm immediately after flashing a photograph of unionists inspecting a spent gas shell.[36]

Another striker from Sheet & Tube, a Czech immigrant named James Eperjesi, was fatally shot shortly after Bogovich and under similar circumstances—he was running for cover when a flare exposed him. Eperjesi died the morning of June 20 at the hospital. Unlike Bogovich, who was struck by a rifle bullet, Eperjesi was killed by a shotgun blast, suggesting that the fatal shot came neither from the mill building nor the police position near Stop 5, but somewhere closer. The journalist Mary Heaton Vorse, who was not a direct eyewitness but was only feet from the scene, claimed that Eperjesi was shot "pointblank, by deputies standing in a truck."[37] Although this may have been the case, it is equally likely that the fatal shot came from behind the railroad embankment that separated the street from plant property. When Eperjesi was killed, another witness close by claimed to see heads popping up and down behind the embankment.[38] A month later, La Follette Committee investigators found the service station near the spot where both men had been killed riddled in a pattern suggesting that a great deal of gunfire had been fired from the direction of the plant and the embankment. Photographs of holes in buildings near where the men were killed, taken by organizer Meyer Bernstein and later acquired by the committee, also indicated that shots had been fired from steel company and railroad property.[39] Several witnesses likewise testified that deadly gunfire came from the mill; and nearly forty years later, still other witnesses continued to repeat this claim.[40] Some of the fire directed at the union people came from high-powered rifles. Although police may not have had any weapons of this kind, Republic had at least four in the plant, along with thirty-five shotguns and eighty-five handguns. For what it is worth, at one point both the police and Republic insisted that their forces fired *no* shots at all that night, only gas, and that the strikers must have shot each other.[41] Nevertheless, in 1944, Republic settled civil claims filed by the estates of Bogovich and Eperjesi—$4,500 for Bogovich and $1,005.25 for Eperjesi.[42]

The fighting continued for nearly five hours. At some point on that night of June 19, Republic's police answered an urgent request from Captain Richmond for more gas munitions.[43] Dozens, perhaps hundreds, of gas shells were discharged, creating a lingering cloud too dense to see through. It sickened numerous people on both sides. The injured poured into local hospitals. Besides the two fatalities, fifty-nine people required emergency medical treatment and several were seriously injured. At least twenty-two people were hit by gunfire (fortunately much of it bird shot); and another twenty-six were overcome by gas. Among the injured were at least seven women, of whom four had been shot. Although initially reported to have been shot and critically injured, Mary Heaton Vorse was only lightly wounded when she was knocked down and struck her head. Eight policemen or deputies were hurt, three by gunfire.[44] Around 6:00 A.M., with the next day dawning, the sheriff met SWOC leaders in the middle of Poland Avenue to implement an "armistice" and organize people to clear the streets of wrecked vehicles and other debris.[45]

Police arrested a dozen people during the riot, mostly on weapons charges.[46] Although most were seized at a distance from the actual fighting, this was not true in every case. The driver of the union sound truck who helped Burke clear the area was apprehended at gunpoint after the vehicle was blasted point-blank with gas projectiles; the man claimed that the truck was wrecked by the sheriff's men while he was in custody. Another person arrested was the Republic spy Ira Albert, picked up at 3:30 A.M. and charged with carrying a concealed weapon. Over the next few days, there would be more arrests of union people.[47] No one with the police, sheriff's office, or Republic Steel (except Albert) was charged in connection with the riot or the deaths of Bogovich and Eperjesi.

The fighting around the Stop 5 gate was the closest that unionists came to holding their own in the episodes of serious violence during the strike. Undoubtedly, union people fired numerous shots into the Republic mill and at police emplacements nearby. The scrapyard worker who initially thought he heard fireworks claimed to have followed a group of armed unionists back toward the mill. They had "every kind of pistol or gun you could imagine."[48] This was consistent with police arrest records, which confirm that a number of weapons were found among the people they interdicted on the way to the scene. During the battle, the strikers managed to overturn and set fire to a police car near Stop 5; and they pushed a city bus across Poland Avenue, using it for cover and to block the road.

The workers' decision to fight was understandable. As far as most union people knew, police, deputies, and company guards had unleashed a nearly unprovoked and deadly attack on women and children. This perception fit with the continual provocation that strikers had experienced in the weeks leading up to the riot. And the events at Monroe and Chicago were examples of what might happen if strikers were not prepared to defend themselves. Even one so far removed from the picket lines as Senator Thomas of the La Follette Committee observed that these earlier episodes invited workers to take steps to defend themselves.[49] Still, the unionists' decision that night to take on several hundred law enforcement personnel and company men required considerable courage. And it came with considerable costs.

Even more than the Memorial Day incident or the events at Monroe, the Stop 5 Riot marked a turning point in the struggle. The riot again put the strike in the national headlines. And in its wake, violence became the paramount concern of politicians, newspapermen, and other elites who increasingly reconfigured discourse on the strike around the need to ensure the peace, even at the expense of strikers' labor rights. But while this development gathered momentum, the struggle at the plant gates continued.

THE SIEGE AT WARREN AND NILES

A key chapter in this struggle unfolded in Warren, where Republic ran an integrated mill with over six thousand workers, and nearby Niles, where Republic had a smaller plant with about one thousand workers. Comprising the furnaces of the old Trumbull Steel Company and the Trumbull-Cliffs Furnace Company, which Republic acquired in 1928 and 1929, the Warren plant boasted what Tom Girdler called "the biggest blast furnace in the world."[50] The plant itself occupied about a square mile of a site nearly twice as large. Located a few miles away, the smaller Niles plant relied on the Warren complex for stock, as it lacked iron- and steel-making furnaces.[51] Unionism and company repression both ran deep in these mills. During the rank-and-file upsurge of 1933–34, three lodges briefly flourished at Warren. By 1936 only one of these, Trumbull Lodge No. 73, remained in place. But when the strike approached, this lodge was among the largest in the SWOC fold.[52]

Republic decided several days before the 1937 strike that it would try to operate both mills during the walkout and hurried to bring in supplies and erect sleeping accommodations. The company placed propaganda ads in the local media and redoubled efforts to shore up support from local commercial and industry groups and local governments. It also increased its police force in the area from thirty-eight at the beginning of the year to forty-six.[53] These preparations did not go unnoticed. On the eve of the strike, unionists observed men moving into the plants with suitcases. They responded by attempting to launch the strike early. But as organizers coursed through the two mills, trying to get men out, they were attacked by company men. It was at Niles that Harold Williams and other SWOC organizers were beaten and had guns drawn on them by company and railroad police. At the Warren plant, the company "lined up a couple of hundred 'loyal' workers and 'bosses' armed with sledge-hammers, pikes, and other weapons," who then coerced employees to stay at their jobs.[54] Company police assaulted organizers as they attempted to spread the strike call among their coworkers, and workers were told that if they walked out they would lose their jobs.[55]

Nevertheless, strikers were able to establish large pickets at the mill gates, patrol their sprawling suburban boundary lines, and, in a short time, effectively blockade both plants. Their chief goal was to prevent loyal employees who remained in the mills from entering and leaving at will. Although company claims that one-third of the workforce remained in the plants were likely inflated, this figure is more accurate than the SWOC's assertion that these mills were nearly empty. Moreover, while some men certainly were bullied to stay on the job, there is little reason to believe strikers' claims that most of those who remained inside were coerced into doing so, for there were plenty of genuine company loyalists at Warren and Niles—a fact consistent with the difficulties the union acknowledged in organizing those plants.[56]

From the outset of the strike, there was considerable tension. On May 28 at the Warren plant, a picketer was shot by a loyal employee. The victim, a twenty-eight-year-old employee of the Works Progress Administration named John Baugh, was shot and wounded by a loyal employee, a black man, who had returned with his gun and shot into the crowd of picketers at the gate after being forcibly prevented from entering the mill earlier that day. Despite these confrontations, the parties were able to negotiate toward an agreement on bringing food into the plants and the situation was, for a brief time, relatively quiet at both plants.[57]

However, violence soon flared again at the Warren mill. It began on the evening of May 31 when several black men ran out of the mill through the picket line at the main gate. Blacks were prominent among loyal employees and poorly represented among the strikers. Within minutes, the men's sorties through the line precipitated an exchange of bricks and other missiles between picketers and hundreds of loyal employees still inside the plant, who had rushed to the gate. Exactly what underlay the fracas is not entirely clear. It is certainly possible that company officials orchestrated the whole thing merely to inflame the strikers. The exchange of missiles continued for some time under the menacing guard of company police, until the sheriff and his men arrived to separate the combatants. The sheriff was actually meeting with SWOC people and Republic officials at the company's nearby Warren headquarters to discuss a system for supplying the plants when bricks started landing on his car, at which "he got mad" and put a stop to the bombardment.[58]

The events that evening ended negotiations with local union leaders on procedures for resupplying the two plants. This presented a problem for

Republic, which had not stocked the plants with nearly enough supplies to carry the two thousand or so loyal employees through the lengthening strike. By the second day of the strike, some men had already been sickened by spoiled or improperly cooked food. After a few days, men began to leave the mills, predicting as they emerged that the plants would have to shut down because of a lack of provisions.[59]

A forced evacuation was a real possibility, and one that Republic was desperate to avoid. So it considered ways of supplying the plants. After rejecting the idea of plowing through the picket lines with a military tank—a notion that Girdler and his men scotched for fear that picketers would blow it up—the company resorted to an even more remarkable scheme to keeps the mills open: aerial resupply with up to fourteen aircraft.[60] Republic had bought the first plane on May 28, several days before the clash on May 31—a fact it initially denied in order to blunt charges by the La Follette Committee that the purchase betokened bad faith on its part. Over the next several weeks, the company bought at least seven other aircraft and leased several more. On June 1, Republic also shipped more weapons into the plants, including ten shotguns and several hundred tear gas and sickening gas shells and grenades. The company likewise provided the Trumbull County sheriff with nearly $3,000 worth of gas ammunition and equipment and contributed about $15,000 to defray the cost of adding special deputies to the sheriff's force.[61]

Although the strikers were surely not eager to approve an agreement on resupplying the mills that would keep the plants running, they might well have been convinced to compromise in the interest of promoting larger, government-sponsored negotiations. Once the planes began to fly, this was out of the question. The contest took on the character of a winner-take-all battle. If the company could even appear to run the mills successfully, it would deliver a devastating blow to the strikers' morale. However, if Republic could not keep the mills stocked, the loyal employees faced, as Girdler put it, "starvation or surrender" and would have to be evacuated—and the union would realize an enormous propaganda victory.[62]

The airlift began inauspiciously. The first flight was dispatched to Niles on May 29 in an airplane owned by a company employee. It left from Cleveland loaded with food in padded sacks. The pilot and his assistant located the plant but mistimed the first drop, landing the supplies on the wrong side of the fence, near picketers who gleefully seized them and posed for local reporters with smashed cans of beef stew and other goods.[63] Subsequent drops on that mission were more successful, however. Convinced that the scheme was feasible, the company then set about finding pilots willing to make the runs. At Warren, employees constructed a landing strip. At the smaller Niles plant, this was impossible and supplies had to be airdropped, as on the first flight. Within days, aircraft were making runs to both plants, sometimes more than a dozen a day. Girdler claimed that over a few weeks the planes delivered more than two hundred thousand pounds of supplies: "newspapers, books and magazines, sides of beef, bunches of bananas, crates of apples, fresh vegetables, milk, freezers of ice cream . . . clothing, bedclothes, and medicines . . . the current movies."[64] Evidently, the company expended $200,000 on the missions.[65]

Republic's resupply efforts did not go unchallenged by the SWOC, however. Within a day of the first regular drops, the union had its own planes in the air harassing Republic's aircraft and trying to determine where they were coming from. For weeks thereafter, there were scattered reports of union planes over Warren and Niles jousting with company planes.[66] Republic also had trouble securing pilots or support services near Warren and Youngstown. Eschewing the company's offer of premium rates, pilots and aircraft operators contented themselves with flying paying sightseers and journalists over the picket lines.[67] Republic was likewise unwilling or unable to fly planes out of the greater Youngstown area. Instead, the company secured pilots and an airfield in the Cleveland area, making each run to the plants a round-trip of about one hundred miles. Two weeks into the campaign, the union pressured Mayor Harold Burton to revoke the company's permit to fly food from Cleveland's Great Lakes Airport, a private field, forcing the company to remove operations to more distant Ashland, Ohio.[68]

Almost from the beginning, local journalists reported gunfire directed at Republic's aircraft from locations near the plants and picketers dodging objects thrown down at them from the planes. Although there was apparently no air-to-air or air-to-ground shooting, there were skirmishes between union snipers and company police stationed in the mills.[69] In one of these exchanges, a Pennsylvania Railroad policeman was hit by a stray bullet. On another occasion, a *New York Times* photographer observing a flight into the Warren plant drew fire from Republic's police and had to flee for his life.[70] So intense was the shooting that the company set up rows of boxcars alongside the landing strip in the Warren mill to protect the planes from incoming fire. At the apex of this struggle, picketers claimed that company airmen were intentionally flying dangerously low over their heads. The SWOC's David McDonald arrived at the plant in Niles just in time to be

FIGURE 14. Loyal employees and aircrew at Republic Steel's plant at Warren, Ohio, pose near an airplane used to supply workers trapped inside by aggressive picketers, June 23, 1937. Courtesy of the Youngstown Historical Center of Industry and Labor.

repeatedly "dive bombed" by company planes as he tried to deliver a speech to cheering picketers from the back of a truck.[71]

No one was seriously hurt in this dangerous contest, but there were other close calls.[72] Republic's district manager for Warren and Niles, Frank Flynn, had to be flown back into the Warren plant after leaving for church and finding he could not get back in past massed picketers. Flynn claimed that his plane was hit by gunfire and that another aircraft landed with twenty-five bullet holes in it.[73] On June 2, two planes crash-landed at Warren, one with a strut severed by a rifle bullet, the other probably because the pilot was distracted during landing by all the shooting.[74] The next day, a United Press reporter got what he called his "money's worth" when the resupply plane he rode in drew twenty shots and was hit by nine bullets, including one that pierced the seat beside him.[75]

Although a remarkable testament to the company's wealth and resolve, the airlift ran up against the practical limits of aerial cargo delivery. As long as Republic dared not try to break the picket lines on the ground, it had trouble delivering adequate supplies into the plants. A bigger problem for

FIGURE 15. Loyal employees hurriedly unload supplies from an airplane inside Republic Steel's Warren, Ohio, plant, June 19, 1937. Courtesy of Youngstown Historical Center of Industry and Labor.

Republic was that however well-supplied they might have been, loyal employees remained imprisoned in the mills, unable to see friends and family or tend to other aspects of private life. Even Flynn, the company's district manager, claimed that the stress surrounding the sieges nearly killed him and forced his eventual evacuation from the Warren plant.[76] The loyal employees' frustrations surfaced in a letter sent to Secretary of Labor Frances Perkins on June 21. An obvious attempt to propagandize the company's position, the letter nevertheless captured the real frustrations faced by the men inside. Its most salient point: "We are sick and tired of having to stay inside this plant."[77]

THE LOGIC OF COERCION AND VIOLENCE

These events at Warren and Niles give further support to the view that, although chaotic and confused, the violence that characterized the Little Steel Strike was seldom random or irrational. Violence originated in attempts by the union to set up effective pickets, and thereby close the plants and keep them closed, and in efforts of the steel companies and their allies to counter this. Other episodes confirm this. On June 14 and 15, around a dozen people were injured and at least seven strikers arrested when police in

Johnstown used gas and firearms to rout a gathering of strikers confronting loyal employees at the gates of Bethlehem's Cambria Works.[78] On July 20, at Republic's small N&G Taylor plant in Cumberland, Maryland, ten people were injured and four hospitalized when some two hundred picketers clashed with police, deputies, and maintenance workers trying to enter the plant.[79] Indeed, similar clashes occurred virtually every day, with prominent flare-ups in Youngstown, Canton, Massillon, and Cleveland.

Violence became the arbiter of the workers' labor rights, not only in major episodes of unrest, but also in grinding contests on and about the picket lines. The essential purposes of picketing—especially mass picketing—were to coerce scabs from entering the mills, draw out those who remained inside, and ultimately prevent the companies from running the plants. To be sure, mass picket lines could also peacefully persuade workers to join the cause, boost strikers' morale, and protect against assaults and harassment by company men. But the coercive aspects were central—and often effective. In Canton in the first days of the strike, mass pickets forced the closure of units that Republic had sought to keep open; and around Youngstown, Warren, and Niles, threatening pickets and barricades were central to the union's efforts from the outset.[80]

For their part, the companies were quite willing to use force to push through the picket lines, intimidate picketers, and provoke them and thus undermine the legitimacy of their cause while paving the way for legal intervention. Ironically, while mass picketing best served the union's purpose if it could be employed to successfully quarantine the plants *without* descending into open violence, it was in the companies' interests to convert the passive coercion of mass picketing into eruptions of violence that could be used to demonize the union and justify further restrictions on picketing—as happened at Republic's South Chicago plant. And there was plenty of provocation. Strikers everywhere complained of heavily armed company police who shot into strikers' homes and at the strikers themselves, occasionally drawing blood.[81] Workers also claimed that company agents infiltrated their picket lines, attempting to frighten them with rumors of impending attacks and blacklists or to instigate violence.[82] John Steuben recalled a man on the line in Youngstown who repeatedly urged "rushing the gates" and criticized strike leaders' supposed "lack of action," only later to be exposed as a member of Republic's police force.[83] In light of these tactics, and mindful of the companies' arsenals, strikers feared that the companies might suddenly overwhelm them with violence.[84]

Although many factors played a role, the SWOC's willingness to pressure loyal employees and fight the companies when push came to shove can be traced to a combination of rank-and-file fervor and local leadership. The events at Warren and Niles are a good example of this, as the union's response was clearly influenced by a tradition of militancy in the area as well as by the leadership of Gus Hall, a colorful and enigmatic figure who would one day graduate from local labor organizer and militant strike leader to national leader of the Communist Party. Born Arvo Kusta Halberg in 1910 in a log cabin in the mining hamlet of Iron, Minnesota, Hall described the rigors of life in mining and logging towns of his youth as a foundation of his political views. "Working in the lumber camps in those days would make a communist out of anyone," he recalled.[85] Easygoing and gregarious, Hall was also, as one striker recalled, "a likeable fellow"—"a fairly decent guy, if you knew him."[86]

Unlike many people accused of being Communists, Hall was not only an actual party member; he spent several years in the early 1930s at the International Lenin School in Moscow, where young people of peasant and working-class origin received revolutionary training. Along with intellectual and political education, Hall supposedly received schooling in sabotage and guerilla tactics. The truth of the latter claim may be questioned not only with respect to Hall's own story, which is characteristically ambiguous on this point, but also because the true scope of the school's curriculum remains steeped in mystery and clouded by anti-Communist propaganda.[87] Whatever he learned there, Hall returned to the United States in 1933. When arrested in 1934 in the Minneapolis teamsters' strike for inciting a riot—a charge for which he was jailed for six months—Hall was well along in establishing himself as an agitator and organizer.

A burly six-footer, Hall lived and worked for a while in northeast Ohio, where he married and also changed his name, in order to avoid an earlier blacklisting, he claimed. Although never specific about his time as a steel worker, Hall did work at Republic's Youngstown mill before he was fired for organizing during the rank-and-file upsurge. In the summer of 1936, Hall was hired to organize for the SWOC. Thomas White, a worker at Republic's Youngstown Works, recalled the circumstance in which Hall was engaged by the SWOC's John Mayo: "Now Warren was hard to organize and John Mayo had sent three or four organizers in there and they couldn't organize Warren[;] and I was in John Mayo's office in the Erie building when they called Gus Hall in and they said, 'Gus, can you organize Warren?' Gus organized Warren."[88]

After the Little Steel Strike, Hall continued a life of confrontation and controversy, jumping bail after being convicted under the anti-Communist Smith Act in 1949 before being recaptured and serving five and a half years in federal prison. After his release, Hall became party leader and headed the party until his death in 2000. In those later years, Hall frequently suggested that his work with the SWOC had been one of the key episodes in his life. Hall was undoubtedly a tough and effective organizer. During the strike, he was as committed to keeping Republic's plants closed as Girdler and company were to reopening them. Unlike Murray and his acolytes in the SWOC, Hall was far less constrained by corporatist ideology or mainstream political commitments in the methods he was prepared to use to achieve this goal. In this regard, Hall contradicted not only the emerging image of the party functionary, slavishly tethered by Popular Front commitments to CIO aims, but also, ironically, a broader conception of doctrinaire service to staid party aims that he would later, as party leader, personify and enforce.

Hall's brand of militancy could be seen not only in the effort to stop Republic's aerial resupply of the mills but also in an equally dangerous bid to close off rail access to the plants.[89] For the companies, railroads were essential to bringing in the huge quantities of raw materials needed to make steel and to bringing out finished products. This was particularly true through much of northeast Ohio, including Warren and Niles, where there was no ready access to waterborne transportation. These mills could not be run if railroads feeding them were closed. Hall and other organizers knew this and focused considerable efforts on stopping the trains.

From positions near where the tracks entered the mills, picketers were able to convince individual train crews to turn back, even though the leadership of the railroad brotherhoods had decided early in the strike not to abrogate their contracts for the sake of sympathy action.[90] Tom Girdler complained that in deference to their workers' wishes, some railroad officials determined to haul only "regular" loads in and out of the mills—raw materials and steel products, but not food or munitions. Girdler also claimed that some lower-level railroad officials had conspired with union people to prevent the movement of any cargoes.[91] For a time, strikers in Warren were indeed able to insist on inspection of railcars for strikebreaking goods before allowing them into Republic's mill.[92] Generally, though, the railroads were willing to defy the picketers. Typically, their crews simply pushed the trains past picketers or, with the help of steel company men, resorted to subterfuge

FIGURE 16. Pennsylvania Railroad police, heavily armed with gas and shotguns, guard the tracks near Warren, Ohio, June 16, 1937. Allied with the steel companies, at least 570 railroad police were active in the strike. © 1937, Associated Press.

or surprise to get through.[93] Squads of railroad and company police, armed with gas and firearms, also patrolled the tracks and drove off picketers. Unable to stop the trains by picketing, unionists blocked the tracks with crossties and other heavy objects and also resorted to more destructive measures.[94]

As the first week of June drew to a close, railroad officials protested to the governor of Ohio that "to all intents and purposes a state of riot" prevailed on the tracks around Youngstown, Warren, and Niles. Officials with the railroads and steel companies complained that picketing and sabotage were preventing the railroads from fulfilling their obligations as common carriers. They were granted several injunctions barring picketers from the tracks.[95] But while the injunctions may have discouraged picketing, they did little to suppress a growing sabotage campaign. On June 15, with one hundred Pennsylvania Railroad police on guard, Republic moved a thirty-five-car train into the Warren mill, offloaded supplies, and sent it out laden with steel products. Less than two hours later, union men dynamited eighty feet of track, including a trestle, on the line between Warren and Niles. The track was repaired under the watch of heavily armed railroad police.[96]

FIGURE 17. Sabotage of railcars by having their pockets opened in the greater Youngstown area, June 15, 1937. Loaded with limestone, the cars have been effectively immobilized. Courtesy of the Youngstown Historical Center of Industry and Labor.

The tracks around the Warren mill witnessed repeated confrontations between picketers and railroad police and were the scene of a number of acts of sabotage like the one just mentioned.[97] In the Canton area, too, what Girdler called a group of "revolutionists" controlled rail access to Republic's mills for a time until driven off by heavily armed Pennsylvania Railroad police.[98] These encounters between picketers and police could be quite violent. On June 8, Joe Morton, president of the SWOC local, and several other picketers were gassed and beaten by railroad police on the tracks leading into Republic's plant just outside of Massillon while trying to inspect boxcars.[99]

Acts of sabotage, often involving explosives, occurred all over northeast Ohio and were not confined to the railroads. These increased in frequency when the mills began to reopen in earnest in late June, but some occurred before this.[100] A fairly typical instance unfolded late on June 1, when someone short-circuited two high-voltage power lines leading into a Republic plant in Canton.[101] Although these acts were usually carried out by union men, in at least a few cases what looked like union sabotage was the work of company agents, intent on aggravating the union's reputation for destruction and violence. Organizer John Johns in Canton recalled how union men there began to suspect a vice president of the lodge named Martin Becker of being a company agent when the man managed to run a train engine into a Republic plant, causing it to smash into a building inside, without getting caught by patrolling company police. The La Follette Committee later determined that Becker was indeed a spy for Republic.[102] Earlier in the strike, *Daily Worker* reporter Adam Lapin described embarking on a tour of the picket lines with Republic worker and SWOC organizer Joseph Gallagher, only to find a block of explosives apparently planted—unarmed—on the driver's seat of Gallagher's automobile.[103] Over the weekend of June 19 and 20, police in Canton discovered eight sticks of dynamite in the possession of four men they had detained for menacing picketers.[104]

Closing off the airways or railroads would have meant little if the mill gates were not continuously picketed. Typically, picketers were organized in four "turns" of six hours, facilitating twenty-four-hour picketing. At the plant level, picketers were under the control of picket heads who presided over picket captains, who actually supervised the individual turns. With over two dozen plants to picket, some with eight or more major gates, strikers did not have the resources to cover the gates at all times with more than a couple of dozen people each, and usually far fewer. Nor was this feasible for other reasons, as large gatherings of picketers were increasingly proscribed by judicial injunctions and police actions. By the time the conflict was several weeks old, exhaustion and boredom were also problems, and organizers risked eroding strikers' morale by setting staffing goals that could not be met. At the same time, not all plants or gates were equally important; nor was any important at all times. And most plants were initially closed by the strike. In this context, local leaders economized by identifying the most critical times and locations and focused their efforts there. Key to this approach were "flying squadrons" of picketers, sometimes under radio control, which strike leaders dispatched by automobile to weak points on the lines when trouble threatened.[105] Although strikers and their families bore the brunt of picket duty, they were aided everywhere by volunteers—other CIO unionists, leftists, and common folk who embraced the spirit of solidarity.

The picket lines were the scene of countless smaller clashes. On June 5, 6, and 7, picketers in Canton were repeatedly accosted by large groups of heavily armed company men and bombarded with missiles thrown from company property. In a separate incident on June 6, picketers in Canton drew gunfire from loyal employees and company police inside one of Republic's mills. The picketers returned fire. According to the *Canton Repository*, 125 shots were exchanged, fortunately without injury, before city police brokered a truce.[106] When the *New York Times*' Pulitzer Prize–winning labor reporter Louis Stark visited the Warren area in early June, he found the picket lines "manned by grim and determined men" who vowed to hold the siege.[107] At Warren and Niles, picketers guarded the plants' boundaries, which at Warren extended for miles from town, through swamps and open country. The union's flying squadrons patrolled the perimeters of the plants, apprehending and roughing up would-be infiltrators. Loyal employees were reduced to trying to creep past picketers under cover of darkness or through secluded areas around the plants' perimeters. One told of wading through a swamp with seven colleagues to attempt entry into the Warren plant, only to be captured by armed SWOC men who partly stripped him and covered him in grease before releasing him with a warning.[108] In fact this practice of abducting scabs, and partly stripping, greasing, and affixing union insignia to them, was not uncommon in northeast Ohio.[109]

Some of the cases involving attacks on loyal employees were brought to light by the Senate and House Committees on Post Offices and Post Roads. The committees became involved in the strike to answer complaints by Republic that unionists were preventing the company and its loyal employees from receiving shipments of food and other supplies mailed to the struck mills. The hearings and floor debates on the issue provided the CIO's opponents in Congress, as well as Girdler himself, who eagerly testified, with a forum in which to publicize union-sponsored violence in the strike.[110]

As these proceedings showed, union people certainly did interfere with the mail. It emerged that anyone approaching the plants at Warren and Niles was required to secure a pass, signed by Gus Hall. Moreover, the U.S. Post Office inspector documented cases where picketers were allowed to examine the contents of mail trucks trying to enter these mills, where local post office officials met privately with local SWOC leaders (including Hall) about delivery policies, and where threatening groups of strikers turned back mail trucks at the gates.[111] One of the couriers in Warren was told by picketers at the plant gate that "they would beat my damned head off if I went in any further."[112] The postmaster in Niles was turned away from a delivery when he encountered a roadblock and four hundred picketers. Although most common around Warren and Niles, similar confrontations occurred elsewhere, including at the gates of the Republic's Dilworth-Porter fabricating plant in Pittsburgh, the smallest facility directly involved in the strike.[113]

Despite these findings, the investigations concluded in July without calling the postmaster general to testify or making official findings of agency misconduct. A majority of committee members were apparently satisfied with the Post Office's contention that its decisions were driven by a neutral assessment of risks to couriers and a reasonable interpretation of federal law giving postmasters discretion to decline to make unsafe or "abnormal" deliveries; or perhaps they were satisfied to know that the Justice Department was already actively investigating reports of criminal interference with the mail by strikers.[114] In fact, it is easy to see why even congressmen with little sympathy for the strikers would have demurred on Republic's complaints, given the company's view that the Post Office essentially be *required* to move truckloads of bread, towels, and the like into the plants and draw its employees into potentially riotous situations in the process. Less easily dismissed, though, were accusations regarding unionists' interference with smaller mailings posted by individuals. Republic presented the La Follette Committee with some fifty cases in which packages containing food, clothing, and toiletries addressed to employees in the mills, sent by their relatives, were rejected by postal employees, some having been opened and inspected.[115] Although unremedied by Congress, the more serious cases of impeding the deliveries did not go unpunished. Several SWOC people were eventually convicted of interfering with the mail. Republic also sued the postmaster general to compel delivery into its plants, but the suit was rendered moot by the end of the strike.[116]

Another tactic common in the Youngstown, Warren, and Niles areas, and sometimes linked to Hall's leadership, involved visits to the homes of the men who were still in the mills or were threatening to go back. These visits involved everything from reasonable attempts to persuade the men to honor the strike to threats of bodily injury and acts of vandalism. As one striker claimed many years later, "Gus Hall and guys like us would break up scab houses and wreck them, just tear them up. We'd look for the company stooges."[117] That union people engaged in this kind of intimate strongarming is corroborated—somewhat—by reports that Republic provided the La Follette Committee, documenting more than 150 reports of violence and coercion throughout the strike zone. Of these, 56 involved verbal threats issued at the homes of nonstriking employees, usually to wives or other family members. The majority of these threats were vague, even incoherent;

a few were presented as death threats; and 16 entailed threats to burn or bomb the employee's home. Only a handful of visits were said to have resulted in physical violence between union people and scabs.[118] While the seriousness of some cases should not be diminished, others were almost certainly contrived or exaggerated, or they rested on the mere fact that someone with the union had visited the employee or his family at home. For example, on June 1, the wife of a Republic employee in Chicago "became hysterical" after being "threatened" by a visitor to her home. Although the nature of the threat was not specified, the race of the visitor—a "negro"—was, suggesting a different and less sympathetic cause for alarm.[119]

As for damage to homes and property, Republic's records describe at least twenty cases of rocks or other objects being thrown through windows and a comparable number of cases of damage to cars. Certainly there were many instances beyond these. But serious property damage was relatively uncommon. Republic's submissions show only a couple of occasions where houses were trashed and none that involved actual dynamiting. In this regard, the evidence provided by Republic seems largely consistent with arrest records from the areas affected by the strike as well as other narratives from both sides about the course of the conflict.[120] While quite a few newspaper accounts document attacks on workers' property, common rumors aside, relatively few of these involved explosives; and none revealed a specific intent to seriously hurt people.[121]

No doubt there were also numerous small skirmishes between strikers and strike supporters and loyal employees, company guards, and police, run-of-the-mill scuffles and fights usually not important enough to find their way into the historical record.[122] The majority of entries of this kind in Republic's records involve claims of violence or threats of violence connected with attempts by unionists to prevent workers from entering the mills or, in some cases, to get them to sign union cards. Occasionally, scabs were severely beaten or, as we have seen, even briefly abducted, sometimes taken to local union headquarters, and interrogated about their intentions or conditions within the plants—sometimes by Gus Hall himself.[123]

Although the vast majority of purely oral threats and other warnings to honor the picket lines were never documented, suspected company loyalists did sometimes receive notes warning them not to betray their fellow workers. Records from Youngstown include a handwritten warning to one Audy Palko, written in crayon on the back of a union handbill: "Someone said you wanted to scab—better not take the chance—A Friend." Another worker was similarly cautioned: "You are supposed to be a union man[.] We hate traitors—you better stay out till we win Tony—Don't be a scab—A Friend."[124] In other instances, unionists sent the men in the mills bogus telegrams announcing family emergencies or imminent marital discord requiring the worker's presence back home. Undoubtedly, some workers were brought out by worries, well founded or not, of trouble back home or concerns that harm might come to the striker or his family. However, not all familial interventions were coerced by the union. Armed with their own views about the conflict, some workers' wives needed no prodding to challenge their husbands on the question of union membership and strike support. On May 31, *New York Times* reporter Louis Stark discovered that a crowd of women had gathered at the main gate of Republic's Warren mill to send notes into the mill "demanding that their husbands leave." Several men emerged, one to an "irate wife" who "slapped her husband's face" and made him sign a union card on the spot.[125]

On June 24, state troops on strike duty in Warren claimed to have narrowly escaped injury when a bomb was thrown at them from a passing automobile.[126] The incident led to the arrest of a union man named A. C. Scott. By the end of June, authorities had also charged Gus Hall and five other men, along with Scott, with conspiring to sabotage steel and railroad company property and to damage private homes, with explosives stolen from mining operations in Pennsylvania.[127] Hall surrendered to authorities in Warren at noon on July 1 in the company of CIO counsel Lee Pressman. In his mug shot, Hall seemed defiant, unworried, and perhaps even bemused.[128]

The men charged with Hall had been picked up earlier and interrogated between June 27 and 30 at the police station by a group that included officers in the Ohio National Guard. One arrestee, a black truck driver and local wrestling standout named Sidney Watkins, claimed to have been recruited by strike leaders who wanted "colored people" on the picket lines but denied even knowing Hall.[129] Another arrestee, George Bund, a Republic employee who had signed up with the SWOC after the strike began, was also evasive about Hall's role in the alleged plot.[130] More useful to authorities was a statement given by John Borawiec (sometimes Orawiec), another Republic employee. Although Borawiec recalled getting gas money from Hall to pick up some explosives, he insisted that Hall mostly dealt with A. C. Scott.[131] For his part, Scott, who was making $90 a month with the CIO after being fired by Republic in March for organizing, claimed that Hall wanted him to set up a crew to blow up houses and that he had another crew sabotaging the railroads.[132] The *Daily Worker* charged, not implausibly, that the confessions had been beaten out of the men. But even if true, this does not mean they were innocent.[133]

Hall initially denied involvement in these schemes and always remained evasive (if slyly suggestive) about his activities. In a 1972 pamphlet, he called the Warren charges a "frame-up."[134] Later, in 1997, he recalled the conflict surrounding the aerial resupply effort: "There was a landing strip in the Republic property and they used planes to bring in scabs and food. Some of the strikers were hunters and had guns. I don't know anything about it, . . . but I'm told that they were pretty good at hitting moving targets—and a plane is bigger than a bird."[135] Youngstown organizer Thomas White struck a similar tone when asked in 1974 how the strikers blocked railroad access and stopped water and power going into Republic's mills. His response: "I don't think I should elaborate too much on that. The idea was to do what had to be done."[136]

The SWOC's top leadership generally opposed militant tactics, at least when it became evident that they would not much benefit from them. The strikers' sieges at Warren and Niles were at least partially lifted by Philip Murray and other higher-ups. Secretary-treasurer David McDonald recalled arriving in Youngstown to discover "several hundred pickets milling about" near a railroad bridge leading into Sheet & Tube's plant who vowed to stop any scabs entering the plant, even as the picketers were periodically scattered by "tear gas assaults" from company police. From his hotel room, McDonald "could see hundreds of armed [company] men, apparently equipped with tear gas, rifles and even a few machine guns, stationed on the roofs of downtown buildings." He blamed the situation on a "fire-eater named Shorty Steuben [who] had convinced the strikers that the whole city stood against them and only by a massive show of force—backed with arms, if necessary— could the workingmen prevail." McDonald claimed that he promptly moved to sideline Steuben and nixed Steuben's plan to organize a massive march though the city to deter the reopening of the plants. The risk of bloodshed, McDonald said, was too great.[137]

McDonald's charges fit with a broader effort by SWOC leaders to blame strike violence on Communists like Hall and Steuben. But this has to be taken with a grain of salt. Not all Communists were as militant as Hall and Steuben, and there is no evidence that any of them was given to wanton violence for its own sake. Quite the contrary: the violence such men were accused of was choreographed to achieve particular purposes, including those that conventional tactics seemed incapable of accomplishing. Nor were all militants Communists. The UMW had forged its own reputation for militancy in the coalfields, and its organizers were hardly unfamiliar with or deeply opposed to violent tactics. Many SWOC organizers and officials, including Philip Murray himself, had given loyal service to the UMW during in the 1920s and early 1930s, in which violence was directed against scabs and company forces as well as leftist union dissidents. If not entirely strategic, the leadership's opposition to violence in the Little Steel Strike had to be rooted in principles of nonviolence of very recent vintage. It is also wrong to think that violence had to be instigated (or could be fully controlled) by Communist Party or UMW organizers in the first place. Many rank-and-file strikers were incensed by the companies' vicious attacks on unionists and understood well that losing the strike portended months and even years of privation. Such men often needed little prodding or ideological justification to escalate the terms of conflict.

Grim though it was, the struggle was punctuated by a few absurd episodes. When Mayor Burton of Cleveland, who actually sided with the strikers in denying Republic the use of Cleveland's Great Lakes Airport, pulled up at the airport, picketers mistook him for a company official and nearly overturned his car.[138] In early June, a brawl broke out at a Youngstown clothing store when union shoppers realized that newly hired special deputies had come to the store to obtain their police uniforms.[139] Little over a week later, the local newspaper in Canton reported that unionists had "seized" a loyal employee who was also a Stark County special deputy and had "divested him of his badge and credentials" before releasing him—and unceremoniously dumping the items at the county jail.[140] Another ridiculous episode involved one Roy Conner, alleged by Republic to be "definitely associated with Communistic activities," who in June repeatedly called at the Warren home of a Republic engineer, posing as a pilot looking to get work in Republic's airlift. Conner's intrepid gambit was not successful; and his exact intention remains unclear.[141]

Not all union tactics involved violence, or even picketing. Strikers also attempted to strengthen their position by fomenting sympathy strikes, including localized general strikes.[142] During the first few days of the strike, the participation of thousands of UAW and other CIO unionists on the picket line helped bring workers out of Republic's mill in Buffalo.[143] In Warren and Niles, Gus Hall defied a court injunction and overcame the hostility of AFL unions to organize a general strike that briefly shut at least

FIGURE 18. Sympathy strikers march past the main gate of Republic Steel's Warren, Ohio, plant under the watch of National Guardsmen, June 23, 1937. Courtesy of the Youngstown Historical Center of Industry and Labor.

eleven manufacturing plants as well as several other businesses in the area, all to protest the intervention of the National Guard against the strikers. Concerned that the sympathy strikes might damage a reputation the CIO was trying build for responsible adherence to contracts, CIO leaders ended them.[144]

Organizers also managed brief sympathy strikes in Youngstown, including a stoppage by over one thousand area truck drivers to protest the Stop 5 killings, which, according to state officials, "blocked all roads into Youngstown."[145] A few days later, workers staged a solidarity parade that prompted area employers to discharge three hundred participants.[146] Similar efforts, already mentioned, involved appeals to railroad workers to refuse to work trains entering Republic's plants and protests of the presence of Pennsylvania Railroad police within the struck plants and to forgo the carriage of strike-related goods on the trains themselves. The SWOC also solicited the CIO's National Maritime Union to tie up ore shipments on the Great Lakes and CIO miners to shut down iron ore mines in the Upper Great Lakes region.[147] The strategy was sound and prevented some shipments into the mills. A few iron mines were struck, and some striking miners ended up staying out longer than most of the striking steel workers.[148] However, these efforts were hampered by the fact that the CIO had yet to effectively organize the miners and seamen.

FIGURE 19. UMW miners, on strike in sympathy with the SWOC, picket the entrance of a Republic Steel coal mine in Connellsville, Pennsylvania, July 15, 1937. © 1937, Associated Press/Bill Allen.

The most promising call to solidarity involved the steel companies' captive coal mines, a number of which were organized by the UMW. On June 13, John L. Lewis ordered somewhere in the neighborhood of ten thousand UMW miners at seventeen captive mines in West Virginia and western Pennsylvania to strike.[149] The CIO had earlier threatened a broader strike against the steel companies' captive mines, after the companies attempted to frustrate the collection of dues used to finance the steel drive; but it pulled back when U.S. Steel began negotiating with the union.[150] The CIO also threatened to strike independent coal providers and other companies if they aided the steel companies.[151] Apparently unwilling to antagonize firms under contract with the UMW or alienate New Deal officials, Lewis backed away from a threat to call out six hundred thousand bituminous coal miners in an industry-wide strike. Nevertheless, over several days in late June and July, thousands of miners, some of them marching arm in arm, joined steel workers' picket lines and rallies in Johnstown.[152]

9

A Change of Heart

CORPORATE POWER AND NEW DEAL STRIKEBREAKING

The prospect of a union victory faded as June unfolded. Increasingly, the very acts of militancy that were so crucial to sustaining the picket lines and keeping the plants closed hurt the unionists' cause in other ways. For the companies were repeatedly able to leverage the disorder and violence associated with these tactics into a wave of government interventions that effectively doomed the walkout. How they managed this in the face of their own overwhelming culpability is a study in the prerogatives of corporate power and the limits of New Deal liberalism. This dynamic was evident throughout the strike zone and at every level of government. But its basic logic was nowhere more apparent than in Johnstown.

JOHNSTOWN AND THE CONSTRUCTION
OF "COMMUNITY" OPPOSITION

Its massive structures strung for miles along the Conemaugh River, Bethlehem's Cambria Works loomed in every way over Johnstown. In 1937, Johnstown was a small city with fewer than 70,000 residents and maybe 125,000 in the entire metropolitan area. The town was devastated by the "Great Flood" of 1889, when over two thousand people died after the collapse of a faulty dam at an upriver retreat founded by none other than Andrew Carnegie and Henry Frick, among others. Even then, the Cambria Iron Works, established back in 1852, dominated the city's landscape. Under the company's overpowering influence, the city evolved into a bastion of antiunionism—"an industrial jail of a city," according to William Z. Foster.[1] The mill became part of Bethlehem in 1922, and by 1937 its thirteen thousand employees exceeded by a factor of ten the number at the city's next largest employer, a U.S. Steel plant.[2]

During the union drive, SWOC organizers in Johnstown were not victims of much violence. But they were harassed by Pinkertons in Bethlehem's employ, and they were targets of an antiunion advertising campaign promoted by the city's business community and political leaders. Organizers also had to contend with an ERP, which was relatively well subscribed and fairly functional but targeted for SWOC infiltration and usurpation. It is not clear how much success organizers had achieved at the plant prior to the strike. As we have seen, by the time the strike loomed only a fraction of the eight thousand workers they claimed to have signed up were paying dues. Nevertheless, although the national leadership chose not to call a strike at Johnstown, local SWOC leaders judged their work sufficiently effective that in mid-May 1937, they authorized a walkout at the mill whenever the national leadership might deem it appropriate to do so.[3]

If the SWOC was not certain of the strength of its position, neither was Bethlehem. By May, a company-wide strike seemed increasingly unlikely, but a strike at the Cambria Works was very plausible, and the company began to prepare. Intending to run the mill during a strike, the company brought in food and bedding. It increased the size of its force of company police in Johnstown and augmented its supplies of gas munitions. It also began to confer in earnest with local officials and business leaders on how to meet to the strike.[4]

When the May 26 strike call omitted Bethlehem's mills, it was left to the local SWOC leaders in Johnstown to decide the next move. The earlier strike vote notwithstanding, for two weeks they seemed content to do nothing, even as rank and filers fretted about organizing efforts and the need for solidarity. But then Bethlehem's conflict with workers at its captive Conemaugh & Black Lick Railroad intervened. The company had unilaterally imposed schedules on these workers and refused to recognize and bargain with the brotherhoods representing them or to sign written contracts, even after federal railway labor administrators ruled in the workers' favor. In frustration, the railroad men walked out on May 10.[5] Faced with a tide of sympathy among steel workers, the local SWOC leadership called a meeting the next day and conducted a vote, which authorized a strike to begin almost immediately.[6] Production workers began walking out at around the 11:00 P.M. shift change, many bearing tools and clothing as they streamed past curious sightseers at the gates. By morning, picketers were patrolling along the plant's extensive perimeter. Hundreds of workers, arriving for the start of the 7:00 A.M. shift, either joined the picket lines or turned for home. Although some workers continued to enter the plant and the mill continued with some processes, production was largely shut down.[7]

Bethlehem's response to the strike was much aided by the mayor of Johnstown, a megalomaniacal bootlegger named Daniel Shields who loathed the CIO. During the drive, Shields presided over a hearing concerning an organizer arrested for distributing the SWOC's newspaper, *Steel Labor*. Shields instructed the man that distributing literature was prohibited in Johnstown and apparently did so with sufficient force that local unionists largely abandoned this tactic in favor of more covert methods of recruitment.[8] Later, the mayor, again acting as jurist, sentenced a picketer to ninety days in jail and a $100 fine for "picking up a rag" with intent to throw it at a policeman.[9]

Shields told union people that he planned to prevent Bethlehem from importing strikebreakers, provoking the strikers, or even running the mill during the strike, as long as the picketers remained peaceful. He lied. On June 13, Shields ordered the arrest of a young man not directly connected to the SWOC because he had yelled the word *scab*. Over the next several days, the strikers perceived that officials and police, both local and company, were taking an increasingly menacing approach. More ominously, picketers confronted threatening gangs of vigilantes, many of them deputized American Legionnaires.[10] In fact, Shields had equipped these men with "nightsticks, helmets, and shields and ordered [them] to patrol residential districts in taxicabs and private cars."[11]

These forces were organized around a "Citizens' Committee," founded on June 14 by town officials and civic leaders with the support of Bethlehem. Although ostensibly neutral, the group clothed itself in the rhetoric of law and order, the right to work, and "Americanism" and did little to hide its real agenda. On June 15, the committee convened a meeting with SWOC field director David Watkins at which members warned that any strike violence would be charged against the CIO and the SWOC and that the committee was already helping recruit deputies to respond to this eventuality. It was at this point that Shields deputized dozens of men to serve with the city police and began working with Bethlehem on obtaining munitions. How many men were recruited and how much weaponry was acquired is unclear, not least because Shields courted contempt of Congress by failing to produce records subpoenaed by the La Follette Committee. Shields claimed that the

deputized vigilantes numbered 600 or 700 men. However, 200 to 300, the number offered by police officials, is a more likely estimate. Bethlehem provided this force with at least $5,000 worth of gas.[12]

There was a fair amount of unrest on June 13 and again the night of June 14, when a fight between picketers and loyal employees at one of the gates resulted in local police using gas and gunfire against unionists. At least ten people were hurt and seven arrested before the state police restored calm. There were other episodes of unrest around this time, too, including a handful of assaults and outbreaks of stone throwing and damage to property. However, serious episodes of violence remained relatively uncommon, given the size of the walkout and the tension in the town. And the situation seemed within the ability of the regular police to control, had local officials been committed to doing so.[13]

Instead, the mayor, the Citizens' Committee, and agents of the company proceeded with their buildup of armed forces and other inflammatory actions. On June 14, Shields issued a proclamation purporting to guarantee the rights of strikers, while condemning "men not residents of our community" who were behind "certain disturbances."[14] On June 16, the *Johnstown Democrat* published the opinion of a local attorney, whom Shield had commissioned to define the boundaries of the right to picket, which concluded that picketing was lawful only if the underlying strike was lawful and the picketing itself completely uncoercive and limited to "reasonable" numbers.[15] That same day, Shields took to the local radio to fulminate about "bullies, hoodlums, yes, cowards" who, he said, were already in Johnstown threatening "defenseless women and children," beating up workers, and otherwise imposing on the rights of "red-blooded Americans." Of course, Shields meant unionists—"Greeks bearing gifts."[16] On June 16, too, the Citizens' Committee ran an advertisement in the *Democrat* touting the "Constitutional Right of every man to work" and indicting strikers for acts of intimidation and disorder and for threatening the "home life" of workers.[17] The next few days brought more of this, including an advertisement on June 17 in which the mayor offered $5,000 for information leading to the arrest and prosecution of six CIO men who had supposedly kidnapped a loyal employee, "stripped him and turned him out, naked," on the street.[18]

Much of this offensive against the SWOC was directly sponsored by Bethlehem, which had established a secret account, ostensibly for the purpose of "maintaining law and order," through the offices of the Citizens' Committee and the mayor. From mid-June through late July, more than $25,000—probably much more—was drawn from the account and placed at the disposal of the committee and the mayor. Some of this money went toward anti-SWOC publicity and paid for gas weapons for the city police. But more than $23,000 went straight into the personal accounts of Shields and his wife, which when revealed prompted a half-hearted grand-jury investigation.[19]

The near-continuous ranting about union violence made good use of news that the UMW was organizing sympathy strikes at captive mines and planning a massive march by forty thousand miners on Johnstown, to be held June 20. While the sympathy strikes were real enough, the march was miscast as an "invasion" that promised to sow mayhem and disorder. What the CIO actually intended was a peaceful rally, half as large, which had been conceived before the strike began in Johnstown. Moreover, its true purpose was to bolster the morale of SWOC supporters. Nevertheless, company operatives and Johnstown officials used the invasion threat, as well as other, specious claims of imminent violence and exaggerated depictions of actual disorder, to back a petition to Governor George H. Earle III to impose martial law, with the hope that this would end picketing and allow the plant to reopen.[20]

Initially, Earle took no action on the request—not least because the situation remained relatively peaceful. Although there was a stabbing at one of the plant's gates on the night of June 16, the *Johnstown Democrat* reported that this "lone disturbance" had been "quelled almost as quickly as it started" and that loyal employees engaged in maintenance work and keeping a few departments running were entering unmolested.[21] On June 18, the *Democrat* reported that police had the situation in hand and that "peace reigned along the miles of Bethlehem mills."[22] But that very day the mayor and his forces escalated their anti-CIO rhetoric and announced their plan to conduct a "back to work" march that would breach the picket lines.[23]

Finally convinced that mass violence loomed, the next day, June 19, the governor declared martial law in Cambria County and dispatched several hundred state police to the area, many on horses and motorcycles, with National Guard units held ready to back them up.[24] Earle's order required that the union dismantle the pickets and requested that the planned rally be canceled, but it also ordered the Cambria mill to keep most of its departments closed.[25] CIO unionists, including many in UMW locals in Pennsylvania, perceived this as a victory and deluged the governor with appreciative letters and telegrams.[26] For the moment, it seemed, Shields and other procompany forces had miscalculated. Just before the order was issued, they joined with Eugene Grace and other company officials in questioning the need for it. To no avail—at 12:30 A.M., June 20, state police "padlocked" the plant.[27]

COMPANY-SPONSORED VIGILANTISM

With events suddenly turned against them, Bethlehem and its allies refocused their efforts on organizing a back-to-work movement. The "Steel Workers Committee," around which this campaign was structured, initially enjoyed little support from the workers themselves. It was funded and organized almost entirely by the Citizens' Committee and thus, in turn, by Bethlehem.[28] Together with the Citizens' Committee, the back-to-work movement quickly accomplished several functions for Bethlehem. These community groups, as they were sometimes generically described, operated as instruments of intimidation and coercion. But they were also used in more subtle ways to legitimate other means of strikebreaking, to lobby and organize more aggressive government intervention, and to purvey propaganda.

Republic and Sheet & Tube sponsored their own community groups. In Canton, Republic attempted to stage a back-to-work meeting on the morning of the first full day of the strike. The company abandoned the venture, which was supposed to feature some sort of poll on whether to continue the strike, only when pressured by the mayor, who feared that it would incite trouble.[29] A few days later, the local chamber of commerce bowed to its "civic duty" and the urgings of a "committee of workers" and commenced its own poll. The organization mailed out ballots to determine whether Republic's workers in Canton desired to return to the plants. The ballots touted the chamber's supposed neutrality but went on about how "it cannot shrink from its duty to preserve the good name of the city of Canton and to use its influence on the side of law and order in the community and the protection of life and property." How this "neutral" body got hold of all the workers' home addresses can be imagined.[30] A week later, the ballot count revealed that a large majority wanted to go back to work. For the chamber, this mandated an end to the strike, even though unionists boycotted the poll and more than twenty-five hundred ballots were declared uncountable by local clergymen who conducted the vote.[31]

With the assistance of the NAM, Republic also organized a Law and Order League in Canton. Working with Republic officials, its public relations firm, Hill & Knowlton, a local Citizens' Committee, and the chamber, the back-to-work movement and the Law and Order League demanded that picketers be disarmed, company men be hired on as deputies, and public officials give "protection" to loyal employees. The back-to-work movement even mounted armed patrols, becoming so threatening that its actions began to worry leaders of the Law and Order League. On June 18, the back-to-work movement set out to smash the picket lines, but the plan unraveled when the few men who showed up were preemptively assaulted by union men.[32]

Groups like these were active elsewhere, including Youngstown, where a company-sponsored back-to-work movement, backed by the Mahoning Valley Citizens' Committee, played an important role in stoking the tensions that led to the Stop 5 Riot.[33] In Cumberland, Maryland, home to Republic's N&G Taylor mill, a back-to-work march organized in part by a company union had to be postponed when several hundred CIO men preemptively seized the meeting site.[34] In Warren and Niles, Republic sponsored a back-to-work movement, a Citizens' Committee, as well as a "John

Q. Public League," which performed the familiar functions of pressuring the strikers while demanding that police and National Guard dismantle the pickets and oversee the full reopening of the mills.[35] For a time, before such schemes were overtaken by other developments, these groups conspired to have as many as five hundred men deputized as special police and to set up patrols of men armed with firearms.[36] In Massillon, Republic helped organize an entity variously known as the Citizens' Committee, the Labor Relations Committee, and the Law and Order League, which worked with a back-to-work group and a revitalized company union to oppose the strike. These groups, which Republic pressed workers to join, propagated fears of a violent CIO invasion, broadcast the company's threat to permanently close the mills, and pushed city officials to deputize company men. As we shall see, these efforts led to considerable bloodshed.[37]

Almost all these community groups represented themselves as independent actors with no particular position on the underlying dispute and few ties to the steel companies. But as the La Follette Committee concluded, the organizations were actually creatures of the steel companies, without much public support and poorly subscribed by the men they claimed to represent.[38] Instead, these groups were disproportionately composed of and led by owners and managers of local businesses, representatives of commercial groups, professionals, and government officials.[39] Often, their leaders were directly bound to the companies by overlapping economic interests, which were inevitable in small- and medium-size mill towns like Monroe, Johnstown, or Massillon—a small city of only twenty-six thousand, where Republic employed the vast majority of wage earners and claimed to pay a $40,000 daily payroll.[40] Just as often, the people who predominated in the community groups embraced a common class identity with the companies and their mangers, reinforced by membership in commercial organizations, churches, social clubs, and the like.

PAID PROPAGANDA AND BIASED MEDIA COVERAGE

During the strike, the companies continued to assail workers and the public alike with propaganda invoking the right to work; the SWOC's supposed domination by radicals, immigrants, and blacks; its alleged penchant for violence; its alleged desire to exploit the steel workers economically; the threat that a long strike or the advent of CIO unions might pose to the viability of particular plants; and a congenial vision of American life and industrial capitalism, which married antiunion views to attractive tropes about traditional patterns of authority and entitlement in the home, the community, and the workplace. As we have seen, much of this program was developed for the companies by the NAM. But key aspects were also devised by professional public-relations firms, in particular Hill & Knowlton, which was on retainer to Republic and Sheet & Tube; and John Price Jones (and its advertising component, Thornley & Jones) and Ketchum, MacLeod & Grove, which were employed by Bethlehem.[41]

Although national in scope, this campaign was also focused locally.[42] Such was evident in Johnstown, as we have just seen. In northeast Ohio, too, both Republic and Sheet & Tube ran full-page newspaper advertisements promising substantial rewards to anyone whose information might lead to prosecution of strikers for acts of violence.[43] Sheet & Tube said that reopening its mills was contingent on whether the workers desired to return to work. As soon as the company could point to the back-to-work movement as evidence of such sentiments, it ran advertisements in which Frank Purnell himself declared union violence the only impediment to a resumption of operations.[44] Another advertisement by Sheet & Tube interwove a critique of SWOC demands with a broader assault, roughly shaped around federalist principles, on the premises of New Deal liberalism.[45] Similarly, the Mahoning Valley Citizens' Committee ran a lengthy piece in the leading Youngstown paper that paired a reminder about the area's economic dependence on the steel industry with a call to settle the strike on the basis of "American principles"—which meant enforcing the law against "rich and poor alike, even though to do so may be politically inexpedient."[46]

Another medium for company propaganda involved the use of letters, written by company officials and ostensibly addressed to loyal employees but intended for wider publication. On June 15, Tom Girdler mailed a rambling, slightly incoherent epistle to all Republic employees in which he railed against CIO duplicity and radicalism, accused the picketers of violence and lawlessness, and touted the local Law and Order Leagues and back-to-work movements. A representative passage asked, "Must Republic and its men submit to the communistic dictates and terrorism of the C.I.O.?" And: "Is America to remain a free country[—]the answer is NO."[47]

By their very existence, the back-to-work movements and citizens' groups suggested that only through violence could unionists prevent the lawful reopening of the mills. This assertion conveniently took as given, and thereby preempted any real investigation of, the underlying premise that so many workers were clamoring to return in the first place. The awkward position that this stratagem put the union in was illustrated later in the strike, when the SWOC itself was reduced to arguing that the plants should *not* reopen because this would certainly result in widespread fighting and bloodshed.[48]

The steel companies' arguments also resonated with an ideological orientation, particularly well rooted among elites, that faulted workers for strike-related violence and was disposed to sacrifice labor rights to the greater good of industrial peace. Even if not loaded in this way, the tendency of elites to abhor disorder and street-level violence conveniently aligned them against the SWOC, since by a very simple calculation, the union and its organizing drive were the proximate cause of all the trouble that summer. Of course, the reality was vastly more complicated. But this was exactly the problem. While the companies could make effective use of simple, though misleading, narratives about the strike, the union had to offer more complicated and less resonant justifications, steeped in testaments about relative fault and claims about workers' allegiances that the SWOC could not easily prove. Nor could the SWOC match the volume of information the companies and their allies distributed. The union was able to take out a few advertisements of its own, but these were never as numerous as the companies'.[49]

A few major outlets, including the *New York Times,* the *Washington Post,* and *Time* magazine, were at times fairly objective in their coverage of the strike. But, ironically, journalistic objectivity could make the union's cause seem more problematic and its position less defensible, as it could yet conceal the complicated considerations involved, including the layers of company provocation that figured in strike clashes. A front-page story in the June 20 *New York Times,* under the headline "C.I.O. Violence Told," is exemplary; it details a loyal employee's testimony to the Senate Committee on Post Offices and Post Roads about being assaulted when trying to enter Republic's mill at Warren so that he could "protect his home."[50] The story was probably true enough, except it said nothing about about how the strikers might well have seen their struggle in equally desperate terms, or about the contempt for the labor law on the part of Republic that had caused the strike. Nor did objectivity of tone always equate to basic accuracy in reporting. The *Times'* front-page coverage of rioting in Johnstown on June 14 and 15 exaggerated the level of disorder and incorrectly implied that the fighting was fostered by the influx of thousands of UMW reinforcements to the "battle-front."[51] Even more damaging to the SWOC, although superficially no less objective, was a nationwide torrent of stories in late June and early July describing the arrests of Gus Hall, Robert Burke, and other union organizers for strike-related misconduct. The problem for the union was not simply that such events were reported, as the arrests were newsworthy, but rather that no comparable stories were run about murderous steel company agents, even though they should have been.

By mid-June, media coverage had begun to turn more strongly against the strikers, even at the more liberal outlets.[52] By June 22, the *Washington Post,* which had earlier condemned the Memorial Day killings, was attacking the CIO for sponsoring violence, irresponsibility, and "dictatorship."[53] Other commentaries were more subtle, but no less critical. On June 6, the *New York Times* featured a prescient piece by legal scholar Dean Dinwoodey on the ambiguities of the right to picket under the Wagner Act, the First Amendment, and other relevant laws. Among the uncertainties Dinwoodey identified was the difficulty in distinguishing "peaceful" picketing, which the law protected, from violent or otherwise unlawful picketing. Without resolving that matter, the professor wryly observed that the picketing in the steel strike had generated more violence than the "illegal" automobile sit-down strikes.[54] Still more prescient was a June 19 piece in the *Times* that castigated the SWOC for striking in the first place, instead of making its case entirely before the NLRB and the courts.[55] On June 22, the *Times* published a digest of editorials from nearly twenty papers from across the country that overwhelmingly condemned Governor Earle's order closing the Cambria mill as foreign to American traditions, a "vicious precedent," "unjust," contrary to the right to work, a concession to "Gangsterism," partisan and politically motivated, and so on.[56]

There may have been more to the favorable coverage enjoyed by the companies than ideological alignments or poor editorial judgment. The La Follette Committee was concerned that the public-relations firms hired by the steel companies might have influenced newspapers like the *Times* to publish company-friendly pieces about the strike, some of them penned by the public-relations firms themselves. The assumption was far from unreasonable, as suggested by an exchange before the La Follette Committee between public-relations man John Price Jones and Senator Thomas, in which Thomas asked whether Jones guaranteed his clients that he would plant news stories favorable to them in the newspapers. When Jones ventured that, although favorable news coverage might appear coincidental with the companies' purchasing of advertisements, this "would be without any understanding with the newspaper." Thomas observed that this would make the arrangement "all the more subtle." And when Thomas pushed Jones to say whether the purchasing of advertisements made the paper more inclined to favor the companies in its news reportage, Jones demurred: "I cannot answer that question."[57]

The strikers did receive much favorable treatment in some publications, including the *Pittsburgh Courier;* left-liberal magazines like *Harper's* and the *Nation;* as well as the *Daily Worker, New Masses,* and other Communist and Socialist papers. There was also *Steel Labor* as well as other CIO organs. Even some local papers in the strike-affected areas, including the *Youngstown Vindicator,* struck a fairly neutral tone, at least early on. But these perspectives were exceptional and reached limited audiences. Of course the CIO's vast corps of organizers and supporters gave it extraordinary advantages when it came to communicating directly with workers, their families, and other members of the affected communities. But while these advantages were central to maintaining rank-and-file support and working-class solidarity, they counted for little when it came to defending the SWOC's agenda in middle-class and elite circles where what appeared first as indifference to the strikers' cause began to build into a tide of opposition.

NEW DEAL LIBERALISM AND THE IRONIES OF STATE INTERVENTION

By the end of the June, eroding support for the strike was reflected not only in the perceptions of newspaper editors and reporters but also in surveys conducted during the strike by the American Institute of Public Opinion, or Gallup.[58] Scientific polling was in its infancy and Gallup did not solicit views about the steel strike. But it did survey overall support for the CIO and unionism in general. A survey conducted between June 16 and June 21 found that 71 percent of respondents had become less supportive of unions over the preceding six months. Fifty-seven percent agreed with the proposition that "the militia should be called out *whenever* strike trouble *threatens.*" The sit-down strikes of the preceding winter and spring were unpopular with survey respondents and many respondents thought such strikes should be forcibly suppressed.[59] But publicity surrounding the ongoing, and much bloodier, steel strike surely influenced the public's views about this later strike—views that in turn affected political developments concerning the conflict.

The union had counted on the support of President Roosevelt and Secretary of Labor Perkins, who had aided the CIO by declining to oust the automobile sit-down strikers and by quietly helping to negotiate a settlement, despite pressure from powerful interests who regarded the strikes as outrageous crimes against property and authority.[60] And of course there was the massive support that the CIO had given Roosevelt and the New Deal in the recent elections. With such facts in mind, many picketers hit the bricks with signs identifying their cause with Roosevelt. On the second day of the strike, the *Chicago Daily News*'s Edwin Lahey observed that local picketers "compensated themselves for their cradle feet by a confident feeling that 'Mr. Big' in Washington, for the first time in their memories, is with them in an industrial fight."[61] This optimism was further piqued early in June when Roosevelt publicly questioned the steel companies' reasons for not signing a contract.[62]

Despite all this, it was unwise for unionists to presume the administration's support. Although a capable administrator, Perkins was moderate in her class politics. Roosevelt himself was opposed to labor militancy and radicalism, and his support for mainstream industrial unionism was contingent. Although happy to ally with the CIO, he was wary of being perceived as too closely associated with the federation, concerned that this might undermine his administration's standing with conservative constituents. Meanwhile, congressional conservatives in both parties had begun to push legislation to outlaw sit-down strikes, drawing a link between strike violence and what they regarded as an overly generous system of labor rights. Then there was the fact that neither the president nor the Perkins Labor Department (as distinct from the NLRB, an independent agency) had clear authority to intervene forcefully in the strike. Intervention by these offices could well be deemed illegal by the steel companies, local authorities, or New Deal opponents.[63]

Similar dynamics reigned at the state level. During the organizing drive, CIO officials and their allies courted the support of governors of the key strike states of Pennsylvania, Indiana, and Ohio, hoping they might pressure the steel companies to recognize the SWOC and sign collective bargaining agreements. All three governors—George Earle of Pennsylvania, M. Clifford Townsend of Indiana, and Martin Davey of Ohio—were New Deal Democrats. Earle especially had a progressive reputation. Elected in

1934 on a ticket that included the UMW's Thomas Kennedy, Earle had led
the enactment of Pennsylvania's own "Little New Deal" and continued to
support various prolabor bills during the Little Steel Strike.[64] Townsend,
too, had been elected with strong support from organized labor and seemed
neither hostile to the CIO's cause nor enamored of Little Steel's hard-line
stance. Although Martin Davey was a businessman—he was the son of
famous tree surgeon John Davey, whose company (now employee-owned)
today remains a giant in the arboricultural and horticultural fields—there
was reason to believe that he might also assist the union. By one account,
Davey had assured SWOC people in Ohio prior to the strike that "if they
[the companies] won't listen to me, I've got an ace in the hole. I'll close
their __ mills for them."[65] But as with Roosevelt, if any of these governors
aided the SWOC, it would be in the face of pressures from business interests
and their allies. Moreover, any move by the governors that favored the
SWOC or the CIO could well alienate AFL unions, which were also politically important, and locked in bitter conflict with the CIO. And like
Roosevelt, none of these governors had any deep affinity for the currents of
labor militancy and radicalism embedded in the SWOC's campaign. Finally,
it was also not clear what legal authority the governors actually had to intervene, particularly if they really intended to aid the union.

On the night of June 2, Davey met for the first time during the strike
with Tom Girdler, as well as with the vice president and the general manager
of Sheet & Tube.[66] At conferences with both union and company representatives on June 11 and 12, Davey proposed a seven-point plan in which the
companies would sign a collective bargaining agreement and the union
would accept members-only representation and forego both a closed shop
and company support in collecting dues (a "check-off" provision). The union
endorsed the proposal but the companies rejected it, agreeing only to maintain the status quo while discussions were ongoing.[67] A week later, Davey
proposed another compromise: Republic and Sheet & Tube would sign a
conditional agreement with the SWOC, pending resolution of the underlying legal issues by the NLRB and the courts. The companies rejected this as
well. In separate communiqués to Davey, Girdler and Purnell invoked the
right to work and challenged Davey to use his authority to reopen the mills,
offering specious excuses to explain why they had not conveyed these sentiments in person.[68]

Faced with this intransigence, on June 17 Davey wired Roosevelt an
"urgent" telegram asking that his administration take the lead in settling the

dispute. Later that day, Roosevelt and Perkins announced the creation of an ad hoc board to mediate the strike, consisting of three members of their choosing: Lloyd Garrison, dean of the University of Wisconsin Law School, former chair of the (first) National Labor Relations Board, and great-grandson of the famous abolitionist William Lloyd Garrison; Edward McGrady, assistant secretary of labor and former AFL official; and Charles Taft II, a Cincinnati lawyer, younger brother of "Mr. Republican" Robert Taft, and son of William Howard Taft. More liberal than his brother and father, Taft, the chair, had helped negotiate two major, violent strikes in 1934. The board drew its authority from the National Mediation Act of 1913, which empowered the secretary of labor to mediate labor disputes and appoint "commissioners of conciliation" to that end. The understanding was that the board would mediate the strike while preparing to offer binding arbitration, should the parties agree.[69]

Representatives of both sides greeted the formation of the board with pledges of cooperation and expressions of optimism. Charles Taft then formally requested that the parties maintain the status quo during negotiations.[70] However, no sooner did he do this than the companies began to agitate against the status quo and cast the board's proper function in terms of facilitating reopening of the mills. As a statement by Republic put it, "The first duty of the Federal board is to investigate this breakdown of law enforcement and to assist in the restoration of law and order." Maintaining the status quo, the company charged, would be "destructive of the rights of the thousands of workers idle for nearly four weeks who want to go back to work."[71] Similar statements followed from the various citizens' committees and back-to-work groups.[72]

On June 19, the same day Earle moved to close the Cambria Works in Johnstown, the mediation board convened in Cleveland's luxurious Hotel Hollenden. The companies were represented by Tom Girdler, Eugene Grace, Frank Purnell, and W. S. Sykes, assistant to Inland's president, as well as various company lawyers. Leading the union's delegation were Philip Murray, John L. Lewis, David McDonald, Van Bittner, and Lee Pressman.[73] From the beginning it was clear that the companies intended to deal with the board as a unified group, with Girdler at the head, and that Girdler had no intention of negotiating. Girdler dismissed Taft as "a man who likes to talk about what his father did" and McGrady as an "office boy" for Roosevelt and Perkins.[74] Citing Lewis's earlier description of him as an "assassin and a monomaniac," Girdler flatly refused to even occupy the same room as Lewis or Murray.[75] The *Nation*'s Paul Anderson cataloged Girdler's conduct during the proceedings: "spouting purple profanity," pounding on the table, and categorically rejecting every effort at compromise. Girdler's performance at a press conference, during which he made "insinuations which are not tolerated in ordinary locker-room conversation," convinced Anderson that the steel man needed "to go to a competent psychiatrist and have his mind washed out with soap and water."[76]

Crazy or not, Girdler's antics aligned with the steel companies' absolute refusal to budge on either signed contracts or CIO recognition. In a move that underscored their intransigence, the companies now refused even any oral agreement with the union and denied ever being amenable to this. Faced with this, the CIO delegation desperately receded from its earlier conditions in hopes of reaching some sort of agreement. They made clear that they were open to several compromises, including the members-only and check-off concessions floated earlier by Martin Davey.[77] On June 21, the board met with the companies' representatives, who again rejected the Carnegie-Illinois contract and repeated their objections to signing written contracts. Negotiations "broke down," leaving Charles Taft desperately trying to restart talks.[78]

That same day, both Republic and Sheet & Tube announced their intention to reopen their mills in the Youngstown area. In Youngstown itself, agents of Sheet & Tube urged participants in the back-to-work movement to arm themselves "with pistols and revolvers and whatever guns they could borrow or buy" and provided them with helmets so they could march through the picket lines.[79] In Warren, a "shotgun army" of four hundred vigilantes, backed by the chamber of commerce and John Q. Public League, prepared to march into Republic's mill, while loyal employees got ready to march out of the plant. Unionists organized the movement of sympathizers into the Youngstown area in order to counter the reopenings. Defying a local judge's injunction, crowds of strikers and supporters gathered at the plant gates, many of them with clubs and some wielding firearms.[80] The *New York Times*' Russell Porter described the scene in Youngstown the next morning: "Thousands of armed pickets stood outside the mill gates, hundreds of police, deputy sheriffs and company guards were at the gates and inside, and perhaps several thousand non-union workers waited near by [sic] to return to work if they could after nearly a month of strike-bound idleness."[81] In Canton, where on the night of June 18, strikers had broken up a back-to-work march, an air of impending battle also prevailed. The local police augmented their regular and special forces; and local SWOC leaders publicly appealed for restraint on the picket lines.[82] Even in the now-quieter Calumet, word of a back-to-work drive brought several thousand strikers streaming back to the picket lines at Inland and Sheet & Tube plants.[83]

CIO leaders telegrammed the president and begged him "in the name of God" to stop the back-to-work marches.[84] Late on the night of June 21, Roosevelt in turn telegrammed both Girdler and Purnell, urging them to delay the reopenings. Purnell responded only after Roosevelt's deadline for a reply had expired; Girdler ignored the president entirely.[85] Clearly the steel men did not care that a number of tragic confrontations were imminent. In fact, they likely welcomed the prospect as something that would aid the companies' efforts to completely break the strike.

Amid these dire developments, both the mediation board and local law-enforcement officials pleaded with Davey to mobilize the National Guard. Finally, late on the night of June 21, a little over a day after the Stop 5 Riot and two days after Earle imposed martial law in Cambria County, Davey declared martial law in Mahoning and Trumbull Counties. Or rather, because the Ohio State Constitution made no provision for martial law, he practically did so by mobilizing the first of several thousand Ohio National Guard troops and dispatching them to those counties—the "Youngstown Military District"—with orders to cooperate with local officials in imposing order, to "prevent riot, blood-shed, and possible loss of life" and to preserve the status quo while the mediation board completed its work. Accordingly, the Guard was ordered to prevent the reopening of the closed mills and to protect the ability of those still operating to continue unimpeded by unionists. Further, Guardsmen were to intercept and disarm "all persons who are not officers of the law" and prevent "invasion of these counties by non-residents, either in small groups or in mass formation."[86] This language was interpreted by the Guard and local law enforcement (whose own proclamations the Guard were expected to enforce, along with court injunctions issued around this time) to limit the number of picketers to no more than ten at each mill gate, to bar the presence of unauthorized persons within one thousand feet of the plants, and to require that any assemblies anywhere else in the affected area occur only with formal approval of the authorities.[87] In some places, picketers were banned from carrying signs and required to remain in constant motion. Even journalists had to register with the Guard or face arrest.[88] The heavily armed troops set up machine guns around the plants and left no doubt that they would use force to carry out their

FIGURE 21. A train, probably with the B&O Railroad, moves a full load of steel from Republic's Warren, Ohio, plant under heavy guard of company and railroad police, June 23, 1937. Courtesy of the Youngstown Historical Center of Industry and Labor.

mission.[89] Although not all unionists welcomed these developments, picketers in Youngstown greeted the Guard jubilantly, some shouting, "We've won the strike."[90]

In some respects, the Guard did judiciously enforce Davey's status quo proclamation against the steel companies. On June 22 and 23, Guardsmen prevented Republic and Sheet & Tube from moving railcars and loyal employees into closed mills. The Guard made the railroads agree to transport only shipments consistent with the order and to provide the Guard with documents confirming this. And the Guard oversaw evacuation of loyal employees long besieged in Republic's mills at Warren and Niles, with the understanding that they could return under protection of the Guard.[91] But the Guard also responded aggressively to reports that picketers were congregating in excessive numbers or were otherwise interfering with loyal employees or company operations. Guardsmen cooperated with local police in conducting warrantless searches of the homes of strikers and sympathizers, ostensibly looking for caches of explosives and other weapons.[92] And they worked with local police in setting up numerous roadblocks and checkpoints, searching for weapons and preparing to interdict union supporters heading into the strike areas.[93]

In Johnstown, Earle's order was enforced mainly by deployment of approximately five hundred state police. Although Earle's proclamation left it to the judgment of the officer in command to determine how best to preserve the peace, the understanding was that this meant, above all, maintaining the status quo.[94] The plant would have to stay closed and the union would have to pull its picketers off the streets. Even more than their brothers in Ohio, unionists in Johnstown viewed this as a victory and quickly acceded. As soon as martial law was declared on June 19, the union ceased picketing. The UMW demonstration planned for the following afternoon—the "invasion"—was canceled by John L. Lewis himself.[95]

Bethlehem's compliance was not so easily obtained. Working with Mayor Shields, the company contrived to delay preparations for the Cambria Works closure.[96] Earle threatened Shields with arrest to force his cooperation. And the colonel in charge served Bethlehem with a curt letter announcing that in view of its failure to abide by the governor's directive, the plant would be closed by state authorities at 12:30 A.M., June 20.[97] The state police oversaw evacuation of the plant, but only after yielding to threats of a lawsuit and granting the company permission to allow eight hundred to one thousand "maintenance" men to unload raw materials, ship out finished products, and keep the furnaces hot.[98] Like Davey's order, Earle's was issued with the understanding that it would remain effective as long as the dispute was before the mediation board.

In both states, the status quo orders immediately came under attack by the steel companies and their allies. In Ohio, company officials, back-to-work movements, and citizens' committees deluged the governor with letters and telegrams demanding that the mills be reopened, while Purnell himself charged Davey with denying the men the "right" to their jobs.[99] Other groups ran newspaper advertisements accusing Davey of violating the right to work, irresponsibility and partisanship, acting without lawful authority, and rewarding union violence.[100] The *Youngstown Vindicator,* which ten days earlier had called on the companies to sign with the union, demanded with a front-page editorial that the mills be allowed to reopen and the union be permitted to pursue its claims against the companies before the NLRB.[101] The mayor of Youngstown, who had earlier played his cards more carefully, also insisted that the mills be allowed to reopen.[102]

In Pennsylvania, Bethlehem and its allies assailed Earle's order as an imposition on the rights of the company and its loyal employees. In the name of the Johnstown Citizens' Committee and the Steel Workers Committee, this coalition placed advertisements in Pennsylvania and other states. These included a June 24 advertisement featured in the *New York Times, Chicago Daily Tribune, L.A. Times,* and several dozen other papers, which opened under the emphatic caption, "WE PROTEST!," and then proceeded to condemn Governor Earle's order as an affront to workers' "constitutional rights." The advertisements, which ran a full page in many papers, cost $65,000—at least $31,000 of which was paid directly by Bethlehem.[103] The *Chicago Daily Tribune,* whose news desk depicted government intervention as a bid to save a doomed strike and advance Earle's presidential ambitions, editorialized that Earle and Davey had perpetrated an "outlandish and anarchical perversion of law" that abetted "armed insurgents" in their attack on the rights of business and working people.[104]

Just before making his decision to close the Cambria mill, Governor Earle received a telegram from Eugene Grace in which Grace invoked the right to work and legal claims about the limits of gubernatorial power and demanded that the mill be allowed to remain open. Mayor Shields also telegrammed Earle, intemperately accusing the governor of "arrogantly" closing the mill to the detriment of local businesses and claiming that "ninety percent of our people are opposed to the CIO." Impugning Earle's motives, he vowed that "we will resist the imposition of communism regardless of the political aspirations of any man."[105] In the days that followed Earle's order, Shields continued to pressure the governor to reopen the plant. The Johnstown Citizen's Committee, which had solicited the support of forty thousand wealthy citizens and petitioned the state legislature to reverse the governor's order, claimed that since the reason for Earle's declaration of martial law was the now-canceled miners' march—and not the committee's own back-to-work stratagems—the martial-law regime should be ended.[106]

Meanwhile, the mediation board continued to seek some sort of agreement. On June 22, the board met again with the CIO delegation, who again underscored their willingness to compromise. The board arranged for the leaders of steel companies already under contract with the SWOC to explain, by phone, how this was "working out reasonably well." The next day, the board tried one last time to get the Little Steel delegation to meet with Murray. They refused. The board then made a final proposal that would have obligated the companies to sign a contract similar to the Carnegie-Illinois agreement and to recognize the SWOC, but only if the SWOC won an NLRB-sponsored "secret ballot election."[107] The contact would "be torn up if the union loses" and in the meantime all strikers would return to work.[108] The companies rejected this out of hand. Exuding disgust, the board's last statement concluded with the following verdict: "We believe that the refusal of the four companies to enter into any agreement with the S.W.O.C. regardless of the number of employees whom it actually represents, which could be demonstrated by a secret ballot election, is not the way to industrial peace."[109] The steel companies parried this with a joint statement that declared the CIO an irresponsible bargaining agent, repeated the claim that the Wagner Act did not require signed contracts, and again denied that they had ever accepted the basic terms of a contract.[110]

With the mediation effort at an end, both Davey and Earle lifted their status quo orders—Davey on June 24, Earle that same day, to take effect the following morning at 7:00 A.M. Davey's new order included this justification: "The right to work is sacred. The right to strike is equally valid. Those who want to return to their employment shall enjoy that privilege without being molested. Those who wish to remain on strike are entitled to do so."[111] Davey's order was a go-ahead to reopen the mills with the protection of state troops.[112] Earle's decision to allow the Cambria mill to reopen was not accompanied by such dramatic rhetoric. But it contemplated that Bethlehem would restart the mill and that state forces would remain to keep the peace.[113]

The companies and their allies exulted over the governors' new orders. The same groups that just hours earlier had been lambasting the governors for closing the mills dispatched a slew of obsequious telegrams to Davey, especially. The Mahoning Valley Citizens' Committee telegrammed Davey that they "wish[ed] to commend your courageous act in the Proclamation of June 24, 1937. Your stand is commensurate with the acts of a true statesman and patriot."[114] Even had they not banked on the status quo orders' providing a springboard for the reopening orders, the companies intended all along to exhaust the governors' willingness to keep the mills closed and then reopen them with the protection of state forces. This was plainly evident to the *Chicago Daily Tribune*'s Wayne Thomis, who on June 23 perceived that the steel executives intended to wait out the status quo orders and then "reopen their plants with the protection of civil authorities and thus yet break the strike."[115]

Although no radical, Earle could not have relished his decision to allow the Cambria mill to reopen, as he continued to publicly blame the steel companies for the strike. He even attended a rally in July, where he pledged to help the strikers while admonishing them not to be tempted to violence.[116]

In return, Earle escaped public criticism by the CIO and enjoyed good relations with organized labor through the remainder of his term. Davey, though, was obviously less troubled by his decision, which prompted the CIO do its best to trouble him. A delegation of twenty labor leaders called on the governor two days after he lifted his order. Unconvinced by Davey's contention that his hands were tied by the law, the delegation issued a statement that adjudged Davey "a low-type politician who made promises and continually violated them" and pointed out that Republic and Sheet & Tube still controlled hundreds of armed men in the strike zone.[117] The CIO vowed that it would make the governor pay politically and named him a target in the next election cycle.[118] The CIO also attempted to have Davey's deployment of the National Guard, as well as other restraints on picketing, enjoined by a federal court in Columbus. The union's primary arguments, which were not trivial, were that martial law had been imposed without legal authority and that picketing was being restrained in a fashion that violated the supremacy of federal labor law and policy. However, the strike ended before the case could be heard.[119] And the CIO's plan to punish Davey was preempted by his decision not to stand for another term.

When the governors lifted their status quo orders, CIO officials pleaded with Roosevelt to intervene directly and stop the mills from reopening.[120] After several days of silence, Roosevelt issued a devastating response. At a June 29 press conference, he summoned Shakespeare and declared the strike "a plague on both your houses."[121] The statement made clear the president's intention to distance himself from capitalists and workers alike and, if possible, to wash his hands of the whole affair. Like thousands of rank and filers, Lewis was deeply betrayed. But he waited until Labor Day to give full vent to his anger. In a nationally broadcast radio address, Lewis warned Roosevelt, "It ill behooves one who has supped at labor's table and who has been sheltered in labor's house to curse with equal fervor and fine impartiality both labor and its adversaries when they become locked in deadly embrace."[122] Roosevelt's decision to denounce the union would seriously erode the administration's alliance with Lewis and the CIO and would reverberate for years to come.[123] His move also hinted at a fundamental political shift. In the words of the *Buffalo Evening News*'s Washington correspondent, it signaled that the New Deal had undergone "a change of heart."[124]

The Roosevelt administration did make some further efforts to resolve the conflict. On June 27, after the mediation board's efforts collapsed, Perkins made a last-minute appeal to Davey to keep the mills closed—and if necessary to subpoena Girdler and Purnell to the capitol in Columbus and hold them till they negotiated in earnest. While Perkins described the exchange as a suggestion, Davey seized the opportunity to criticize Perkins and Roosevelt while holding forth on the limits of his own legal authority to keep the mills closed and the perils of "confiscat[ing] private property" and using "high-handed" dictatorial power in the fashion "we condemn in Germany, Italy and Russia."[125] A few days later, in another somewhat conciliatory gesture, Perkins concurred with Roosevelt's Shakespearean dictum but also reiterated the view that the parties should be made to bargain in good faith. Moreover, she publicly cited the mediation board's final report as proof that the CIO was not "irresponsible." Well into July, CIO officials continued to press Perkins to intervene more decisively in the strike, but without success.[126]

In the days following the reopening order, the number of Guardsmen on strike duty in Ohio increased dramatically. The size of the contingent stationed in the Youngstown area reached a high of 2,319 on June 28 before beginning to decline. Seeing that the troops would now serve to break the strike, government officials and antistrike forces in Canton and Massillon began to push for martial law in those cities as well. On June 25, the sheriff of Stark County wrote National Guard general William L. Marlin, declaring that the situation was becoming "dangerous" and fairly demanding that troops be moved there.[127] That same day, the sheriff sent a similar letter to the mayor of Canton, James Seccombe—who had sparred with Davey over the sufficiency of Seccombe's efforts to rein in violence—urging that Seccombe make more aggressive use of city police to prevent violence and enforce a court order limiting picketing.[128] In fact, Seccombe, along with Henry Krier, mayor of nearby Massillon, also wrote General Marlin asking that he send troops to Stark County.[129] On June 29, the issue was settled when Davey ordered deployment of the Guard in the "Canton-Massillon Military District."[130] On July 3, Davey pledged to use the Guard to open all mills in Ohio that were still shut. A week into July, after receiving requests from Republic as well as Mayor Harold Burton and the local sheriff, Davey sent fifteen hundred Guardsmen to Cleveland to reopen the mills in that city.[131] In all, thirty-three hundred Guardsmen were deployed in Ohio and oversaw reopenings at all the major struck mills in that state.[132]

Only a few days after Davey and Earle lifted their status quo orders, some national headlines were proposing that the CIO, fresh from its sensational victories over a slew of open shop bastions like General Motors, Chrysler, and U.S. Steel, had met its "first defeat."[133] Journalists reported workers' streaming back into the mills under the protection of state troops.[134] In fact, the plants could not be returned to production overnight. Furnaces had to be relighted and other systems laboriously restarted before production could resume. Moreover, because the local back-to-work movements represented far fewer workers than they claimed, the companies and their allies had to actually mobilize workers to return to the mills. Of course, the governors' orders convinced many that the strike was doomed and primed them to return. But despite all the pressures to give up the struggle, thousands remained staunchly committed to the strike and continued to picket the mills, unwilling to surrender.

This dogged determination set the stage for numerous clashes with Guardsmen and police. This was certainly true in Ohio, even before Davey ordered the mills reopened. No sooner had the National Guard arrived in Youngstown than it arrested 150 steel, mine, and rubber workers as they arrived from other towns to support the strikers—and claimed to have turned away another 3,000. The Guard carried out this policy aggressively, seizing such unthreatening figures as Rose Stein, a writer for the *Nation* who neglected to obtain necessary credentials and was thrown "into a cell with a demented woman."[135] The Guardsmen also set about disarming the strikers—although, as the union delegation had complained to Davey, not the company police or the special police and deputies.[136]

Even before Davey's new order came down, the Guard moved to support the reopenings.[137] On June 23, as thousands of local workers struck in sympathy with the steel strikers, Guardsmen armed with machine guns and drawn bayonets pushed aside picketers and broke the month-long siege of Republic's plants at Warren and Niles. The next day, workers were said to be "pouring" back to work.[138] On June 25, Guardsmen at one of Sheet & Tube's gates in Campbell pushed aside four hundred picketers to allow seven hundred employees to enter the plant.[139] After reducing the pickets and demolishing union barricades, National Guard officers set about controlling when the plants reopened as well as how they managed changes in shifts, movements of rail and truck shipments, and disbursements of payrolls.[140]

Over the next two weeks, National Guard reports and communiqués documented steady increases in the number of men going to work and weakening of the picket lines at most of the struck plants in Ohio. Nevertheless, local strike leaders continued to insist that the strike could be won if only the men could hold out.[141] Organizers worked hard to bolster morale. A meeting in Youngstown on June 26 drew an animated crowd of 800. The

FIGURE 22. National Guard machine-gun position in Youngstown, Ohio, June 25, 1937. Courtesy of the Youngstown Historical Center of Industry and Labor.

next day, another meeting drew 700 and prompted a call to the Guard by Republic's police, who described how speeches by John Steuben, Robert Burke, and "some Slovak" had generated considerable enthusiasm. The June 27 meeting was followed that evening by another meeting at Rumanian Hall attended by another several hundred.[142] That same night, at least 2,500 (maybe as many as 8,000) people rallied in Canton; 1,000 in Massillon; and 1,200, many of them CIO rubber workers, in Akron.[143] In addition to condemning the companies and extolling the union's cause, speakers at these gatherings questioned the number of men back in the mills and accused the companies of burning tar paper in the furnaces to create the illusion that the mills were truly up and running.[144] Union leaders also assured the strikers that the SWOC was receiving ample political and financial support from other unions and that the strikers need not fear going hungry or losing their homes or cars.[145]

Unionists resorted to other methods to shore up the strike. A Guard report on a June 27 union meeting in Youngstown describes how Robert Burke urged strikers to make anonymous telephone calls to the homes of "rats" at work in Republic's plant and, if possible, to enlist their wives

FIGURE 23. Their numbers limited by injunctions and police proclamations, weary picketers in Youngstown, Ohio, protest the reopening of area mills as National Guardsmen and police stand by, July 1, 1937. © 1937, Associated Press.

"in calling them out."[146] National Guard records also document incidents in which workers wanting to go back were threatened with injury, either by telephone or written note, or by union men on the streets or at their homes.[147] But these efforts could only do so much to counter the growing worries and frustrations of men who had gone weeks without pay and, in some cases, given hours to picket duty only to see their lines pushed aside, and who risked being blacklisted if they did not return soon. As efforts to resuscitate the strike foundered, a tone of victimization and resignation began to accompany the usual defiance of SWOC statements. "Our hands are empty and our belts are being pulled tighter each day, but we are determined to remain on strike until Tom Girdler learns that the laws are made for him to obey"—so said a July 5 proclamation by the SWOC's regional director for Ohio.[148]

The Guard did keep the peace. But even by evenhandedly enforcing the law, the Guard favored the steel companies, inasmuch as the law itself was proving to be biased against the strikers. And evenhandedness was hardly the norm. The La Follette Committee deemed the Ohio National Guard "guilty of intemperate application of the law."[149] While they held the field, the troops cooperated with local police in assaulting strikers, breaking up pickets, sacking and shuttering union halls, invading strikers' homes, and detaining anyone suspected of entering the strike areas for the purpose of giving any kind of support to the strikers, including people who were unarmed and otherwise posed no apparent threat. Even the discovery that CIO lawyers were in Youngstown providing arrested unionists with legal counsel provoked suspicion from the Guardsmen.[150] The CIO's director in Ohio, a former miner named John Owens, described the Guard's work as a "terror campaign" and threatened that strikers would "take all means necessary to protect themselves" if such practices did not cease.[151]

The reopenings did feature a good deal of union violence, often directed at the companies and their loyal employees. While much of this involved minor scuffles and property damage, there were quite a few serious episodes. The Guard uncovered an amazing amount of explosives in the strike zone.[152] But the Guard did not find all of it. In the course of several days in late June, a bomb wrecked a highway bridge near Warren; another went off near the gates of Republic's open hearth furnace operation in Youngstown; another damaged a bridge in Warren.[153] In the early morning hours on the last day of the month, a water main in Canton was blown up.[154] There were numerous smaller bombings in the Youngstown and Canton-Massillon areas in late June and early July, most of them designed to harm property but not people. But there were also reports of sniping at authorities or workers trying to enter the mills, as well as continued shooting at aircraft still operating around Warren.[155]

A serious clash between unionists and Guardsmen occurred in Canton on the morning of June 30. Although initial reports claimed that the Guard-supervised reopenings were orderly, by that afternoon considerable trouble had erupted. At least seventy-five picketers were arrested and a number of people injured by Guardsmen who forced aside picketers at two of Republic's plants.[156] A Guardsman likely killed a Republic striker during the mêlée. The Guard, the police, and the local coroner all asserted that the striker, a forty-one-year-old Spanish immigrant from Massillon named Crisanto Lopez, had died of a heart attack. But union people, who claimed to have seen the Guard beating someone where Lopez was later found near death, and whose accounts of widespread beatings by the Guard were backed up by journalists, said that Lopez was fatally bludgeoned about the head by one of the troopers.[157]

The Guard supported its operations in northeast Ohio with considerable espionage.[158] The intensity of this effort is evident in the Guard's field orders and reports. Alongside fairly innocuous estimates of the number of men working in the mills and the rate at which the mills resumed production are trivial notations, such as the kind of license plate on Gus Hall's car, an attempt to determine the intentions of "Mike the Greek," and ruminations about various "bad actors" and suspicious characters.[159] A report describing John Steuben, compiled in late June, verges on the ridiculous. Steuben, who at this point would have been easily recognized by almost anyone in the area, was described by height and weight; he was said to have a "sheep eye," a "shifty eye," and a "swarthy complexion"; also, said the reports, he "always has a woman."[160]

Other reports speculated about the dates and whereabouts of union meetings and rallies, attendance at these events, and the contents of speeches delivered there, often with inane but revealing commentary. In his report on a June 26 rally in Campbell, 1st Lieut. John Cianflona reached the uninspired conclusion that Robert Burke was "a radical in my estimation." The journalist Mary Heaton Vorse was "not very effective" in her speech; "very ineffective," too, was "a negro named Curley Jackson." Another speaker "spoke Romanian, or Slavish," and yet another "seems to have enjoyed the visit to the city house of correction."[161] Two days later, other Guardsmen submitted similar reports about an open-air meeting in the Youngstown area, this one at a baseball field in Struthers.[162]

Although the Guard's records reveal little interest in company arsenals or the possibility that company agents planted contraband on unionists, its intelligence reports were much concerned with the possession of explosives and weapons by union people.[163] The field reports also highlight the Guard's preoccupation with "invading" armies of sympathetic unionists. Guard agents in the Canton area closely monitored other workers for signs of sympathy with the SWOC, especially those affiliated with the United Rubber Workers of America, a CIO union gaining a hold in the region's tire plants. The Guard's espionage reports also chronicle episodes of union-authored sabotage.[164] Among these are incidents in which the Guardsmen themselves were targets, including an amusing episode in which someone cut the telephone lines serving a Canton schoolhouse occupied by the Guard.[165]

These intelligence reports occasionally refuted accusations of union-sponsored violence and sometimes affirmed the frustrations that fueled the strikers' bitterness toward the troops.[166] However, for every instance of candor and empathy there is something that underscores the Guard's partisan role in the strike. The reports filed by 1st Lieut. Robert Boyd consistently referred to the strikers as the "enemy." His account of the funeral of one of the men killed in the Stop 5 Riot described the 230-car procession as an "enemy movement" of which an improbable "40%" were outsiders from Pennsylvania.[167] Elsewhere, Boyd claimed that the "enemy (CIO) have our telephone numbers," and urged that codes would have to be adopted; and a few days later, that "the enemy ... intend to await our withdrawal to start any trouble or gorilla [sic] operations."[168]

Other sources underscore the unease and tension that underlay the relative peace the Guard imposed during the reopenings. Guard records from June 27 describe "several brawls" and "considerable hostility among the workingmen" who returned to work at Sheet & Tube's Campbell Works. The plant's managers found that the men "do not talk much. They are all worried what will happen when [the] guard leave." The same document observed that "there are many strong CIO men who say they will not go back until [a] contract is signed. Sgt. Burkett is of the opinion that if the troops leave there will be considerable disorder."[169] And so there was. On July 6, employees heading to work in Republic's plants at Warren and Niles had to run gauntlets of stone- and brick-throwing unionists positioned along the roads.[170]

The reopening of Bethlehem's Johnstown mill also generated conflict and disorder. On June 25, the day Earle's status quo order was lifted, fifteen hundred picketers resumed patrols at Bethlehem's Cambria Works, among them hundreds of CIO miners. However, two days later, the mill was reopened and took in about a third of the usual complement of workers. On the night of June 28 and the early morning of June 29, explosions ruptured vital water pipelines leading into the Cambria mill, forcing it to bank its furnaces and stop production for several days.[171] In the wake of this spectacular act, Mayor Shields arrested the SWOC's subregional director as well as a local railroad unionist and brought them to "trial" before forty or fifty "citizens." When a local attorney who volunteered to represent the men was himself arrested for questioning the legality of the proceedings, the affair degenerated into a confused ritual aimed at warning the men to leave town if they valued their safety. Probably more helpful to the mayor's purpose was a decision by state police to enforce a limit of only two to six picketers at each of the mill's dozen gates. There was scattered violence in Johnstown in the days ahead. But by the close of June, the picket lines had dwindled, most workers had returned, and the strike there was broken.[172]

Within a couple of days of Davey's reopening order, mills in the Youngstown area were reporting large complements of workers on the job. According to Lieutenant Boyd, by June 25 or 26 "enemy strength" in Youngstown had been "depleted by 9000 desertions."[173] By that time, Republic and Sheet & Tube claimed to have taken in 18,556 returning workers in their Youngstown plants. Although this may have been an exaggeration, over the next two weeks several other plants idled by the strike were relighting their furnaces, and newspapers were reporting a commensurate thinning of picket lines.[174] The Guard reports of conflict between rival factions of workers inside the mills prove that many workers who went back after the reopenings remained staunch unionists. But unionists or not, they got the mills running.

10

Let's Bust Them Up

LAST STRUGGLES AND DEFEAT

By the end of the first week of July, the strike was collapsing. The plants not already reopened were relighting their furnaces and preparing to resume production; and, overall, far fewer picketers patrolled the gates. There were notable exceptions, however. Almost two weeks into July, Sheet & Tube's large mill at Indiana Harbor and the company's smaller plant in South Chicago both remained closed and under threat from strikers prepared to vigorously resist any effort to reopen them. Together with the small N&G Taylor plant in Cumberland, Maryland, these were the last mills to reopen.[1] But for a time, picketers stood fast even in some places where the mills had reopened. As the Ohio National Guard recognized, in early July "heavy pickets" could still be found in a number of locations in that state, including Cleveland, Massillon, and Niles.[2] These pockets of resistance set the stage for a chaotic and violent conclusion to the walkout.

THE RIOT AT MASSILLON

In 1937, Republic dominated life in Massillon, where its four thousand employees represented a large majority of the city's wage earners. The company ran two operations there: Union Drawn Steel, within the city itself; and the much larger and more integrated Massillon Works, just outside of town. Republic had invested heavily in ERPs in Massillon and employed a familiar array of repressive tactics to thwart the SWOC. Massillon was one of the places where organizers convened some of their meetings in darkened parks and fields.[3] Nevertheless, SWOC organizers recruited large numbers of workers in both mills. It was in response to this success that the company imposed a lockout at the Massillon Works before the strike even began.

Despite some attempts by Republic to stock and staff the mills in anticipation of a shutdown, both the Massillon Works and the Union Drawn plant were closed by the combination of lockout and strike.[4] But Republic immediately undertook steps to break the strike and open the mills with loyal employees. The company sponsored a back-to-work movement and a citizens' group variously known as the Law and Order League, the Labor Relations Committee, and the Citizens' League. Besides the usual functions of running advertisements, holding meetings, and orchestrating petitions, these groups joined company officials in a campaign "to conscript the Massillon police department to break the strike."[5]

Early in the strike, a Republic official approached the police chief, former steel worker Stanley Switter, to inform him that the town was about to be overrun by union "hoodlums" and ask why the police did not "take such action as the Chicago police in putting them where they belonged."[6] If Switter did not act, the man suggested, Republic might have to reconsider its commitment to Massillon. Later, members of the Law and Order League also demanded that Switter deputize some men and smash the picket lines. But the chief again demurred, noting that the department was making fewer arrests during the strike than in "normal times," that the Massillon Works was outside his jurisdiction, and that, in any case, his department was not a "strikebreaking outfit."[7] Not satisfied, on June 21 nearly three hundred men "stormed the City Hall" and demanded to meet with Switter and the mayor and interrogated them about their continued refusal to build up the police and break the strike. A few days later, Republic officials in Massillon communicated to Switter a false rumor that five thousand to ten thousand CIO unionists were about to "invade" the town. Despite Switter's protests, several thousand loyal employees, American Legionnaires, and other anti-CIO figures assembled to meet the phantom army of unionists. The mob dispersed only when National Guardsmen arrived and validated Switter's assurance that no unionists were approaching—and only after mob leaders had photographed the scene to document the town's enthusiastic support for Republic.[8]

In the days that followed, representatives of the Law and Order League and back-to-work movement continued to hector Switter and other city officials, railing about supposed acts of union violence, police bias in favor of the strikers, and the threat that Republic might pull out of Massillon. They demanded that city officials enlarge the police force and deploy it against the strikers; and they promised to raise money to pay for this. At last these efforts began to bear fruit when Switter accepted a modest donation of weapons directly from Republic. Toward the end of June, Switter also agreed to appoint a contingent of seven special police, although he culled those candidates whose records suggested excessive procompany bias.[9]

On July 2, several hundred Guardsmen oversaw the reopening of the Massillon plants. Some troops were billeted within the Massillon Works, but they neither encountered nor caused much trouble. Although they arrested some strikers, including the president of the local lodge, there was nothing like what happened in Canton and Youngstown. And the Guard withdrew from the town over several days beginning on July 8.[10] Nevertheless, when the withdrawal began, a considerable number of workers remained out, particularly at the Massillon Works, where even the company claimed less than two-thirds normal staffing. This situation left Republic unable to resume full production and faced with a powerful symbol of union resistance.[11]

On July 6, a delegation representing the Law and Order League, the back-to-work movement, and Republic itself visited Switter and other city officials and again requested that special police be appointed from a list of loyal Republic employees. Meeting renewed objections, the delegation telephoned Republic's office in Canton to demonstrate that officials there were then, as they spoke, swearing in part of a contingent of fifty-six company men as special police. On July 7, Switter conceded, agreeing to deputize about forty men, as many as thirty-two of whom were Republic employees preselected by the company itself, and to arm them with revolvers and billy clubs. Republic itself bonded twenty-seven of the recruits; and, as on other occasions when it planted its men with the local police, the company continued to pay them.[12] Switter had not changed his mind about the wisdom of appointing Republic's men to the police force but rather had succumbed to unrelenting pressure and simple exhaustion. As he told the La Follette Committee, his thinking was, "Well, if they wanted trouble, let them have it; there was no way to stop it."[13]

Leading this group of deputies was a hot-headed Legionnaire, one Harry O. Curley, who liked to be called by his military rank, "Major" Curley.[14] Retired from the army, Curley himself was never actually deputized by the police or legally authorized by anyone to wield any official authority at all—the belated realization of which would throw him into a panic during the disorder to come. Contradicting persistent claims that strikers in the area were threatening people in their homes, Curley repeatedly posted the deputies near the picket lines. From his new position, he set about publicly denouncing the strikers and their supporters, calling for strong action against them, and figuring ways to provoke them.[15]

The picketers in Massillon were not much armed, even with sticks, by this point in the strike. Nor had there recently been any major outbreaks of violence, besides a "small riot" on June 7 when union people attacked a man gathering signatures for a back-to-work petition. Even when the mills reopened, there were only a few scuffles and instances of vandalism.[16] And things were quiet around the Massillon Works on the evening of July 11, where a crowd of maybe two hundred people, including fifty or sixty picketers and many women and children, were gathered near the union's local headquarters, a few hundred feet from Republic's office and the plant's main gate. As was usual on Sunday nights during the strike, the union had organized festivities at the building, including an orchestra that had earlier played out in the street, and some dancing. The headquarters also housed a strike kitchen where people were eating and casually socializing.[17]

After Switter's inspection earlier that evening revealed things to be orderly, Curley pressured the chief to leave the city in order to get some rest. Sometime before 10:00 P.M., with Switter gone, Curley countermanded Switter's orders to give the union building a wide berth and directed the special police as well as city police—over whom he seemed to wield unquestioned authority—to station themselves within a few feet of union headquarters. Against Switter's instructions, Curley also increased from six to twenty the number of police on duty at the main gate and had these men augment their usual sidearms and gas with nearly every weapon in the department's stocks. Curley outfitted one man, a machine gunner in the Great War, with a Thompson submachine gun. At about 10:00 P.M., Curley deployed his men in a rough semicircle fifty to one hundred feet from, and partly encompassing, the union people gathered in front of the headquarters. Around the same time, someone in league with Curley summoned at least eight Pennsylvania Railroad police to the scene.[18]

Despite these unsettling measures, the unionists were entirely peaceful and initially at ease with the situation, as even Republic's own witnesses tended to confirm. Once the unionists noticed the deployment of special police around them, a few of the leaders considered sending their people home before deciding differently.[19] They should have done so, for Curley fully intended to provoke a clash. This was the understanding of the men under his command, one of whom testified that he expected trouble, since otherwise "I would not have been sent down there."[20] Another of Curley's men remembered the major's making statements that night like, "I am going to clean out that God Damned Hall tonight."[21]

With all of this, it was only a question of what particular event would set things off. Sometime after 10:30 P.M., a drunk man antagonized picketers near the main gate. Just before 11:00 P.M., another ruckus developed after two cars were involved in an accident, also near the gate. Most likely the crash was part of a scheme by some union people to impede access to the plant, since that was its immediate effect and the accident occurred during a shift change. Whatever the circumstances, police at the scene fired several live rounds while trying to capture one of the drivers who had fled. Adding to the confusion, several people who were apparently connected to the union began throwing rocks and bottles at other cars in the area. However, with the help of union leaders, police stationed near that spot were able to apprehend the fleeing driver and settle things down.[22]

Some of Curley's men refused to believe that the shooting down the street was the work of the police and insisted on believing that it heralded the outbreak of serious union-sponsored violence. Just as the commotion near the gate was settling down, Curley's men confronted a striker who had just parked his car near union headquarters, with the headlights illuminating the police formation. The police demanded that he extinguish the lights or have them shot out. Moments after the man responded by either cutting the lights or possibly only dimming them, several of the police could be heard shouting, "Let them have it," "Break them up," and "Let's bust them up." The submachine gunner fired into the car while other police dropped to the ground and unleashed a volley of gunfire and gas, first at the car and then in the direction of the union headquarters. The people gathered about the building fled in panic, even though some of them, disbelieving that the police could have resorted to lethal force with so little reason, initially thought the shots were blanks.[23] Frank Hardesty, the SWOC's subregional director for Canton and Massillon, who was on the headquarters' steps, recalled taking a moment to realize that live ammunition was being fired before fleeing with "bullets flying through the air and bouncing off the buildings like a hailstorm."[24]

Curley's force engulfed the union headquarters and surrounding areas with gunfire and gas. The police claimed to have done so to suppress gunfire coming from the unionists, but this was untrue. Equally unfounded was a claim that the police had begun shooting because the SWOC people had been preparing to rush the police or the plant. What is certain, instead, is that just after the shooting broke out, police lay violent siege to the headquarters. For more than a half hour, they discharged firearms and gas intermittently toward the building and at targets in the surrounding darkness. The shooting trapped a number of men and women inside the headquarters. When the firing momentarily died down and one man tried to exit the front door, he was immediately shot through the leg. During another brief lull, a group of men left the building to help a man who had been shot down in the street out front. They drew fire and one of them was seriously injured. Several hundred gunshots and around one hundred gas shells were fired in the small area surrounding the union building.[25]

Curley's men were soon reinforced by two dozen police from Canton, including Republic employees serving as special police. The Canton police brought in an armored car, which drove up and down the street in front of the union headquarters shooting gas to "clear the street."[26] At 11:30, just as the shooting seemed to be dying down, around sixty Guardsmen joined the police. A motley but heavily armed force of police and deputies, Guardsmen, railroad police, company police, and loyal employees then "raked the headquarters" with gunfire before storming the building and arresting everyone inside. They ransacked the place and looted the union's records, including signed SWOC membership cards that were carried off by a Republic official. The "mopping up squad" went door-to-door through nearby residential buildings, destroying personal property and arresting more people thought to be with the union. They "arrested all persons within a radius of three or more blocks" and, in the words of the NLRB, held them "for several days, for the crime, apparently, of belonging to the Union."[27] In all, about 165 people were seized, none with the benefit of a warrant or any concern for probable cause. A number of arrestees were treated roughly; and some were not released for several days, in many cases only after waiving any legal claims against the police. Where arrest charges were announced, they were trumped up: suspicion, disorderly conduct, resisting an officer, and at least one case of reckless driving. In the end, only fourteen were ever formally charged.[28]

Two workers were killed in the assault. Fulgencio Calzada, a thirty-seven-year-old Spanish immigrant and former Republic worker, died on the scene, shot in the back of the head; and Nicholas Vathiaz (or Vadios, or Valdas), a forty-seven-year-old immigrant striker from Greece, succumbed the next morning at the hospital to a gunshot through the pelvis. Around a dozen people were injured, including two men shot in the back (one who barely survived), another shot in the cheek, and several shot in the legs.[29] When a Hungarian immigrant striker named Loggin Drosz, age forty-seven, died on July 18 after falling ill at a union meeting, friends and family charged that his death was caused by the delayed effects of gas inhalation during the riot. However, the Stark County coroner—the same Doctor Edward Reno who attributed the June 30 death of the Canton striker to a heart attack— concluded that Drosz died of heart failure unrelated to the riot. Nevertheless, it is quite possible that Drosz's life was cut short by the gas. Several authorities, including the NLRB and the La Follette Committee, considered his death a result of the riot.[30]

Most likely there was not any shooting at all by union people during the fray. As the NLRB and La Follette Committee determined, police claims that they were provoked by gunfire directed at Curley's men near the union headquarters or by a planned attack on the plant were certainly contrived. Of all the people arrested that night, only one was "armed"—with a small pocket knife. And police found no weapons in the headquarters or homes they ransacked. Indeed, nothing about the unionists' disposition suggests anything provocative, beyond the efforts of a handful, well removed from Curley's group, to harass workers leaving the plant.

In testimony before the NLRB and the La Follette Committee, several special police not only confirmed the violence of the attack but also expressed doubts as to whether their actions were justified. Although the Pennsylvania Railroad contended that its men were not actively involved in the events of that night, quite a few railroad police contradicted this claim, testifying that they participated in the shooting and the assault that followed.[31] In the end, as the NLRB put it, "the strikers were the victims, and not the aggressors, in an unprovoked attack."[32] Both the NLRB and the La Follette Committee concluded that the entire affair was the fault of Republic, which had armed the police, sponsored the appointment of the special police, facilitated Curley's assumption of control over the city police, and cultivated the violent antiunion sentiments that led to the riot.[33]

The morning after the clash, police and Guardsmen marched their throngs of prisoners to jail, some without shirts or shoes, before crowds of onlookers. The mayor of Massillon immediately banned all public meetings.[34] A few days later, U.S. marshals began hunting for Joe Morton, president of New Deal Lodge No. 1124 at the Massillon Works; Kenneth

Steed, president of Square Deal Lodge No. 1566 at Union Drawn; and Leo Cox, picket captain—all on charges of interfering with mail deliveries in the area. The marshals found Morton, who had been gassed in the attack on the union hall, a few days later in Columbus.[35]

On July 14, Socialist Party leader and several-times presidential candidate Norman Thomas arrived in town for Fulgencio Calzada's funeral and delivered a speech to a large group of unionists, advocating further investigations of Little Steel by the La Follette Committee and urging strikers to abstain from violence. Nicholas Vathiaz was buried the next day, after a Greek Orthodox service held at the rooming house where he resided. Even the local paper, which had little good to say about the strikers, seemed impressed that the poor man's procession to the cemetery entailed 165 automobiles. He was buried just across the Tuscarawas River from the Massillon Works.[36]

The workers in Massillon could also have laid to rest any hope of defeating Republic on the picket lines. The day after the riot, the local paper ran a picture on the front page of helmeted Guardsmen, rifles on their shoulders, surveying the destruction of the union headquarters.[37] It was a shambles: papers and shattered glass all about, the furniture broken, and blood from the wounded everywhere. The strike kitchen was closed indefinitely. As the La Follette Committee concluded, "The riot resulted in the breaking of the morale of the strikers, followed shortly by the end of the strike."[38]

CLASHES IN CLEVELAND

As in Massillon, violence in Cleveland erupted after a relatively quiet period through June and much of July.[39] Republic had moved its headquarters to Cleveland in 1936 and operated four plants there with about seven thousand workers. The company had closed these mills when the strike began but late in June moved to reopen them. On July 6, some two thousand Guardsmen, along with nearly five hundred city police and sheriff deputies, stood guard at the reopenings. There was little trouble, in part because authorities had already limited the union to only twelve picketers per gate and required that their names be provided in advance. On July 13, the Guard began to pull out of Cleveland and by July 16 had largely withdrawn.[40]

Despite the reopenings, the union's assertion that the strike remained "effective" in Cleveland was not entirely unfounded.[41] As of July 17, the city police estimated that about 40 percent of Republic's workers remained out.

FIGURE 24. Workers enter Republic Steel's Upson Nut plant in Cleveland, Ohio, under the protection of city police and National Guardsmen, probably July 7, 1937. © 1937, Bettmann/Corbis/Associated Press.

These stalwarts were angry at the company and resentful of the workers who crossed over, especially at the largest plant: the Corrigan-McKinney Works, with about thirty-seven hundred employees. Further inflaming the strikers was the fact that the Corrigan-McKinney plant was one of the few mills to have taken on a sizable contingent of outside replacement workers: 394 by mid-July, many of them blacks newly arrived from the South. However, CIO diligence in integrating blacks and a tradition of black militancy in the area ensured that black workers fought on both sides of the line that summer.[42]

Cleveland was primed for conflict in other ways, too. Home to robust communities of Communists and other radicals, the city was regarded by many as the nation's premier union town. By the time of the strike, the CIO had made solid advances among the city's industrial workers. And some of the violence could be traced to striking knitting mill and textile workers, about five thousand of whom were also out. But the steel strike was the focal point of discord, and in the last week of July that conflict appeared to be reigniting. By mid-July, the *Cleveland Plain Dealer* was reporting a surge in skirmishes between unionists and loyal employees, including fights, incidents of bricks and rocks thrown through windows, and damage to automobiles.[43] On the evening of July 22, a vacant house was dynamited and three Republic strikers were charged with the crime. Earlier the same day, police had responded to numerous fights and cases of property damage and other vandalism.[44]

On July 21, SWOC members voted to reestablish large pickets at Republic's Cleveland plants. The move accompanied the lifting of the sheriff's proclamation limiting the number of picketers. The lines were increased dramatically, particularly at the gates of the Corrigan-McKinney plant, where by July 26 some two thousand to three thousand people picketed. As hundreds of loyal employees and strikebreakers (many of them blacks) attempted to enter and leave the mill during the shift change, they clashed repeatedly with the massed unionists. The main battleground was near the intersection of Independence Avenue and Dille Road. Unrest there gave rise to a tragedy on the afternoon of July 26, when a car driven by a loyal employee burst through the line, striking and killing a forty-five-year-old striker, a Slovak immigrant named John Orecny, who was dragged along the pavement before horrified witnesses. Unionists claimed that the episode occurred after a police sergeant at the scene instructed workers entering the plant to "run over them" if they did not yield.[45]

After Orecny's death, enraged strikers began bombarding the cars of loyal employees as they tried to pass through for the evening shift change. While SWOC picket captains desperately attempted to rein in the crowd, belligerent company loyalists gathered near the scene, inside the plant, hurling taunts and invectives. Rocks and bricks began to rain down on both sides of the line. Police officials mustered several hundred officers to the scene. For a time they were able, with horses and gas, to open some distance between unionists and loyal employees. However, the semi-peace would not hold. Around 11:00 P.M., at another gate, perhaps five hundred loyal employees armed with clubs and wearing identifying armbands rushed out of the plant and attacked a group of one hundred picketers and then rampaged through surrounding neighborhoods, assaulting any unionists they could get hold of. The company men sacked the nearby union headquarters, throwing a young woman through a window. Union people rallied to the scene and fighting raged, as gangs from either side hunted each other on the darkened streets, fighting vicious skirmishes till dawn. Some eighty people received hospital care for injuries that night and several were critically injured, including another striker run down by a car.[46]

FIGURE 25. Police attempt to separate loyal employees from mass picketers at Republic Steel's Corrigan-McKinney Works in Cleveland, Ohio, July 26, 1937. © 1937, Associated Press.

Years later, Tom Girdler still exulted in how "our men" had taken the fight to the "trouble makers" around the Corrigan-McKinney Works—agitators, he said, who could not have been actual strikers. Even the tossing of the young woman through the window met with his approval.[47] As with other outbursts of violence, Republic denied that its managers or police had played a role in organizing the mob. However, it seems clear that the captain of the company police in Cleveland, Dewey Jones, had led the attacks that night. The staff of the La Follette Committee was familiar with Jones from earlier assaults on union people and deemed him "a man of vicious temper, quick in the use of force." Jones was nearly prosecuted by federal authorities for beating two garage mechanics who, during the organizing drive, had discovered in Jones's car a company espionage report on SWOC organizers and had turned it over to the committee.[48] In any event, the company's denial of responsibility for the riot on the night of July 26 was of little avail, as both Republic and Jones would later be successfully sued by dozens of victims of that fray.

The morning of July 27 brought renewed conflict at the Corrigan-McKinney gates when police and scabs tried again to force their way through a series of picket lines and blockades. Again, stones and bricks were thrown and at least twenty more people were injured. Police also made a number of arrests. According to strikers, police inspector Martin Horrigan warned the picketers that "I'll fill St. Alexis' Hospital with you people if you don't get out of here."[49] By midmorning, union leaders on the scene were able to restrain their people. Apparently, so were Republic's police, as there was little evidence of mob activity inside the plant. SWOC leaders took most of the picketers away from the plant on a peaceful march to city hall. In the meantime, the city's public-safety director, Eliot Ness (of Prohibition fame), banned any groups from assembling near the Corrigan-McKinney Works. Lawyers for Republic petitioned a court for an injunction limiting the size of pickets near all its mills in Cleveland.[50] And by the next day, the conflict had diminished along with the size of the picket lines.

On the evening of July 29, at least six thousand people rallied at the Public Square in downtown Cleveland in support of the major strikes in the city.[51] Although Mayor Burton brushed off CIO appeals to order Republic's Cleveland plants closed on grounds that he lacked such authority, earlier that day he convened a meeting of his fellow mayors from Massillon, Canton, Niles, and Warren to discuss the strike situation at Republic. The mayors relayed to Republic a proposal from the CIO to temporarily settle the strike—one that Canton's mayor, James Seccombe, adjudged "very fair." But finding itself on the verge of complete victory, Republic categorically rejected the deal.[52] In the meantime, workers streamed back into the plants, unimpeded. There were still instances of vandalism and isolated fights, but nothing like the previous days. On August 6, a final episode of serious strike-related violence flared near Republic's Upson Nut plant in Cleveland when four loyal employees brazenly stabbed a man named Mike Kelly inside the CIO's headquarters, seriously injuring him.[53]

SETTLEMENT AND SETBACK IN THE CALUMET

Not everywhere were the last weeks of the strike so violent. At Inland it ended with something of a settlement. Negotiations that led to this occurred in the last days of June, facilitated by Indiana governor Clifford Townsend, who earlier had called unsuccessfully for a conference of governors of Indiana, Illinois, Michigan, and Ohio to devise a settlement in the strike.[54] As June drew to an end, Inland became increasingly insistent that it would reopen its big Indiana Harbor mill, and the union became more vocal in threatening to do whatever might be necessary to prevent this from happening. Townsend responded by mobilizing, but not deploying, thirty-nine hundred members of the Indiana National Guard. Fearing the Guardsmen would break the strike, SWOC people pleaded that he not deploy them. But the threat of violence, combined with a continued inability to reopen its mill, also pressured Inland to reach a settlement. Just before midnight on June 30, an agreement was reached.[55]

The terms of the settlement were announced the next morning. The parties had actually not entered a bilateral agreement but rather had separately pledged to honor a memorandum underwritten by the Indiana Labor Board. The union agreed to end the strike. Inland would recognize the SWOC as bargaining agent only for its members and would take back the strikers without discrimination; the company's prestrike labor policies (which resembled the SWOC's terms with U.S. Steel) would remain in place, except that major grievances arising under the agreement could be submitted to the state labor board. All other issues would await resolution of charges pending against Inland before the NLRB.[56] On July 1, Inland reopened the Indiana Harbor mill amid cries of victory from thousands of jubilant workers, some sporting beards they had vowed to grow until the strike ended. The *Daily Worker* joined the chorus, likening the "triumph" to the victory of the patriots over British tyranny and parroting the claims of SWOC leaders that the agreement represented a real coup.[57] The "truce," as it was called, was less a triumph than a restoration of the status quo ante. But it would be the union's only victory that summer.

Sheet & Tube had been a party to the talks that led to the Inland agreement but withdrew just as an accord was reached. Undaunted, Townsend's staff continued to confer with company officials. However, the company, which was then ramping up production at its Ohio mills, remained publicly obstinate. On July 2 and 3, Sheet & Tube's district manager sent Townsend two letters, for the governor's eyes only, in which he explained the company's refusal to enter any agreement.[58] On July 3, Frank Purnell also sent a letter to Sheet & Tube's employees in the Calumet region urging them to demand "protection" to return to work. The next day, the company fully restarted its smaller plant on the Illinois side of the border.[59] That day, too, a committee of local churchmen as well as representatives of the company union at the Indiana Harbor mill telegrammed the governor demanding that Guardsmen be deployed.[60] The following days brought more petitions like these, along with company announcements that the mill would soon reopen, one way or another. But Townsend held fast, insisting that if the steel companies thought violence was truly impending, then they should continue to negotiate.[61]

Sheet & Tube's strategy in the Calumet placed union leaders in a now-familiar bind. They could promote forcible resistance to the reopening. But beyond undermining the leadership's bid for respectability and support of elites, the resulting violence would likely guarantee the deployment of Guardsmen, who would eventually reopen the mills themselves. And while the threat of violence might spur a settlement, a major incident would probably foreclose any agreement. In the end, SWOC leaders demurred. After warning repeatedly about the certainty of violence, even a "bloodbath," they acquiesced to the reopening when the hour arrived.[62]

On the evening of July 12, crowds gathered near Sheet & Tube's Indiana Harbor plant to celebrate news that the plant was about to reopen under an agreement between the company and the SWOC. The next day, thousands of workers streamed into the plant under the protection of railroad police and company guards.[63] But the company denied there had been any settlement. Indeed, it posted signs at the gates that read, "Notice[:] We have not made any agreement or contract with any official person or organization[.] This plant is open for work on the conditions which existed when work was stopped on May 26th 1937."[64]

However, there is more to the story. Months after the strike ended, the SWOC published in the records from its first convention a letter from Townsend, dated July 10, 1937, and addressed to Van Bittner, which appeared to confirm Sheet & Tube's agreement to a deal similar to the one agreed to by Inland. About two years after the strike, the union republished the letter along with a note from Bittner to the governor, dated the same day, which indicated the union's endorsement of the proposal.[65] Although these documents were annotated to suggest that an enforceable agreement was therefore in place, the more obvious purpose in publishing them was to deny that the union had capitulated and to prove the company's bad faith. Ultimately, it seems the letter was an artifact of Sheet & Tube's use of the negotiations as a hedge against unfavorable state intervention and to buy time to implement its reopening plan.

In early August, the SWOC formally called off the strike at all the companies except Republic. As of October, as many as 12,850 Republic workers remained out on strike; in Warren and Niles, hundreds would picket into the spring. But these workers faced exhaustion and a rapidly worsening economy, and Republic made clear that if they did not return to work within a certain number of days after the mills reopened, they would lose their jobs.[66] Around 8,000 workers either defied this threat or reported for work and were turned away because of their role in the union or the strike. Later, when smaller numbers of holdouts applied for reinstatement after the deadlines, they were also refused reemployment. Despite their bids for reinstatement, many of these men insisted they were still out on strike—or locked out—through the end of 1937 and into 1938. There were also continued picketing and scattered violence, including an incident at Republic's Niles plant in the early morning of September 29, when four carloads of men descended on a picket post, smashed the picket shanty, and overturned a picketer's automobile.[67] But while picketing gave proof of the unionists' determination, it did little to bother the operation of Little Steel's plants.[68] The strike was broken.

PART III

The Aftermath

The anthem learned by the steel is:
Do this or go hungry.

CARL SANDBURG
Smoke and Steel (1920)

A Steel Strike Is Not a Picnic

THE ANATOMY OF FAILURE

The Little Steel Strike is rightly remembered as a model display of the effective use of company-sponsored repression to break a strike. Even today, the SWOC's battle with Little Steel stands as the deadliest strike in America since the 1920s.[1] But to a far greater degree than expressed in conventional accounts of the strike, including the works of Irving Bernstein and Walter Galenson and the reports of the La Follette Committee, the companies' victory was based not only on repression but on the success with which they integrated violence and its effects with maneuverings in the fields of politics, law, and public relations, all while drawing on their overwhelming economic power. These advantages were abetted by shortcomings in the way the strike was conducted by the SWOC, as well as by the actions of radical organizers and militant rank and filers, whose more confrontational tactics, unaccompanied by a workable alternative strategy, also played into the companies' strengths.

Although evident in the course of the strike itself, this assessment of the conflict draws additional support from a postmortem that uncovers the strike's immediate costs, including the remarkable number of deaths, injuries, and arrests that resulted, as well as the considerable financial expenses incurred by both sides. Equally useful in understanding why the companies prevailed are closer reflections on the everyday struggles that workers endured during the strike, on the way unionists organized and conducted the strike, and on relations between SWOC leaders and radicals through the course of the conflict.

At least sixteen people were killed as a direct result of the strike. All were men and all were strikers or union sympathizers. Fourteen victims were shot to death: ten in the incident on Memorial Day in South Chicago; two in the Stop 5 Riot in Youngstown; and two more on July 11 outside of Republic's Massillon Works. There was also the death of John Orecny, the picketer run over on July 26 in Cleveland. The sixteenth victim was a Greek immigrant named George Mike, thirty-nine years old, who died a day after being struck in the head by a deputy sheriff's tear gas canister on June 28 in Beaver Falls, Pennsylvania, during a scuffle that occurred when company executives and loyal employees penetrated a picket line at a Union Drawn Steel (Republic) plant. A disabled veteran and union man from the Aliquippa area, Mike was in Beaver Falls that day to sell tickets to a CIO dance. Although authorities denied that the deputy had fired intentionally at Mike, there is no question that the canister killed him.[2] As we have seen, the death of Crisanto Lopez, who died in the mêlée at Canton on June 30, was likely caused by National Guardsmen; and that of Loggin Drosz, the striker who succumbed a week after the Massillon riot, may also have been caused by the strike.[3]

Actually, the strike claimed at least one other life. In December 1947, a former striker named John Voida, fifty-nine, was shot and killed in a bar near Republic's Massillon Works by Zaki Filip, fifty-eight, another Republic employee who had remained loyal to the company during the strike. The killing was the culmination of a series of nasty arguments between the men about the strike.[4] Who can say if this is the only time that rage and resentments generated during the strike later exploded in lethal violence, years after the plants reopened, and that no other workers' lives were cut short by the traumas they endured?

How many people were injured in the strike is even less certain than the death toll. The only accounting was conducted by La Follette Committee investigators, who identified 323 significant, nonfatal injuries. Of these, 58 involved gunshot wounds and 10 entailed serious and possibly permanent injuries. Only 40 of those injured were police, of whom none was permanently disabled. The committee reported no injuries among company loyalists, although it is obvious that many were hurt in fistfights and other clashes. In fact, the committee's tally surely undercounts all categories of nonfatal casualties, as the committee made no effort to count injuries sustained around Warren and Monroe, where dozens of people were hurt, and its

FIGURE 26. Demonstrators injured in the Memorial Day Massacre, held in jail for three days, are finally brought before a judge, June 2, 1937. Bond was set at $500 per defendant. © 1937, Corbis.

tabulation was largely limited to cases involving hospital visits.[5] Union people, especially, refrained from seeking medical help, fearing arrest. Hospital records from across the strike zone reveal that when people did seek medical help, they often attempted to conceal their identity, the cause of their injury, or the nature of their connection to the strike; or they left in haste.[6] Given these factors, and the intensity and scale of the conflict, a truly accurate accounting of all nontrivial injuries might well run into the thousands.

Union people also bore the brunt of arrests. Testifying before a U.S. Senate committee in 1939, Lee Pressman estimated that some 2,000 strikers and sympathizes had been arrested during the strike. Of these, he said, over 900 were ultimately charged with "offenses of one kind or another, ranging from disorderly conduct to kidnapping."[7] Although higher than estimates Pressman gave right after the strike, these figures are consistent with records provided to the La Follette Committee by local courts and police. In the immediate Youngstown area alone, authorities recorded nearly 400 strike-related arrests during the first month of the strike; and as the mills reopened, a similar number of strikers and supporters were arrested. As was typical throughout the strike, most charges involved trespass, disorderly conduct, simple assault, inciting to riot, damaging property, carrying concealed weapons, and suspicion. Courts in Warren and surrounding Trumbull County actually disposed of almost 60 strike-related criminal cases, suggesting that many times this number were arrested and released without being formally charged. In Canton there were well over 200 documented strike-related arrests. Following the July 11 killings in Massillon, there were about 165 arrests; and around 100 unionists were arrested in Chicago in the days surrounding the Memorial Day Massacre. In Johnstown and nearby jurisdictions, there were at least 63 strike-related arrests.[8] According to Pressman, the amount of bail the union paid during the strike exceeded $250,000.[9]

The circumstances of these arrests reflect the nature of the struggle as a grinding contest punctuated by spectacular episodes. For instance, picketers at Republic's plant in Buffalo, where things were relatively quiet, were repeatedly arrested in small numbers following run-of-the-mill conflicts with police or company men.[10] Other arrests were more dramatic, as in the aftermath of the Memorial Day Massacre, the Stop 5 Riot, and the July 11 riot in Massillon. And many arrests were made in connection with efforts to reopen the mills. On June 10, police in Youngstown seized over a dozen strikers after resorting to gas to force a supply of food through a line of several hundred picketers at a Republic gate. In the last part of June in Canton, Guardsmen arrested at least 75 picketers for blocking access to Republic's mills.[11] And then from June 30 through July 9, troops in Canton arrested at least 164 people, most without formal charges or access to legal counsel.[12] On June 30 alone, Canton city police arrested 103 people on disorderly conduct charges.[13] On some occasions, large groups of unionists were arrested preemptively, as in Youngstown on June 22, when police seized 150 union supporters to prevent their joining the picket lines.[14]

Local union officials, organizers, and picket captains were singled out for arrest. Almost every prominent organizer in the Youngstown area was arrested in June, including Fred Fortunato, John Steuben, and Robert Burke.[15] Burke's experience stands out. After Burke was arrested on June 9 on the dubious charge of shooting a heckler, the sheriff gave some indication of the nature of the case against him when he declared that Burke faced no specific charges, only being "mixed up in all the trouble"—before later charging him with the shooting. Afterward, Burke was also charged with inciting a riot and criminal syndicalism. In October, he was convicted on the riot charge and sentenced to a fine plus a short jail term, which was suspended.[16]

Fortunato and Steuben faced various charges of rioting, interfering with (sabotaging) railroad property, and in Steuben's case, criminal syndicalism. Steuben's trial in October before a packed courtroom apparently adduced more evidence of his peaceful purposes than any intention to wreck railroad tracks. Nevertheless, he was convicted and sentenced the same as Burke.[17]

Youngstown was not the only place where police focused on leaders and organizers. Chicago police hunted down union leaders after the Memorial Day Massacre. Once company supporters established control over the local police in Massillon, lodge president Joe Morton was arrested at least twice before the July 11 Riot and then again afterward.[18] On July 26, in Cumberland, police arrested several CIO organizers at the N&G Taylor mill, under an ordinance—adopted by the city council in compliance with threats from Republic and the chamber of commerce that the mill would otherwise be closed—that limited the number of picketers to six, required them to remain in constant motion, and required that they be employees of the place picketed.[19]

The companies and their allies obtained numerous judicial injunctions throughout the strike zone that limited picketing and facilitated entry of loyal employees into the plants.[20] The companies were also the beneficiaries of proclamations against picketing promulgated by sheriffs or other local executive officials, often (but not always) in supposed compliance with court orders limiting picketing.[21] While most of these measures regulated the size and conduct of the picket lines, some were even more specific. In addition to ordering picketers to keep moving, Buffalo police banned them from picketing the homes of loyal employees.[22] Throughout northeast Ohio, authorities required picket captains to identify picketers in advance and mandated that picketers carry proof of identity, and they arrested scores of workers for violating these strictures.[23]

Occasionally, CIO lawyers convinced courts to void injunctions and proclamations on grounds that they violated picketers' constitutional rights.[24] In Stark County, Ohio, the union convinced the same judge whose injunctions had earlier limited the size and conduct of its picket lines to enjoin Sheriff Nist and other local police from barring all picketing, as they later did—although not until the strike was effectively broken there.[25] In nearby Trumbull County, union lawyers frustrated Republic's bid for an antipicketing injunction when they convinced the court to order Republic to produce records showing the company's expenditures for weapons and espionage services. Although it barred coercion and limited the size of picket detachments, the injunction eventually issued by the court was judicious in tone; it validated the strikers' right to picket and enjoined the company from sponsoring violence against the picketers.[26] However, neither in Trumbull County nor anywhere else did unionists effectively challenge the authority of local judges to limit the size and conduct of pickets. The strike concluded amid lingering uncertainty on how state and federal law governed the question.

Quite a few unionists ended up facing serious felony charges. Dozens of demonstrators who survived the Memorial Day Massacre (and, initially, some who did not) faced felony conspiracy charges that could have resulted in prison sentences.[27] Probably they would have been prosecuted on these charges had not the La Follette Committee's investigation and protests of union people cast light on the authorities' conduct. On December 20, 1937, about sixty of the demonstrators pleaded guilty to unlawful assembly and were assessed token fines by a judge who lectured them on the perils of radicalism.[28]

Thirteen people, including Gus Hall, were formally charged with crimes related to possessing or transporting explosives in the Warren area. Nine, including Hall, pleaded guilty to lesser charges and received fines and probation; the other four were convicted and sentenced to terms of one to twenty years in prison.[29] In Cleveland, four other unionists were convicted on charges related to possessing a bomb and also sentenced to one to twenty years.[30] A total of nine SWOC members and supporters were convicted on federal charges of obstructing the mail and several were imprisoned. Several union men were also arrested and charged with attempted murder for shooting at Republic's food planes; however, it appears they were never prosecuted on these charges.[31]

In general, authorities were less aggressive in prosecuting unionists than they were in arresting them in the first place. The cases were often dropped and, if not, the sentences imposed were typically relatively light. This is consistent with the view that the primary purpose of the arrests was to harass strikers and sympathizers and to move them off the streets, rather than to go through the costly, time-consuming, and uncertain process of vindicating the law's punitive aspirations.[32] Lee Pressman claimed that there would have been many more prosecutions in Ohio had the union not acceded to a practice by which local authorities ransomed arrested unionists for set fees.[33]

Nowhere were serious charges pressed against police or company men. On occasion, company police were arrested by local police after picket line scuffles or other capers, but the charges were invariably dismissed. On a few other occasions, loyal employees were arrested as well. For example, the men who

FIGURE 27. Mug shot of Communist organizer Gus Hall after his surrender to authorities in Warren, Ohio, on charges related to sabotage, July 1, 1937. Courtesy of the Youngstown Historical Center of Industry and Labor.

stabbed Mike Kelly in the Cleveland CIO office in early August were charged with assault.[34] Authorities in Cleveland prosecuted a fair few Republic men for assaults and gun crimes related to the strike.[35] But the only nonunionist to face a very serious charge stemming from the strike was Fritz Swanson, who ran down the picketer at the Corrigan-McKinney Works in Cleveland. Swanson was charged with manslaughter, but the charge was later dropped.[36]

The one thing the steel companies did pay for their conduct was money. The La Follette Committee figured that an incomplete accounting of the cost of the strike—limited to the direct, calculable expenses of Republic and Sheet & Tube; the Pennsylvania Railroad and the Ohio National Guard; Mahoning, Stark, and Trumbull Counties in Ohio, and the cities within those counties; as well as Monroe, Michigan—totaled over $4 million. Republic and Sheet & Tube alone expended $1,950,000 and $1,593,000, respectively. Much of this went toward police services. The La Follette Committee estimated that during the strike in Ohio, Republic and Sheet & Tube employed over two thousand private guards. Records from Republic showed that from May through September 1937, it spent nearly $375,000 on "patrol duty," of which $232,263 was spent in June alone. In November, by comparison, with the strike essentially over, the company spent only $200 on such functions. Sheet & Tube's strike-related expenses on "police and watchmen" were just as impressive: $319,160.[37]

The companies' bottom lines were also affected.[38] Bethlehem claimed to have incurred $1.2 million in costs related to the strike but did not elaborate on their nature; and Inland said that the strike "adversely affected" earnings, but also did not elaborate.[39] Sheet & Tube allowed that it "lost substantial potential profits" because of the strike, without saying what this entailed.[40] In its annual report for 1937, Republic made no specific mention of strike-related expenses. However, in an internal memorandum, Republic confessed some reduction in income per share—although quite modest compared to what happened to company income during the recession that set in in the summer of 1937.[41] There was also some evidence that manufacturing consumers shifted orders to other companies during the strike.[42] In addition, as we will see in the next chapter, several years after the strike Republic and Sheet & Tube were required by the NLRB to compensate workers who were unlawfully kept from their jobs after the strike. Republic paid about $1.5 million for this purpose; Sheet & Tube, $170,000. In aggregate, all these costs were considerable—in total, Republic alone incurred about $4 million in expenses. But these costs were nowhere near enough to throw the companies into crisis, let alone break them: Republic reported a net profit of over $9 million in 1937; Inland and Sheet & Tube both realized profits for the year in excess of $12 million; and Bethlehem made over $30 million.[43]

Republic also paid damages as a result of civil lawsuits filed by people injured in the strike. According to company records, injured strikers and the relatives of those killed filed over two hundred lawsuits. Most of these concerned the major riots in Cleveland, Massillon, Youngstown, and South Chicago; and virtually all named Tom Girdler and other officials as defendants along with Republic itself. One of the most notable—apparently the only one to go to a jury—was filed in Cleveland and charged the company with responsibility for the unrest there on July 26 and 27. The plaintiff in that case was awarded $20,000 in damages. However, it was not till 1944 that Ohio appellate courts upheld the verdict.[44] This delay was typical. It was not until 1944 or 1945 that most suits were finally settled. The 210 cases described in the company's files settled for a total of $322,885.26, an average of $1,537 per claim.[45]

Republic paid a total of $50,015.25 to the estates of fifteen men killed in the strike. Elizabeth Orecny collected $6,500 for the death of her husband,

John, the man run over in Cleveland; and the estates of Memorial Day victims Otis Jones, Kenneth Reed, and Joseph Rothmund each collected $5,000. But the estates of their fellow demonstrators Hilding Anderson and Earl Handley received only $1,500 and $1,000, respectively. Worst of all was the company's liability for the death of Fulgencio Calzada, shot dead at Massillon on the night of July 11, which cost Republic only $250. Katherine Nelson, who was partially paralyzed on Memorial Day received only $2,500; and Frank Stenken, whose injuries that day resulted in the amputation of his leg, received only $1,350. Some plaintiffs did fare considerably better. Harold Williams, whose skull was fractured in the beating he took from company officials as he tried to rally workers in the Niles plant as the strike began, was paid $12,500. Harry Harper, who lost an eye on Memorial Day, received $20,000. And Paul Castman, severely beaten by company men in Cleveland, five weeks before the strike, was also paid $20,000.[46] But these are definite exceptions.

Republic and its supporters attempted to turn the tables on the unionists. They filed lawsuits against the CIO, the SWOC, and their officers and supporters, seeking damages for union-sponsored violence.[47] The most remarkable of these was a $7,500,000 suit that Republic filed in May 1939 under federal antitrust laws. It charged the CIO, the SWOC, the AA, ten local lodges, John L. Lewis, Philip Murray, and virtually every other officer of these organizations, as well as seven hundred members from the lower ranks, with unlawful restraint of trade by using violence to force the company to close its plants during the strike.[48] Had this action succeeded, it could have resulted in every one of these people and organizations being held "jointly and severally" liable for the entire judgment. However, before the claim could go to trial, the legal theory on which it rested was rejected by the U.S. Supreme Court in a case involving a violent sit-down strike.[49] Still, the suit forced SWOC and CIO legal staffers to take frantic steps to plan a defense. CIO negotiators remained sufficiently worried about the prospect of renewed prosecution that they later got the company to agree, in settling strike-related claims, to forever foreswear any such suit.[50]

HUNGRY FAMILIES AND THE BURDENS OF THE STRIKE

Writing some thirty years after the strike, David McDonald recalled the scene at a union kitchen in Canton, during the waning days of the struggle.

The place was "filled with people, mostly women, and they had a beaten, hopeless look about their eyes. They were waiting for food to arrive." What they got instead, recalled McDonald, was "a very short speech from headquarters, delivered in a voice that quavered," announcing that there was "no more money" and that the kitchen would have to be closed. McDonald suggested that "if an epitaph is ever written for the Little Steel strike, that would have to be it: 'We have no money and we'll have to close down the kitchens.' It was a simple as that."[51]

McDonald had a penchant for melodrama, but he was right. The union had established strike kitchens and commissaries throughout the strike zone. However, by late June organizers were having difficulties nearly everywhere keeping the strikers and their families housed and fed, even in the Chicago area, where the economy was diversified and strikers had the backing of many unions and social organizations.[52] It is unclear exactly how much money was paid in strike benefits, by the SWOC, by other unions, or by civic groups and fraternal organizations. A few months after the strike, McDonald reported that the SWOC had spent "hundreds of thousands of dollars . . . to purchase food and clothing for the strikers and their families and to defray the expenses of active pickets." On three occasions, the union appealed to steel workers at other companies to donate money for such proposes.[53] But this was not enough.

Homelessness and hunger were pitiless companions to the many worries that troubled strikers in this drawn-out struggle. Their leaders in and out of jail, their rights of speech and assembly curtailed, their organization and tactics tarred as criminal, strikers were hounded by constant threats of violence on the picket lines and, at home, by mounting domestic worries. Compounding strikers' troubles, many local governments either expressly disqualified strikers from receiving government relief benefits or simply did not have the resources to provide them.[54] Some sympathetic landlords, local merchants, and even banks and finance companies allowed the strikers grace on payments and, occasionally, even donated money. But grace was usually extended for only one month, which meant that by late June thousands of workers and their families were facing real trouble.[55] Nor were all businessmen so sympathetic. Some just wanted their money, some identified with the steel companies, and others blamed the strikers for a shutdown that was costing them a lot of business. There is also evidence that steel companies dissuaded some landlords and businesses from extending credit during the strike, the better to force workers back to work.[56] On the other hand,

<small>FIGURE 28.</small> Strikers and members of their families queue for food benefits at a union facility in Youngstown, Ohio, June 23, 1937. © 1937, Associated Press.

strikers in Warren, Ohio, at least, were accused of turning the tables: forcing local business people to make cash and in-kind contributions to the union.[57]

Interviewed in 1974, Youngstown striker Danny Thomas wanted "everybody to know that a steel strike, or any type of strike, is not a picnic." The struggle against Little Steel, he said, "started a period of misery." Thomas recalled that he was "more fortunate" than most strikers to live with his parents and was therefore able to turn down the food at UMW relief stations— "so somebody else could have it."[58] It is clear that many strikers were driven back to work by necessity.[59] And in this period—when few married women held regular jobs outside the home, families tended to be larger, and food and other necessities were relatively more expensive—married strikers were indeed especially vulnerable. This dynamic did not always weaken the resolve of family men, however. Youngstown organizer and striker, Augustine Izzo, who was single and in his midtwenties, marveled at the courage of strikers who put themselves and their families "on the line." Indeed, Izzo recalled that "we had more older people fighting than we had younger ones."[60] In some cases the responsibilities of family life seemed to strengthen union support. Years after the strike, Chicago-area organizer George Patterson recalled, "The reason I got interested in the union was that I got married in the middle of that Depression, and then along came my son and I didn't have enough money to buy a bottle of milk."[61] Izzo's observation that married men fought hard jibes with the ages and marital status of the people who were killed or seriously injured during the strike. Of the twenty-three people killed or seriously injured in the Memorial Day Massacre who are identifiable as steel workers, eighteen were married and eight were at least forty years old. Likewise, the last plant to reopen (on August 12) was the N&G Taylor mill in Cumberland, whose workforce was supposed to be 95 percent married.[62] Such resolve is impressive. But in the end, misery loomed over all.

A FLAWED GAMBIT?

In early July, AFL president William Green delighted in the strike's failure, declaring it "ill-advised and untimely" and the CIO defeated in "its first major test."[63] Although motivated by contempt for the new federation and its founder, John L. Lewis, Green's judgment was perhaps more than half right. Despite all that was arrayed against it, the strike might conceivably have ended differently had it been better organized. For instance, it is possible that the SWOC would have been more successful if, instead of demanding company-wide recognition, it had demanded recognition only at those mills where it was better organized. Doing so may have concealed the SWOC's weaknesses at the less-organized mills and prevented those mills becoming showpieces in back-to-work propaganda. But counterfactual speculation cuts both ways, and it is also possible that such a strategy would have allowed the companies to better focus their resources, perhaps further isolating organizers and union supporters in the most repressive plants.

The contours of the strike were problematic in a different way. The strike closed Sheet & Tube and Inland for a month, but the bigger companies— Republic and especially Bethlehem—were only partially affected. Meanwhile, U.S. Steel and Jones & Laughlin, which accounted for about half of all production and where the union was already recognized, were not targeted at all. In this way, the union's effort proved both too small and too big. The strike was too small in that it was never able to reduce overall steel production enough to bring collateral pressures on the steel companies—total ingot production fell by only about 15 percent.[64] The strike was too big in that a campaign focused on only one company might have put it at a real competitive disadvantage and forced it to recognize the union, all at less expense and risk to the union and its members—a point that finds support in the union's successful campaign against Jones & Laughlin. Nevertheless, it bears recalling that the SWOC's leadership was not especially well positioned to shape the boundaries of the strike.

Although this, too, was largely beyond the leadership's control, the timing of the strike likewise proved inopportune. While a summer strike eased the hardships endured by the strikers, it coincided with a seasonal slack in the demand for steel.[65] The strike also began right at the start of the second major downturn of the Great Depression. The "Roosevelt Recession" had begun to set in as the strike began. New orders for steel were already in decline in May and by late summer demand for steel had fallen sharply.[66] In August, when thousands of Republic workers were still on strike, steel production was at 83 percent of capacity and unsold product was steadily accumulating; by November, production had fallen to 50 percent of capacity.[67] The rapidly slowing economy relieved pressure on the companies to reopen the mills. And had the main walkouts lasted longer, the recession alone would have doomed the strike.

Leftist commentators and rank and filers charged the CIO and SWOC leadership with undermining the strike by isolating themselves from the rank and file, by dictating strategy and tactics in an authoritarian way, and by suppressing the militancy of striking steel workers and their supporters in order to better court favor with New Deal politicians.[68] Workers in northeast Ohio demanded—unsuccessfully—that John L. Lewis appear in person to address such charges.[69] Had the leadership been more inspiring and less authoritarian, and had it better cultivated the support of teamsters, rubber workers, and other sympathetic union people, these critics argue, the strikers could have more successfully confronted the police and National Guard and prevented the mills from reopening.

Again, conjecture cuts both ways. A more confrontational strategy might well have increased the number of bloody clashes and further weakened the union without changing the ultimate outcome. Nevertheless, it is hard to see how more solidarity would have hurt the strike. And it seems clear that Murray and other union leaders misapprehended the function that police, the National Guard, and government officials would play in ending the strike; and that the strike leadership proved inept and uninspiring in the face of Little Steel's fierce and sophisticated attacks. Preoccupied, too, with dictating strategy and tactics and dissuading workers from pursing broader political concerns, the leadership was only partially successful in sustaining workers' morale, particularly at the crucial moments following the major riots, the entry of state police and the Guard, and the dramatic reopenings.[70] Indeed, SWOC leaders concerned themselves little with picketing and street-level protest, except, it seems, for the purpose of discouraging militancy—as when Murray eventually vetoed efforts by Gus Hall and others to quarantine Republic's mills at Warren and Niles and reined in local sympathy strikes there and in Youngstown.

For their part, CIO and SWOC leaders claimed that the strike was actually undermined by militancy, and especially by a Communist penchant for confrontation.[71] In some ways, the charge is certainly true. Although hardly the only authors of such tactics, Communists like Gus Hall supported violent tactics, like the sabotage campaign in northeast Ohio, as well as other militant measures that engendered and justified company-sponsored violence, undermined the SWOC's legitimacy, and facilitated intervention by government forces that broke the strike. Nevertheless, to rationalize defeat in these terms is problematic. For as we have also seen, militancy was often a response to provocations and outright assaults by the companies and their allies; and it invariably drew on workers' frustrations with Little Steel's ruthless intransigence, the companies' economic and political might, and the failure of the leadership's own program or the labor law to overcome these conditions. And, of course, for all their post hoc criticisms of the excesses of "hotheads" and "fire-eaters," CIO leaders like Murray and McDonald had no fundamental opposition to militancy as such, nor even to the supposed imprudence and recklessness of such actions. Rather, what they seemed to reject was the possibility that in the hands of radical organizers and rank and filers, these tactics portended intensification of the struggle with the steel companies and potential expansion into a broader contest between workers and capitalists that might not be resolved by the signing of collective bargaining agreements and the exercise of industrial statesmanship.

The role of local organizers and rank and filers in pushing for the strike has also been invoked to defend Murray and other CIO leaders from charges that they mismanaged the walkout. The idea is that Murray and other leaders were pressured to call the strike by the rank and file and also deceived by men from the lower ranks into thinking that the union commanded a greater level of support than was actually the case—which, ironically, is also essentially the justification that Girdler and company advanced to support Little Steel's refusal to treat with the union in the first place.[72] A variation of this larger theme was advanced by others, including journalist and CIO sympathizer Benjamin Stolberg, who claimed that "Stalinist" organizers like Gus Hall and Robert Burke, eager for a "chance for entrenchment," duped the SWOC leadership into calling the strike by providing them with inflated membership estimates.[73]

These charges are also problematic. For the strike was scarcely planned by anyone. And while it is true that the union would likely have prevailed had organizers enlisted vast support at every mill, even with the benefit of hindsight it is unclear how organizers could have reliably counted such support, let alone developed it in the first place, in the face of company repression. After all, the strike was provoked by such repression. Moreover, other successful CIO strikes in this period, including the Jones & Laughlin strike and automobile sit-down strikes, did not begin with the union already backed by overwhelming numbers of workers. In any case, when the strike began the SWOC probably enjoyed the substantial support of somewhere near half the workers at the struck mills. Given that thousands of others weakly supported the union or were undecided, this could have been enough to prevail had other factors unfolded differently.

It is also important to recall that by early May, Murray himself had gathered authorizations to strike from a number of prominent lodges and had begun publicly threatening the steel companies with a strike. As David McDonald's later confession regarding the union's inflation of enrollment numbers at U.S. Steel suggests, SWOC leaders were complicit in exaggerating the level of support for the union at the other companies. It is significant, too, that Murray called the strike without consulting John L. Lewis. Lewis, McDonald, and Lee Pressman all speculated that Murray did this to assert his independence from Lewis, who had marginalized him in negotiations with U.S. Steel.[74] If this is true, Murray may well have seen the strike itself as an opportunity to assert his ambitions. In any case, it seems that in the afterglow of the CIO's triumphs at General Motors and U.S. Steel, the *Jones & Laughlin* ruling, and other victories, Murray and his lieutenants did not fully appreciate the weakness of their position in Little Steel. Otherwise, maybe they would have actually opposed the strike in May, rather than claiming years later to have had misgivings.

In the course of criticizing the role of poor leadership in undermining the rank-and-file movement that preceded the birth of the SWOC, New Left scholar Staughton Lynd has also suggested that Lewis, Murray, and their colleagues in the CIO, SWOC, and UMW leadership, as well as Communist Party leaders, who uncritically embraced the CIO's overall program, all betrayed the strike's radical potential.[75] This thesis, which presumes that the workers themselves were poised for radicalism, and had been for several years prior to the creation of the SWOC, asserts a different kind of failure. It is at odds with the views of liberal historians Irving Bernstein, Walter Galenson, and others who have depicted the conservative evolution of steel unionism—which the strike both embodied and entrenched—as a natural and, from the standpoint of workers' interests, appropriate accommodation to prevailing social and economic conditions. It contradicts the work of John Bodnar and others who contend there was little appetite for radicalism among the rank and file. And it is inconsistent with James Rose's argument, based on his study of a U.S. Steel plant, that the rank and file alone was not strong enough to defeat the companies anyway.[76] And yet Lynd's thesis bears closer consideration.

Although a fair number of steel workers were avowedly revolutionary, the majority were certainly not affiliated with any radical leftist organizations. But this observation does not fully address whether the strikers were fundamentally amenable to radicalism or conservatism, not least because the question itself wrongly supposes that these affiliations are easily conceptualized and applied. In an essay on the origins of steel unionism, David Brody endorses Robert Brooks's observation that the rank-and-file leaders of the Little Steel Strike were indeed united around a coherent ideology: industrial unionism. Even if not a call to abolish wage labor and private property, this perspective was radical enough in the eyes of industrialists like Tom Girdler, Eugene Grace, and Frank Purnell. Perhaps even more apt is Brody's judgment that "for the great majority outside the activist ranks . . . either/or terms" simply do not apply.[77] Writing in 1935, journalist Harvey O'Connor observed in a similar vein that, among the diversity of political views evident in the ranks of the steel workers, there was an openness to both militant tactics and radical aims, born as much out of raw anger as any particular program. "When will there be an end to this goddamned system?" a worker asked him. Another avowed that "it'd be better to blow the whole god-damned mill to pieces than keep on this way, starving and wanting."[78] All of this goes to the essential truth of Rick Fantasia's injunction that class consciousness is best conceptualized, not abstractly, but by the way it expresses itself in moments of conflict.[79]

With this in mind, one can reflect on the strikers' accomplishments in ways that support Lynd's charge. In the face of extraordinary resistance, strikers shut down almost every plant struck, idling eighty thousand steel workers. In many locations, strike support remained very strong after it was plainly evident that the companies would not yield. Even when workers did return to the mills, this often said more about their material needs than their political commitments. And then there was the sympathy of other workers. Although never overwhelming in numbers, miners, rubber workers, steel workers from other companies, and various other workers descended on the mill towns by the thousands, to the point that interdicting them became a major concern for the companies and their allies in government. And this happened despite the ambivalence of the SWOC leadership. For all its disorganization and messiness, few strikes better highlight the spirit of worker solidarity that so flourished in the 1930s. On the racial front, an area of long-standing difficulty and further ambivalence on the part of the leadership, organizers made impressive gains, and workers remade their own views on the subject.[80] Notwithstanding the difficulties organizers encountered recruiting blacks, the strike certainly was not lost for lack of black participation. Indeed, for the first time, blacks played a crucial role in advancing steel unionism. It was an ugly accomplishment but an accomplishment nonetheless that blacks fought each other on the picket lines. Through all of this, strikers and sympathizers alike courageously defied both poverty and well-armed police, vigilantes, and Guardsmen, without any promise and little immediate prospect of practical gain. These actions reflect a kind of radicalism in some ways more profound and, frankly, more authentic than what can be found in membership cards, reading lists, and meeting records.

With more ambiguous implications for Lynd's thesis, the strike also demonstrated how unstable political commitments could be in the context of a bitter episode of class struggle. For example: in Monroe, where a small contingent of unionists engineered a dramatic walkout that garnered mass support and immediately shut Republic's plant, only to see their numbers reduced in a few days to a small, isolated minority, whom the company and its agents quickly routed; or in Massillon, where a spirit of solidarity and defiance endured well into July, only to be deflated by the July 11 killings and the rampage that followed; or in the strikers' views of radicals like Hall and Burke, which showed a definite contingency, responsive to the ebb and flow of the campaign as well as the overall results of these men's efforts. Workers' conceptions of the strike and the social order generally were in a state of conflict and flux, being shaped by the strike as much as they shaped the strike. Such was the nature of the strike as a fluid contest—a contest over the very ideals that the debate about whether steel workers were conservative or radical tends to misrepresent, portraying workers' beliefs as static features in their lives and experiences.

The steel workers certainty had the potential to advance a more ambitious program. However, in the end, as Lynd himself acknowledges, it is difficult to believe that the rank and file could have challenged Little Steel without some national organization. Unfortunately, the national organization they got, the SWOC, was stifling. For Murray and his acolytes, the strike presented legal and political action as effective alternatives to "direct action" in the battle to attain union representation and develop effective collective bargaining. For them, this course was obviously the better one. Not only were militancy and radicalism ideologically suspect and potentially uncontrollable; from the leadership's vantage, they seemed increasingly impractical. And of course there was the SWOC's single-largest victory that year, its contract with U.S. Steel, conspicuously achieved though backroom negotiations among elites. In Brody's words, this act of "industrial statesmanship" could not "have been more remote from the shop floor"—or the picket lines.[81]

THE PURGE OF COMMUNIST ORGANIZERS

Without the support of Communist organizers, the SWOC would have stood no chance against Little Steel and might even have failed to organize U.S. Steel and other firms. Nevertheless, before the strike was over, SWOC leaders were denouncing Communist influences in the labor movement and moving to purge the SWOC's own ranks of radicals. By early July, Communist organizers in the Youngstown area, including Hall, Burke, and Steuben, had been dismissed.[82] The SWOC leadership denied the purge, with its suggestions of the AFL's repudiation of William Z. Foster and others in 1920; and a few days later the Communist Party's general secretary reiterated party support for the CIO campaign.[83] Hall himself asserted that he had not been purged, albeit unconvincingly, as he and the others henceforth no longer worked with the union.[84] Communist organizers in the Chicago area, including Joe Weber, were soon pushed out, too.[85] In both regions, the immediate architects of these purges were local SWOC directors—John Mayo in the Youngstown area and a group led by Joe Germano and Nick Fontechhio in Chicago.[86] But surely Murray and other top leaders approved the moves.

The purges conspicuously accompanied vows to expel all members guilty of lawlessness during the conflict. And the purges were publicly justified by associating the Communists with strike-related crimes—which, although true enough in some cases, amounted to the union doing with its own people what its lawyers were then urging the NLRB to block the companies from doing. The purges also converged with broad cuts in staff instituted in the wake of the Little Steel Strike. As one student of union politics in this period points out, "While the leftists were laid off, right-wingers such as Joe Germano were kept on and promoted."[87] In some areas, party members were given the choice of resigning from the party or leaving the union. In general, they left the union. But in some places, including Chicago, they had to be forced out.[88] Nor were the purges always immediately successful. It was one thing to fire prominent, paid organizers like Hall and Burke, but another to root out unpaid shop floor leaders. At mills in the Calumet and northeast Ohio, a few Communists leaders held on into the 1940s, when many met another round of purges associated with mandates of the Taft-Hartley Act.[89]

Besides the usual human shortcomings and foibles, the Communists belonged to an organization that was opportunistic and frequently sacrificed the most basic of radical commitments to narrow party interests and dictates. As Lynd argues, this made them complicit, along with John L. Lewis and others, in the failure to effectively organize the rank-and-file upsurge that preceded the formation of the CIO and the SWOC. Indeed, the purge of Communist organizers was in many ways the culmination of the party's decision several years earlier to cast its lot with Lewis and company in the first place. Nevertheless, Communist organizers had performed well. Unlike in other CIO drives where party members alienated fellow unionists with unceasing party-line proselytizing, Communists in the steel drive were remarkably focused on basic organizing and engaged in little gratuitous political work. Moreover, the values they did bring to bear were generally universalist and constructive. Even in this, the Popular Front period, the Communists in steel were more disposed to bold and militant tactics that had the potential, at least, to put real pressure on the companies, even as these tactics fed the companies' political stratagems and propaganda campaigns. As the Communists' role in organizing general strikes and other solidary acts demonstrates, they embraced an ideology of industrial solidarity that transcended the narrow calculations and diffident social vision that otherwise defined steel unionism. For these reasons, organizers like Burke and Hall earned the respect of many workers with no particular affinity for the Communist program, and black workers, especially, long revered the Communists for their commitment to racial equality and social justice.[90]

But even if the men who were purged adhered to bolder tactics and a different social vision, like Communists elsewhere they remained captive to a party leadership not poised to support much deviation from the CIO's overall platform. Nor is it evident that the Communists themselves possessed a clear strategy for how to effectuate their vision. Militancy plus social vision does not equal a program, and the party had given up any real program of its own when it decided in 1934 to abandon its efforts to organize an independent union. Had the Communists remained in the SWOC, or had they been unrestrained, it is unlikely that their presence would have dramatically changed the course of steel unionism. In any event, given the union's failure on the picket lines and its subsequent turn to law and mainstream politics, these radicals became an encumbrance for a SWOC leadership already wary of their ideology and appeal among the rank and file.

THE SWOC IN DEFEAT AND CRISIS

Deeply in debt when the strike began, by the time the mills had begun to reopen, the SWOC's financial situation was desperate as it struggled to cover the rapidly mounting costs of legal expenses, publicity and travel, and material support for strikers and their families. By the time the strike ended in late summer, the SWOC had spent around $2.5 million organizing steel. This included $601,000 borrowed from the UMW and around $960,000 from the CIO. The union had also received about $1 million in in-kind donations from the UMW, including the UMW's payment of the salaries of dozens of SWOC staffers from Philip Murray on down.[91] And the SWOC had few other sources of funding. In the summer of 1936, initially poor organizing gains and weak dues collection convinced the leadership to virtually suspend collection of dues from enlistees until April 1937, when the

SWOC attained recognition at U.S. Steel and a number of smaller operators. Even then, the amounts collected were modest and actually diminished during the strike and the months that followed. In May, in the Calumet region, the union collected over $28,000 in dues from just over fifty thousand members. But by late summer, the SWOC was collecting only about $15,000 a month; by the following year, less than $10,000 a month. In the Cleveland area, where the SWOC counted 18,632 members, it only collected $3,615 in February 1938.[92] Meanwhile, neither the UMW nor the CIO itself was able or inclined to provide more funds. As David McDonald put it, "Our line of credit with the UMW had just run out."[93] Financial problems reigned for years. Not until 1941 was the SWOC able to establish a meaningful flow of dues, repay its debt to the UMW, and begin to operate as a self-sustaining organization.[94]

Faced with these conditions, the union curtailed operations. Full-time field-workers were reduced from 256 in July 1937 to 213 in November 1937, while part-time field-workers were reduced over the same period from 108 to 75; and many remaining staffers were put on reduced pay.[95] The union's distress is evident in a letter McDonald sent in September 1938 to the financial secretaries of the various SWOC lodges urging that they collect dues from unemployed men on government relief.[96] Chicago-area organizer Sam Evett bluntly described the effect of "financial trouble" in his district: "There was no money to pay the staff with. . . . We were down to eight staff-representatives for the whole Chicago-Calumet area."[97] When employment did pick up, the union established "dues pickets" at the gates of better-organized plants in order to collect sufficient funds.[98]

The strike left many workers ambivalent about steel unionism.[99] And in the strike's wake, membership plummeted. Although definitive numbers are elusive, a few decades after the strike, economic historian Barbara Newell was able to extrapolate membership levels in the Calumet from records on dues payment. She found that effective membership in the SWOC's District 31 peaked at around 32,000 in April and May 1937, before falling to around 21,000 in July and only 7,500 in December of that year. Membership declined further by the middle of 1938 before beginning to rise in 1939. Even then, by the end of 1939 effective membership was only about 21,000.[100] Further examination of these records reveals even deeper problems. The proportion of members at the Little Steel plants in the Calumet who paid their dues declined from 14 percent in August 1937, to 12 percent the following February, to 9 percent by July 1938—as nominal membership numbers remained roughly constant. Even as late as August 1939, two years after the strike, only just over half the roughly 14,000 members claimed at Little Steel plants in the area paid their dues.[101] Meanwhile, reformulated "independent" unions under the control of the companies sniped at the SWOC, accusing it of having squandered workers' pay in the failed strike. Under these circumstances, it seemed possible that the SWOC might not long survive its bruising battle with Little Steel.[102]

Kind of a Victory

NEW DEAL LABOR LAW ON TRIAL

In the archives of the Republic Steel Corporation is a remarkable document, dated August 4, 1941. A memorandum to the company's ten district managers authored by top company officials, it decrees that "there must be *no* Labor Board cases in the corporation arising from any unfair labor practices of any of our supervisory forces, for as good Americans we must all obey the laws of the land and the orders issued by the Supreme Court." The memorandum goes on to say that a "meeting of all supervisors should be held in each of our plants and these employes [sic] are to be told again that there must be no discrimination in any manner against any employe [sic] on account of his union affiliations." It notes that copies of the Wagner Act "were being sent to each plant to be distributed to all supervisors."[1]

Several years earlier, the SWOC had charged the Little Steel companies with numerous strike-related violations of the Wagner Act, including discriminatory firings and refusals to reinstate workers, antiunion violence, and failure to recognize the SWOC. The NLRB aggressively prosecuted these charges in the face of strident company resistance. Its eventual victories in these cases coincided with the decision by Republic and the other struck companies to behave like "good Americans"—to abide the labor law and, eventually, recognize the union and commence collective bargaining. The story of how the NLRB prosecuted Little Steel reveals both the value of the new regime of labor rights and, in this, its first major test after the Supreme Court's *Jones & Laughlin* decision, the regime's limitations as a means of effectuating labor rights.

A year after the end of the Little Steel Strike, Philip G. Phillips, the NLRB's regional director for Cincinnati, dispatched to the NLRB office in Washington, DC, a letter criticizing the timid way that an agency judge, a "trial examiner," was dealing with the labor board's case against ARMCO. Phillips advocated that the NLRB make "Little Steel realize that we are just a little bit bigger than they are."[2] The letter featured in 1940 congressional hearings aimed at undermining the NLRB and revising the Wagner Act, where it was presented as evidence of the agency's bullying of the Little Steel defendants.[3] The charge was unfounded. But Phillips's statement captures the aggressive way the board initially dealt with Little Steel, while the response it triggered also anticipates the price the agency would pay for this approach.

Although established in 1935, when the Little Steel Strike began the NLRB was only emerging as a functional institution. Until the *Jones & Laughlin* decision in April 1937, the NLRB's activities were hamstrung by numerous lawsuits challenging the constitutionality of the Wagner Act. But no sooner was the case decided than the NLRB encountered another wall of resistance: a campaign, orchestrated by Little Steel, to test the agency's authority and reform the new regime of labor law.[4] This contest between the NLRB and Little Steel was shaped by uncertainty surrounding the functions of the agency and the nature of the law it was charged with enforcing.

For the first twelve years after its creation, the NLRB was structured around a three-member board. The "board" in this narrow sense was charged with several functions: presiding over the agency's prosecution of violations of basic labor rights, or unfair labor practices; conducting union elections and other procedures for determining whether a union legally represented a group of workers; and adjudicating internal appeals of cases. In most instances, the first two functions were delegated to other offices within the agency; however, ultimate authority rested with the board proper. The agency also included a general counsel, whose main function was to prosecute unfair labor practice cases. However, the actual administration of unfair labor practices and representation issues usually fell to a corps of regional directors, like Phillips, and their staffs. Most NLRB cases were initially adjudicated, not by the board itself, but before the trial examiners.

The text of the Wagner Act offered surprisingly little instruction on exactly how the agency should carry out these functions amid the complex realities of industrial conflict. The statute's key substantive provisions—

Section 7 (outlining basic labor rights), Section 8 (defining unfair labor practices), and Section 9 (concerning union representation)—were fairly broadly worded and somewhat ambiguous; and, though thoughtfully drafted, the statute's procedural sections were very terse. These characteristics reflected the drafters' intention that the agency enjoy considerable flexibility in enforcing the statute. But in its early days, the Wagner Act's ambiguities gave rise to great contention and not a little trepidation.[5] Crucially, the law denied the agency the authority to initiate an unfair labor practice prosecution unless a written charge was first filed by a private party against the employer.[6]

The Little Steel companies' assertion that the law did not require that they enter written agreements with the union left the union's lawyers uncertain about how this position contravened the act, which contributed to the main charges against the companies being filed weeks into the strike and via a sequence of unusual and controversial proceedings. On June 1, CIO lawyer Lee Pressman and SWOC president Philip Murray telephoned the assistant general counsel for the NLRB's review section, Nathan "Nat" Witt, about the prospect of bringing strike-related charges against the companies. Witt, a leftist and friend of Pressman, flew to Pittsburgh the next day to confer on how to proceed. Witt, Pressman, and Murray developed an argument by which the refusal to sign a contract as well as Little Steel's overall conduct could be presented as violations of the act, and the trio agreed that Witt would expedite the cases.[7] As the next chapter recounts, when brought to light a few years later, these maneuvers grounded an attack on the NLRB and the Wagner Act by conservative congressmen. However, at the time they represented a reasonable attempt to compel Little Steel's adherence to the law.

These dealings between Witt, Pressman, and Murray concerned the case against Inland, which provided the best occasion to assert that refusal to sign written contracts violated the labor law. The argument rested on the assumption that Inland had a duty under the Wagner Act to engage in collective bargaining in the first place; and this, according to the law, depended on the union having the support of a majority of the employees. These conditions were easiest to demonstrate at Inland, where strike support was strong and organizers claimed to have enlisted about 85 percent of the workers.[8]

Hearings in the NLRB case against Inland commenced in Chicago on June 28, 1937, only to be disrupted several times when company lawyers walked out in a huff over relatively trivial procedural objections.[9] The hearings eventually resumed. And by the time they closed in October, the board had marshaled considerable evidence to demonstrate majority support for the SWOC and to back the union's charge that Inland maintained an illegal company union. This left the question of signed contracts. The NLRB conceded that the duty to bargain in good faith imposed by Section 8(5) of the Wagner Act did not require that the parties necessarily reach any contract, as it left this to be decided by the relative bargaining strength of the employer and union. But the board distinguished this issue from whether a party otherwise willing to agree on a contract could withhold signature or refuse to commit the agreement to writing. In light of Inland's professed adherence to the essential terms of the Carnegie-Illinois contract, and the fact that signed contracts were customary in labor relations, the board concluded that Inland's position could only be interpreted as an attempt to circumvent the Wagner Act. On November 12, 1938, the board therefore ordered the company to dismantle its ERP; cease and desist from otherwise interfering with its workers' rights under the labor law; and, above all, begin bargaining in good faith with the SWOC and commit to a written and signed contract for any agreement reached by this process.[10] Although the board's decision was set aside two years later by the Seventh Circuit Court of Appeals, in 1941 the Supreme Court resolved the underlying issue of signed and written contracts in the agency's favor.[11]

The NLRB's *Inland Steel* decision did not deal at all with questions surrounding company-sponsored violence, discriminatory discharges, mass refusals to reinstate strikers, and other strong-arm tactics, as Inland was not much involved in such conduct. However, these issues were central to the board's main case against Republic, concerning its Ohio plants. On July 16, 1937, the board issued a formal complaint against the company, denoting its decision to prosecute the charges brought by the CIO. Hearings were held between July 21 and September 27, first before the board itself in Washington, DC, and then before a trial examiner in Canton, Cleveland, and Youngstown in August and September.[12] In all, the agency took testimony from over two hundred witnesses. Even these proceedings occurred in the shadow of company repression, as the NLRB was compelled to hide some witnesses amid rumors that company agents might find and kill them.[13]

This investigation was followed by months of procedural wrangling, marked by the board's issuance of an order on April 8, 1938, which it ultimately withdrew, followed by Republic's unsuccessful appeal to the Supreme Court on the propriety of this move and then oral arguments before the

FIGURE 29. Luther Day (right), lawyer for Republic Steel; Stanley Switter, chief of police in Massillon, Ohio (center); and Edwin Smith, one of three members of the NLRB, examine maps during an NLRB hearing in Washington, DC, late July 1937. Library of Congress, Prints and Photographs Division, photograph by Harris & Ewing, LC-H22-D-1981.

board itself.[14] At last, on October 18, 1938 the board issued a final order in which it found Republic guilty of a vast array of unfair labor practices, including using discriminatory discharges and threats of discharge to undermine the organizing campaign; maintaining company unions; locking out workers at the Canton and Massillon mills prior to the strike in retaliation for their support for the SWOC; threatening to close mills in retaliation for organizing; using false or inflammatory propaganda to slander the union and miscast its aims; fortifying its plants and building up its police forces for the purpose of intimidating workers not to organize or strike; using beatings, gunplay, and physical threats against its workers, with the intent to deny the right to organize and strike; employing force and threats of job loss to coerce workers to subscribe to back-to-work movements; and refusing to reinstate workers who supported the strike when they attempted to return to work. Although the board's decision ignored the murkier episodes of lethal violence at Youngstown, Cleveland, and Canton, it devoted extensive attention to the July 11 riot at Massillon and determined that Republic bore responsibility for the killings there.[15]

Backed by several thousand pages of transcripts of witness testimony and documents, and by straightforward readings of the law, these findings were incontrovertible. The only real question concerned how far the board would go in trying to remedy Republic's transgressions. An important factor was the board's determination that the strike was "provoked" by Republic's violations of the law. This conclusion allowed the board to focus discussion of remedies on restoration of prestrike conditions while nullifying the board's policy whereby strikers who walked out for economic reasons (rather than to protest violations of the labor law) could be permanently replaced and lose their right to reinstatement. And yet Republic could not be said to have provoked the strike simply by refusing to bargain with the union or sign a contract, when the union had not yet demonstrated that it enjoyed the support of a majority of Republic's workers.[16] Casting the strike as the result of a broader array of unlawful layoffs, threats, and violence resolved this issue, not only for the board but, importantly, for the Third Circuit Court of Appeals. In rejecting the company's appeal of the NLRB order, the court endorsed the board's reasoning that even if the strike had been motivated by Republic's unwillingness to sign a contract, the pursuit of a contract was an extension of the union's struggle against the company's campaign of unfair labor practices.[17]

In addition to ordering Republic to cease and desist from its unlawful conduct, and to dismantle its company unions, the board's order required the company to "repair the damage" its actions had done to the workers' rights. In the board's determination, the "most effective method" for doing so was "to reinstate to their former positions those employees who have gone out on strike as a consequence of the respondent's unlawful conduct."[18] The reinstated workers would also be entitled to back-pay from Republic. Even before the board attempted to administer these findings, it was clear that these remedies would apply to more than five thousand workers in Ohio alone.[19]

The process of administering the remedies would prove drawn out and complicated. In several dozen instances, the board identified specific workers who had been discriminated against and was able to establish definite parameters for calculating reinstatement and back-pay. Its determination that Republic was liable for the May 1937 lockouts at Canton and Massillon had the same effect for workers involved in those affairs. However, most of the workers that the board's decision deemed eligible for these remedies were not so well identified and fell into a different category. These were strikers who had asked for their jobs back after the strike, either in the summer of 1937 or, at Warren and Niles, in the spring of 1938, but were denied reinstatement en masse.[20]

The board's orders of April 8 and October 18 both made clear that, in the several dozen cases where specific evidence of discrimination had been adduced, as well as in the lockout cases, reinstatement and back-pay would be calculated based on when those workers were discharged, locked out, or otherwise denied reentry to their jobs. However, for those workers whose rights were violated but did not fall into these categories, a less favorable procedure would apply. The board ordered Republic to offer them reinstatement and back-pay, provided, first, that any back-pay would accrue only from the time, beginning *after* the board's order, that they had again been denied reinstatement; second, that the company would then be granted five days to reinstate applicants without incurring *any* back-pay liability; and third, that any workers whom the company had offered reinstatement to prior to the board's order would also not receive any back-pay. Workers whose positions had been eliminated in the interim were to be put on a preferential hiring list. And all workers who had been unlawfully fired or denied reinstatement were entitled to compensation for vacation time on account of the company's decision to deprive all of them, regardless of whether they had since been reinstated, of the service credits necessary to qualify for this benefit.[21]

When the board issued its April 8 order, the union immediately distributed to the sixty-five hundred Republic workers who were still on strike in Ohio printed applications for reinstatement, with instructions to complete and send them by registered mail to Republic. Most workers mailed the forms only to have the company return them, signaling that it had no intention to take the men back. When the board issued its revised order on October 18, the union and its members repeated this procedure.[22] This time, Republic promptly reinstated over 80 percent of applicants within the five days specified in the board's order. These workers were eligible for vacation pay, albeit not for 1937. But they could receive no back-pay at all, even though Republic had unlawfully denied them their jobs. When SWOC staff objected to this outcome, the board dismissed the complaint, saying it did not have the resources to pursue a more comprehensive remedy.[23]

These rules for determining reinstatement and back-pay initially applied only to Republic's Ohio plants, and not those in the Calumet, Buffalo, and

FIGURE 30. Republic Steel strikers in Cleveland, Ohio, receive forms with which to apply for reinstatement and back-pay, April 14, 1938. © 1938, Corbis.

Monroe. However, the SWOC subsequently filed charges against the company for its actions at these plants, and formal complaints were issued beginning in early 1940. These cases as well as the litigation of the board's Ohio case, which was on appeal, were then overtaken that fall by the parties' decision to settle all pending cases. Republic and the SWOC negotiated the terms of these settlements in October and November 1940, eventually developing a framework for resolving issues involving reinstatement and back-pay, as well as vacation and seniority, at all these plants, based on the precepts laid out in the board's October 18 order in the Ohio case. The resulting stipulations, as these settlements were called, were subsequently approved by the board.[24]

For several years, a union team built around attorney Lee Pressman and former organizer Meyer Bernstein worked with Republic's lawyers and its employment and labor staff to administer the stipulations. Adjustments had to be made for claimants whose jobs had been eliminated as a result of the recession or automation. Then there were workers the company was not obliged to reinstate or compensate because they were unavailable to resume their old jobs, had refused employment, or were fired for good cause. Deductions also had to be made for money received during the back-pay period from relief agencies or Social Security. All of this had to be figured with respect to the nearly three thousand individual reinstatement cases from all of Republic's plants that remained unresolved, as well as almost twelve hundred lockout cases from Canton and Massillon. In negotiating this process, the union's staff was aided first by "knowledgeable" individual workers and then, later, by "NLRB committees" of workers chosen at each of the affected plants.[25]

It was during this time, between early 1939 and mid-1941, that Republic ceased most active discrimination against SWOC workers. However, the company was not yet resigned to recognizing and bargaining with the union. That would come later in 1941, via further stipulation. But Republic gradually rehired nearly all the workers it had initially refused to reinstate in the wake of the board's October order, leaving back-pay as the main concern for those administering the stipulations. As we shall see in the next chapter, these moves by Republic were very much abetted by the war, which changed the landscape of labor relations.

It has long been unclear how much money Republic paid in remedies, with leading authorities offering divergent numbers. After the board's initial order against Republic, the SWOC forecast that the back-pay awards from Ohio alone might reach $5 million, and rumors had the company poised to pay as much as $7.5 million.[26] A document in the union's archived records, which appears to have been drafted after the basic formula had been decided, concluded that net back-pay for Republic would total $2,304,913.46.[27] Later, when the checks were finally being mailed in November 1941, the union's *Steel Labor* forecast that workers would get around $1.5 million, on top of $600,000 in vacation pay, paid out the previous December.[28] Former USW president and SWOC secretary-treasurer David McDonald later cited a total of $500,000 paid by Republic, as does one of the union's postwar hagiographies.[29] CIO scholar Walter Galenson set the company's total back-pay liability at $2 million, while Robert Zieger said the cases "produced back pay awards totaling millions of dollars."[30]

In fact, Republic paid a total of $1,501,413.72, of which $875,609.13 was actual back-pay. The remainder, $625,804.59, was vacation pay. And the back-pay figure apparently included some money separately paid to men whose departments had been eliminated (especially at Warren, Niles, Canton, and Monroe) and some who, because unfairly deprived of seniority, had been prematurely laid off during the slack period. In accordance with the board's final order in the Ohio case and the stipulations agreed to in its wake, a total of some 7,733 Republic employees were reinstated—not counting several thousand holdouts whom the company voluntarily reinstated *prior* to the board's October 18 order. Of the 7,733, about 2,900 received some form of back-pay. Another 1,189 awards of lockout pay were made—some to people who also received back-pay—totaling $30,370.09. Twenty-four men for whom there was specific proof of discrimination also got back-pay, totaling $20,066.28.[31]

Not all Republic plants were covered by the October 18 order and the stipulations based on it. Republic's Union Drawn Steel subsidiary in Beaver Falls was covered by a separate board order that mandated back-pay and reinstatement for a handful of workers.[32] However, workers at Republic's N&G Taylor plant, who held out longer than most, got neither back-pay nor their jobs back, as the company closed the plant and the board dismissed their case.[33] Meanwhile, after extensive hearings the board also found Bethlehem guilty of unfair labor practices at a number of its plants, including the Cambria mill in Johnstown, and ordered it to stop supporting its ERPs and to cease and desist from coercing its employees. But the board dismissed the charges related to Bethlehem's use of armed vigilante groups during the strike.[34] The board's case against Bethlehem concluded without ordering the company to make reinstatement or back-pay, as had its earlier case against Inland.

The board's litigation against Sheet & Tube was resolved by another negotiated settlement, which the parties began to work on around the same time that negotiations with Republic commenced. The remedies in the Sheet & Tube case were easier to administer, because they involved only three hundred claims and because the parties specifically identified the workers entitled to back-pay *and* prescribed the amount to be paid: $170,000.[35] The NLRB's case against Sheet & Tube also differed from that against Republic in that it involved a much higher proportion of claims of discriminatory layoffs and discharges, as opposed to mass refusal-to-reinstate claims. Accordingly, the union's records in the Sheet & Tube case document the program of discrimination and harassment that followed in the wake of the strike, as well as the pretexts the company used to justify its actions. Some men who were fired attested they were "merely told [they] no longer had a job," that they were "over weight," or that a younger man had been hired in their place; or they were asked why they had not reported for work earlier—meaning, during the strike. Others were let go because they were on the picket lines, wore union buttons, or refused to renounce the CIO. While some firings rested on grounds that the worker had participated in violent or otherwise criminal conduct during the strike, many of these incidents were minor, if they could be substantiated at all.[36]

NLRB REMEDIES AND THE VALUE OF THE WAGNER ACT

Were it not for the NLRB prosecution of the Wagner Act, most all strikers who were effectively fired by the companies would have lost their jobs permanently, and none of these men would have received any payment. Nor would the companies have been compelled to recognize and bargain with the union. The board's Little Steel cases may be the most outstanding example of the agency's effort to enforce the labor law against large, powerful, and intransigent employers; and these cases' role in advancing labor rights is significant. However, the board's prosecutions of Little Steel also reveal crucial shortcomings in the Wagner Act and the agency's power to enforce labor rights.

One outstanding weakness is the size of the remedies paid out by the companies. Bethlehem and Inland paid nothing, not because they had abided the law, but because the act allowed for monetary damages only to "make whole" workers who had suffered specific economic injury as a result of the company's violation of their labor rights. Moreover, the amounts that Republic and Sheet & Tube paid were, relatively speaking, quite small. The $170,000 paid by Sheet & Tube in the spring of 1941 comes out to an average of about $660 per recipient, while the company made $12 million in profits in 1937 and $16 million in 1941.[37] At Republic, over 3,000 workers who had been unlawfully denied reinstatement collected no back-pay (although some got vacation compensation). The 2,900 or so who did received, on average, about $300. And there were great disparities in how this was allocated. Nearly half the back-pay money went to the workers at the South Chicago Works, where $391,078.81 was split among 216 men, including one who got the largest payment of all—more than $6,000. On the other hand, 660 workers at the Canton complex received only $29,182.56; and 436 men who battled the company at Warren and Niles and picketed well after all others had given up divided $21,423.94—in both cases not even $50 per man.[38] Although the $1.5 million that Republic paid in back-pay and vacation pay remains among the largest remedial awards ever enforced under the labor law, the figure represents only 0.6 percent of the $252 million in revenue and

17 percent of the $9 million in company profits the year of the strike. For the five years from the time of the strike to final settlement, company revenues were $1.4 billion and profits, $67 million.[39]

The back-pay checks from Republic were mailed on Thanksgiving Day, November 27, 1941. Hundreds of workers then began sending the union letters of complaint, often addressed to Philip Murray himself.[40] For example, in March 1942, Mrs. Matte Yelich wrote to Murray on behalf of her husband, a worker at Republic's South Chicago Works, as well as his coworker, John Mayerle. Noting that they had "done a lot of suffering during the strike," Mrs. Yelich wanted to know why these men had neither been reinstated nor received any back-pay when so many others had, and what they might do to remedy the situation. A CIO lawyer wrote back, explaining simply that the union was constrained by the terms of the board order and settlement and that Yelich should contact local union representatives about getting the men reinstated.[41] That December, Mrs. Joseph Hudak wrote David McDonald, complaining that her husband, who worked in Monroe, had received only $14.85 in vacation pay and nothing in back-pay. Mrs. Hudak was especially perturbed that Joseph, whom she had picketed alongside, had been "thrown off the list" while others from the plant had gotten substantial payments. "I would like to know which has the right," she asked, "those members who were on the picket line during the riot, or when it was broken, or those who hid themselves & came round when everything was over." A few weeks later, the union's legal department wrote back, pointing out that Mr. Hudak had returned to work prior to October 18, 1938, and therefore could not collect any back-pay.[42]

The legal department's records contain scores of letters like these as well as lists with the names of dissatisfied workers. One list from Cleveland identifies five hundred workers who wished to have their cases reviewed or reconsidered.[43] Even John Mayo, district director in Youngstown and loyal supporter of the SWOC's leadership, was compelled to relay the displeasure of the men under him, writing to Meyer Bernstein that he had "received your postal card and was very, very glad to hear from you because I wanted the privilege of saying that the settlement of the Republic Steel Case is a **??# & (*%$?** no-good settlement." He continued, "The men say they hate everyone who had any part of it."[44] Although there is no way of measuring how much workers' dissatisfaction eroded their support for the union, undoubtedly this did occur. John McCreay and Steve Kovach, employees at Republic's Youngstown Works, were so disgusted with the checks they received for $4.64 and $3.89 that they mailed them back to the union, addressed to Philip Murray, with a suggestion from McCreay that the funds be used to "buy a contract with Republic Steel Corp."[45]

Following so much talk about how many millions of dollars were forthcoming, the paltry payments aggravated workers' frustrations with losing the strike and going so long without work. Everett Smith, an employee from Warren, complained that his check for $503.90 was far below the $2,900 that, by his calculation, he should have received. "I feel that there has been a mistake somewhere so I am writing you for advise [sic]." Smith noted that he had been "out of the mill 2 ½ years" and had lost "not only [his] radio and Frigidaire but automobile, horses, cows and finally my home." The union staff explained to Smith, "We were unable under the terms of the Labor Board settlement to collect as much as we should have liked to for our members."[46] Tony Traficant, a laborer at Republic's Youngstown Works, wrote David McDonald in January 1942 to ask why he had not gotten any backpay. Traficant pointed out that his "losses during the strike were big. I lost a car 6 (six) months old and a home." Traficant said he had "filed every paper that [there] was to be filed" and yet received nothing. But again, the union staff simply wrote back explaining the formula that had to be followed and expressing regrets that more could not be done.[47]

The union legal department did look into possible mistakes, but most complaints went nowhere. The union was ready to move on. Several weeks after the United States entered the war, Meyer Bernstein, who had been inducted into the army a few months earlier and was doing his best to finish his work with the SWOC by mail, received a letter from union official Harold Ruttenberg, who assured Bernstein that most of the complaints "were sunk at Pearl Harbor."[48]

Long waits for inadequate settlement money was not the only hardship that these workers faced. Many were blacklisted during their unemployment. Youngstown striker Danny Thomas, a leader at Sheet & Tube's Brier Hill Works, recalled that, "No one would give us a job, credit, or anything." Thomas "wound up eventually ginny dancing for the Pennsylvania Railroad," saying, "I lasted there for a week or two, until they found out who I was." Thomas described how he and others who were denied reinstatement "struggled along" with rent and other expenses. He could only "visualize what happened to married people."[49] According to union records, Thomas finally received $788 in back wages.[50] Thomas White, who had been fired from his job at Republic's Youngstown Works after being exposed by a spy, described similar experiences during the thirty-eight months he was denied work: "Anywhere I tried to get a job, the Republic Steel [Corporation] was there." White recalled finally landing a position in a nearby town, only to have Republic send "an emissary out . . . to see that I was discharged." When eventually he received $1,500 in back-pay, which was comparatively generous, White was disappointed. Asked how he and other blacklisted workers survived their years of hardship, White invoked the solace that came with knowing they were "fighting back."[51]

For many workers, the NLRB's prosecution of the companies did constitute a way of fighting back. Warren organizer John Grajciar put his finger on an important and intangible benefit of the remedial scheme that transcended the practical deficiencies of reinstatement and back-pay. According to Grajciar, Tom Girdler himself publicly announced after the strike that Grajciar and fellow organizer Harry Wines would never work at Republic again. And so for Grajciar "it was kind of a victory for us to go back" to work in the plant, despite how little money he and Wines received in back-pay. Although Grajciar was going to work for the SWOC full-time, he resumed work for Republic for just a couple of days, to underscore his victory.[52]

The value of the NLRB's monetary remedies has to be understood in light of the notion that back-pay would perform a key function in the Wagner Act's scheme for enforcing labor rights, not only as compensation for the men whose rights were impinged, but as a deterrent for the companies. It is doubtful that the amounts in the Little Steel cases were large enough to serve these purposes, given that the board was unable to reconstitute broken picket lines, reorganize ransacked offices, or rebuild unionists' shattered nerves. In fact, the Wagner Act prohibited the board from using its principal remedies of back-pay or reinstatement to punish the steel companies for their treatment of workers, no matter how egregious.[53] Even the board's attempt in the Ohio case to force Republic to reimburse work-relief agencies for wages paid to strikers wrongfully denied reinstatement was rejected by the Supreme Court as an effort to redress "an injury to the public," which transgressed the Wagner Act's narrow focus on "making whole" individual employees.[54]

The inadequacy of these remedies reflects the Wagner Act's broader failure to redress the fundamental inequality of economic and political power that defines labor relations. Although the opening section of the act explicitly recognized this disparity, and although the statute was conceived in part to redress it, the law was built around a naïve and contradictory view of the right to strike that envisaged the strike as the prime "economic weapon" with which workers could alter this disparity.[55] The statute's drafters conceived that the right to strike would anchor all other rights, constituting the most basic means by which workers might press employers for meaningful representation and effective collective bargaining. However, the Wagner Act did little to ensure that the right to strike itself would actually be effective against powerful employers determined to resist, even where this resistance contravened other provisions of the statute. Instead, the statute essentially defined the right as a right merely to withhold labor and publicize the strikers' cause, in the hope that these tactics alone would overcome employers' resistance. Beyond this, the law strongly protected the right of employers to carry on business notwithstanding a strike. While the statute did give the NLRB authority to order reinstatement of strikers who strike because of an employer's unfair labor practices, and to prevent the employer from otherwise discriminating among strikers seeking to return to work (effectively giving the board the power to end some strikes), the act did not authorize the board to prevent an employer from reopening or continuing to run its struck business, whatever the circumstances.[56]

This last point is important, as the reopenings sealed the companies' victory over the strikers. Once the companies were sufficiently supported by police and National Guardsmen, they were able to send workers right through the most robust picket lines. Mass picketing, strikes in coal and shipping, general strikes, lawsuits—everything the union did to rein in the Guard and police and thwart the reopenings failed, with devastating effect. In the plain words of one Youngstown striker, when the gates reopened, "I was disillusioned. I was heartbroken because I never dreamed my fellow workers would return back to work."[57]

Little Steel's success in this regard raises the question, Did Republic or the other companies rely on James Rand's Mohawk Valley Formula in undermining the organizing drive and breaking the strike? The La Follette Committee concluded that they had, based on how fully the companies' methods complied with the formula and how thoroughly the formula had been advertised by Rand and the NAM. The committee pointed to a pamphlet circulated during the strike by the National Industrial Council of the NAM, in which the tenets of the Mohawk Valley Formula were said to counsel ways in which the SWOC might be stopped. As the committee mentioned (and as the NAM's pamphlet related), during the strike Philip Murray also charged the companies with implementing elements of the formula.[58] A number of commentators, including Irving Bernstein and Mary Heaton Vorse, agreed with the committee's conclusion about the formula's influence.[59] Nevertheless, the evidence is equivocal. It is possible that Little Steel's methods aligned with the Mohawk Valley Formula simply because similar interests, ideology, and resources took them down the same path. After all, could men like Girdler, so practiced in the arts of labor repression, have really needed Rand's counsel in deciding how to deal with the SWOC?

Notably, none of the Little Steel firms had to hire large numbers of replacement workers to facilitate their mills reopening—something that might have been difficult anyway, given the sizes of their workforces. Nor were the workers who streamed back into the plants as the strike unwound driven there at gunpoint, as had happened in 1919. Despite his exaggerated view of workers' loyalties to the companies, historian James Baughman's contention that most strikers were forced back to work by exhaustion and economic distress is fundamentally correct.[60] Baughman has in mind the reopenings in June and July. But the same can be said about the men from Republic who sought reinstatement in the months that followed. Of course all of this occurred in the context of an awesome display of power by the companies, underscored by their readiness to use force. But even had the steel companies not resorted to violence, exhaustion would eventually have supplied enough men to reopen the mills. And there is nothing the law could have done to block this. For although the Wagner Act authorized the NLRB to order the reinstatement of strikers, notwithstanding the companies' use of strikebreakers—provided the strike was caused by unfair labor practices—the law offered picketers no effective way to stop the use of strikebreakers in the first place and no alternative means by which to keep the plants closed and pressure the companies. Moreover, the law did nothing to prevent exhausted strikers from crossing over. In fact, the Wagner Act probably should have, in legal terms, "preempted" the one policy that kept the mills temporarily closed: the governors' status quo orders, which they enforced for a time with their state police and National Guardsmen.[61]

A certain irony can also be noted in the La Follette Committee's conclusions about the right of the unionists to picket in large numbers, which they successfully used for a time to check the companies' prerogatives to run the plants. This is particularly evident in the committee's excoriation of the Chicago police for causing the Memorial Day Massacre by enforcing its ban on mass picketing. In fact, the legality of mass picketing was already in doubt at the time of the strike. The Wagner Act implicitly established a right to picket without clarifying its permissible extent or the degree to which picketing might be limited by local authorities. A struggle over this ambiguity defined many clashes during the strike, including the one on Memorial Day. In due time, the position that the police, the Guard, and the companies successfully instituted on the ground—that in the name of public safety they could dramatically limit the number of picketers, even if this eviscerated workers' labor rights—would be fully validated by the courts and Congress.[62]

And while the use of Guardsmen and police to keep the mills closed was probably contrary to the labor law, their role in overseeing the reopening of the mills was perfectly consistent with the labor law. So was the authorities' role in issuing and enforcing injunctions that limited the size and location of the SWOC's pickets. Not that the injunctions were entirely unproblematic: they were often issued without proper notice, credible findings of fact, or due consideration that the party seeking the injunction have "clean hands." Occasionally, the companies' having unclean hands was successfully raised by CIO lawyers challenging injunctions in northeast Ohio as well as by board members in oral arguments in the *Republic Steel* (Ohio) case. In a board hearing, Republic's attorney, the famous corporate lawyer Luther Day, attempted to evade the question of clean hands but stumbled, conceding that "the conduct of all those engaged in the situation should be considered." Member Edwin S. Smith pounced, asking if by that Day also meant the company.[63] Nevertheless, the injunctions themselves did not violate the Wagner Act or the 1932 statute limiting the power of federal courts to intervene in labor disputes, the Norris-LaGuardia Act. In the years to come, the validity of such injunctions would become even clearer.

As we have seen, strikers committed many criminal acts of destruction and violence. Not only were these used to justify the companies' actions and undermine union support, they also presented the NLRB with a dilemma involving its remedial authority. If the board ordered the reinstatement of strikers irrespective of their participation in criminal acts, it jeopardized its political legitimacy and risked having the courts deny enforcement of the order on the grounds that Congress could not have contemplated such a result.[64] But if the agency simply declined to reinstate anyone implicated in criminal behavior, it would have made police, prosecutors, and provocative employers the true arbiters of labor rights. Aside from vague suggestions in its legislative history, the Wagner Act provided little guidance on how the board should negotiate this dilemma.[65] However, the statute's drafters did broadly orient the act to the containment of disorder involving labor disputes. Encoded in the statute's first sentence, this precept was enhanced by the Supreme Court's decision in *NLRB v. Jones & Laughlin Steel,* which elevated the protection of the flow of interstate commerce above the statute's other stated purposes of redistributing wealth and equalizing power between employers and employees.[66]

The board earnestly attempted to negotiate this dilemma. In its main case against Republic, it ordered strikers implicated in crimes reinstated, except where the crimes were proved by a conviction or guilty plea *and* were especially serious. The board's reasoning emphasized Republic's ultimate responsibility for the violence, the fact that the company condoned strike-related violence by antiunion employees, and the board's congressional mandate to effectuate labor rights as opposed to performing the work of local law enforcement and prosecutors. The board also reasoned that Republic should not be allowed to profit from its outrageous violations of the labor law. Although logical and sincere, and less harsh than what the courts and Congress would later require, the NLRB's approach was fraught, as its argument called for deference to convictions by local officials whose biases and vulnerabilities to manipulation by powerful employers were abundantly evident in the Little Steel cases.[67]

There was also the problem of delay, despite efforts to expedite the cases. Charges in the key cases were first filed while the strike was still very much under way. But initial rulings by the NLRB's trial examiners were not issued until the following fall and winter and final rulings not until a year or more after the strike ended. The reinstatements ordered by the board did not occur until late 1938 and 1939. The stipulated vacation pay and back-pay claims were not paid until the end of 1941. Prolonged further by appeals to the circuit courts and Supreme Court, the cases were not finally closed until 1942—five years after the strike.[68] Ironically, anticipation of such delays was one factor that led many unionists, including SWOC leaders, to support a strike in the first place.[69]

Unreconciled

WAR, VICTORY, AND THE LEGACIES OF DEFEAT

Despite the shortcomings of the Wagner Act and the crippling effects of the strike on the SWOC, Little Steel's adherence to the open shop did not survive the war. By the end of the summer of 1942, every one of the companies involved in the strike had signed collective bargaining agreements with the SWOC, which had since reorganized as the USW. Over the next several decades, these developments positioned the USW to become an institutional cornerstone of the American labor movement at the pinnacle of its postwar influence. And yet as this victory unfolded, the Little Steel Strike remained a malignant presence, reshaping steel unionism and then playing a prominent role in a successful campaign, authored in part by the steel industry, to rein in the NLRB and radically reform the Wagner Act.

THE WAR AND THE COLLAPSE OF THE OPEN SHOP

News of the outbreak of war in Europe reached Bethlehem's Eugene Grace on a company-owned golf course, on the outskirts of Bethlehem, Pennsylvania. Grace reacted by remarking to his companions, "Gentlemen, we are going to make a lot of money."[1] In the emerging militarized economy, Bethlehem certainly did "make a lot of money." During the years of direct U.S. involvement in the war, Bethlehem realized total revenues averaging more than $1.5 *billion* per year; and its total net income was $670 million—in contrast to only $136 million for the period from 1935 through 1939. Nor was Bethlehem's experience unique, despite its significant involvement in shipbuilding and armament production. Republic's annual raw steel output nearly doubled between 1937 and 1942.[2] Its net income, $59 million from 1935 through 1939, totaled

$311 million during the war years. For all six Little Steel companies, total net income increased from $439 million from 1935 through 1939 to $1.6 *billion* during the war years. Between 1938 and 1941, total employment in steel also roughly doubled.[3] Wartime price control and taxes on excessive profits did limit the companies' profits. However, the main institution for regulating wartime production, the National War Labor Board (WLB), also limited pay increases. In essence, the government guaranteed profits while subsidizing research and plant development.[4]

What Grace likely did not prophesy that day on the links was that the advent of global war signaled the end of the open shop. By increasing and stabilizing production, the war increased the steel companies' willingness to absorb the costs associated with union recognition and collective bargaining. By vastly improving the employment situation, wartime production also enhanced the ability of workers to organize and make demands on the companies. Furthermore, increasing reliance on government contracts exposed the steel companies to government efforts to rationalize war production and mandate adherence to the Wagner Act. Philip Murray and other CIO leaders and allies failed in their effort to invest this new regime with a genuine central-planning function that would encompass the full participation of organized labor in managing the industrial economy, or to have companies automatically disqualified from government contracts if they flouted the labor law.[5] Nevertheless, government officials made clear to the companies the risks of continued defiance.[6]

In the meantime, the SWOC gradually recovered from its poststrike crisis. It rebuilt its membership, paid off its debt to the UMW, and finally attained financial independence from the CIO. To be sure, as late as the fall of 1940 the union could count perhaps only 250,000 dues-paying members out of a total workforce (including fabricating firms) of about a million.[7] But a definite turnaround was under way, as both membership and payment of dues increased.[8]

The SWOC resumed organizing in the late summer of 1939, this time focusing on Bethlehem Steel. But as Robert Brooks pointed out at the time, "The enthusiasm built up by the whirlwind successes of the 1937 campaign had been dissipated in the futile and unplanned strike against Bethlehem's Cambria plant." Patterned on the earlier drive, the new campaign foundered and so organizers reverted to a slower, more deliberate program. This approach paid off. In the spring of 1941, Bethlehem stipulated to a series of twelve NLRB-sponsored elections at its mills, every one of which the union won.[9] Almost 70 percent of voters favored representation by the SWOC.[10] The union also made progress elsewhere. In May 1941, David McDonald assured Lee Pressmen that the union would win elections at all but a few of Republic's plants, mostly in the South or at more isolated mills in the North.[11] That summer, union officials resumed communicating to the companies their formal demands for recognition and contract negotiations.[12]

The stipulations concerning reinstatement and back-pay claims against Sheet & Tube and Republic also addressed the issue of union recognition. On July 9 and July 25, 1941, respectively, those companies agreed with the SWOC and the NLRB to resolve the question by cross-checking union membership rolls against payroll lists. Although the SWOC already enjoyed recognition at Inland, a similar procedure was agreed to that summer to decide whether workers at the Indiana Harbor plant and the Chicago Heights operation would form a single bargaining unit.[13] These checks demonstrated strong support for the SWOC at every one of the three companies—about 70 percent at Republic's plants, about 74 percent at Sheet & Tube, and 75 percent at Inland.[14] Counting those polled at Bethlehem, these procedures tested the views of some 140,000 workers at the four companies, of whom roughly 99,000 aligned with the SWOC. The numbers suggest how much latent support there probably had been for the SWOC around the time of the Little Steel Strike, and how effective company repression had been. Interestingly, without doing anything spectacular in the way of poststrike organizing, the union garnered nearly as much support at Republic as at Inland—even though at the time of the strike, Inland was much more fully organized than Republic. Four years after the strike and five years after it launched its organizing drive, the CIO had finally secured the right to represent the workers at these companies.

An initial round of bargaining conferences with the four companies began in September 1941 in Pittsburgh and continued that fall and winter in New York, Cleveland, Youngstown, and Indiana Harbor. The negotiations were intensive and difficult.[15] Initially, the union made little headway; but by the time the parties met again in January 1942, the United States was fully involved in the war and the negotiations were subject to the jurisdiction of the WLB. Instead of simply threatening employers with disqualification from government contracts if they remained in violation of federal laws, the WLB subjected the parties to compulsory resolution of labor disputes, including issues regarding union representation as well as wages and basic conditions of employment.[16] In effect, the WLB could preempt collective bargaining and impose the functional equivalent of collective bargaining agreements. Wartime excess profit taxes further diminished the companies' antipathy to concessions in collective bargaining, as the taxes created a sizeable margin of funds from which wage increases could be granted without affecting bottom-line profits—meaning that wage increases were basically paid by the government itself.[17]

In July 1942, the WLB issued a far-reaching, precedent-setting ruling concerning Little Steel. The decision featured a formula on wage increases and granted the union a dues check-off provision and a "maintenance of membership" provision. Although the decision did not impose the "union shop" that union people had demanded, it did substantially improve the organization's position. For the check-off provision guaranteed the union a continuous flow of dues, and the maintenance of membership clause required that workers remain with the union representing them at the time the agreement went into effect. Together, these provisions relieved pressure on the union to engage in continuous recruitment, retention, and dues-collection work.[18]

In the meantime, a series of NLRB-sponsored elections held to settle the question of exclusive representation at other steel firms, including U.S. Steel, resulted in overwhelming victories for the union and set the stage for uniform, nearly industry-wide labor standards to be instituted through collective bargaining. These events left the four principle Little Steel companies with few remaining reasons not to sign. Inland signed on August 5, 1942, Sheet & Tube on August 12, and Bethlehem and Republic on August 13. Tom Girdler himself never did sign—he left this to other executives. The substantive terms of the contracts, which were very similar, embodied the dictates of the WLB decision issued earlier that year.[19] And they were brief: the master contract between the USW and Republic entailed only thirty-one pages.[20] Nevertheless, the contracts marked the defeat of the open shop in steel.

Had it not been for the war, the companies might well have continued to flout their workers' demands for recognition and collective bargaining, even in the face of NLRB orders. They certainly would have pushed the union hard at the bargaining table—where the NLRB had no authority to force a settlement—and probably would have tested the SWOC's stomach for another big strike. In any event, Tom Girdler described his company's acquiescence to the WLB's Little Steel ruling as a grudging act of patriotism.[21] The contract with the USW a few weeks later brought forth even more telling responses. Writing only a year or so later, Girdler purported to speak for many industry officials and stockholders when he said that "my opinions have not changed." "In our private discussions my associates and I find ourselves unreconciled" to the new regime. Girdler ventured that "many thoughtful people" agreed with his views on labor and the CIO. "But under the present circumstances, what are they going to do about it?"[22] Elsewhere, Republic rationalized its eventual recognition of the USW as the result of there finally being reliable proof of majority support for the union among its workers.[23] But times had changed. No sooner were the companies under contract than they began touting their fidelity to federal labor law.[24]

There were some strikes in this period, but they were relatively small and not especially important to the overall course of events. One occurred in Lackawanna, New York, in February 1941, when thousands of union militants shut Bethlehem's plant in protest of the company's response to wildcat strikes spawned by the company's refusal to negotiate grievances with the union.[25] A tempestuous affair, the strike ended with a settlement negotiated by the federal Office of Production Management, an early creation for managing defense production. Although the victory was very limited, a throng of workers, blacks and whites together, paraded back into the mill under the banners of American flags and CIO pennants.[26]

There were uprisings that spring at other Bethlehem mills.[27] And just as the Lackawanna strike was unfolding, several hundred men at Republic's Youngstown Works walked out in solidarity with crane operators who had left their jobs over a grievance.[28] A week earlier, there had been a brief strike of the blast furnace department at Sheet & Tube's Brier Hill Works in Youngstown, over a local grievance.[29] Nor was the more compliant U.S. Steel immune to unrest, as that fall its massive Gary Works was hit by several sit-down strikes of modest proportions.[30]

These conflicts were consistent with David Brody's claim that a "guerilla war for unionism" raged in many steel mills in the several years following the Little Steel Strike.[31] Although these episodes embodied the usual conflicts between rank-and-file workers and managers, they also reflected increasing discord between workers and the union itself over the legitimacy of strikes as means of securing labor rights. The wartime economic regulations being embraced by the SWOC/USW and the CIO often did not align with the interests of rank and filers, who pulled wildcat strikes to protest the long hours, rigid wages, and onerous work rules that were part of this bargain.[32]

During the years leading to the war, the union also developed a policy of never striking a company under contract. Already evident in the union's rhetoric during the early days of the steel drive and in the leadership's failure to support sympathy actions during the strike, this antistrike stance was a central theme at the SWOC's inaugural convention in December 1937 and became a standard term in its contracts.[33] The aggressive and large-scale shop floor and street-level organizing that characterized the 1936–37 drive was clearly no longer preferred.[34] As Lee Pressman's biographer describes it, Pressman and other CIO leaders determined even before the Little Steel Strike was over that the union's best course was to try to "win through the New Deal administrative state what it could not in a sheer test of economic strength."[35] Ironically, in 1938 Pressman himself warned the CIO leadership against overreliance on the NLRB's machinery in lieu of building strength by more direct means.[36]

As we saw in the last chapter, for several years after the Little Steel Strike, the union did not have the resources to mount an aggressive organizing campaign. However, the same union records that show this also reflect a qualitative shift in strategy marked by the union's preoccupation with litigation and the administration of lodges and local unions already organized.[37] When organizing efforts were restarted in 1939, the campaign was methodical and uninspired. From the fall of 1937 through 1941, *Steel Labor* regularly celebrated the NLRB's cases against the steel companies while only occasionally reporting actual organizing efforts.[38] In June 1939, the paper described the "new" campaign in Little Steel almost entirely in terms of how the leadership was pressing its cases with the board.[39] During this period, legal victories against the companies were even cast as "renew[ed] drive[s]."[40] In 1940, SWOC leaders reorganized the SWOC itself, disbanding the lodges inherited from the AA and replacing them with less autonomous committees.[41] And at its first convention two years earlier, the SWOC had instituted a policy by which the national office retained three-quarters of all dues collected by the locals.[42]

Even as it weakened steel unionism, the union's embrace of a legalistic, bureaucratic program in the wake of the failed strike against Little Steel strengthened the leadership relative to the locals and the rank and file, as it gave the leadership exclusive access to the institutions now most vital to the union's survival. The war entrenched these tendencies. During the war, strikes by industrial workers were all but categorically prohibited by the WLB and other war production agencies, further empowering union leadership and heightening conflicts between it and the membership. By now, also leader of the CIO, Philip Murray went further, playing a key role in instituting a comprehensive no-strike pledge. Issued just after Pearl Harbor, the no-strike pledge was not entirely effective either in the CIO generally or in the SWOC/USW. Least of all did it prevent wildcat strikes motivated by local rank-and-file grievances. In steel, there were hundreds of wartime wildcat strikes: over 350 mainly small walkouts (averaging about thirty workers) in 1942 and almost 1,000 in 1943.[43] Nevertheless, the leadership took its commitment to "patriotic labor statesmanship" seriously and Murray "did not hesitate to 'dirty his hands' in the suppression of even minor work stoppages at obscure mills and mines."[44] He purged the entire leadership of the union's militant local at Sheet & Tube's Brier Hill Works in Youngstown because of wildcat strikes during and shortly after the war.[45]

Patriotic rhetoric aside, the no-strike pledge prevented steel workers from taking greater advantage of wartime labor scarcity and employer prosperity. Instead, the WLB's Little Steel Formula, articulated in the ruling that imposed on the companies the framework for contracting with the SWOC/USW, became the basis of a policy that, to fight inflation, suppressed industrial wages for the duration of the war. Despite complaints and protests, the no-strike pledge largely held, as labor leaders reckoned it the price of government-sponsored union recognition.[46] In the meantime, enforcing the pledge habituated union leaders to the role of suppressing strikes and disciplining their membership—while leaving management's prerogatives basically unchallenged.[47] The war production regime would be no entrée to the system of social or industrial democracy (or socialism) that many workers and labor leaders had hoped would follow from a decade of sacrifice and struggle.[48]

TAFT-HARTLEY AND THE LEGACY OF LITTLE STEEL

By the second half of 1937, the New Deal faced escalating resistance from conservative politicians and commentators, as well as from elements of the business community who, with increasing confidence, resisted new reforms and sought to roll back those already enacted. Although the 1938 election left President Roosevelt's party nominally in control of both houses, and although many newly elected conservatives secured their victories by embracing popular New Deal initiatives, the New Deal had reached its limit. There were no major statutory reforms after 1938 and many reforms already enacted were stalled. The next two election cycles brought more losses for liberals. And by the close of 1943, key initiatives of the New Deal, including the Works Progress Administration and the Civilian Conservation Corps, had fallen victim to a continued rightward shift in Congress.[49]

In fact, from the beginning, the Second New Deal featured what historian Alan Brinkley has called "a declining hostility towards corporate power," marked by an ideological shift from an earlier faith in structural reform to an increasing commitment to Keynesian and Keynesian-like economic theories.[50] This new political economy would oversee a startling economic recovery, albeit one rooted in massive war-related spending and a legacy of debt and unresolved social conflicts. The Wagner Act was essential to the Second New Deal, and its overt goals of "restoring equality of bargaining power between employers and employees" and raising "wage rates and the purchasing power of wage earners" embodied this new orientation. But as the NLRB's prosecutions of Little Steel showed, in practice the statute still impinged on the ideology and interests of powerful businesses that wanted it repealed or radically amended.[51]

Enacted in 1947, the Labor-Management Relations Act, or Taft-Hartley Act, reversed the New Deal's reformist approach to labor relations. Its many amendments to the Wagner Act reconfigured the labor law along more conservative, business-friendly lines and its enactment is often considered a watershed moment in American history. But not widely known is that Taft-Hartley's overall program was conceived much earlier, as part of an effort by congressional conservatives in the late 1930s and early 1940s that made prominent use of the Little Steel Strike to justify new restraints on the rights of workers and the prerogatives of the NLRB.

This bid to turn the strike against labor rights began while steel workers were still on the picket lines. As the NLRB was developing its cases against them, the Little Steel companies, joined by the NAM and the U.S. Chamber of Commerce, publicly questioned the agency's authority and competency, as well as its fairness.[52] While the strike was still under way, this campaign coalesced in a call to amend the Wagner Act.[53] When the strike ended, the Little Steel companies quietly took the lead in a program, also spearheaded by the NAM, to draft amendments to the labor law and press for their adoption. In this, they were supported by AFL conservatives who resented the CIO's successes and attributed its gains to biases in the statute and on the part of the NLRB. Later in 1938, a group of attorneys from Republic, Inland, Weirton, and ARMCO formed a committee to work on these proposals.[54] Their efforts paid off in the summer of 1939 when congressional conservatives created a special committee to investigate the NLRB.

The "Smith Committee," known by the name of its chair, Representative Howard K. Smith of Virginia, embarked on a sweeping investigation of "anti-American affiliations and associations of board personnel" and "extra-legal" or otherwise improper acts of NLRB members and staff. Besides weakening the agency's legitimacy and forcing changes in its personnel, the committee's work was geared to generating a package of proposed amendments to the Wagner Act and a record to support their passage.[55] Although occasionally concerned with actual instances of abuse or impropriety, the committee mainly mined the board's records for cases that could be manipulated to cast the agency and its staff as biased or incompetent.[56]

The efforts of attorney Nat Witt (then head of the NLRB review section) to initiate the board's prosecution of Inland, although undertaken with the partial approval of the board itself, provided the Smith Committee with such an opportunity. As Witt tried to explain, his actions were undertaken in the context of an extraordinary and unprecedented situation. When he engaged in ex parte communication with CIO people, ten unionists had already been killed or fatally wounded in Chicago, the threat of further violence loomed elsewhere, and there was no indication the companies would be held to any account. Similarly, the technical violation with which Witt was charged—initiating proceedings without a *written charge* being filed by a private party—was conspicuously analogous to the board's argument that Inland violated the Wagner Act by refusing to sign a *written agreement* with the SWOC. But none of this impressed the Smith Committee's conservative majority, who pilloried Witt.[57]

The committee also charged Witt, other NLRB staff, and the board itself with bias and ex parte dealings with the CIO regarding the case against Sheet & Tube.[58] And it impugned the board's attempt to require Republic to reimburse relief programs for money paid to unfairly discharged steel workers. Showing remarkable sympathy for the company, the committee painted the board's "staggering penalty" against Republic as "reprehensible" and an "invention" and suggested—with little evidence to back the claim—that radicals in the agency had conspired with CIO operatives in formulating it. The committee's final report intimated that it was only Republic's vast economic power that had protected the company from even greater injury.[59]

The Smith Committee also faulted the NLRB for ordering reinstatement and back-pay for employees implicated in strike violence. Committee members questioned board personnel about the *Republic Steel* (Ohio) case and repeatedly implied that extending these remedies to such workers was unconscionable.[60] The committee's attention to this matter was complicated by the board's nearly concurrent decision ordering the reinstatement of scores of workers—SWOC men, organized in part by the same Joe Weber who played a prominent role at Republic's South Chicago Works—who were involved in a violent sit-down strike in February 1937 at a small plant near Chicago operated by a company called Fansteel Metallurgical.[61] Although the Supreme Court had overturned the board's order to reinstate the strikers, the Fansteel case offered the committee a ripe occasion to press the claim of NLRB excesses, as it lacked the outrageous, employer-sponsored violence that characterized *Republic Steel*.[62]

The board's remedies in the Republic case were also raised in a parallel investigation of the board and the Wagner Act by the Senate Committee on Education and Labor. There, too, industry representatives were allowed to criticize how the board enforced the act in the Little Steel cases. A representative of the Iron and Steel Institute testified that the industry's loyal employees were victims of "interference, restraint, or coercion," against which local laws had proved inadequate, and that the board had overstepped in reinstating Republic strikers. He called for statutory changes to preclude reinstatement of employees found guilty of "interference, restraint, or coercion."[63] Other witnesses asserted that NLRB regional director Philip G. Phillips, whom the Smith Committee had charged with bias, had unfairly prosecuted ARMCO and that the board's back-pay remedy against Republic was punitive and therefore excessive.[64]

These investigations exposed the NLRB, the SWOC, and the CIO to considerable negative publicity, including high-profile news stories that painted the agency and the unionists as incompetent, corrupt, and subversive.[65] This contributed to a dramatic changeover in board membership and staff, in line with the Smith Committee's recommendation to purge the agency of "a large group" who adhered to a conception of the "employer-employee relationship based upon class conflict rather than cooperative enterprise," and its claim that the NLRB had been corrupted by "alien and subversive doctrines."[66] Unfortunately, as the Little Steel Strike so clearly showed, labor relations are inherently an arena of class conflict and not an intrinsically "cooperative enterprise." The removal of NLRB personnel attuned to this fact weakened the agency and diminished its enforcement efforts.

The investigations produced efforts at legislation. The lead House bill, the Smith Bill—which would have barred reinstatement of strikers implicated in violence, made unions liable for strike violence, weakened an employer's duty to bargain, and restructured the NLRB to limit its prosecutorial abilities—passed the House in June 1940, but died in the Senate. Similar legislation in the Senate did not advance either. Neither did scores of bills that were subsequently introduced between 1940 and 1947. All failed to overcome both opposition from Roosevelt and New Dealers in Congress and the distractions of the war. But the Smith Bill in particular would resurface as a template for more successful reform.[67]

By 1946, Franklin Roosevelt had been succeeded by Harry Truman; and in both houses of Congress, the New Deal coalition had been displaced by blocks of conservative Democrats and increased numbers of Republicans. Postwar demobilization and reconversion had spurred a massive wave of strikes in 1945 and 1946, which were disruptive and adverse to powerful business interests. In this climate, industrial firms, industry groups, and their political allies finally succeeded in changing the Wagner Act. Enacted the following summer, the Taft-Hartley Act drew heavily on the work of the Smith Committee. But Congress also held new hearings in developing Taft-Hartley, at which conservatives again invoked the Little Steel Strike to support their efforts.

The House report on Representative Fred Hartley's bill had the NLRB's *Republic Steel* case squarely in mind when it fulminated about the agency's efforts to "reinstate, with back pay, strikers whom employers discharge for what the Board seems to regard as minor crimes, such as interfering with the United States mail, obstructing railway rights-of-way, discharging firearms, rioting, carrying concealed weapons, malicious destruction of property, and assault and battery."[68] Of course, the bill's proponents completely ignored the predominant role that employers played in provoking this conduct. With the exception of objections from labor leaders, the only prominent rejoinder to this rhetoric came from the board's rather conservative chairman, Paul Herzog, who argued before both the House and Senate committees that the NLRB had long since repudiated the jurisprudence it was accused of improperly adhering to.[69] Herzog intimated that what was actually at hand was an effort to foreclose the balanced approach to enforcing the law that underlay the board's *Republic* case.[70]

In line with employer resentments about the Little Steel Strike, the new law eroded the right to strike, making it easier for employers to fire workers because of strike-related violence and workers' participation in the kind of mass picketing that had been so central in their efforts to contest Little Steel.[71] Taft-Hartley also limited the NLRB's authority to directly premise unfair labor practices on employer propaganda, something the agency had done in its main case against Republic.[72] The new statute prohibited "secondary boycotts," foreclosing the kind of broad-based solidarity the SWOC called on to aid its cause. Under this provision, the SWOC probably could not have called out workers from other companies in sympathy strikes or even, perhaps, picketed some of Little Steel's own subsidiaries.[73] Taft-Hartley also barred Communists from holding union office, largely banishing them from the labor movement. And it transformed the structure of the NLRB in a bid to further impede the aggressive enforcement efforts that the board had engaged in during the strike.[74] Not surprisingly, when Senator Robert Taft visited Youngstown soon after passage of the law bearing his name, crowds of steel workers greeted him with vulgar invectives.[75]

Conclusion

THESE THINGS THAT MEAN SO MUCH TO US

Among the many memorable subjects of Studs Terkel's oral history of the Depression, *Hard Times,* is a union organizer named Larry Van Dusen. Having come of come of age in the 1930s, Van Dusen reckoned himself different from the young workers of the late 1960s. Those "who come into the shop," he told Terkel, knew little about "what we've been through." "You tell them about the Memorial Day Massacre . . . you tell them about the troops in Flint and sit-down strikes. . . . Well, they listen, if they're polite. But it doesn't really touch them, these things. These things that mean so much to us."[1]

When Van Dusen offered this doleful judgment about struggle and memory, barely thirty years had elapsed since the SWOC's campaign to organize steel had exploded in conflict and bloodshed. From where we stand, a lifetime has passed. In the meantime there have been other large, often contentious strikes. Among these were a number of big steel strikes, including one in 1959 that stands as the largest work stoppage in American history in terms of man-days out. But there has been no strike anywhere in America like Little Steel—none so awash in violence, so rooted in the most basic questions of class prerogatives and raw power. The Little Steel Strike was the last strike of its kind. In many ways it was the last great strike.

As the strike receded into the past, the USW emerged as the archetype of a dominant brand of industrial unionism, its relative conservatism on both political issues and bargaining contrasting with the more social democratic orientation of the postwar UAW and even more so with the mild socialism once promoted by the United Electrical, Radio and Machine Workers and the International Longshore and Warehouse Union.[2] In this mode, the USW achieved remarkable success. It organized nearly all the workers in basic steel, as well as many in the fabricating firms and ore mines. And with

U.S. Steel once again in a leadership role, the union entered a period of "pattern bargaining" that achieved nearly uniform contracts throughout basic steel. By the 1960s, when Van Dusen found that only the more polite young workers indulged his memories of the 1930s, these contracts were more lucrative than anyone could have imagined back then.[3]

There were definite shortcomings in this program. It was not until the mid-1950s that the majority of steel workers and their families lived above the official poverty line, and not until the early 1960s that most achieved something resembling middle-class security and comfort.[4] For black workers especially, the promises of equality that accompanied the CIO's assault on the open shop in the 1930s were frustratingly distant, as blacks often remained mired in low-paying, dangerous jobs with limited upward mobility and faced discrimination in union governance and the processing of grievances. However, for most workers (including many blacks) the gains achieved in postwar collective bargaining were genuine.[5]

In 1970, USW district director John Johns, who had been in the thick of the struggle in Canton back in 1936 and 1937, offered an interviewer a statement that perfectly captured the apparent stability of postwar labor relations: "I think they're [the companies] very well reconciled now to our ways, the same way we're reconciled to their ways." Johns acknowledged and even celebrated the abandonment of the militant spirit that defined much of the 1937 strike. The two sides, he said, had come to "get along fairly well."[6] What Johns did not seem to realize was how much remained unresolved by three decades of "mature" bargaining and "responsible" unionism.

Even as Johns spoke, a number of developments were conspiring to tear away this façade of stability. Among these was the increasing difficulty that well-established American producers experienced in adopting more efficient technologies—like continuous casting machines and basic oxygen furnaces—as successfully as newly capitalized European and Asian concerns. America's share of the world market in basic steel, which had been utterly dominant, steadily eroded.[7] Even domestically, the big legacy firms yielded market share to newer, smaller, more flexible, and union-free "mini-mills."[8] On top of this, they faced the practice by foreign producers of "dumping" cheap steel into the American market.

Deteriorating plant equipment, combined with anxieties about the companies' viability, eventually led many workers to believe the companies were letting the mills run down: squeezing out profits, shareholder dividends, and executive compensation without adequate reinvestment for long-term

viability. When the advent of a strong dollar in the early 1980s simultaneously undermined the competitiveness of American steel on the world market, deterred improvements in plants, *and* made financial reinvestment of
dollars elsewhere very lucrative (dollars that could be drawn out of the mills),
many workers were sure the companies were engaged in a "capital strike"—a
term once levied at industrialists who withheld investment to undermine
the New Deal.[9]

It may not have helped the American companies' viability (though it certainly did the workers') that they were under contract with the USW, while
the mini-mills remained union-free and foreign producers, unionized or
not, often paid lower wages.[10] But far from impeding the companies' quest
to maintain competitiveness, as many critics charged, the USW actually
agreed to substantial concessions on wages, benefits, and staffing, particularly in the 1980s; and it repeatedly accommodated companies' demands for
more efficient work rules. Nor could the USW leadership or rank and file be
faulted for suspecting that the companies' pleas for concessions were greedy
stratagems—not when executives and top managers continued to command
extraordinarily lucrative pay and bonuses.[11] Decades of commitment to
industrial stability at the expense of failing to confront conflicts in the
plants left a legacy of rampant worker alienation, which coexisted symbioti-
cally alongside a dominant management philosophy premised on entrenched
contempt for workers.[12]

In September 1977, the corporate successor to Sheet & Tube stunned the
people of Youngstown when it suddenly announced closure of the company's
Campbell Works. Within five years, nearly all the major steel plants in the
area had been shuttered, including the Brier Hill Works and Republic's
Youngstown Works, scenes of such conflict and violence in 1937. In the decades that followed, nearly every other big mill involved in the Little Steel
Strike also closed: Republic's plants at Massillon and South Chicago and
most of its mills in Canton, near which more than a dozen victims lost their
lives in the 1937 strike; Bethlehem's Cambria Works in Johnstown; Sheet &
Tube's South Chicago and Indiana Harbor plants. By the mid-1980s the
USW's image as an anchor of middle-class security was undone by the spec-
tacle of tens of thousands of laid-off steel workers queuing for unemployment
benefits, welfare and food stamps, and even donations at private food banks,
and by the desperation of others trying to hustle minimum wage jobs.[13]

U.S. Steel and ARMCO, now called AK Steel, are the only major producers involved in the SWOC organizing drive that are still in business.

One by one, the others fell victim to merger, bankruptcy, and dismember-ment.[14] A few plants emerged still operating, usually in the hands of foreign producers like the industry's new giant, the Indo-European firm ArcelorMittal. But the major consequence of realignment was the closure of plants, large and small. Nationwide, from 1974 to 1987 the industry shed 337,000 jobs. Between 1989 and 2008, the number of production and pri-mary maintenance workers in basic steel declined by nearly half, so that today there are only about 100,000 such workers in the entire industry.[15]

As these changes took hold, the true shortcomings of the USW showed in its inability to stem the layoffs and closings. It was reluctant even to press for palliative social reforms and welfare policies, in part because the leader-ship associated these with the radicals it had purged four or five decades earlier.[16] Rather, the union was reduced to begging favors of local and fed-eral governments that had long renounced the economic policies that once aided the industry and the union.[17] Such was the sad legacy of a dependency on the state that evolved directly out of the struggle with Little Steel.

Facing all of this, many steel workers found themselves yearning for radi-cal ideals and militant tactics of the sort that their union had begun to repu-diate even before defeat at the hands of Little Steel was final. Indeed, some organized against the closures, occupying company offices, picketing at executives' homes, and proposing to run the factories themselves. But the companies were able to dismiss their demands as sentimental foolishness.[18] When David Roderick took over as chairman of U.S. Steel in 1979, he famously declared that "U.S. Steel is not in the business of making steel. It is in the business of making money."[19] Meanwhile, not even with the lyrical support of music legend Bruce Springsteen could the people of Youngstown preserve for posterity the last prominent symbol of the city's steel-making heritage, the "Jeannette" blast furnace, centerpiece of the Brier Hill Works, which was demolished in 1997 after standing nearly eighty years.

In addition to those of U.S. Steel and AK Steel, the mills now owned by ArcelorMittal and some of the other foreign-owned firms remain somewhat unionized, albeit mainly because the new owners inherited USW workers and their contracts. Even where they have not been closed down, the union mills have all hemorrhaged workers for several decades, in part because of declining orders, in part because of relentless automation. Union density among all workers in steel has fallen to near 20 percent, and most of the USW's 600,000 members are not in steel.[20] Seventy-five years after Little Steel, unionism today is just hanging on in the industry.

FIGURE 31. Idled blast furnace at what was once Republic Steel's Warren, Ohio, plant, seen from an abandoned house, 2009. Photograph courtesy of Michael S. Williamson, previously published in Dale Maharidge and Michael S. Williamson, *Someplace Like America: Tales from the New Great Depression* (Berkeley: University of California Press, 2011).

South Chicago, Youngstown, Canton—almost everywhere the battle against Little Steel raged, weeds and saplings rise up among the crumbled footprints of the old mills and through the streets where union people once protested. I visited the scene of the Memorial Day Massacre for the first time on a brilliant Saturday morning in early July 2009. The once-imposing steel plant was gone, its remains partly occupied by a scrapyard. The only traffic on 116th Street, which leads past the scene of the clash, consisted of a couple of beaten-up trucks, driven by beaten-down people, carrying scrap to sell at the yard. The only other person there was a Chicago police officer, randomly parked on 116th Street and chatting on the phone. Friendly enough and oblivious to both my purpose and the small irony of his words, he advised me not to stray onto the property of the railroad or scrap company, as he "wouldn't be able to stop them from charging me with trespass."

The desolate "prairie" those men and women strode across on that warm Sunday afternoon, chanting supposedly un-American slogans under the banner of American flags, was not much changed. Bathed in a silence broken only by chirping birds and distant industrial noises, the scene remained strikingly familiar to anyone who knew the story. It was easy to conjure the events of that Sunday afternoon, seven decades earlier, to visualize the police, stirring about, agitated; the few picketers over by the gate with their oversized sandwich boards; and of course the demonstrators, falling like cut wheat, writhing or crawling in the grass as the police beat white women, too. The union hall built years after the strike a few hundred yards away, and on a fairly busy street, was evocative in different ways. Slightly run-down, the building had become a community center, as the USW local that resided there died with the mills. Still out front, at the base of a lamp post on the street side of the building, was a memorial plaque installed in 1967, the names of the ten "martyrs" and the words of tribute all the more compelling for the corrosion that blighted some of the letters.

Surveying these relics, one is tempted to draw strong connections between the Little Steel Strike and the state of labor in our time. Indeed, it is tempting to follow Staughton Lynd in tracing the USW's failure to better respond to the crisis that engulfed it in recent decades to its antipathy to the radicalism that flared during the strike—to lament the failure to build from the discontent of that time a radical challenge to capitalism itself, one that might have created a society intolerant of the capricious events that laid the industry and its workers so low and hostile to the notion that the purpose of industry is to make money. One can likewise see in these ruins the legacy of labor laws whose commitment to managing, but not resolving, the conflicts between workers and capitalists was thoroughly exposed during the strike, and further revealed in the years to follow. It is actually very hard to imagine that the profound traumas that attended the birth of the SWOC and the first major test of the NLRB and the Wagner Act were not significant in all these ways. But while there is surely truth in these conjectures, conjectures they may have to remain, as the influence of the strike, though powerful, is simply too attenuated and too intermingled with everything else that has happened to give final proof to them.

What the strike does provide is an opportunity to do what those young workers whose indifference so troubled Van Dusen would not: to remember the Little Steel Strike with all its intense tragedies and traumas and to draw from it a crucial lesson about this world of alienation and deep inequality we inherited from its protagonists. Decades later, veterans of the strike, even the conservative, bread-and-butter unionists among them, were still engrossed with the conflict. In interview after interview about their lives as workers, they came back around to Girdler, to signed contracts and Stop 5, to Little Steel—always Little Steel, Little Steel. The epic struggle remained a source of pride and proof of their own potency as workers. But it also confirmed for them the power of the capitalists, the fickle role of law and the state in the arena of labor relations, the double-edged sword of militancy, the contradictions of industrial unionism, and the precariousness of any functional system of labor rights in modern society. In testament to the strike's historical significance, these insights survived the postwar détente of labor and capital, the reinvention of the strike in official reflections, and the incessant disputations of a culture that persistently denies that class could ever constitute an authentic framework of identity and consciousness. It is in these workers' impressions that one finds the essential truth of the Little Steel Strike and its profoundest lesson for all Americans, imprinted so delicately in Van Dusen's reflections, and with such bluntness in Upton Sinclair's judgment about Little Steel: "The purpose of the strike is to teach you what capitalism really is; to free you from the accepted falsehoods of your class."[21]

Appendix

Struck plants by region or city, with approximate sizes of workforce, May 1937

Youngstown, Ohio, and Nearby Areas

Republic Steel

Warren Works, Warren, OH	6,500
Youngstown Works, Youngstown, OH	6,000
Niles Steel Fabricating Plant, Niles, OH	1,000

Youngstown Sheet & Tube

Campbell Works, Campbell, Struthers, and Youngstown, OH (including small, nearby Hubbard Furnace)	12,000
Brier Hill Works, Youngstown and Girard, OH	2,000

Calumet Region

Inland Steel

Indiana Harbor Works, East Chicago, IN	12,000
Chicago Heights Works, Chicago Heights, IL	500

Republic Steel

South Chicago Works, Chicago, IL	2,200
Grand Crossing Works, Chicago, IL	400

Youngstown Sheet & Tube

Indiana Harbor Works, East Chicago, IN	8,000
South Chicago Works, Chicago, IL	1,000

Johnstown, Pennsylvania

Bethlehem Steel

Cambria Works	13,000

Canton, Ohio

Republic Steel

Stark Rolling Mills	3,500
Steel Division—Plants A and B	2,000
Berger Manufacturing	1,200

Canton Tin Plate	650
South Plant	400
Canton Culvert Division	100
Cleveland, Ohio	
Republic Steel	
Corrigan-McKinney Works	3,700
Upson Nut	1,700
Truscon Steel	750
Steel & Tubes Plant	500
Massillon, Ohio	
Republic Steel	
Massillon Works	3,200
Union Drawn Steel	400
Buffalo, New York	
Republic Steel	
Buffalo Works	3,000
Monroe, Michigan	
Republic Steel	
Newton Steel Plant	1,400
Cumberland, Maryland	
Republic Steel	
N&G Taylor Plant	475
Beaver Falls, Pennsylvania	
Republic Steel	
Union Drawn Steel Plant	350
Pittsburgh, Pennsylvania	
Republic Steel	
Dilworth-Porter Plant	250
Total Workers Employed at Struck Plants	88,175
Approximate Number on Strike at Height of Conflict	81,500

ABBREVIATIONS

AA   Amalgamated Association of Iron, Steel, and Tin Workers

ACHRC   American Catholic History Research Center and University Archives

AFL   American Federation of Labor

CHS   Chicago History Museum/Chicago Historical Society

CIO   Committee for Industrial Organization/Congress of Industrial Organization

ERP   Employee representation plan

IWW   Industrial Workers of the World

LCH   La Follette Committee Hearings (hearings before a U.S. Senate subcommittee of the Committee on Education and Labor)

NAM   National Association of Manufacturers

NIRA   National Industrial Recovery Act

NLB   National Labor Board

NLRB   National Labor Relations Board

NRA   National Recovery Administration

OHS   Ohio Historical Society

PSU-HCLA   Penn State University's Historical Collections and Labor Archives

SMWIU   Steel and Metal Workers Industrial Union

SWOC   Steel Workers Organizing Committee

UMW   United Mine Workers of America

USW	United Steelworkers of America
WLB	National War Labor Board (Second World War)
WRHS-RSC	Western Reserve Historical Society, Republic Steel Collection
YHCIL	Youngstown Historical Center of Industry and Labor
YSSR	Youngstown Steel Strike Records (Ohio Historical Society)
YSU-OHP	Youngstown State University, Oral History Project

NOTES

INTRODUCTION: LABOR, LITTLE STEEL, AND THE NEW DEAL

1. Ruth Needleman, *Black Freedom Fighters in Steel: The Struggle for Democratic Unionism* (Ithaca, NY: Cornell University Press, 2003), 191; George Patterson, Jesse Reese, and John Sargent, "Your Dog Don't Bark No More," in *Rank and File: Personal Histories of Working-Class Organizers,* ed. Alice Lynd and Staughton Lynd (New York: Monthly Review, 1988), 95 (quotation).

2. Paul Y. Anderson, "Armed Rebellion on the Right," *Nation,* August 7, 1937, p. 146.

3. NLRB v. Jones & Laughlin Steel, 301 U.S. 1 (1937).

4. For a review of shortcomings in the literature, see Joseph M. Turrini, "The Newton Steel Strike: A Watershed in the CIO's Failure to Organize 'Little Steel,'" *Labor History* 38, nos. 2–3 (1997): 229–31. Notable studies include William J. Adelman, *The Memorial Day Massacre of 1937* (Chicago: Illinois Historical Society, 1975) (locally published and out of print); Donald G. Sofchalk, "The Memorial Day Incident: An Episode in Mass Action," *Labor History* 6, no. 1 (1965): 3–43; Carol Quirke, "Reframing Chicago's Memorial Day Massacre, May 30, 1937," *American Quarterly* 60, no. 1 (2008): 129–57; James L. Baughman, "Classes and Company Towns: Legends of the 1937 Little Steel Strike," *Ohio History* 87 (1978): 175–92; Michael Speer, "The 'Little Steel' Strike: Conflict for Control," *Ohio History* 78 (1969): 273–87. The strike is briefly mentioned in business histories of the steel industry. See, for example, Kenneth Warren, *Bethlehem Steel: Builder and Arsenal of America* (Pittsburgh: University of Pittsburgh Press, 2008), 201–2. For treatments of the strike in broader histories, see Robert Zieger, *The CIO, 1935–1955* (Chapel Hill: University of North Carolina Press, 1995), 60–65; Irving Bernstein, *The Turbulent Years: A History of the American Worker, 1933–1941* (Boston: Houghton Mifflin, 1969), 478–97; and Walter Galenson, *The CIO Challenge to the AFL: A History of the American Labor Movement, 1935–1941* (Cambridge, MA: Harvard University Press, 1960), 96–109.

5. Michael Dennis, *The Memorial Day Massacre and the Movement for Industrial Democracy* (New York: Palgrave Macmillan, 2010). More recently, Dennis

published another, similar book: *Blood on Steel: Chicago Steelworkers and the Strike of 1937* (Baltimore: Johns Hopkins University Press, 2014).

6. Donald G. Sofchalk, "The Little Steel Strike of 1937" (PhD dissertation, Ohio State University, 1961).

7. See, for example, Philip Dray, *There Is Power in a Union: The Epic History of Labor in America* (New York: Doubleday, 2010), 270–71; Galenson, *CIO*, 112; William T. Hogan, *Economic History of the Iron and Steel Industry in the United States* (Lexington, MA: Lexington Books, 1971), 85–89; William E. Leuchtenburg, *Franklin Roosevelt and the New Deal: 1932–40* (New York: Harper, 1963), 241; Mary Heaton Vorse, *Labor's New Millions* (New York: Modern Age, 1938), 131; Zieger, *CIO*, 62–65; and Philip Taft and Philip Ross, "American Labor Violence: Its Causes, Character, and Outcome," in *Violence in America,* ed. Hugh D. Graham and Ted R. Gurr (New York: Signet, 1969), 270, 342.

8. Joseph G. Rayback, *A History of American Labor* (New York: Free Press, 1959), 343–45.

9. David J. McDonald, *Union Man* (New York: Dutton, 1969), 119.

10. United Steelworkers of America, www.usw.org/union/history (last visited February 14, 2015). See also Vincent D. Sweeney, *The United Steelworkers of America: The First Ten Years* (Pittsburgh: USWA, 1947), 32.

11. Richard W. Nagle, "The Little Steel Strike," in *Encyclopedia of American Business History and Biography: The Iron and Steel Industry,* ed. Bruce Seely (New York: Facts on File, 1994), 279–80.

12. Alan Brinkley, *The End of Reform: New Deal Liberalism in Recession and War* (New York: Vintage, 1996).

CHAPTER 1: LIKE A PENITENTIARY

1. Carl Sandburg, "Smoke and Steel," in *Smoke and Steel* (New York: Harcourt, Brace and Company, 1921), 5.

2. Paul Krause, *The Battle for Homestead, 1880–1992* (Pittsburgh: University of Pittsburgh Press, 1992), 32–33.

3. John Andrews Fitch, *The Steel Workers* (Pittsburgh: University of Pittsburgh Press, 1989), 78.

4. William T. Hogan, *Economic History of the Iron and Steel Industry in the United States* (Lexington, MA: Lexington Books, 1971), 85–89, 227–29; Fitch, *Steel Workers,* 76–86.

5. Krause, *Homestead,* 205–6. See also David Brody, *Steelworkers in America: The Nonunion Era* (Cambridge, MA: Harvard University Press, 1960), 50–51; U.S. Senate, Committee on Education and Labor, *Violations of Free Speech and the Rights of Labor: Labor Policies of Employers' Associations: Part IV, The "Little Steel" Companies,* Report No. 151, 77th Cong., 1st Sess. (Washington, DC: GPO, 1941) (hereafter *Little Steel Companies*), 33–34; and James Holt, "Trade Unionism in the

British and U.S. Steel Industries, 1880–1914: A Comparative Study," *Labor History* 18, no.1 (1977): 5, 9–10, 14–15.

6. Hogan, *Economic History*, 231–32; Fitch, *Steel Workers*, 124–27; *Little Steel Companies*, 36.

7. Fitch, *Steel Workers*, 133.

8. Brody, *Steelworkers*, 60–68; Hogan, *Economic History*, 443–49.

9. David Brody, *Labor in Crisis: The Steel Strike of 1919* (Urbana: University of Illinois Press, 1965), 13–14.

10. Although some technical distinctions can be made, the differences between iron and steel were very much shaped by commercial considerations. Thomas J. Misa, *A Nation of Steel* (Baltimore: Johns Hopkins University Press, 1995), 29–39.

11. Hogan, *Economic History*, 1–5, 11–13, 53–76 (quotation p. 11). See also Robert B. Gordon, *American Iron: 1607–1900* (Baltimore: Johns Hopkins University Press, 1996), 171–84.

12. Hogan, *Economic History*, 5–7, 27–38. See also Misa, *Nation of Steel*, 5–38.

13. Krause, *Homestead*, 288–89; Fitch, *Steel Workers*, 86–89.

14. Hogan, *Economic History*, 216–24, 835, 837 (table 26–3); Kenneth Warren, *Bethlehem Steel: Builder and Arsenal of America* (Pittsburgh: University of Pittsburgh Press, 2008), 87–88.

15. Gordon, *American Iron*, 15–18, 27, 33–54, 90–170; Warren, *Bethlehem Steel*, 5–12.

16. Hogan, *Economic History*, 419–31; Fitch, *Steel Workers*, ch. 6.

17. Hogan, *Economic History*, 839–58.

18. Misa, *Nation of Steel*, 50–55.

19. Brody, *Steelworkers*, 17–26.

20. Krause, *Homestead*, 285–86.

21. Misa, *Nation of Steel*, ch. 4; Hogan, *Economic History*, 463–537; Thomas K. McCraw and Forest Reinhardt, "Losing to Win: U.S. Steel's Pricing, Investment Decisions, and Market Share, 1901–1938," *Journal of Economic History* 64, no. 3 (1989): 593–94, 598 (table 2).

22. Warren, *Bethlehem Steel*, 17, 72–78 (quotation pp. 77–78); Hogan, *Economic History*, 557 (table 21–16).

23. Hogan, *Economic History*, 561–643.

24. Ibid., 236–39.

25. Jones & Laughlin Steel, 1 NLRB 503, 507 (1936); *The Men Who Make Steel* (Pittsburgh: American Iron and Steel Institute, 1936), 18.

26. *Little Steel Companies*, 9; *Statistical Abstract of the United States, 1931* (Washington, DC: GPO, 1931), 831–32 (table 814); *Statistical Abstract of the United States, 1920* (Washington, DC: GPO, 1920), 194, 203 (table 139).

27. Kenneth Warren, *Big Steel: The First Century of the United States Steel Corporation, 1901–1921* (Pittsburgh: University of Pittsburgh Press, 2001), 246 (table 18.1).

28. Earle C. Smith, "History of Republic Steel Corporation (1937)," pp. 1–2, Series 8, Public Relations Division, Container 342, Folder 30, WRHS-RSC.

29. Misa, *Nation of Steel*, 29–39.

30. Katherine Stone, "The Origins of Job Structures in the Steel Industry," *Review of Radical Political Economics* 6 (1974): 148–49.

31. Krause, *Homestead*, 141–46, 178–83.

32. Fitch, *Steel Workers*, 102.

33. Krause, *Homestead*, 143–44.

34. Misa, *Nation of Steel*, ch. 5.

35. Fitch, *Steel Workers*, 140–41.

36. James D. Rose, *Duquesne and the Rise of Steel Unionism* (Urbana: University of Illinois Press, 2001), 17–18. Later, both the proportion of unskilled workers and overall number of workers in the industry fell as automated machinery became more capable and complicated to operate.

37. *Statistical Abstract of the United States, 1935* (Washington, DC: GPO, 1935), 305–10 (table 343).

38. Interview of Dan Thomas, August 1, 1974, p. 1, YSU-OHP.

39. Fitch, *Steel Workers*, 6.

40. Brody, *Steelworkers*, 52.

41. Hogan, *Economic History*, 228–29.

42. Holt, *Trade Unionism*, 27–29.

43. See "Memorandum of Union Jurisdiction in the Steel Industry," June 25, 1936, Congress of Industrial Organization Records, Box 19, Folder 6, ACHRC.

44. Brody, *Steelworkers*, 50–52, 58.

45. Misa, *Nation of Steel*, 175–76.

46. *Men Who Make Steel*, 18.

47. *Little Steel Companies*, 253.

48. On Republic's overall size in 1937, see *Annual Report of Republic Steel Corporation, 1937* (Cleveland: Republic Steel Corporation, 1938), 6–10, 24–27.

49. John Hennen, "E.T. Weir, Employee Representation, and the Dimensions of Social Control: Weirton Steel, 1933–1937," *Labor Studies Journal* 26, no. 3 (2001): 25, 28.

50. Fitch, *Steel Workers*, 229–31. See also John Bodnar, *Workers' World: Kinship, Community, and Protest in an Industrial Society, 1900–1940* (Baltimore: Johns Hopkins University Press, 1982), 69; and Kenneth Casebeer, "Aliquippa: The Company Town and Contested Power in the Construction of Law," *Buffalo Law Review* 43, no. 3 (1995): 617, 633–34.

51. U.S. Senate, *Hearings before the Committee on Education and Labor: Violations of Free Speech and the Rights of Labor,* 76th Cong., 1st–3rd Sess. (Washington, DC: GPO, 1937) (hereafter LCH), 11400 (exhibit 4597), 13893–97 (exhibits 5200–5206).

52. Ibid., 12667–69, 12676, 12878–79 (exhibits 4949–50).

53. Fitch, *Steel Workers*, 214–20.

54. U.S. Senate, *Report on Conditions of Employment in the Iron and Steel Industry,* 62nd Cong., 1st Sess., Report No. 110, vol. 3 (Washington, DC: GPO, 1913), 83–84; Horace Cayton, *Black Workers and the New Unions* (Chapel Hill: University of North Carolina Press, 1939), 19 (table 8).

55. Lizabeth Cohen, *Making a New Deal: Industrial Workers in Chicago, 1919–1939*, 2nd ed. (New York: Cambridge University Press, 2009), 18–19 (table 3).

56. Horace Bancroft Davis, *Labor and Steel* (New York: International, 1933), 29; Barbara Warne Newell, *Chicago and the Labor Movement: Metropolitan Unionism in the 1930's* (Urbana: University of Illinois Press, 1961), 117.

57. See, for example, interview of John N. Grajciar (1 of 2), July 2, 1968, pp. 11–12, USWA–Labor Oral History Collection, PSU-HCLA.

58. James C. Kollros, "Creating a Steel Workers Union in the Calumet Region, 1933–1945" (PhD dissertation, University of Illinois–Chicago, 1998), 26–27; Thomas Joseph Sabatini, "A Nation Made of Steel: The Remaking of the White Republic in Ohio's Mahoning Valley, 1915–1942" (PhD dissertation, University of Minnesota 2006), 198–200.

59. Cohen, *Making a New Deal*, 21–27.

60. Davis, *Labor and Steel*, 27–34; Fitch, *Steel Workers*, ch. 2.

61. Cayton, *Black Workers*, 19 (table 8).

62. Bruce Nelson, *Divided We Stand: American Workers and the Struggle for Black Equality* (Princeton, NJ: Princeton University Press, 2001), 145–85.

63. "Problems Faced in Building Organization in a Steel Town," *Party Organizer* 6, no. 2 (February 1933): 16.

64. Brody, *Steelworkers*, ch. 3.

65. Fitch, *Steel Workers*, 144–49.

66. Robert Bruno, *Steelworker Alley: How Class Works in Youngstown* (Ithaca, NY: Cornell University Press, 1999); Jack Metzgar, *Striking Steel: Solidarity Remembered* (Philadelphia: Temple University Press, 2000); Sherry Lee Linkon and John Russo, *Steeltown U.S.A.: Work and Memory in Youngstown* (Lawrence: University of Kansas Press, 2002), ch. 1. See also Nelson, *Divided We Stand*, 145–50.

67. Nelson, *Divided We Stand*, 156.

68. See, for example, Cassandra Vivian, *Monessen: A Typical Steel Country Town* (Charleston, SC: Arcadia, 2002).

69. Charles Rumford Walker, *Steel: The Diary of a Furnace Worker* (Warrendale, PA: Iron and Steel Society, 1999), 57.

70. See, for example, interview of Sam Camens, May 8, 1991, Video Oral History Collection, at approx. min. 1–2, 50–51, YHCIL; interview of A.J. Carter, September 29, 1991, Video Oral History Collection, at approx. min. 44–48, YHCIL; interview of John Occhipinti, September 19, 1991, Video Oral History Collection, at approx. min. 2–3, YHCIL.

CHAPTER 2: THEY SHOULD HONOR US

1. Charles Rumford Walker, *Steel: The Diary of a Furnace Worker* (Warrendale, PA: Iron and Steel Society, 1999), 33.

2. Mary Heaton Vorse, *Men and Steel* (New York: Boni and Liveright, 1920), 18, 21.

3. John Andrew Fitch, *The Steel Workers* (Pittsburgh: University of Pittsburgh Press, 1989), 3.

4. Fitch, *Steel Workers,* 3 (emphasis added).

5. Vorse, *Men and Steel,* 18–19.

6. Horace Bancroft Davis, *Labor and Steel* (New York: International, 1933), 18.

7. Fitch, *Steel Workers,* 191.

8. Kenneth Casebeer, "Aliquippa: The Company Town and Contested Power in the Construction of Law," *Buffalo Law Review* 43, no. 3 (1995), 617, 642. See also Davis, *Labor and Steel,* 53–54.

9. Richard Edwards, *Contested Terrain: The Transformation of the Workplace in the Twentieth Century* (New York: Basic, 1979).

10. Harvey O'Connor, *Steel-Dictator* (New York: John Day, 1935), 86–88.

11. Fitch, *Steel Workers,* 91–95, 166–68, 171–77.

12. Ibid., 201.

13. Ibid., ch. 8. See also Charles Hill, "Fighting the Twelve-Hour Day in the American Steel Industry," *Labor History* 15, no. 1 (1974): 19, 20–21.

14. Thomas Bell, *Out of This Furnace* (Pittsburgh: University of Pittsburgh Press, 1976), 32, 167.

15. See, for example, John Wexley's play, *Steel,* written, revised, and produced several times between 1931 and 1937. See also Susan Duffy, *American Labor on Stage: Dramatic Interpretations of the Steel and Textile Industries in the 1930s* (Westport, CT: Greenwood 1996), 109–13, 119; and Ann Banks, *First Person America* (New York: Norton, 1991), 78.

16 Carl Sandburg, "Smoke and Steel," in *Smoke and Steel* (New York: Harcourt, Brace and Company, 1921), 6.

17. Walker, *Diary of a Furnace Worker,* 33.

18. Fitch, *Steel Workers,* 59–60, 64–66.

19. Interchurch World Movement, *Report on the Steel Strike of 1919* (New York: Harcourt, Brace and Howe, 1920), 64.

20. Joseph M. Turrini, "The Newton Steel Strike: A Watershed in the CIO's Failure to Organize 'Little Steel,'" *Labor History* 38, nos. 2–3 (1997): 244.

21. Fitch, *Steel Workers,* 60.

22. Lucian W. Chaney, "Accident Frequency Rates in the Iron and Steel Industry, by Causes, 1913 to 1921," *Monthly Labor Review* 13, no. 3 (1921): 488–92 (tables 1–3); Ellie Wymard, *Talking Steel Towns: The Men and Women of Steel Valley* (Pittsburgh: Carnegie Mellon University Press, 2007), 17–25

23. "Killed or Maimed, 17,700; Year's Casualties in Pittsburgh Exceed Those in Some Big Battles," *New York Times,* January 14, 1906, p. 1.

24. David Brody, *Steelworkers in America: The Nonunion Era* (Cambridge, MA: Harvard University Press, 1960), 158–59.

25. "Had Warning of Explosion," *New York Times,* January 14, 1907, p. 18.

26. Davis, *Labor and Steel,* 39; "Blast Furnace Death Toll Twenty-Two," *Massillon Evening Independent,* March 22, 1926, p. 2.

27. "10 Dead, 60 Hurt, in Gary Explosion," *New York Times,* June 15, 1926, p. 1.

28. U.S. Senate, Committee on Education and Labor, *Report on Strike at Bethlehem Steel Works,* Report No. 521, 61st Cong., 2nd Sess. (Washington, DC: GPO, 1910), 124.

29. See, for example, U.S. Senate, *Report on Conditions of Employment in the Iron and Steel Industry,* Report No. 110, 62nd Cong., 1st Sess., vol. 4 (Washington, DC: GPO, 1913), 19–102.

30. See Chaney, "Accident Frequency Rates," 488–92 (tables 1–3).

31. Max D. Kossoris and Swen Kjear, "Injury Experience in the Iron and Steel Industry, 1934 and 1935," *Monthly Labor Review* 43, no. 6 (1936): 1370; "Accident Experience of the Iron and Steel Industry in 1928," *Monthly Labor Review* 29, no. 4 (1929): 32–42.

32. Interview of John Occhipinti, September 19, 1991, Video Oral History Collection, at approx. min. 19–21, YHCIL.

33. Interview of Joe Kerrigan, April 11, 1991, Video Oral History Collection, at approx. min. 13–14, YHCIL. See also interview of Pat Schialdone, April 18, 1991, Video Oral History Collection, at approx. min. 18–20, YHCIL; and interview of A.J. Carter, September 26, 1991, Video Oral History Collection, at approx. min. 19–20, YHCIL.

34. Vorse, *Men and Steel,* 113–14. On company boasts, see *The Men Who Make Steel* (New York: American Iron and Steel Institute, 1936), 35–41.

35. O'Connor, *Steel-Dictator,* 294–95 (quotation); *Statistical Abstract of the United States, 1935* (Washington, DC: GPO, 1935), 305–12 (table 343); *Statistical Abstract of the United States, 1924* (Washington, DC: GPO, 1924), 315–20 (tables 306–9).

36. Davis, *Labor and Steel,* chs. 3 and 5.

37. Interchurch World Movement, *Report on the Steel Strike,* 85–118.

38. Ethelbert Stewart, "Are Average Wage Rates Keeping Pace with the Cost of Living?" *Monthly Labor Review* 22, no. 4 (1926): 750–51.

39. Interchurch World Movement, *Report on the Steel Strike,* 11–15.

40. See, for example, John Bodnar, *Workers' World: Kinship, Community, and Protest in an Industrial Society, 1900–1940* (Baltimore: Johns Hopkins University Press, 1982); and Walker, *Diary of a Furnace Worker,* 39, 118–19.

41. George Patterson, Jesse Reese, and John Sargent, "Your Dog Don't Bark No More," in *Rank and File: Personal Histories of Working-Class Organizers,* ed. Alice Lynd and Staughton Lynd (New York: Monthly Review, 1988), 98.

42. Autobiographical narrative, in Carl "Jerry" Beck Papers, Box 2, Folder 9, MSS 0143, YHCIL. See also interview of Gilbert Peterson Sr., September 19, 1991, Video Oral History Collection, at approx. min. 8–9, YHCIL.

43. William T. Hogan, *Economic History of the Iron and Steel Industry in the United States* (Lexington, MA: Lexington Books, 1971), 526–27, 574–75, 642–63; Davis, *Labor and Steel,* 221–22.

44. Hogan, *Economic History,* 554–55 (table 21–15).

45. Kenneth Warren, *Bethlehem Steel: Builder and Arsenal of America* (Pittsburgh: University of Pittsburgh Press, 2008), 132.

46. Walker, *Diary of a Furnace Worker,* 138.

47. Ibid., 135–36.

48. Bell, *Out of This Furnace,* 195–96.

49. Jack Metzgar, *Striking Steel: Solidarity Remembered* (Philadelphia: Temple University Press, 2000), 33.

50. Interview of Erwin Bauer, August 18, 1991, Video Oral History Collection, at approx. min. 1–12, YHCIL; interview of Sam Camens, May 8, 1991, Video Oral History Collection, at approx. min. 9–11, YHCIL.

51. Fitch, *Steel Workers,* 17–19, 232 (quotation).

52. See Rick Fantasia, *Cultures of Solidarity: Consciousness, Action, and Contemporary American Workers* (Berkeley: University of California Press, 1988), 3–24.

53. Fitch, *Steel Workers,* 217–20.

54. Kenneth Warren, *Big Steel: The First Century of the United States Steel Corporation, 1901–1921* (Pittsburgh: University of Pittsburgh Press, 2001), 112–13.

55. Brody, *Steelworkers,* 61–63.

56. Ibid.

57. Ibid., 67–68.

58. Ibid., 68–77, 114–15.

59. Ibid., 86–91, 154, 167–68; Fitch, *Steel Workers,* 192–99, 207–14; James D. Rose, *Duquesne and the Rise of Steel Unionism* (Urbana: University of Illinois Press, 2001), 22.

60. Upton Sinclair, *Little Steel* (New York: Farrar and Rinehart, 1938), 63.

61. On the Pressed Steel strike, see Melvyn Dubofsky, *We Shall Be All: A History of the Industrial Workers of the World,* 114–21 (Urbana: University of Illinois Press, 2000). On the East Youngstown strike, see Thomas Joseph Sabatini, "A Nation Made of Steel: The Remaking of the White Republic in Ohio's Mahoning Valley, 1915–1942" (PhD dissertation, University of Minnesota, 2006), 71–81; and Davis, *Labor and Steel,* 238–40. On the Bethlehem strike, see Robert Hassen, "The Bethlehem Strike of 1910," *Labor History* 15, no. 1 (1984): 3–18.

62. Quoted in Hogan, *Economic History,* 862–63.

63. David Brody, *Labor in Crisis: The Steel Strike of 1919* (Urbana: University of Illinois Press, 1965), 54–60.

64. Ibid., 49, 70–71, 186–87.

65. James R. Barrett, *William Z. Foster and the Tragedy of American Radicalism* (Urbana: University of Illinois Press, 1999), 71–82.

66. William Z. Foster, *The Great Steel Strike and Its Lessons* (New York: Arno, 1969), ch. 3; Brody, *Steelworkers,* 217–18.

67. Brody, *Steelworkers,* 236–40; Foster, *Great Steel Strike,* 76–85.

68. Brody, *Labor in Crisis,* 87–90, 159; U.S. Senate, Committee on Education and Labor, *Violations of Free Speech and the Rights of Labor: Labor Policies of Employers' Associations; Part IV, The "Little Steel" Companies,* Report No. 151, 77th Cong., 1st Sess. (Washington, DC: GPO, 1941) (hereafter *Little Steel Companies*), 44; Interchurch World Movement, *Report on the Steel Strike,* 170–72, 209–21.

69. Foster, *Great Steel Strike,* 97–101, 222–24; Interchurch World Movement, *Report on the Steel Strike,* 23–28, 235–42.

70. Barrett, *William Z. Foster,* 91–92; Brody, *Labor in Crisis,* 148–49, 164; Foster, *Great Steel Strike,* 53–63, 111–16, 188–89.

71. Interchurch World Movement, *Report on the Steel Strike,* 34–35.

72. U.S. Senate, *Hearings before the Committee on Education and Labor: Investigation of Strike in Steel Industries,* 66th Cong., 1st Sess. (Washington, DC: GPO, 1919); Barrett, *William Z. Foster,* 92–93.

73. Robert Justin Goldstein, *Political Repression in Modern America from 1870 to 1976* (Urbana: University of Illinois Press, 2001), 151–54; Brody, *Steelworkers,* 243–46.

74. Brody, *Labor in Crisis,* 63–66.

75. Interchurch World Movement, *Report on the Steel Strike,* ch. 6; Brody, *Labor in Crisis,* 66–69.

76. See, for example, "Steel Unions in Last Move for General Strike," *Chicago Daily Tribune,* November, 2, 1919, p. 4; and "Leaders Urge 25 More Unions to Join Strike," *Chicago Daily Tribune,* September 25, 1919, p. 2.

77. Ruth Needleman, *Black Freedom Fighters in Steel: The Struggle for Democratic Unionism* (Ithaca, NY: Cornell University Press, 2003), 19–22.

78. Brody, *Labor in Crisis,* 74–75; Foster, *Great Steel Strike,* 35, 194–205; Brody, *Steelworkers,* 222–24.

79. Foster, *Great Steel Strike,* 207–8; Needleman, *Black Freedom Fighters,* 21–24, 188; Brody, *Steelworkers,* 223–25.

80. Lizabeth Cohen, *Making a New Deal: Industrial Workers in Chicago, 1919–1939,* 2nd ed. (New York: Cambridge University Press, 2009), 40–41; Interchurch World Movement, *Report on the Steel Strike,* 177–78; Vorse, *Men and Steel,* 110–11.

81. Brody, *Steelworkers,* 223–25.

82. Ibid., 228–34, 238–41; Brody, *Labor in Crisis,* 101–28, 172–74.

83. Foster, *Great Steel Strike,* 213–22; Interchurch World Movement, *Report on the Steel Strike,* 177–79; Vorse, *Men and Steel,* 120–27.

84. Brody, *Labor in Crisis,* 112–13; Foster, *Great Steel Strike,* 65–67, 234–65; *Little Steel Companies,* 43–44.

85. Foster, *Great Steel Strike,* 192–93.

86. For this assessment, see, for example, Rose, *Duquesne and the Rise of Steel Unionism,* 35–36; and O'Connor, *Steel-Dictator,* 108.

87. Davis, *Labor and Steel,* 265.

88. *Little Steel Companies,* 45.

89. See, for example, "Think Steel Labor Opposed to Unions," *Wall Street Journal,* July 21, 1923, p. 2.

90. See, for example, Robert H. Zieger, *American Workers, American Unions, 1920–1985* (Baltimore: Johns Hopkins University Press, 1986), 3–10; and Irving Bernstein, *The Turbulent Years: A History of the American Worker, 1933–1941,* rev. ed. (Boston: Houghton Mifflin, 2010).

91. *Statistical Abstract of the United States, 1933* (Washington, DC: GPO, 1933), 284–94 (table 318); Colin Gordon, *New Deals: Business, Labor, and Politics in America, 1920–1935* (New York: Cambridge University Press, 1994), 52–53. See also Cohen, *Making a New Deal,* 56, 102–3, 184–86; Robert Lynd and Helen Lynd, *Middletown: A Study in Modern American Culture* (New York: Harcourt, Brace and World, 1929); and "Accident Experience of the Iron and Steel Industry," 34 (table 3).

92. Brody, *Steelworkers,* 250–55.

93. Ibid., 225–29; *Little Steel Companies,* 46–47.

94. *Little Steel Companies,* 104. On King's views of industrial relations, see W. M. MacKenzie King and F. A. McGregor, *Industry and Humanity: A Study of the Principles Underlying Industrial Reconstruction* (New York: Houghton Mifflin, 1918).

95. *Characteristics of Company Unions,* Bureau of Labor Statistics Bulletin No. 634 (Washington, DC: GPO, 1935). See also Daniel Nelson, "The Company Union Movement, 1900–1937: A Reexamination," *Business History Review* 56, no. 3 (1982): 335–57.

96. *Little Steel Companies,* 46–48, 60–61; Hogan, *Economic History,* 866–72.

97. Davis, *Labor and Steel,* ch. 7.

98. Robert R. R. Brooks, *As Steel Goes . . . Unionism in a Basic Industry* (New Haven, CT: Yale University Press, 1940), 42.

99. "Labor Federation Ousting Radicals," *New York Times,* November 18, 1920, p. 1; "Gompers Charges Plot by Foster," *Washington Post,* April 13, 1922, p. 1.

100. Bernstein, *Turbulent Years,* 93; Louis Adamic, *My America: 1928–1938* (New York: Harper and Brothers, 1938), 348.

101. Cohen, *Making a New Deal,* 184–204; Gordon, *New Deals,* 36–37, 45–55.

102. A plan in 1922 to merge Republic, Sheet & Tube, Inland, Brier Hill Steel, Lackawanna Steel, and Midvale Steel into one giant corporation was preempted by Bethlehem's merger with the latter two firms; and a 1930 venture to merge Sheet & Tube with Bethlehem was rejected by stockholders. *Little Steel Companies,* 13, 22. On the posture of the Little Steel companies in the 1920s, see Hogan, *Economic History,* 899–990 (table 28–24). On Republic's overall developments, see Earle C. Smith, "History of Republic Steel Corporation (1937)," Series 8, Public Relations Division, Container 342, Folder 30, WRHS-RSC.

103. Thomas J. Misa, *A Nation of Steel* (Baltimore: Johns Hopkins University Press, 1995), 256 (fig. 7.2); Gertrude G. Schroeder, *The Growth of Major Steel Companies, 1900–1950* (Baltimore: Johns Hopkins University Press, 1953), 197 (table 16).

104. Thomas K. McCraw and Forest Reinhardt, "Losing to Win: U.S. Steel's Pricing, Investment Decisions, and Market Share, 1901–1938," *Journal of Economic History,* vol. 64, no. 3 (1989): 597–98 (tables 1–2).

105. Hogan, *Economic History,* 1119, 1134–42 (tables 34–1, 34–3, 34–5), 1167.

106. Warren, *Bethlehem Steel,* 135–36; Hogan, *Economic History,* 1225–95 (tables 36–19, 36–24, 36–38, 36–45, 36–48).

107. Hogan, *Economic History,* 1181 (table 35–1), 1272 (table 36–36). See also *Statistical Abstract of the United States, 1937* (Washington, DC: GPO, 1938), 742 (table 780).

108. Bernstein, *The Lean Years: A History of the American Worker, 1920–1933* (Boston: Houghton Mifflin, 1960), 506–7. Supposedly, in 1932, only 18,938 of the

158,000 workers on the U.S. Steel payroll were employed full-time. O'Connor, *Steel-Dictator*, 283.

109. Bodnar, *Workers' World*, 146.

110. Gerald Markowitz and David Rosner, *"Slaves of the Depression": Workers' Letters about Life on the Job* (Ithaca, NY: Cornell University Press, 1987), 5.

111. O'Connor, *Steel-Dictator*, 123–24.

112. Adamic, *My America*, 263–97. A Farm Security Administration photographer, Rothstein captured striking images of the daily lives of steel workers in the late 1930s, many of which may be viewed at the website of the Library of Congress.

113. Interview of Augustine Izzo, March 26, 1991, Video Oral History Collection, at approx. min. 1:09–1:11, YHCIL. See also interview of William Brown Jr., April 15, 1991, Video Oral History Collection, at approx. min. 7, YHCIL; and interview of Gilbert Peterson Sr., September 19, 1991, Video Oral History Collection, at approx. min. 8–9, YHCIL.

114. Metzgar, *Striking Steel*, 35.

115. Witt Bowden, "Labor in Depression and Recovery," *Monthly Labor Review* 45, no. 5 (1937): 1061 (table 4); Witt Bowden, "Employment, Earnings, Production, and Prices, 1932 to 1936," *Monthly Labor Review* 42, no. 4 (1936): 851, 876 (table 4).

116. O'Connor, *Steel-Dictator*, 270–71, 286.

117. William J. Adelman, *The Memorial Day Massacre of 1937* (Chicago: Illinois Historical Society, 1975), 15. See also reply to statements of the American Iron and Steel Institute in regard to wages, August 3, 1936, Congress of Industrial Organizations Collection, Box 19, Folder 6, ACHRC.

118. Patterson, Reese, and Sargent, "Your Dog Don't Bark No More," 91.

119. Markowitz and Rosner, *"Slaves of the Depression,"* 3.

120. Robert S. McElvaine, *The Great Depression: America, 1929–1941* (New York: Three Rivers 1993), 79–81, 92, 171–79; Anthony J. Badger, *The New Deal* (New York: Farrar, Straus and Giroux 1989), 19.

121. Caroline Bird, *The Invisible Scar* (New York: McKay 1966), 28.

122. James C. Kollros, "Creating a Steel Workers Union in the Calumet Region, 1933–1945" (PhD dissertation, University of Illinois–Chicago, 1998), 92–96. See also Wymard, *Talking Steel*, 40. In 1934, U.S. Steel claimed to have expended, to that point, $577,000 in direct relief and $2,690,000 in credits and loans to its employees. O'Connor, *Steel-Dictator*, 267–70, 283–84.

123. O'Connor, *Steel-Dictator*, 261–66.

124. Interview of Dan Thomas, August 1, 1974, p. 16, YSU-OHP.

CHAPTER 3: SURE, WE HAVE GUNS

1. "'Sure, We've Got Guns'—Girdler," *Steel Labor*, June 21, 1937, p. 6.

2. U.S. Senate, Committee on Education and Labor, *Violations of Free Speech and the Rights of Labor: Private Police Systems*, Report No. 6, pt. 2, 76th Cong., 1st Sess. (Washington, DC: GPO, 1939) (hereafter *Private Police*), 4–11; U.S. Senate,

Committee on Education and Labor, *Violations of Free Speech and the Rights of Labor: Strikebreaking Services,* Report No. 6, pt. 1, 76th Cong., 1st Sess. (Washington, DC: GPO, 1939) (hereafter *Strikebreaking Services*), 1–13; U.S. Senate, Committee on Education and Labor, *Violations of Free Speech and the Rights of Labor: Industrial Munitions,* Report No. 6, pt. 3, 76th Cong., 1st Sess. (Washington, DC: GPO, 1939) (hereafter *Industrial Munitions*), 5–13.

3. Fraser M. Ottanelli, *The Communist Party of the United States: From the Depression to World War II* (New Brunswick, NJ: Rutgers University Press, 1991), 33–34; Irving Bernstein, *The Lean Years: A History of the American Worker, 1920–1933* (New York: Houghton Mifflin, 1960), 432–34.

4. Philip Taft and Philip Ross, "American Labor Violence: Its Causes, Character, and Outcome," in *Violence in America,* ed. Hugh D. Graham and Ted R. Gurr (New York: Signet, 1969), 335–38.

5. Sidney Lens, *The Labor Wars: From the Molly Maguires to the Sit-Downs* (New York: Doubleday, 1973), 273; Robert Justin Goldstein, *Political Repression in Modern America from 1870 to 1976* (Urbana: University of Illinois Press, 2001), 226.

6. Remington Rand, 2 NLRB 626, 635–42, 644–48, 663–64, 666n31 (1937); *Strikebreaking Services,* 117–19.

7. *Remington Rand,* 2 NLRB at 664–66.

8. *Strikebreaking Services,* 119–20.

9. U.S. Senate, Committee on Education and Labor, *Violations of Free Speech and the Rights of Labor: Labor Policies of Employers' Associations; Part IV, The "Little Steel" Companies,* Report No. 151, 77th Cong., 1st Sess. (Washington, DC: GPO, 1941) (hereafter *Little Steel Companies*), 88.

10. Ibid., 89; *Private Police,* 127–28, 130.

11. *Private Police,* 129–30.

12. *Little Steel Companies,* 89–90; *Private Police,* 130–44. See also U.S. Senate, *Hearings before the Committee on Education and Labor: Violations of Free Speech and the Rights of Labor,* 76th Cong., 1st–3rd Sess. (Washington, DC: GPO, 1937) (hereafter LCH), 9779–10306.

13. *Industrial Munitions,* 111–15, 223 (appendix G).

14. *Little Steel Companies,* 88–91; *Industrial Munitions,* 144–52; LCH, 10068, 10078–80.

15. William T. Hogan, *Economic History of the Iron and Steel Industry in the United States* (Lexington, MA: Lexington Books, 1971), 1217 (table 32–12), 1235 (table 36–19), 1239 (table 36–20), 1270–78 (tables 36–36, 36–37), 1289–93 (tables 36–45, 36–46, 36–47).

16. A. F. Hinrichs and Harry Brenner, "Trends in Manufacturing Employment, 1929 to 1937," *Monthly Labor Review* 50, no. 6 (1940): 1308, 1312.

17. LCH, 9839 (exhibit 4300). For slightly lower numbers, see Hogan, *Economic History,* 1178–79. In 1937, the steel industry's half million wage-earning employees in basic production made it the largest manufacturing industry by scale of employment. *Statistical Abstract of the United States, 1940* (Washington, DC: GPO, 1941) 825 (table 830).

18. Hogan, *Economic History*, 1178–79.

19. Bethlehem also operated and built ships and shipyards. *Little Steel Companies*, 26–32.

20. *Annual Report of Republic Steel Corporation, 1937* (Cleveland: Republic Steel Corporation, 1938), 24–27; Republic Steel, 9 NLRB 219, 226–27 (1938); *Little Steel Companies*, 16; LCH, 9733.

21. *Little Steel Companies*, 22.

22. *Annual Report of Youngstown Sheet & Tube Company, 1937* (Youngstown, OH, Youngstown Sheet & Tube Company, 1938), 16–19.

23. *Annual Report of Bethlehem Steel Corporation, 1937* (Wilmington, DE: Bethlehem Steel Corporation, 1938), 32–33.

24. *Annual Report of Inland Steel Company, 1937* (Chicago: Inland Steel Company, 1938), 11.

25. Norman R. Collins and Lee E. Preston, "The Size Structure of the Largest Industrial Firms, 1909–1958," *American Economic Review* 51, no. 5 (1961), 986, 1004–11 (appendix).

26. *Private Police*, 116, 123–34, 153–94; LCH, 10434–39, 10449–55, 10879–10999.

27. *Little Steel Companies*, 128–29, 171–76.

28. LCH, 11497, 11499, 11612 (exhibit 4676).

29. *Industrial Munitions*, 19–45, 217–21 (appendices C–F). The company purchased two of the machine guns after the 1916 strike at East Youngstown; the other six it inherited when it acquired Brier Hill Steel in Youngstown. LCH, 11174–75.

30. LCH, 8630–38 (exhibits 3943–54).

31. *Industrial Munitions*, 46–49, 61–65.

32. Ibid., 203–4.

33. LCH, 11460 (exhibit 4649), 11380 (exhibit 4588).

34. *Industrial Munitions*, 63–65, 194, 215.

35. See "NLRB Will Investigate Steel Workers' Charge of Shooting, 'Arsenals,'" *Washington Post*, July 19, 1937, p. 1; "Shoot-to-Kill Order Laid to Republic Boss," *Steel Labor*, June 5, 1937, p. 1; and "Always Had Guns on Hand, Girdler Says," *Cleveland Plain Dealer*, June 2, 1937, p. 1.

36. *Industrial Munitions*, 54, 69–105.

37. *Little Steel Companies*, 128–29, 171–76; *Industrial Munitions*, 121–55; LCH, 12136–38 (exhibit 4777). The SWOC was well aware of these efforts even before the strike began. "SWOC Demands Deputy Records, Youngstown Vindicator," May 21, 1937, p. 1.

38. Irving Bernstein, *The Turbulent Years: A History of the American Worker, 1933–1941* (New York: Houghton Mifflin, 1969), 479–80.

39. Carl Becker, "Charles Ruffin Hook," in *Encyclopedia of American Business History and Biography: The Iron and Steel Industry*, ed. Bruce Seely (New York: Facts on File, 1994), 199; John Tebbel, *The Human Touch in Business: The Story of Charles R. Hook* (Dayton, OH: Otterbein, 1963).

40. Alec Kirby, "Ernest T. Weir," in *Encyclopedia of American Business History and Biography: The Iron and Steel Industry*, ed. Bruce Seely (New York: Facts on

File, 1994), 466; Frederick Rudolph, "The American Liberty League, 1934–1940," *American Historical Review* 56, no. 1 (1950): 19–33; "Two Boards Listed by Liberty League," *New York Times,* January 9, 1935, p. 17.

41. Benjamin Stolberg, "Big Steel, Little Steel, and the C.I.O.," *Nation,* July 31, 1937, p. 119.

42. Bernstein, *Turbulent Years,* 480. The La Follette Committee and the NLRB secured much evidence to support this characterization. LCH, 13903–9 (exhibits 5210–11), 13921–24 (exhibit 5224); *Republic Steel,* 9 NLRB at 322–23.

43. James A. Gross, *The Making of the National Labor Relations Board* (Albany: SUNY Press, 1974), 8.

44. Tom Girdler, with Boyden Sparkes, *Boot Straps: The Autobiography of Tom Girdler* (New York: Scribner's, 1943), 5, 39. See also Carol Poh Miller, "Tom M. Girdler," in *Encyclopedia of American Business History and Biography: The Iron and Steel Industry,* ed. Bruce Seely (New York: Facts on File, 1994), 161.

45. Girdler, *Boot Straps,* 27.

46. Ibid., 110.

47. Ibid., 96–97.

48. Ibid., 449–50 (emphasis in original).

49. James A. Gross, *The Reshaping of the National Labor Relations Board* (Albany: SUNY Press, 1981), 7–8.

50. Untitled memorandum, n.d., Series 6, Legal Division, Subseries A, Administrative File, Republic Iron and Steel Company, Minutes of Directors, 1929–37, Container 215, Folder 11, WRHS-RSC.

51. Girdler, *Boot Straps,* 177.

52. Ibid., 169–72, 176.

53. Kenneth Casebeer, "Aliquippa: The Company Town and Contested Power in the Construction of Law," *Buffalo Law Review* 43, no. 3 (1995), 617, 633–34.

54. *Little Steel Companies,* 71–74; *Private Police,* 117–18.

55. Address to the American Iron and Steel Institute, May 24, 1934, reprinted in LCH, 9738, 9897 (exhibit 4303) (quotation p. 9738).

56. *Little Steel Companies,* 29–30 (table 5).

57. LCH, 9853–54, 9881–85 (table 21, charts 4–5).

58. *Annual Report of the Attorney General, 1935–1936* (Washington, DC: DOJ, 1936), 25–26; *Annual Report of the Attorney General, 1936–1937* (Washington, DC: DOJ, 1937), 27; Ellis W. Hawley, *The New Deal and the Problem of Monopoly: A Study in Economic Ambivalence* (New York: Fordham University Press, 1995), 373.

59. *Little Steel Companies,* 54–55; LCH, 7540–41 (exhibit 3799), 11407 (exhibit 4602).

60. Hawley, *New Deal,* 19–46.

61. Anthony J. Badger, *The New Deal* (New York: Farrar, Straus and Giroux, 1989), 85–86.

62. Ibid., 93; U.S. Senate, Committee on Education and Labor, *Violations of Free Speech and the Rights of Labor: Labor Policies of Employers' Associations; Part I, The National Metal Trades Association,* Report No. 6, pt. 4, 76th Cong., 1st Sess.

(Washington, DC: GPO, 1939), 49–69; U.S. Senate, Committee on Education and Labor, *Violations of Free Speech and the Rights of Labor: Labor Policies of Employers' Associations; Part III, The National Association of Manufacturers,* Report No. 6, pt. 6, 76th Cong., 1st Sess. (Washington, DC: GPO, 1939), 75–153.

63. Bernstein, *Turbulent Years,* ch. 7; Peter H. Irons, *The New Deal Lawyers* (Princeton: Princeton University Press, 1993), 243–47; James Gray Pope, "Worker Lawmaking, Sit-Down Strikes, and the Shaping of American Industrial Relations, 1935–1958," *Law and History Review* 24, no. 1 (2006): 45–113.

64. Mary Heaton Vorse, *Labor's New Millions* (New York: Modern Age, 1938), 132.

65. *Little Steel Companies,* 49–51; Bernstein, *Turbulent Years,* 480; Benjamin Stolberg, *The Story of the CIO* (New York: Viking, 1938), 80–81; Paul Y. Anderson, "Armed Rebellion on the Right," *Nation,* August 7, 1937, p. 146. An even more incendiary claim, raised by Communists but impossible to verify, is that the companies worked hand in hand with overtly fascist groups, including the infamous Volksbund and Silver Legion, to oppose the strike. "Republic Steel Backs Cleveland Silver Shirt, Nazi Groups," *Daily Worker,* August 5, 1937, p. 2.

CHAPTER 4: I NEVER GAVE THAT GUY NOTHIN'

1. Irving Bernstein, *The Lean Years: A History of the American Worker, 1920–1933* (New York: Houghton Mifflin, 1960), 334–57; Gerald Markowitz and David Rosner, *"Slaves of the Depression": Workers' Letters about Life on the Job* (Ithaca, NY: Cornell University Press, 1987), 3.

2. Ellie Wymard, *Talking Steel Towns: The Men and Women of Steel Valley* (Pittsburgh: Carnegie Mellon University Press, 2007), 41.

3. Ellis W. Hawley, *The New Deal and the Problem of Monopoly: A Study in Economic Ambivalence* (New York: Fordham University Press, 1995), 13.

4. Robert Zieger, *The CIO, 1935–1955* (Chapel Hill: University of North Carolina Press, 1995), 17 (quotation); Harvey O'Connor, *Steel-Dictator* (New York: John Day, 1935), 134; Peter H. Irons, *The New Deal Lawyers* (Princeton: Princeton University Press, 1993), 203, 227.

5. James A. Gross, *The Making of the National Labor Relations Board* (Albany: SUNY Press, 1974), 10–12.

6. Interview of Ruben Farr, March 27, 1968, pp. 5–6, USWA–Labor Oral History Collection, PSU-HCLA.

7. Gross, *Making of the NLRB,* 122–30.

8. Hawley, *New Deal,* 55–62, 95–97, 108.

9. Gross, *Making of the NLRB,* 25–30, 53–61, 73–88.

10. Ibid., 7–39.

11. John Hennen, "E. T. Weir, Employee Representation, and the Dimensions of Social Control: Weirton Steel, 1933–1937," *Labor Studies Journal* 26, no. 3 (2001): 29–36. See also Irving Bernstein, *The Turbulent Years: A History of the American*

Worker, 1933–1941 (New York: Houghton Mifflin, 1969), 177–78; Gross, *Making of the NLRB,* 38–39; Staughton Lynd, "The Possibility of Radicalism in the Early 1930s: The Case of Steel," *Radical America* 6, no. 6 (1972): 37–64; and United States v. Weirton Steel, 7 F. Supp. 255 (D.C. Del. 1934), 10 F. Supp. 55 (D.C. Del. 1935).

12. Zieger, *CIO,* 16–17; Bernstein, *Turbulent Years,* 32–35.

13. Gross, *Making of the NLRB,* 23–24, 46–51; U.S. Senate, Committee on Education and Labor, *Violations of Free Speech and the Rights of Labor: Labor Policies of Employers' Associations; Part IV, The "Little Steel" Companies,* Report No. 151, 77th Cong., 1st Sess. (Washington, DC: GPO, 1941) (hereafter *Little Steel Companies*), 69; Lewis L. Lorwin and Arthur Wubnig, *Labor Relations Board: The Regulation of Collective Bargaining under the National Industrial Recovery Act* (Washington, DC: Brookings, 1935), 143.

14. William T. Hogan, *Economic History of the Iron and Steel Industry in the United States* (Lexington, MA: Lexington Books, 1971), 1167; *Little Steel Companies,* 53; Bernstein, *Turbulent Years,* 455.

15. Horace Cayton, *Black Workers and the New Unions* (Chapel Hill: University of North Carolina Press, 1939), ch. 5; *Little Steel Companies,* 51–53, 83–88, 104–5.

16. On the workings of the ERPs, see "Plan of Employees' Representation at the Cambria Plant of Bethlehem Steel Company," Minutes of the General Body, January 28, 1937, Howard Curtiss Papers, Box 4, Folder 7, PSU-HCLA.

17. Bernstein, *Turbulent Years,* 456–57; Max Gordon, "The Communists and the Drive to Organize Steel, 1936," *Labor History* 23, no. 2 (1982): 258.

18. Robert S. McElvaine, *The Great Depression: America, 1929–1941* (New York: Three Rivers, 1993), 252–63; Anthony J. Badger, *The New Deal* (New York: Farrar, Straus and Giroux, 1989), 127–28.

19. Gross, *Making of the NLRB,* 143–49; Hawley, *New Deal,* 154–55, 190.

20. U.S. Senate, *Report on the National Labor Relations Board,* Report No. 573, 74th Cong., 1st Sess., pp. 4–6, reprinted in *Legislative History of the National Labor Relations Act, 1935* (Washington, DC: GPO, 1949), 2300–2305.

21. James Gray Pope, "Worker Lawmaking, Sit-Down Strikes, and the Shaping of American Industrial Relations, 1935–1958," *Law and History Review,* 24, no. 1 (2006): 94–96. See also Karl E. Klare, "Judicial Deradicalization of the Wagner Act and the Origins of Modern Legal Consciousness," *Minnesota Law Review* 62, no. 6 (1978): 265.

22. NLRB v. Jones & Laughlin Steel, 301 U.S. 1, 34–35, 41–43 (1937).

23. Bernstein, *Turbulent Years,* 400–424.

24. See, for example, "The Tasks of the Communist Party in the Youngstown Section," *Party Organizer* 7, no. 4 (April 1934): 11; J. D., "Some Experiences in Concentrating on Republic Steel, Youngstown," *Party Organizer* 6, no. 3 (March 1933): 13; "Recruiting Experiences During the Ambridge and Greenburg Steel Strikes," *Party Organizer* 6, no. 12 (December 1933): 11; "Lessons of the Acme Steel Strike," *Party Organizer* 6, nos. 8–9 (August–September 1933): 13; and "Problems Faced in Building Organization in a Steel Town," *Party Organizer* 6, no. 2 (February 1933): 16.

25. See Judith Stepan-Norris and Maurice Zeitlin, *Left Out: Reds and America's Industrial Unions* (New York: Cambridge University Press, 2002).

26. Frances Peterson, *Strikes in the United States: 1880–1936* (Washington, DC: GPO, 1938), 61–62 (table 28), 71–76 (table 30).

27. See Walter Galenson, *The CIO Challenge to the AFL: A History of the American Labor Movement, 1935–1941* (Cambridge, MA: Harvard University Press, 1960), 583–92.

28. Zieger, *CIO*, 24–25. See also Christopher L. Tomlins, *The State and the Unions: Labor Relations, Law, and the Organized Labor Movement in America, 1880–1960* (New York: Cambridge University Press, 1985), 141–43; and Galenson, *CIO*, 76–77, 79.

29. Lizabeth Cohen, *Making a New Deal: Industrial Workers in Chicago, 1919–1939* (New York: Cambridge University Press, 2009), 84–187, 293–95.

30. McElvaine, *Great Depression*, 6–7, 170–87, 196–202.

31. Randi Storch, *Red Chicago: American Communism at Its Grassroots, 1928–1935* (Urbana: University of Illinois Press, 2008), 154–44, 186.

32. Cayton, *Black Workers*, ch. 6; Horace Bancroft Davis, *Labor and Steel* (New York: International, 1933), 264–65; Gordon, "Communists," 258; James C. Kollros, "Creating a Steel Workers Union in the Calumet Region, 1933–1945" (PhD dissertation, University of Illinois–Chicago, 1998), 135–38; interview of John N. Grajciar (1 of 2), July 2, 1968, pp. 5–6, 20–21, USWA–Labor Oral History Collection, PSU-HCLA.

33. Storch, *Red Chicago*, 180.

34. Gordon, "Communists," 258; Storch, *Red Chicago*, 180–85.

35. Fraser M. Ottanelli, *The Communist Party of the United States: From the Depression to World War II* (New Brunswick, NJ: Rutgers University Press, 1991), 53–55; Lynd, "Possibility of Radicalism," 43–44, 46–52.

36. Bernstein, *Turbulent Years*, 197–98.

37. Louis Adamic, *My America: 1928–1938* (New York: Harper and Brothers, 1938), 350; interview of John N. Grajciar (1 of 2), July 2, 1968, USWA–Labor Oral History Collection, PSU-HCLA.

38. James D. Rose, *Duquesne and the Rise of Steel Unionism* (Urbana: University of Illinois Press, 2001), 84–85; O'Connor, *Steel-Dictator*, 186.

39. O'Connor, *Steel-Dictator*, 185–89; Kenneth Casebeer, "Aliquippa: The Company Town and Contested Power in the Construction of Law," *Buffalo Law Review* 43, no. 3 (1995): 617, 653–54.

40. Zieger, *CIO*, 35; *Little Steel Companies*, 53; Ottanelli, *Communist Party*, 53–54; Cayton, *Black Workers*, 126.

41. Cayton, *Black Workers*, ch. 7.

42. U.S. Senate, *Hearings before the Committee on Education and Labor: Violations of Free Speech and the Rights of Labor*, 76th Cong., 1st–3rd Sess. (Washington, DC: GPO, 1937) (hereafter LCH), 12701–3.

43. "Labor Starts Drive to Halt Wage Cuts," *New York Times*, May 14, 1931, p. 1.

44. Peterson, *Strikes in the United States*, 125 (table 37).

45. O'Connor, *Steel-Dictator,* 196.

46. Ibid., 196–98.

47. On the threat of a large strike in 1934, see ibid., 212–18; Lynd, "Possibility of Radicalism," 48–51; Adamic, *My America,* 351–54; and Barbara Warne Newell, *Chicago and the Labor Movement: Metropolitan Unionism in the 1930's* (Urbana: University of Illinois Press, 1961), 124–25. The Steel Labor Relations Board—as well as both the (first) National Labor Relations Board and many other industry-specific boards—were created by Public Resolution No. 44, Joint Resolution of Congress, June 19, 1934, 14 U.S.C. 702(a)–(f) and Presidential Executive Order No. 6763, June 29, 1934.

48. O'Connor, *Steel-Dictator,* 239–42. See also Hogan, *Economic History,* 1168–69.

49. Lynd, "Possibility of Radicalism," 54–59.

50. Rose, *Duquesne and the Rise of Steel Unionism,* 5–6.

51. Memorandum of agreement between the Amalgamated Association of Iron Steel and Tin Workers and the Committee for Industrial Organization, June 3, 1936, Congress of Industrial Organizations Collection, Box 19, Folder 6, ACHRC; chairman's report, Steel Workers Organizing Committee, "Reports of Officers to the Wage and Policy Convention in Pittsburgh," 1937, pp. 3, 5–6, Harold Ruttenberg Papers, Box 5, Folder 17, PSU-HCLA. .

52. Memorandum of agreement between the Amalgamated Association of Iron Steel and Tin Workers and the Committee for Industrial Organization, June 3, 1936, Congress of Industrial Organizations Collection, Box 19, Folder 6, ACHRC; Bernstein, *Turbulent Years,* 437–42; Galenson, *CIO,* 79–83.

53. "Steel Union Lodges Ask Cooperation with C.I.O.," *Union News Service,* April 27, 1936; "Industrial Drive Urged by Steel Workers Lodge," *Union News Service,* March 2, 1936; "Steel Workers Plead for Organization," *Union News Service,* February 17, 1936.

54. Zieger, *CIO,* 37; Bernstein, *Turbulent Years,* 435–41.

55. Bernstein, *Turbulent Years,* 441. See also Zieger, *CIO,* 34–39; and Galenson, *CIO,* 86–87. The AA was formally absorbed into the SWOC before the SWOC was reconstituted as the USW. Memorandum from David McDonald to officers and members of all SWOC lodges, July 25, 1940, David McDonald Papers, Box 197, File 2, PSU-HCLA. Various documents concerning the formation of the SWOC may be found in Congress of Industrial Organizations Collection, Box 19, Folder 6, ACHRC.

56. Minutes of the organizational meeting of the SWOC, June 17, 1936, Congress of Industrial Organizations Records, Box 19, Folder 6, ACHRC; "The Organizational Set-Up for the Steel Organizing Campaign," n.d., ibid.; Zieger, *CIO,* 36–37; Galenson, *CIO,* 84.

57. George Lipsitz, *Class and Culture in Cold War America* (New York: Praeger, 1981), 143.

58. On Murray's background and disposition, see Bernstein, *Turbulent Years,* 441–47; Elizabeth C. Sholes and Thomas E. Leary, "Philip Murray," in *Encyclope-*

dia of American Business History and Biography: The Iron and Steel Industry, ed. Bruce Seely (New York: Facts on File, 1994), 325.

59. Minutes of the organizational meeting of the SWOC, June 17, 1937, p. 2, Congress of Industrial Organizations Collection, Box 19, Folder 6, ACHRC; report by Philip Murray to the SWOC, September 29, 1936, Congress of Industrial Organizations Collection, Box 19, Folder 7, ACHRC.

CHAPTER 5: TO BANISH FEAR

1. David Brody, "The Origins of Modern Steel Unionism: The SWOC Era," in *Forging a Union of Steel,* ed. Paul F. Clark et al. (Ithaca, NY: ILR Press, 1987), 21.

2. Statement by Philip Murray, November 8, 1936, "The Problem before the SWOC on June 17, 1936," pp. 1–2, Howard Curtiss Papers, Box 5, Folder 17, PSU-HCLA.

3. William Z. Foster claimed that sixty organizers were Communists. William Z. Foster, *History of the Communist Party of the United States* (New York: Greenwood, 1968), 349–50. Benjamin Stolberg, an anti-Communist, claimed there were seventy or eighty. Benjamin Stolberg, *The Story of the CIO* (New York: Viking, 1938), 86–87. See also "Steel Campaign Under Way as 200 Organizers Take Field," *Union News Service,* June 22, 1936.

4. Sherry Lee Linkon and John Russo, *Steeltown U.S.A.: Work and Memory in Youngstown* (Lawrence: University of Kansas Press, 2002), 38.

5. Randi Storch, *Red Chicago: American Communism at Its Grassroots, 1928–1935* (Urbana: University of Illinois Press, 2008), 107–27; John Williamson, *Dangerous Scot: The Life and Work of an American "Undesirable"* (New York: International, 1969), 80–93.

6. Max Gordon, "The Communists and the Drive to Organize Steel, 1936," *Labor History* 23, no. 2 (1982): 255–56.

7. Interview of Ruben Farr, March 27, 1968, p. 21, USWA–Labor Oral History Collection, PSU-HCLA.

8. Williamson, *Dangerous Scot,* 125.

9. See interview of John N. Grajciar (1 of 2), July 2, 1968, pp. 32, 37–38, USWA–Labor Oral History Collection, PSU-HCLA.

10. Interview of John N. Grajciar (2 of 2), March 21, 1969, p. 4, USWA–Labor Oral History Collection, PSU-HCLA.

11. Interview of James Gallagher, October 17, 1967, p. 6, USWA–Labor Oral History Collection, PSU-HCLA.

12. Interview of John Johns (2 of 2), March 3, 1978, p. 20–21, USWA–Labor Oral History Collection, PSU-HCLA.

13. Bill Gebert, "The Steel Drive and the Tasks of Communists in Mass Organizations," *Party Organizer* 9, no. 9 (September 1936): 12.

14. Storch, *Red Chicago,* 31–98.

15. Gordon, "Communists," 254.

16. James C. Kollros, "Creating a Steel Workers Union in the Calumet Region, 1933–1945" (PhD dissertation, University of Illinois–Chicago, 1998), 193–95. See also interview of Sam Evett, April 1, 1971, pp. 4–5, USWA–Labor Oral History Collection, PSU-HCLA.

17. Walter Galenson, *The CIO Challenge to the AFL: A History of the American Labor Movement, 1935–1941* (Cambridge, MA: Harvard University Press, 1960), 84–85, 110.

18. Statement by Philip Murray, November 8, 1936, "The Problem before the SWOC on June 17, 1936," pp. 1–2, Howard Curtiss Papers, Box 5, Folder 17, PSU-HCLA. See also memorandum from Clinton Golden to Harold Ruttenberg, August 6, 1936, in SWOC/Hubbard Strike, Harold Ruttenberg Papers, Box 3, Folder 13, PSU-HCLA.

19. "Steel Drive Progress Alarms Employers, S.W.O.C. Meet Hears," *Union News Service,* October 6, 1937.

20. George Patterson, Jesse Reese, and John Sargent, "Your Dog Don't Bark No More," in *Rank and File: Personal Histories of Working-Class Organizers,* ed. Alice Lynd and Staughton Lynd (New York: Monthly Review, 1988), 99.

21. Horace Cayton, *Black Workers and the New Unions* (Chapel Hill: University of North Carolina Press, 1939), 195; "Mass Meetings and Staff Assignments Start Steel Drive," *Union News Service,* June 29, 1936; "Some Notes on the Big Steel Drive," *Union News Service,* June 22, 1936.

22. James D. Rose, *Duquesne and the Rise of Steel Unionism* (Urbana: University of Illinois Press, 2001), 138–39; Irving Bernstein, *The Turbulent Years: A History of the American Worker, 1933–1941* (Boston: Houghton Mifflin, 1969), 454–55; "Prominent Negroes Push Steel Drive," *Steel Labor,* February 20, 1937, p. 5; "Negroes Urged to Join Steel Union Drive," *Steel Labor,* October 10, 1936, p. 7; "The Steel Drive Gets Going," *Steel Labor,* August 1, 1936, p. 2.

23. Bruce Nelson, *Divided We Stand: American Workers and the Struggle for Black Equality* (Princeton: Princeton University Press, 2001), 160–61; Robert B. Gordon, *American Iron: 1607–1900* (Baltimore: Johns Hopkins University Press, 1996), 34, 86, 118, 244.

24. Nelson, *Divided We Stand,* 160–62.

25. Ibid., 164–67; Lizabeth Cohen, *Making a New Deal: Industrial Workers in Chicago, 1919–1939,* 2nd ed. (New York: Cambridge University Press, 2009), 205–6.

26. Linkon and Russo, *Steeltown U.S.A.,* 27.

27. Nelson, *Divided We Stand,* 167–69; Horace Bancroft Davis, *Labor and Steel* (New York: International, 1933), 28–29.

28. Even asking about being assigned a "white" job could get a black worker fired. Nelson, *Divided We Stand,* 169–70. On the theory about heat resistance, see Cayton, *Black Workers,* 30–35.

29. On the ghettoization of black steel workers, see Nelson, *Divided We Stand,* 172, 178–82; and Dennis C. Dickerson, *Out of the Crucible: Black Steelworkers in Western Pennsylvania, 1875–1980* (Albany: SUNY Press, 1986), 56–60, 118–26.

30. Cayton, *Black Workers,* 81.

31. Rose, *Duquesne and the Rise of Steel Unionism,* 64–72; Cayton, *Black Workers,* 176–77; Dickerson, *Out of the Crucible,* 132–34.

32. Cayton, *Black Workers,* 209–10.

33. *Struggle in Steel,* directed by Tony Buba and Raymond Henderson, DVD (San Francisco: California Newsreel, 1996), at approx. min. 12:30.

34. Nelson, *Divided We Stand,* 182–84.

35. Steven R. Scipes, "Trade Union Development and Racial Oppression in Chicago's Steel and Meatpacking Industries, 1933–1950" (PhD dissertation, University of Illinois–Chicago 2003), 175–79.

36. Eleanor Rye, "Women in Steel," *Chicago Defender,* September 12, 1936, p. 4.

37. Patterson, Reese, and Sargent, "Your Dog Don't Bark No More," 99; Ruth Needleman, *Black Freedom Fighters in Steel: The Struggle for Democratic Unionism* (Ithaca, NY: Cornell University Press, 2003), 97–98.

38. Memorandum from Lee Pressman to staff members, July 1, 1936, Harold Ruttenberg Collection, Box 3, Folder 18, PSU-HCLA.

39. Republic Steel, 9 NLRB 219, 241 (1938).

40. Robert R. R. Brooks, *As Steel Goes . . . Unionism in a Basic Industry* (New Haven: Yale University Press, 1940), 116–17; "Pennsylvania State Authorities Won't Harass Orderly Labor Activities," *Steel Labor,* August 1, 1936, p. 6; Vin Sweeney, "Steel Workers' Rights Will Be Protected, Says Kennedy," *Union News Service,* July 13, 1936.

41. Kollros, "Creating a Steel Workers Union," 154–81.

42. Several of these points are made by Brody in "Origins of Modern Steel Unionism," 21.

43. Thomas R. Brooks, *Clint: A Biography of a Labor Intellectual* (New York: Atheneum, 1978), 160–61.

44. See, for example, "Maloy Unmasked" (handbill), in Employee Representation, 1937–42, Harold Ruttenberg Papers, Box 4, Folder 6, PSU-HCLA.

45. Memorandum from Philip Murray to subregional directors, September 11, 1936, p. 3, Howard Curtiss Papers, Box 5, Folder 17, PSU-HCLA.

46. Statement by Philip Murray, November 8, 1936, "The Problem before the SWOC on June 17, 1936," p. 3, Howard Curtiss Papers, Box 5, Folder 17, PSU-HCLA.

47. Employee Representation, 1937–42, Harold Ruttenberg Papers, Box 4, Folder 6, PSU-HCLA; SWOC, 1937–1941, Howard Curtiss Papers, Box 2, Folder 2, PSU-HCLA; letter from Elmer Cope to Harold Ruttenberg, October 20, 1936, in SWOC, Harold Ruttenberg Papers, Box 3, Folder 19, PSU-HCLA; remarks of Colonel Bohne, opening of meeting, September 25, 1936, in Employee Representation, 1937–42, Harold Ruttenberg Papers, Box 4, Folder 6, PSU-HCLA.

48. Richard S. Tedlow, "The National Association of Manufacturers and Public Relations during the New Deal," *Business History Review* 50, no. 1 (1976): 25–45.

49. See, for example, "To the Public and Employees in the Steel Industry" (advertisement), *Chicago Daily Tribune,* July 1, 1937, p. 15. See also Frank Blumenthal,

"Anti-Union Publicity in the Johnstown 'Little Steel' Strike of 1937," *Public Opinion Quarterly* 3, no. 4 (1939): 676–82.

50. U.S. Senate, Committee on Education and Labor, *Violations of Free Speech and the Rights of Labor: Labor Policies of Employers' Associations; Part IV, The "Little Steel" Companies*, Report No. 151, 77th Cong., 1st Sess. (Washington, DC: GPO, 1941) (hereafter *Little Steel Companies*), 302–3; U.S. Senate, *Hearings before the Committee on Education and Labor: Violations of Free Speech and the Rights of Labor*, 76th Cong., 1st–3rd Sess. (Washington, DC: GPO, 1937) (hereafter LCH), 7766–78, 14386–479, 7895–908 (exhibit 3853), 7910–23 (exhibit 3858), 8031–50 (exhibit 3873), 8069–85 (exhibit 3885).

51. There were also quite a few Mexican and Mexican American workers in steel, concentrated in the Calumet, especially at Inland's large plant. Nelson, *Divided We Stand*, 168; Kollros, "Creating a Steel Workers Union," 22–33. On efforts to organize them, see SWOC Fieldworkers Notes, Calumet District, Box 1, Folder 2/3, PSU-HCLA; and George Patterson Papers, Box 6, Folder 7, CHS.

52. For a ground-level view of organizers' efforts on these fronts, see, generally, SWOC Fieldworkers Notes, Calumet District, Box 1, PSU-HCLA.

53. Statement by Philip Murray, November 8, 1936, "The Problem before the SWOC on June 17, 1936," p. 5, Howard Curtiss Papers, Box 5, Folder 17, PSU-HCLA. See also Nelson, *Divided We Stand*, 185; and Kenneth Casebeer, "Aliquippa: The Company Town and Contested Power in the Construction of Law," *Buffalo Law Review* 43, no.3 (1995): 667–68.

54. See, for example, "'No Discrimination' Murray Tells Negroes," *Steel Labor*, February 20, 1937, p. 5.

55. Dickerson, *Out of the Crucible*, 135–40; Cohen, *Making a New Deal*, 335; "Prominent Negroes Push Steel Drive," *Steel Labor*, February 20, 1937, p. 5; "Phil Murray Urges Negro Workers to Join Great Steel Industry Union," *Pittsburgh Courier*, February 13, 1937, p. 1; "Negroes Urged to Join Steel Union Drive," *Steel Labor*, October 20, 1936, p. 1; "Race in Drive to Unite Steel," *Chicago Defender*, August 29, 1936, p. 4.

56. Erik S. Gellman, *Death Blow to Jim Crow: The National Negro Congress and the Rise of Militant Civil Rights* (Chapel Hill: University of North Carolina Press, 2012), 35–47; Nelson, *Divided We Stand*, 192–93.

57. "Negro Steel Workers Support Movement," *Steel Labor*, August 1, 1936, p. 1.

58. On the UMW's favorable reputation among black steel workers, see Nelson, *Divided We Stand*, 189–90; and Cayton, *Black Workers*, 199–201.

59. Casebeer, "Aliquippa," 668; "Police Clubs Rout 200 Defiant Reds," *New York Times*, April 26, 1931, p. 2.

60. Cayton, *Black Workers*, 84–87, 111–22. See also Jack Johnstone, "The Work of the Steel Unit in the Main Mill of Concentration," *Party Organizer* 7, nos. 5–6 (May–June 1934): 19.

61. See, for example, "Steel and Metal: How to Develop Permanent and Intimate Contacts," *Party Organizer* 6, no. 2 (February 1933): 10, 12.

62. Storch, *Red Chicago*, 39, 50–54, 76–78.

63. See Nelson, *Divided We Stand,* 188–89; George Schuyler, "Negro Workers Lead in Great Lakes Steel Drive," *Pittsburgh Courier,* July 31, 1937, p. 1; and "CIO Drives to Organize Race Steel Workers," *Chicago Defender,* August 8, 1936, p. 4.

64. "Race in Drive to Unite Steel Workers," *Chicago Defender,* September 12, 1936, p. 11.

65. Needleman, *Black Freedom Fighters,* 122–23, 190–91.

66. Gellman, *Death Blow to Jim Crow,* 35–36; Kollros, "Creating a Steel Workers Union," 193–95; "NNC to Give Cooperation to CIO Drive," *Chicago Defender,* August 29, 1936, p. 4. See also interview of Dan Thomas, August 1, 1974, pp. 2–5, YSU-OHP.

67. Such tactics are mentioned almost weekly in the union's fieldworkers' notes from the Chicago area. SWOC Fieldworkers Notes, Calumet District, Box 1, PSU-HCLA.

68. See, for example, "CIO Investigator Scores Steel Industry Jim-Crow," *Pittsburgh Courier,* August 29, 1936, p. 3.

69. Cayton, *Black Workers,* 180–89, 207–9.

70. See, for example, "Phil Murray Urges Negro Workers to Join Great Steel Industry Union," *Pittsburgh Courier,* February 13, 1937, p. 1; "Efforts to Organize Steel Men Interests Race," *Pittsburgh Courier,* August 1, 1936, p. 13.

71. Dickerson, *Out of the Crucible,* 136–37.

72. Ernest Rice McKinney, "The Negro Worker and Labor Unions," *Pittsburgh Courier,* August 29, 1936, p. 12. See also "Industrial Unionism Marches On," *Pittsburgh Courier,* March 13, 1937, p. 10.

73. Scipes, "Trade Union Development," 173–74. See also, for example, "Continue Drive to Unite Race Steel Workers," *Chicago Defender,* March 6, 1937, p. 6; "Race in Drive to Unite Steel Workers," *Chicago Defender,* September 12, 1936, p. 11; "The Black Workers," *Chicago Defender,* August 29, 1936, p. 16; and "CIO Drives to Organize Race Steel Workers," *Chicago Defender,* August 8, 1936, p. 4.

74. Schuyler, "Negro Workers Lead in Great Lakes Steel Drive"; George Schuyler, "Race Feeling Tense Where C.I.O. Is Flaunted, Schuyler Finds," *Pittsburgh Courier,* July 24, 1937, p. 1.

75. Cayton, *Black Workers,* 202, 205.

76. January 21, 1937, SWOC Fieldworkers Notes, Calumet District, Box 1, Folder 2/3, PSU-HCLA.

77. Nelson, *Divided We Stand,* 191–92.

78. Organizer Ruben Farr recalled that black support for the SWOC during the drive was strong in Alabama. Interview of Ruben Farr, March 27, 1968, pp. 6–9, USWA–Labor Oral History Collection, PSU-HCLA. But other sources reveal difficulties in this region. See USWA District 36 Records, Box 1, File 4, Box 5, File 44, PSU-HCLA; and letters from Noel Beddow to David McDonald, December 1, 11, 12, 1936, David McDonald Papers, Box 197, File 2, PSU-HCLA. Because the southern mills were not involved in the Little Steel Strike, I have left it for others to elaborate on the course of unionism in this region.

79. Dickerson, *Out of the Crucible,* 143–44; Schuyler, "Negro Workers Lead in Great Lakes Steel Drive"; Schuyler, "Race Feeling Tense Where C.I.O. Is Flaunted, Schuyler Finds."

80. On the effect of the General Motors sit-down strikes, see memorandum from Clinton Golden to subregional directors, February 25, 1937, in SWOC, Harold Ruttenberg Papers, Box 3, Folder 15, PSU-HCLA. On the fear they engendered among black workers, see February 1, 1937, SWOC Fieldworkers Notes, Calumet District, Box 1, Folder 2/3, PSU-HCLA. Apparently, once GM capitulated, this sentiment diminished. February 15, 1937, SWOC Fieldworkers Notes, Calumet District, Box 1, Folder 2/3, PSU-HCLA.

81. November 2, 1936, SWOC Fieldworkers Notes, Calumet District, Box 1, Folder 1, PSU-HCLA.

82. Schuyler, "Negro Workers Lead in Great Lakes Steel Drive"; Romare Bearden, "The Negro in 'Little Steel,'" *Opportunity,* December 1937, reprinted in *The Black Worker: A Documentary History from Colonial Times to the Present,* ed. Philip S. Foner and Ronald L. Lewis (Philadelphia: Temple University Press, 1983), 7:98.

83. Gertrude G. Schroeder, *The Growth of Major Steel Companies, 1900–1950* (Baltimore: Johns Hopkins University Press, 1953), 216–24 (appendix tables 1–3, 5, 7–8).

84. October 15, 1936, SWOC Fieldworkers Notes, Calumet District, Box 1, Folder 1, PSU-HCLA.

85. Statement, November 28, 1936, George Patterson Papers, Box 6, Folder 3, CHS.

86. January 27, 1937, SWOC Fieldworkers Notes, Calumet District, Box 1, Folders 1, 2/3, PSU-HCLA.

87. February 1, 1937, SWOC Fieldworkers Notes, Calumet District, Box 1, Folder 2/3, PSU-HCLA.

88. See SWOC Fieldworkers Notes, Calumet District, Box 1, PSU-HCLA. On the support of "saloon keepers," see October 15, 1936, SWOC Fieldworkers Notes, Calumet District, Box 1, Folder 1, PSU-HCLA.

89. Bernstein, *Turbulent Years,* 462–66; "Steel Union Men Win in Mill Voting," *Steel Labor,* April 10, 1937, p. 1; "50 More Representatives Bolt to SWOC," *Steel Labor,* February 6, 1937, p. 3; "Two Men Win at Bethlehem Steel: Company Union Picks SWOC Men to Meet Bosses," *Steel Labor,* January 23, 1937, p. 1; "Company Union Representatives Press Hard for Wage Increases as S.W.O.C. Lends Inspiration and Authority to the Movement," *Steel Labor,* September 25, 1936, p. 1; "U.S. Steel's Ben Fairless Suffers Another Set-Back," *Steel Labor,* September 25, 1936, p. 3; "S.W.O.C. Encourages Company Unions to Make Wage Demands," *Steel Labor,* September 1, 1936, p. 2; "Company Union Representatives Join Steel Union Movement," *Steel Labor,* August 1, 1936, p. 6.

90. See "Company Union Representatives Join Steel Union Movement," *Steel Labor,* August 1, 1936, p. 6. See also "Company Union Representatives Press Hard for Wage Increase as S.W.O.C. Lends Inspiration and Authority to the Movement,"

Steel Labor, September 25, 1937, p. 1; "U.S. Steel's Ben Fairless Suffers Another Set-Back," *Steel Labor,* September 25, 1936, p. 3; and "Carnegie-Illinois Workers Ask Wage Raise through S.W.O.C.," *Union Daily News,* August 31, 1936.

91. Bernstein, *Turbulent Years,* 465; Brooks, *Clint: A Biography,* 165.

92. Galenson, *CIO;* "Steel Union Passes 125,000; Start Plan for Convention," *Steel Labor,* January 9, 1937, p. 1.

93. November 2, 1936, SWOC Fieldworkers Notes, Calumet District, Box 1, Folder 1, PSU-HCLA; "Steel Workers Sweep Polls; FDR Majorities in All Towns," *Steel Labor,* November 20, 1936, p. 6.

94. Bernstein, *Turbulent Years,* 449–50.

95. "Steel Workers Win" (poster), in SWOC, Harold Ruttenberg Papers, Box 3, Folder 12, PSU-HCLA; November 5, 1936, SWOC Fieldworkers Notes, District, "Box 1, Folder 1, PSU-HCLA; "Steel Workers Defy Bosses with Huge Roosevelt Majorities," *Union News Service,* November 9, 1936.

96. On Taylor's position, see Kenneth Warren, *Big Steel: The First Century of the United States Steel Corporation, 1901–1921* (Pittsburgh: University of Pittsburgh Press, 2001), 145–47. On Lewis and Taylor, see Melvyn Dubofsky and Warren Van Tine, *John L. Lewis* (Urbana: University of Illinois Press, 1986), 171–80, 198–99.

97. Warren, *Big Steel,* 148–49.

98. Brody, "Origins of Modern Steel Unionism," 22; Colin Gordon, *New Deals: Business, Labor, and Politics in America, 1920–1935* (New York: Cambridge University Press,1994), 226–27; Staughton Lynd, "The Possibility of Radicalism in the Early 1930s: The Case of Steel," *Radical America* 6, no. 6 (1972): 37, 42.

99. David J. McDonald, *Union Man* (New York: Dutton, 1969), 104–5.

100. The CIO's lead lawyer, Lee Pressman, agreed with McDonald's characterization of the situation at U.S. Steel. Saul Alinsky, *John L. Lewis* (New York: Vintage, 1949), 149.

101. Bernstein, *Turbulent Years,* 472–73; William T. Hogan, *Economic History of the Iron and Steel Industry in the United States* (Lexington, MA: Lexington Books, 1971), 1173–77. There were two signings: a preliminary agreement on March 3 and a more permanent "initial" contract on March 17.

102. Bruce E. Seely, "Myron C. Taylor," in *Encyclopedia of American Business History and Biography: The Iron and Steel Industry,* ed. Bruce Seely (New York: Facts on File, 1994), 422.

103. Galenson, *CIO,* 93.

104. "Ohio Steel Workers Hear C.I.O. Leaders," *Daily Worker,* March 12, 1937, p. 1; "C.I.O. Wins Union Agreement, Higher Wages and Shorter Hours from U.S. Steel Company; Gains Cover Industry," *Union Information Service,* March 8, 1937.

105. "New Spirit Grips Mahoning Valley," *Daily Worker,* March 28, 1937, p. 5; "C.I.O. Moves Fast in Canton Area," *Daily Worker,* March 28, 1937, p. 5; Adam Lapin, "Steel Trust Stooges Frantic at Union Rise," *Daily Worker,* March 14, 1937, p. 5.

106. Jones & Laughlin Steel, 1 NLRB 503, 510 (1936); John Bodnar, *Workers' World: Kinship, Community, and Protest in an Industrial Society, 1900–1940* (Baltimore: Johns Hopkins University Press, 1982), 124–25; Brooks, *As Steel Goes,* 117–20.

107. "J. & L. Representatives Turn to Steel Union," *Steel Labor,* January 8, 1937, p. 1.

108. Brooks, *As Steel Goes,* 117–20.

109. Hogan, *Economic History,* 1254–55.

110. Brooks, *As Steel Goes,* 123–27. See also Louis Stark, "Peace Plan Drawn in Big Steel Strike; More Plants Close," *New York Times,* May 14, 1937, p. 1; "C.I.O. Spreads Steel Strike; Seeks to Stir 200,000 Men to Join Walkout," *Chicago Daily Tribune,* May 14, 1937, p. 1; and "C.I.O. Steel Strike Shuts Two Plants of Jones-Laughlin: 27,000 Men Idled," *New York Times,* May 13, 1937, p. 1.

111. LCH, 11241–42; Robert Zieger, *The CIO, 1935–1955* (Chapel Hill: University of North Carolina Press, 1995), 60–61; "CIO Victorious in Sharon Vote," *Canton Repository,* May 26, 1937, p. 1; "SWOC Wins by 10,000 at J-L; Sharon Steel Vote May 25," *Steel Labor,* May 24, 1937, p. 1.

112. "The Union Mills," *Steel Labor,* June 5, 1937, p. 2; "The Union Mills," *Steel Labor,* May 15, 1937, p. 2; "Wheeling Steel, Timken Roller, 86 Others Sign," *Steel Labor,* May 1, 1937, p. 1; "51 Steel Mills Signed as Lodges Climb to 492," *Steel Labor,* April 10, 1937, p. 1; "23 More Corporations Sign with Steel Union," *Steel Labor,* March 20, 1937, p. 1.

113. Letter from Philip Murray to SWOC staff, January 12, 1937, in SWOC, Harold Ruttenberg Papers, Box 3, Folder 11, PSU-HCLA.

114. LCH, 16630–31 (exhibit 7420).

115. U.S. Senate, Committee on Education and Labor, *Violations of Free Speech and the Rights of Labor: Private Police Systems,* Report No. 6, pt. 2, 76th Cong., 1st Sess. (Washington, DC: GPO, 1939) (hereafter *Private Police*), 178–79.

116. LCH, 16631–32 (exhibit 7421).

117. Ibid., 16632–34 (exhibits 7422–23) (quotation p. 16632).

118. Ibid., 11029–30.

119. "Organizers of CIO Attacked," *Zanesville (OH) Signal,* November 14, 1936, p. 1.

120. On Burke's experience at Columbia, see Stephen H. Norwood, "Complicity and Conflict: Columbia University's Response to Fascism, 1933–1937," *Modern Judaism* 27, no. 3 (2007): 273–75.

121. LCH, 11027.

122. Interview of Thomas White, July 9, 1974, p. 14–15, YSU-OHP.

123. SWOC Fieldworkers Notes, Calumet District, Box 1, Folder 2/3, PSU-HCLA.

124. *Little Steel Companies,* 96–98; *Private Police,* 187–94; LCH, 11043, 11051–57, 11072–73.

125. *Private Police,* 191–93; LCH, 11074–77.

126. *Republic Steel,* 9 NLRB at 374.

127. Weirton Steel, 32 NLRB 1145, 1163–75 (1941); Adam Lapin, "Steel Union Organizers' Courage Winning Up-Hill Battle in Weirton Domain," *Daily Worker,* May 12, 1937, p. 6.

128. LCH, 16640–50 (exhibits 7424–35A).

129. *Little Steel Companies,* 229.

130. *Private Police,* 179–80; Gordon, "Communists," 264.

131. Letter from Meyer Bernstein to Nick Gatto, February 23, 1937, Meyer Bernstein Papers, Box 1, Folder 2, PSU-HCLA.

132. Needleman, *Black Freedom Fighters,* 31.

133. Gordon, "Communists," 264.

134. *Private Police,* 154–60; LCH, 10931–44; interview of Thomas White, July 9, 1974, p. 2, YSU-OHP.

135. *Private Police,* 170–77 (quotation p. 170).

136. LCH, 10452–53, 10882–89.

137. Casebeer, "Aliquippa," 677.

138. *Little Steel Companies,* 166–67.

139. Bethlehem Steel, 14 NLRB 539, 626–28 (1939); *Weirton Steel,* 32 NLRB at 1163–75.

140. See, for example, October 29, 1936, SWOC Fieldworkers Notes, Calumet District, Box 1, Folder 1, PSU-HCLA.

141. Interview of Thomas White, July 9, 1974, pp. 1–2, YSU-OHP.

142. Affidavit of Gus Ritchie, September 14, 1938, United Steelworkers Collection, Legal Department, Box 1, "Republic Steel—Miscellaneous Correspondence," PSU-HCLA.

143. Refusal to reinstate, Legal Department Records, Box 3, Youngstown Sheet & Tube Company, PSU-HCLA.

144. On the way that "spatial fragmentation" frustrated union organizing, see Rose, *Duquesne and the Rise of Steel Unionism,* 18–19.

145. Cohen, *Making a New Deal,* 318–19.

146. Interview of John Johns (2 of 2), March 3, 1978, p. 8, USWA–Labor Oral History Collection, PSU-HCLA.

147. Williamson, *Dangerous Scot,* 126.

148. Memorandum from Clinton Golden to all staff members, June 24, 1936, in SWOC, Harold Ruttenberg Papers, Box 3, Folder 11, PSU-HCLA.

149. Memorandum from Philip Murray to subregional directors, September 11, 1936, in SWOC/Hubbard Strike, Harold Ruttenberg Papers, Box 3, Folder 13, PSU-HCLA.

150. Gordon, "Communists," 264 (quotation); "Steel and Metal: How to Develop Permanent and Intimate Contacts," *Party Organizer* 6, no. 2 (February 1933): 10, 11.

151. Gordon, "Communists," 259–65 (quotations pp. 262–63).

152. Needleman, *Black Freedom Fighters,* 28–29.

153. *Republic Steel,* 9 NLRB at 241–47, 260–72, 319–24, 354–72, 328–45 (quotations pp. 241, 319, 332); LCH, 12703–4. See also "Steel Workers Hear Pittsburgh Speaker," *Canton Repository,* March 8, 1937, p. 1; and "Steel Unit for CIO Calls Meeting Here," *Canton Repository,* March 5, 1937, p. 41.

154. Dues reports, 1937–43, USWA District 31 Records, Box 43, Folder 3, CHS.

155. See Brooks, *As Steel Goes,* 135; Inland Steel, 9 NLRB 783 (1938); and interview of John Johns (1 of 2), 1970, pp. 6–7, USWA–Labor Oral History Collection, PSU-HCLA.

156. ARMCO, 43 NLRB 1021 (1942).

157. Benjamin Stolberg, "Big Steel, Little Steel, and the C.I.O.," *Nation,* July 31, 1937, p. 119. See also Adam Lapin, "Steel Union Crashing through Domain of Economic Royalism in Weir's Industrial Kingdom," *Daily Worker,* May 11, 1937, p. 3.

158. Adam Lapin, "Weir Hatchet Men Attack 30 Unionists," *Daily Worker,* May 7, 1937, p. 1. See also Adam Lapin, "Weir Thugs Beat Up Unionists Inside Mill," *Daily Worker,* August 27, 1937, p. 4; and Adam Lapin, "Steel Union Organizers' Courage Winning Up-Hill Battle in Weirton Domain," *Daily Worker,* May 12, 1937, p. 6.

159. Hogan, *Economic History,* 1216–17 (table 36–12), 1235–39 (table 36–20), 1277–78, 1291.

160. Galenson, *CIO,* 100; "Expect Local Steel Mill Output Gain," *Chicago Daily News,* May 22, 1937, p. 23; "Demand for Five Steel Products Sets New Record," *Chicago Daily News,* May 20, 1937, p. 27.

161. See, for example, autobiographical narrative, Carl "Jerry" Beck Papers, Box 2, Folder 9, MSS 0143, YHCIL.

162. Memorandum to staff members, local lodge officers, and members— Northeast Region, Harold Ruttenberg Papers, Box 3, Folder 18, PSU-HCLA.

163. See Gordon, "Communists," 261–62.

164. McDonald, *Union Man,* 108. For detailed records of UMW and CIO financing of the organizing drives, see, for example, letters of M. Bernice Welsh, secretary to John Brophy, to David McDonald, David McDonald Papers, Box 197, File 2, PSU-HCLA (accompanying series of checks in amounts of as much as $50,000).

165. Memorandum from David McDonald to all field directors, July 23, 1937, Howard Curtiss Collection, Box 5, Folder 36, PSU-HCLA.

166. Dues reports, 1937–43, USWA District 31 Records, Box 43, Folder 3, CHS.

CHAPTER 6: THE SPIRIT OF UNREST

1. For the letter and proposed contract, see U.S. Senate, *Hearings before the Committee on Education and Labor: Violations of Free Speech and the Rights of Labor,* 76th Cong., 1st–3rd Sess. (Washington, DC: GPO, 1937) (hereafter LCH), 11435–26 (exhibits 4635–36).

2. U.S. Senate, Committee on Education and Labor, *Violations of Free Speech and the Rights of Labor: Labor Policies of Employers' Associations; Part IV, The "Little Steel" Companies,* Report No. 151, 77th Cong., 1st Sess. (Washington, DC: GPO, 1941) (hereafter *Little Steel Companies*), 116–18, 130; LCH, 11239–43, 11269–86 (quotation p. 11241).

3. LCH, 11438 (exhibit 4639).

4. Neither lockout was complete. Meyer Bernstein, report to Mr. Philip Murray on the settlement of the Republic Steel Corporation Labor Board cases, pp. 2–4, United Steelworkers of America, Legal Department Records, Box 1, Republic Steel Corporation, PSU-HCLA. Republic attempted to describe the May 20 stoppage as a layoff because of equipment failure, but the NLRB disagreed. *Republic Steel*, 9 NLRB 219, 249–51 (1938).

5. *Little Steel Companies*, 118–24; LCH, 11414–19 (exhibits 4614–16).

6. *Little Steel Companies*, 118–24; Inland Steel, 9 NLRB 783, 795–96 (1938); "Bargaining with C.I.O. Spurned by Inland Steel," *Chicago Daily News*, May 25, 1937, p. 1; "Terms Given by Republic Are Rejected," *Steel Labor*, May 24, 1937, p. 2; "Independent Steel Companies Refuse to Sign Contracts with CIO, but Continue Talks on Labor Problems with SWOC Groups," *Wall Street Journal*, May 6, 1937, p. 1. See also telegram from Clinton Golden to J. A. Voss, Republic Steel, May 6, 1937, Harold Ruttenberg Papers, PSU-HCLA; and Walter Galenson, *The CIO Challenge to the AFL: A History of the American Labor Movement, 1935–1941* (Cambridge, MA: Harvard University Press, 1960), 98–100.

7. Irving Bernstein, *The Turbulent Years: A History of the American Worker, 1933–1941* (Boston: Houghton Mifflin, 1969), 480–83 (quotations pp. 481, 483); *Little Steel Companies*, 131.

8. Donald G. Sofchalk, "The Little Steel Strike of 1937" (PhD dissertation, Ohio State University, 1961), 380–81; Mary Heaton Vorse, *Labor's New Millions* (New York: Modern Age, 1938), 130–32.

9. LCH, 11238–43; Wheeling Steel, 8 NLRB 102, 106 (1938); "Crucible Steel Signs Contract, Averts Strike," *New York Times*, May 25, 1937, p. 1.

10. LCH, 11259–86.

11. See *Republic Steel*, 9 NLRB at 222, 247–48; and *Inland Steel*, 9 NLRB at 794.

12. "Open Shop Upheld by Republic Steel," *New York Times*, May 13, 1937, p. 4.

13. LCH, 11414–19 (exhibits 4614–16); *Inland Steel*, 9 NLRB at 794.

14. LCH, 11258–59, 11398 (exhibit 4593).

15. *Little Steel Companies*, 125–31; LCH, 10452–53, 10884–87, 11246–56, 11286–94, 11300–302, 11817–58, 11834–35, 12682–91.

16. *Little Steel Companies*, 167–68, 215–16; *Republic Steel*, 9 NLRB at 251; LCH, 11183–85.

17. "Steel Strike Looms at 3 Independents," *Daily Worker*, May 14, 1937, p. 1; "Youngstown Sheet Welcomes Inquiry after Workers Appeal to La Follette," *New York Times*, May 13, 1937, p. 4.

18. LCH, 8347–48.

19. "Open Shop Upheld by Republic Steel," *New York Times*, May 13, 1937, p. 4.

20. *Little Steel Companies*, 130, 206–7, 301–3; LCH, 11258–59, 11424–25 (exhibits 4624–26); Frank Blumenthal, "Anti-Union Publicity in the Johnstown 'Little Steel' Strike of 1937," *Public Opinion Quarterly* 3, no. 4 (1939): 677.

21. Directive from Van Bittner, January 21, 1937, SWOC Fieldworkers Notes, Calumet District, Box 1, Folder 2/3, PSU-HCLA.

22. See, for example, May 6, 1937, SWOC Fieldworkers Notes, Calumet District, Box 1, Folder 1, PSU-HCLA. These records feature many examples of such sentiments.

23. *Little Steel Companies,* 229–30; *Republic Steel,* 9 NLRB at 249–51; LCH, 12706; May 24, 1937, SWOC Fieldworkers Notes, Calumet District, Box 1, Folder 1, PSU-HCLA; Philip Murray, "Labor and Responsibility," *Virginia Quarterly* 16 (Spring 1940): 275.

24. "Strike 'Inevitable' at Inland Steel, Says CIO Leader," *Wall Street Journal,* May 26, 1937, p. 1; "'We'll Close,' Local Plants Warn Steel Union," *Youngstown Vindicator,* May 16, 1937, p. 1; Adam Lapin, "31,000 Steel Men Open War on 'Big 5,'" *Daily Worker,* May 14, 1937, p. 1; "Steel Workers and Producers Seem Adamant," *Youngstown Vindicator,* May 9, 1937, p. 1; "Republic Men Approve Strike," *Youngstown Vindicator,* May 8, 1937, p. 1.

25. LCH, 12705; "Peace in Steel Threatened by Leaders of CIO," *Canton Repository,* May 12, 1937, p. 1; "Strike Threat Clouds Bright Steel Picture," *Canton Repository,* May 9, 1937, p. 47; "'Big Steel Strike' Warned by Murray," *Johnstown Democrat,* May 7, 1937, p. 26; "Crisis of 'Captive Mines' Threatened Independents," *Johnstown Democrat,* May 6, 1937, p. 1.

26. "Strike at 5 Mills of Republic Steel," *New York Times,* May 26, 1937, p. 1; "Steel Union Set for Showdown," *Daily Worker,* May 16, 1937, p. 1; "Local Lodges Delay Action," *Youngstown Vindicator,* May 13, 1937, p. 1.

27. LCH, 12706–7; *Little Steel Companies,* 216, 230; *Republic Steel,* 9 NLRB at 250–51.

28. "Strikes Threaten Four Big Independents in Steel Industry," *New York Times,* May 16, 1937, p. 1; Edwin A. Lahey, "100 C.I.O. Chiefs Begin War on 2 More Steel Companies," *Chicago Daily News,* May 15, 1937, p. 3; "Republic Steel Aide Offers to Meet C.I.O.," *New York Times,* May 6, 1937, p. 17.

29. Interview of Dan Thomas, August 1, 1974, p. 2, YSU-OHP; Adam Lapin, "Set Steel Strike Zero Hour for Today in Independent Mills," *Daily Worker,* May 26, 1937, p. 1.

30. Robert R. R. Brooks, *As Steel Goes . . . Unionism in a Basic Industry* (New Haven, CT: Yale University Press, 1940), 137.

31. "Youngstown Is Next in Steel Drive," *Daily Worker,* May 17, 1937, p. 1.

32. Ibid.

33. Ibid.

34. David J. McDonald, *Union Man* (New York: Dutton, 1969), 109.

35. Enrollment report for Northeast Region, November 1, 1936, in SWOC, David McDonald Papers, Box 197, File 2, PSU-HCLA.

36. Memorandum from David McDonald to all field directors, July 23, 1937, Howard Curtiss Collection, Box 5, Folder 36, PSU-HCLA.

37. Edwin A. Lahey, "Strike On in Steel Mills; Chicago Men Out Tonight," *Chicago Daily News,* May 26, 1937, p. 1.

38. LCH, 4869.

39. "Republic, S-T Next for SWOC," *Youngstown Vindicator,* May 24, 1937, p. 1; "Steel Strike Seen Imminent," *Youngstown Vindicator,* May 23, 1937, p. 1; "Power Voted for Strike Call," *Cleveland Plain Dealer,* May 16, 1937, p. 1.

40. LCH, 12705–7.

41. John Steuben, *Strike Strategy* (New York: Gaer, 1950), 119.

42. LCH, 12706–28

43. Louis Stark, "27 Big Steel Mills Darkened by Strike," *New York Times,* May 27, 1937, p. 1; "Strike Hits Steel Mills in 5 States," *Cleveland Plain Dealer,* May 27, 1937, p. 1; "Steel Strike Closes 21 Plants of Three Large Companies; Auditorium Vote Canceled," *Canton Repository,* May 27, 1937, p. 1; "Thousands Idle in Steel Strikes," *Youngstown Vindicator,* May 27, 1937, p. 1.

44. Steuben, *Strike Strategy,* 122–24. See also "80,000 Steel Workers Strike in 5 States," *Daily Worker,* May 27, 1937, p. 1; and "90,000 Men Idle in Five States as Output Drops," *Chicago Daily News,* May 27, 1937, p. 1. On waterfront picketing, see LCH, 6848 (exhibit 3511), 6857.

45. Some smaller installations at other companies continued to run, including, for example, Sheet & Tube's forge in Evanston, Illinois. "Ohio Governor Acts for Steel Peace," *Chicago Daily Tribune,* May 28, 1937, p. 1.

46. Interview of George Richardson, September 21, 1991, Video Oral History Collection, at approx. min. 1:10–1:14, YHCIL.

47. Interview of John Stenthal, September 23, 1991, Video Oral History Collection, at approx. min. 13, YHCIL.

48. "32,000 Men Jobless in CIO Valley Steel Mill Strikes," *Youngstown Vindicator,* May 27, 1937, p. 1.

49. Edwin A. Lahey, "Workers Leave Jobs at 8 Mills in Chicago Area," *Chicago Daily News,* May 27, 1937, p. 1.

50. Bethlehem Steel, 14 NLRB 539, 612–13 (1939); "Cambria Mill of Bethlehem Goes on Strike," *Steel Labor,* June 21, 1937, p. 1; "Cambria Mill Hit by Railway Strike," *New York Times,* June 11, 1937, p. 5.

51. See this book's appendix. See also *Little Steel Companies,* 4–5.

52. *Little Steel Companies,* 170.

53. Ibid., 170–71; Adam Lapin, "Steel Thugs Open Fire on Pickets," *Daily Worker,* May 29, 1937, p. 1.

54. *Little Steel Companies,* 203.

55. LCH, 12707.

56. *Little Steel Companies,* 204–5; LCH, 12728–30; John N. Grajciar (1 of 2), July 2, 1968, pp. 5–6, 20–21, 32, USWA–Labor Oral History Collection, PSU-HCLA; Lapin, "Steel Thugs Open Fire on Pickets."

57. "7 Republic Plants Shut in Ohio," *Daily Worker,* May 27, 1937, p. 3.

58. "Steel Strike Closes 21 Plants of Three Large Companies; Auditorium Vote Canceled," *Canton Depository,* May 27, 1937, p. 1; "CIO Picket Lines Barricade Plants of Republic Steel," *Canton Repository,* May 26, 1937, p. 1.

59. *Little Steel Companies,* 217.

60. "Republic Official Accidentally Shot," *Canton Repository,* May 31, 1937, p. 1; Lapin, "Steel Thugs Open Fire on Pickets."

61. *Little Steel Companies,* 218; LCH, 13035, 13139–40 (exhibits 5056F–G).

CHAPTER 7: IN THE NAME OF THE PEOPLE

1. "90,000 Men Idle in Five States as Output Drops," *Chicago Daily News,* May 27, 1937, p. 1.

2. "4 Pickets Hurt at Inland Steel," *Youngstown Vindicator,* May 30, 1937, p. 1; "Clash at Indiana Plant," *New York Times,* May 30, 1937, p. 3; "Labor: Steel Strikes," *Chicago Daily Tribune,* May 30, 1937, p. 8; Edwin A. Lahey, "Steel Strikers Battle Guards at Indiana Mill," *Chicago Daily News,* May 29, 1937, p. 1; "Twenty Picketers Arrested in Chicago," *New York Times,* May 27, 1937, p. 1.

3. William J. Adelman, *The Memorial Day Massacre of 1937* (Chicago: Illinois Historical Society 1975), 2–10.

4. Michael Dennis, *The Memorial Day Massacre and the Movement for Industrial Democracy* (New York: Palgrave Macmillan, 2010), 73–78; Randi Storch, *Red Chicago: American Communism at its Grassroots, 1928–1935* (Urbana: University of Illinois Press, 2008), 11.

5. U.S. Senate, Committee on Education and Labor, *Violations of Free Speech and the Rights of Labor: The Chicago Memorial Day Incident,* Report No. 46, pt. 2, 75th Cong., 1st Sess. (Washington, DC: GPO, 1937) (hereafter *Memorial Day Incident*), 2–5 (quotation p. 5); U.S. Senate, *Hearings before the Committee on Education and Labor: Violations of Free Speech and the Rights of Labor,* 76th Cong., 1st–3rd Sess. (Washington, DC: GPO, 1937) (hereafter LCH), 4684–88, 4863–66; Edwin A. Lahey, "Workers Leave Jobs at 8 Mills in Chicago Area," *Chicago Daily News,* May 27, 1937, p. 1.

6. *Memorial Day Incident,* 5; LCH, 4684–88, 4863–66, 4875–78; report of the Citizens Joint Commission of Inquiry on the South Chicago Memorial Day Incident, 1937, pp. 5–6, CHS; "Rout Strikers at Steel Mill," *Chicago Daily Tribune,* May 28, 1937, p. 1; "85,000 Strike; Police Act," *Chicago Daily Tribune,* May 27, 1937, p. 1.

7. The exact number of strikers versus loyal employees remains uncertain. See Dennis, *Memorial Day Massacre,* 112–13.

8. LCH, 4867–68, 4883–84.

9. Ibid., 4643–44, 4686–87, 5002–5 (exhibit 1329).

10. "Police Repulse March of 1,000 on Plant in South Chicago," *Washington Post,* May 29, 1937, p. 1.

11. *Memorial Day Incident,* 5–7; Dennis, *Memorial Day Massacre,* 117; "Ohio Governor Acts for Steel Peace," *Chicago Daily Tribune,* May 28, 1937, p. 1; "Chicago Cops Fire on Picket Line at Republic Steel," *Daily Worker,* May 29, 1937, p. 5. See also Lawrence Jacques Papers, Box 1, Folder 1, CHS, describing medical treatment of those injured that day.

12. George Patterson, Jesse Reese, and John Sargent, "Your Dog Don't Bark No More," in *Rank and File: Personal Histories of Working-Class Organizers,* ed. Alice Lynd and Staughton Lynd (New York: Monthly Review, 1988), 95 (quotation). Patterson's archived papers contain vivid photographic clippings of the event. George Patterson Papers, Box 6, Folder 4, CHS. See also LCH, 4883–86.

13. Lahey, "Steel Strikers Battle Guards at Indiana Mill"; "Picture Story of Vicious Clash of Striking Steel Workers and Police in South Chicago Labor War," *Chicago Daily News,* May 29, 1937, p. 28.

14. *Memorial Day Incident,* 6–7; Donald G. Sofchalk, "The Memorial Day Incident: An Episode in Mass Action," *Labor History* 6, no. 1 (1965): 12–13.

15. "Police Kill 4 Pickets; 100 Wounded at Republic Steel," *Daily Worker,* May 31, 1937, p. 1.

16. Lizabeth Cohen, *Making a New Deal: Industrial Workers in Chicago, 1919–1939,* 2nd ed. (New York: Cambridge, 2009), 346–47; Wendy L. Wall, *Inventing the "American Way": The Politics of Consensus from the New Deal to the Civil Rights Movement* (New York: Oxford University Press, 2009), 42–48.

17. Carol Quirke, "Reframing Chicago's Memorial Day Massacre, May 30, 1937," *American Quarterly* 60, no. 1 (2008): 132.

18. LCH, 4893.

19. *Memorial Day Incident,* 8–18; Sofchalk, "Memorial Day Incident," 13–15.

20. LCH, 4903–5; report of the Citizens Joint Commission of Inquiry on the South Chicago Memorial Day Incident, 1937, pp. 8–9, CHS.

21. *Memorial Day Incident,* 15–17.

22. Tom Girdler, with Boyden Sparkes, *Boot Straps: The Autobiography of Tom Girdler* (New York: Scribner's 1943), 245.

23. LCH, 4912–13, 4970–71.

24. Dennis, *Memorial Day Massacre,* 140–41 (quotation p. 140); Paul Y. Anderson, "Armed Rebellion on the Right," *Nation,* August 7, 1937, p. 146.

25. Dennis, *Memorial Day Massacre,* 140–50.

26. Patterson, Reese, and Sargent, "Your Dog Don't Bark No More," 95. See also LCH, 11418 (exhibit 4616).

27. LCH, 4959–64 (quotation p. 4961).

28. Ibid., 4912–13.

29. Ibid., 6787 (exhibit 3447), 6813–14 (exhibits 3473–74), 6826 (exhibit 3486).

30. *Memorial Day Incident,* 33–35; LCH, 4742–43, 4950–53, 4966–68.

31. LCH, 5008 (exhibit 1331), 5168–69 (exhibits 1629A–B, 1630); F. Raymond Daniell, "900 Chicago Police Guard Strike Area as Riots are Hinted," *New York Times,* June 2, 1937, p. 1.

32. *Memorial Day Incident,* 37; LCH, 5007–9 (exhibit 1331).

33. LCH, 4927–31; "Rioters Freed on Bail as Police Hunt Inciters," *Chicago Daily News,* June 2, 1937, p. 4; "Forty Pickets Arraigned on Conspiracy Charge," *Chicago Daily News,* June 2, 1937, p. 36.

34. "Murder in South Chicago," *Chicago Daily Tribune,* June 1, 1937, p. 12; "4 Dead, 90 Hurt in Steel Riot," *Chicago Daily Tribune,* May 31, 1937, p. 1. See also

"Pin Steel Riot on Red Agents; 6th Victim Dies," *Chicago Daily Tribune*, June 2, 1937, p. 1; "Chicagoans Led in Steel Strike by Outsiders," *Chicago Daily Tribune*, June 1, 1937, p. 2; "Riots Blamed on Red Chiefs," *Chicago Daily Tribune*, June 1, 1937, p. 1; and "The Law Defended," *Chicago Daily Tribune*, May 31, 1937, p. 14.

35. Jerold S. Auerbach, *Labor and Liberty: The La Follette Committee and the New Deal* (Indianapolis: Bobbs-Merrill, 1966), 121–22; Carol Quirke, *Eyes on Labor* (New York: Oxford University Press, 2012), 168.

36. LCH, 4777–79 (quotation p. 4779).

37. LCH, 4802.

38. *Memorial Day Incident*, 13; LCH, 4767–70. Both sources note the witness's "Mexican Army" reference.

39. William Grogan, *John Riffe of the Steelworkers* (New York: Coward-McCann, 1959), 30–31. See also David J. McDonald, *Union Man* (New York: Dutton, 1969), 114; and interview of Sam Evett, April 1, 1971, pp. 20–22, USWA–Labor Oral History Collection, PSU-HCLA.

40. Storch, *Red Chicago*, 128, 155; LCH, 4917–21, 6753–54 (exhibit 3422); Edwin A. Lahey, "Mayor Orders Steel Crews from Mill," *Chicago Daily News*, June 5, 1937, p. 1.

41. Dennis, *Memorial Day Massacre*, 130–31.

42. Interview of Sam Evett, April 1, 1971, pp. 13–22, USWA–Labor Oral History Collection, PSU-HCLA.

43. *Memorial Day Incident*, 9.

44. Ibid., 37.

45. LCH, 4713.

46. *Memorial Day Incident*, 36–38; LCH, 5009–10 (exhibits 1332–33).

47. LCH, 4972–76, 5065–67 (exhibit 1436).

48. *Memorial Day Incident*, 12–13, 21–22, 32; LCH, 4718–20, 4738, 4839–40, 4852–54, 4893–94, 4986–97.

49. Even today it is not completely clear how the violence began. Dennis, *Memorial Day Massacre*, 138–42.

50. "Chicago Riot Films Stun Audience Here," *New York Times*, July 3, 1937, p. 5.

51. Quirke, *Eyes on Labor*, 163–64. See also "Riot Film Backed by New Witnesses," *New York Times*, July 3, 1937, p. 5; "Riot Films Banned Here by Censors," *Chicago Daily News*, July 2, 1937, p. 1; "Chicago Riot Film Studied in Inquiry," *New York Times*, June 17, 1937, p. 3; and "Chicago Riot Film Seized," *New York Times*, July 11, 1937, p. 2. The Chicago police also seized films taken, separately, by two clergymen on the field. LCH, 4898–902; Dennis, *Memorial Day Massacre*, 144–45; Adelman, *Memorial Day Massacre*, 19.

52. Quirke, "Reframing Chicago's Memorial Day Massacre,"139–44.

53. *Memorial Day Incident*, 14–15; Quirke, "Reframing Chicago's Memorial Day Massacre," 134. See also Dennis, *Memorial Day Massacre*, 208.

54. *Memorial Day Incident*, 30–31.

55. The most complete and poignant testimony to this effect was offered by Lupe Marshall, a social worker of Mexican nationality, who was roughed up by

police and placed in a patrol wagon. LCH, 4950–55. See also Ibid., 4991–93, 4991–92; and Quirke, "Reframing Chicago's Memorial Day Massacre," 137–39.

56. *Memorial Day Incident,* 34.

57. Ibid., 5–7; U.S. Senate, Committee on Education and Labor, *Violations of Free Speech and the Rights of Labor: Industrial Munitions,* Report No. 6, pt. 3, 76th Cong., 1st Sess. (Washington, DC: GPO, 1939), 146–47.

58. *Memorial Day Incident,* 147.

59. "Chicago's Brutal Police," *Washington Post,* July 2, 1937, p. 8; "Suppressed Film Reveals Police as Aggressor in Strike Riot," *Washington Post,* June 17, 1937, p. 1. See also Louis Stark, "Riot Film Backed by New Witnesses," *New York Times,* July 3, 1937, p. 5; and "Chicago Riot Films Stun Audience Here," *New York Times,* July 3, 1937, p. 5.

60. Quirke, *Eyes on Labor,* 164–68.

61. Sofchalk, "Memorial Day Incident," 28–29, 31, 40–41.

62. 81 Cong. Rec. 6155, 6162–63, 6766–67 (1937).

63. Girdler, Boot Straps, 240–69; "Steel Riot Plot is Revealed," *Chicago Daily Tribune,* June 7, 1937, p. 1.

64. The four men who died on Memorial Day were Causey, Handley, Reed, and Popovich. Rothmund died on May 31, Tagliori on June 1, Anderson on June 3, Jones on June 8, and Francisco on June 15. "Steel Strike Diary," *Steel Labor,* June 21, 1937, p. 7; Daniell, "900 Chicago Police Guard Strike Area as Riots are Hinted." On the presence of National Maritime Union picketers, see Lahey, "Steel Strikers Battle Guards at Indiana Mill."

65. On the backgrounds of the strikers, see Dennis, *Memorial Day Massacre,* 161, 193; and "Steel Strike Diary," *Steel Labor,* June 21, 1937, p. 7. On their ages, see LCH, 5075–89 (exhibits 1441–49).

66. "Riots Blamed on Red Chiefs," *Chicago Daily Tribune,* June 1, 1937, p. 1.

67. Nan Pendrell and Ernest Pendrell, "They Used to Call Him Tony," *Daily Worker,* September 5, 1937, p. 8.

68. "Riots Blamed on Red Chiefs," *Chicago Daily Tribune,* June 1, 1937, p. 1.

69. Hays Jones, "10,000 Honor Victims of Police Attack at Chicago Steel Mill—Picket Republic Steel Office," *Daily Worker,* June 4, 1937, p. 1; Hays Jones, "Police in Chicago Yield to Strikers on Picket Rights," *Daily Worker,* June 2, 1937, p. 1; "Protest Steel Slayings at Chrysler Bldg.," *Daily Worker,* June 1, 1937, p. 1.

70. Edwin A. Lahey, "Seventh Riot Victim Dies as C.I.O. Holds Rites for Five," *Chicago Daily News,* June 3, 1937, p. 9.

71. "Hold Funeral for 3 Riot Dead; 7th Victim Dies," *Chicago Daily Tribune,* June 4, 1937, p. 19.

72. Lahey, "Mayor Orders Steel Crews from Mill."

73. "Eighth Victim Dies from Chicago Riot," *New York Times,* June 9, 1937, p. 2; "Must Steel Sign Contract? Labor Board Asked to Rule," *New York Times,* June 9, 1937, p. 3.

74. "Stadium, Half Filled, Hears CIO Campaign," *Chicago Daily Tribune,* June 18, 1937, p. 1; "Calls Killing of 9 'Brutal Massacre,'" *New York Times,* June 18, 1937, p. 4.

75. "Funeral for Slain Steel Worker Held," *Chicago Defender*, July 3, 1937, p. 6.

76. "Horner Intervenes in Chicago Strike; Fifth Death in Riot," *New York Times*, June 1, 1937, p. 1.

77. "Rioter's Widow Threatens to Kill Herself," *Chicago Daily News*, June 12, 1937, p. 4. See also Quirke, "Reframing Chicago's Memorial Day Massacre," 139.

78. *The I.L.D. News* 2, no. 1 (January 1939): 2; Pendrell and Pendrell, "They Used to Call Him Tony."

79. George Schuyler, "Negro Workers Lead in Great Lakes Steel Drive," *Pittsburgh Courier*, July 31, 1937, p. 1.

80. "Horner Intervenes in Chicago Strike; Fifth Death in Riot," *New York Times*, June 1, 1937, p. 1; "Riots Blamed on Red Chiefs," *Chicago Daily Tribune*, June 1, 1937, p. 1.

81. See, for example, "Youngstown Strikers Bitter over Massacre," *Daily Worker*, June 1, 1937, p. 4.

82. Lahey, "Mayor Orders Steel Crews from Mill."

83. Edwin A. Lahey, "Mayor Orders New Checkup at Republic Steel," *Chicago Daily News*, June 7, 1937, p. 1; Jerry Greene, "Life Goes On Its Serene Way as 1,000 Steel Workers Toil," *Chicago Daily News*, June 2, 1937, p. 8.

84. "Must Steel Sign Contract? Labor Board Asked to Rule," *Chicago Daily News*, June 9, 1937, p. 3.

85. Daniell, "900 Chicago Police Guard Strike Area as Riots Are Hinted"; "Republic Steel Plant Guarded by 948 Police," *Washington Post*, June 2, 1937, p. 1; "Pin Steel Riot on Red Agents; 6th Victim Dies," *Chicago Daily Tribune*, June 2, 1937, p. 1; "Barbed Wire Stretched at Republic Corp.," *Chicago Daily News*, June 2, 1937, p. 4.

86. "Horner Intervenes in Chicago Strike; Fifth Death in Riot," *New York Times*, June 1, 1937, p. 1 (quotation); "Riots Blamed on Red Chiefs, *Chicago Daily Tribune*," June 1, 1937, p. 1. On Mooney's threatening behavior, see interview of Sam Evett, April 1, 1971, pp. 21–22, USWA–Labor Oral History Collection, PSU-HCLA.

87. Daniell, "900 Chicago Police Guard Strike Area as Riots are Hinted"; "Horner Intervenes in Chicago Strike; Fifth Death in Riot," *New York Times*, June 1, 1937, p. 1; "Riots Blamed on Red Chiefs," *Chicago Daily Tribune*, June 1, 1937, p. 1.

88. "Steel Aftermath," *Time*, August 2, 1937, p. 13; "The Vindication of the Police," *Chicago Daily News*, July 22, 1937, p. 10. See also LCH, 6869–912 (exhibits 3526–45).

89. Report of the Citizens Joint Commission of Inquiry on the South Chicago Memorial Day Incident, 1937, pp. 12–14, CHS; Dr. Louis Andreas, in *Hard Times*, ed. Studs Terkel (New York: New Press, 1970), 143.

90. Thomas F. Patton, "Recollections of Some of the Highlights of the History of Republic Steel Corporation, 1930–1971," September 1, 1981, p. 23, Series 8, Public Relations Division, Container 345, Folder 9, WRHS-RSC.

1. U.S. Senate, *Hearings before the Committee on Education and Labor: Violations of Free Speech and the Rights of Labor,* 76th Cong., 1st–3rd Sess. (Washington, DC: GPO, 1937) (hereafter LCH), 9771–72, 9923 (exhibit 4312).

2. U.S. Senate, Committee on Education and Labor, *Violations of Free Speech and the Rights of Labor: Labor Policies of Employers' Associations; Part IV, The "Little Steel" Companies,* Report No. 151, 77th Cong., 1st Sess. (Washington, DC: GPO, 1941) (hereafter *Little Steel Companies*), 142–44; LCH, 11353–54. See also Joseph M. Turrini, "The Newton Steel Strike: A Watershed in the CIO's Failure to Organize 'Little Steel,'" *Labor History* 38, nos. 2–3 (1997): 236–43.

3. LCH, 11473–76 (exhibits 4665–68), 11516–47, 11749–56 (exhibits 4693–98).

4. *Little Steel Companies,* 149; LCH, 11471–72 (exhibits 4660–63), 11549–75, 11738–38 (exhibits 4691A–D), 11763–69 (exhibits 4701–12), 11757–62 (exhibit 4699).

5. LCH, 11588–91; Turrini, "Newton Steel Strike," 238–40.

6. *Little Steel Companies,* 151–54; Edwin A. Lahey, "C.I.O. Organizer Beaten as Mill Plans to Reopen," *Chicago Daily News,* June 10, 1937, p. 1.

7. "Hundreds Move to Storm Picket Line at Steel Mill," *Chicago Daily News,* June 10, 1937, p. 1 (Red Streak edition).

8. *Little Steel Companies,* 157–58; LCH, 11789, 11796.

9. *Little Steel Companies,* 157–59; LCH, 11792–96.

10. *Little Steel Companies,* 156–61; U.S. Senate, Committee on Education and Labor, *Violations of Free Speech and the Rights of Labor: Industrial Munitions,* Report No. 6, pt. 3, 76th Cong., 1st Sess. (Washington, DC: GPO, 1939) (hereafter *Industrial Munitions*), 150–55; LCH, 12059–61 (exhibit 4731); Turrini, "Newton Steel Strike," 255–60; F. Raymond Daniell, "Conflict Is Brief," *New York Times,* June 11, 1937, p. 1; Edwin A. Lahey, "'Army' Halted, Monroe Ruled by Vigilantes," *Chicago Daily News,* June 11, 1937, p. 1.

11. Turrini, "Newton Steel Strike," 259–60; "Bloodshed Feared: City Calls on Murphy to Send in Troops by Tomorrow," *New York Times,* June 12, 1937, p. 1.

12. *Little Steel Companies,* 161–63; Turrini, "Newton Steel Strike," 253; F. Raymond Daniell, "Monroe Picketing Restored by Pact," *New York Times,* June 16, 1937, p. 7; "Vigilantes Guard Lone Road to Mill," *New York Times,* June 14, 1937, p. 3; "Bloodshed Feared," *New York Times,* June 12, 1937, p. 1; "The Strike Fronts," *Chicago Daily Tribune,* June 13, 1937, p. 18.

13. *Little Steel Companies,* 164–70; Republic Steel, 9 NLRB 219, 373–75 (1938).

14. *Little Steel Companies,* 188–91; LCH, 12256–57.

15. Letter from Meyer Bernstein to Nick Gatto, May 28, 1937, Meyer Bernstein Papers, Box 1, Folder 2, PSU-HCLA.

16. *Little Steel Companies,* 169, 171–73. See also Adam Lapin, "Union Accuses Sheriff in Ohio," *Daily Worker,* June 13, 1937, p. 2; and Adam Lapin, "Ohio Sheriff Boasts Arsenal for Violent Attack on Strikers," *Daily Worker,* June 9, 1937, p. 1.

17. LCH, 11499.

18. "'We'll Close,' Local Plants Warn Steel Union," *Youngstown Vindicator,* May 18, 1937, p. 1.

19. LCH, 11919–25, 12841–45 (exhibit 4922), 12848–49 (exhibit 4924) (quotations pp. 12841, 12849); interview of Thomas White, July 9, 1974, pp. 14–15, YSU-OHP; "Burke Is Held to Grand Jury," *Youngstown Vindicator,* June, 11, 1937, p. 1; "14 Jailed, 3 Hurt in Mill Gate Clash," *Youngstown Vindicator,* June 10, 1937, p. 1.

20. Adam Lapin, "Mahoning Valley Labor Lines Up With Strikers," *Daily Worker,* June 12, 1937, p. 1.

21. *Little Steel Companies,* 174; LCH, 15934 (exhibit 6750).

22. "Thomas Refuses Back-to-Work Truce," *Youngstown Vindicator,* June 18, 1937, p. 1; "Back-to-Work Group Awaits Company Order," *Youngstown Vindicator,* June 17, 1937, p. 1; "9,000 S.&T. Men Demand Plants Re-open," *Youngstown Vindicator,* June 14, 1937, p. 1.

23. "Purnell Delays Answer on Re-openings," *Youngstown Vindicator,* June 16, 1937, p. 1; "'Mills Can't Work Without Protection'—Purnell," *Youngstown Vindicator,* June 3, 1937, p. 1; "Girdler Asks Protection for Workers," *Youngstown Vindicator,* June 2, 1937, p. 1.

24. Richmond's claim that he only threw the gas because he was first bombarded with rocks and bricks by fifteen nearby union men was contradicted by other witnesses, including police. *Little Steel Companies,* 188–89; LCH, 12218–27, 12262–80, 12575 (exhibit 4903) (quotation p. 12224); interview of Fred A. Fortunato, January 6, 1983, pp. 10–11, 34–35, YSU-OHP; interview of Thomas White, July 9, 1974, p. 3, YSU-OHP.

25. *Little Steel Companies,* 189–90.

26. Interview of Angela Campana, December 13, 1982, pp. 3–4, YSU-OHP.

27. Interview of Joseph J. Petaccio, December 30, 1982, pp. 1–2, YSU-OHP.

28. Donald G. Sofchalk, "The Little Steel Strike of 1937" (PhD dissertation, Ohio State University, 1961), 321–22; interview of Joseph J. Petaccio, December 30, 1982, pp. 2–4, YSU-OHP.

29. Interview of Clingan Jackson, July 6, 1977, p. 8, YSU-OHP. Richmond was injured by the projectiles. LCH, 12229, 12359 (exhibit 4906).

30. Ibid., 12227–35, 12259.

31. Ibid., 12243–45; John Steuben, *Strike Strategy* (New York: Gaer, 1950), 217; interview of James McPhillips and Charles Shea, November 7, 1967, p. 16, USWA–Labor Oral History Collection, PSU-HCLA.

32. LCH, 12246–47 (quotation p. 12247).

33. Ibid., 12248–49; interview of Fred A. Fortunato, January 6, 1983, pp. 11–12, YSU-OHP.

34. LCH, 12244–48.

35. *Little Steel Companies,* 190–91; LCH, 12270–71, 12302–3.

36. Interview of Clingan Jackson, July 6, 1977, p. 8, YSU-OHP (quotation); LCH, 12539 (exhibit 4906); "Ohio Strife Halted by One-Day Truce," *New York Times,* June 21, 1937, p. 1.

37. Mary Heaton Vorse, *Labor's New Millions* (New York: Modern Age, 1938), 143.

38. LCH, 12515–18 (exhibits 4874, 4876), 12240–41, 12575–79 (exhibits 4904–5).

39. LCH, 12831–36 (exhibits 4911–18); letter from Meyer Bernstein to Joseph Gallagher, February 2, 1938, Meyer Bernstein Papers, Box 1, Folder 2, PSU-HCLA.

40. Interview of Thomas White, July 9, 1974, pp. 3, 5–6 YSU-OHP. See also interview of Fred A. Fortunato, January 6, 1983, pp. 13, 15, YSU-OHP.

41. *Industrial Munitions*, 217 (appendix C); LCH, 12283, 12286, 12291–94; "Ohio Strife Halted by One-Day Truce," *New York Times*, June 21, 1937, p. 1.

42. Docket of the Republic Steel Strike, May 1937, Series 5, Industrial Relations, Subseries A, Administrative Files, Strikes, Docket of Republic Steel Corporation, Container 77, Folder 30, WRHS-RSC.

43. *Industrial Munitions*, 144.

44. *Little Steel Companies*, 188–91; LCH, 12516–17 (exhibit 4875), 12539–40 (exhibit 4886), 16046–59 (exhibits 6882–905); Dee Garrison, *Mary Heaton Vorse: The Life of an American Insurgent* (Philadelphia: Temple University Press, 1989), 184–86; "Pitched Battle in Youngstown Follows Gassing of C.I.O. Women," *New York Times*, June 20, 1937, p. 1.

45. LCH, 12233–34; "Ohio Strife Halted by One-Day Truce," *New York Times*, June 21, 1937, p. 1.

46. LCH, 16076 (exhibit 6926), 16079 (exhibit 6931), 16083–86 (exhibits 6935–37, 6939), 16095 (exhibit 6948), 16102 (exhibit 6955), 16105–9 (exhibits 6961–62).

47. *Little Steel Companies*, 196–97; LCH, 12251–55, 16108 (exhibit 6962).

48. Interview of Joseph J. Petaccio, December 30, 1982, p. 3, YSU-OHP.

49. U.S. Senate, Committee on Education and Labor, *Violations of Free Speech and the Rights of Labor: The Chicago Memorial Day Incident*, Report No. 46, pt. 2, 75th Cong., 1st Sess. (Washington, DC: GPO, 1937), 41.

50. Tom Girdler, with Boyden Sparkes, *Boot Straps: The Autobiography of Tom Girdler* (New York: Scribner's, 1943), 288.

51. Republic Steel Corporation, Mahoning District, Warrant Plant, n.d., Series 8, Public Relations Division, Mahoning Valley District, Warren Ohio, History File, Container 347, Folder 19, WRHS-RSC; "New Republic Tin-Plate Mill at Niles Starts," *Western Reserve Democrat* (Warren, OH), February 11, 1937, p. 1.

52. *Little Steel Companies*, 75–80; LCH, 12701–3. On events in 1933 and 1934, see interview of John N. Grajciar (1 of 2), July 2, 1968, pp. 20–21, USWA–Labor Oral History Collection, PSU-HCLA; and interview of John N. Grajciar (2 of 2), March 21, 1969, p. 1, ibid.

53. *Little Steel Companies*, 200–202; LCH, 12894 (exhibit 4964).

54. *Republic Steel*, 9 NLRB at 356. See also Louis Stark, "Steel Strike Food Landed Under Fire," *New York Times*, June 2, 1937, p. 1; and "Planes Carry Food to Mills, *Youngstown Vindicator*," May 29, 1937, p. 1.

55. *Little Steel Companies*, 203; *Republic Steel*, 9 NLRB at 356; Republic Steel Corp. et al. v. Amalgamated Ass'n of Iron, Steel, and Tin Workers of America et al.,

No. 41767, June 1937, in "Legal Documents Pertaining to Suits against the Nat'l Guard, the Governor, and the Steel Companies," Youngstown Steel Strike Records (hereafter YSSR), Box 1, Folder 11, Series 167, OHS.

56. *Republic Steel,* 9 NLRB at 356; LCH, 12695–97; "77,000 on Strike!," *Steel Labor,* June 5, 1937, p. 1; David Lurie, "Strikers at Warren Mill Patrol 11 Mile Picket Line Front," *Daily Worker,* June 2, 1937, p. 7; "Says Republic Mills Operate," *Youngstown Vindicator,* May 27, 1937, p. 1.

57. *Little Steel Companies,* 203–4; Adam Lapin, "Steel Thugs Open Fire on Pickets," *Daily Worker,* May 29, 1937, p. 1; "Bystander Shot in Picket Line Fight," *Youngstown Vindicator,* May 28, 1937, p. 1.

58. Interview of John N. Grajciar (1 of 2), July 2, 1968, pp. 5–6, 20–21, 32, USWA–Labor Oral History Collection, PSU-HCLA; *Little Steel Companies,* 204–5; LCH, 12728–30.

59. *Republic Steel,* 9 NLRB at 356; "Planes Carry Food to Mills," *Youngstown Vindicator,* May 29, 1937, p. 1.

60. Girdler, *Boot Straps,* 300–301, 304.

61. *Little Steel Companies,* 126–27 (table 11), 203; LCH, 11510, 11730 (exhibit 4686), 12932–33 (exhibits 4988–89).

62. Girdler, *Boot Straps,* 299.

63. Ibid., 301–2; "Both Sides Use Planes in Strike," *Youngstown Vindicator,* May 30, 1937, p. 1; "Planes Carry Food to Mills," *Youngstown Vindicator,* May 29, 1937, p. 1.

64. Girdler, *Boot Straps,* 304.

65. LCH, 11613–33 (exhibit 4674).

66. "Work Sheet[s] of Ohio National Guard, June 21–July 7," YSSR, Box 1, Folder 13, Series 167, OHS; Adam Lapin, "Steel Union Planes Block Landing of Food for Scabs," *Daily Worker,* May 31, 1937, p. 1; "Both Sides Use Planes in Strike," *Youngstown Vindicator,* May 30, 1937, p. 1.

67. "Airplane Operators See Busy Week-End," *Youngstown Vindicator,* May 29, 1937, p. 2.

68. "Republic Uses Secret 'Base,'" *Youngstown Vindicator,* June 12, 1937, p. 1; "CIO Gets Warrant to Halt Food Planes," *Youngstown Vindicator,* June 5, 1937, p. 1; "Assail Use of Field Here by Strike Planes," *Cleveland Plain Dealer,* June 3, 1937, p. 1.

69. "Tells of Ride in Food Plane," *Youngstown Vindicator,* June 3, 1937, p. 1; Louis Stark, "Air Crashes Halt Strike Food Supply in Steel Struggle," *New York Times,* June 3, 1937, p. 1; Stark, "Steel Strike Food Landed Under Fire"; "Shoot at Planes Landing Food in Warren Plant," *Youngstown Vindicator,* June 1, 1937, p. 1; "Both Sides Use Planes in Strike," *Youngstown Vindicator,* May 30, 1937, p. 1. See also transcript of record, respondent's exhibit no. 50, pp. 6072, 6075–77, Republic Steel Co. v. NLRB, 311 U.S. 7 (1940) (docket no. 14).

70. "Thugs Fail to Break Steel Picket Lines," *Steel Labor,* June 5, 1937, p. 1; Louis Stark, "Rail Unions to Act over Steel Strike," *New York Times,* June 1, 1937, p. 9; "Fire at Plane, Shot Hits Man," *Youngstown Vindicator,* May 31, 1937, p. 1.

71. David J. McDonald, *Union Man* (New York: Dutton, 1969), 113–14; "Shoot at Planes Landing Food in Warren Plant," *Youngstown Vindicator,* June 1, 1937, p. 1.

72. A Warren employee was lightly wounded by stray gunfire during this fray. "Fire at Plane, Shot Hits Man," *Youngstown Vindicator,* May 31, 1937, p. 1. The shooting apparently died down after SWOC leader Philip Murray visited the plant. Sofchalk, "Little Steel Strike," 157.

73. LCH, 12697–98.

74. "Air Crashes Halt Strike Food Supply in Steel Struggle," *New York Times,* June 3, 1937, p. 1; Adam Lapin, "Planes with Food for Steel Scabs Crash," *Daily Worker,* June 3, 1937, p. 1; "Warren Goes into Second Strike Week," *Western Reserve Democrat* (Warren, OH), June 3, 1937, p. 1; "2 Planes Crash in Plant," *Youngstown Vindicator,* June 2, 1937, p. 1.

75. "Tells of Ride in Food Plane," *Youngstown Vindicator,* June 4, 1937, p. 4.

76. LCH, 12698.

77. "268 in Niles Plant Ask Perkins Help," *New York Times,* June 22, 1937, p. 5.

78. Russell B. Porter, "Johnstown Swept by Strike Rioters throughout Night," *New York Times,* June 15, 1937, p. 1; "Police Bullets Rout Strikers at Johnstown," *Chicago Daily Tribune,* June 15, 1977, p. 1; "15 Injured in Riot at Cambria Plant," *New York Times,* June 14, 1937, p. 2.

79. "10 Hurt in Riot at Steel Plant in Cumberland," *Washington Post,* July 21, 1937, p. 16; "Quiet Today at Scene of Yesterday's Riot," *Cumberland Evening Times,* July 21, 1937, p. 11.

80. "Steel Union Planes Block Landing of Food for Scabs," *Daily Worker,* May 31, 1937, p. 1; "Republic Shuts Its South Plant," *Canton Repository,* May 29, 1937, p. 1.

81. LCH, 13135–43 (exhibit 5056A–N), 13143–48 (exhibits 5058–65). See also "3 Hurt, 3 Held in Strike Clashes," *Cleveland Plain Dealer,* August 7, 1937, p. 1; and "Vandals Fire 4 Shots into Home," *Cleveland Plain Dealer,* August 2, 1937, p. 1.

82. Steuben, *Strike Strategy,* 141; interview of Dan Thomas, August 1, 1974, pp. 10–11, YSU-OHP; interview of James McPhillips and Charles Shea, November 7, 1967, pp. 6, 10–11, USWA–Labor Oral History Collection, PSU-HCLA.

83. Steuben, *Strike Strategy,* 142.

84. Interview of Dan Thomas, August 1, 1974, p. 14, YSU-OHP.

85. Michael Riley, "Last of the Red-Hot Believers," *Time,* September 9, 1991, p. 2.

86. Interview of John Johns (1 of 2), 1970, p. 5, USWA–Labor Oral History Collection, PSU-HCLA; interview of John Johns (2 of 2), March 3, 1978, p. 20, ibid.

87. Gidon Cohen, "Propensity Score Measures and the Lenin School," *Journal of Interdisciplinary History* 36, no. 2 (2005): 209, 215; Gidon Cohen and Kevin Morgan, "Stalin's Sausage Machine: British Students at the International Lenin School," *Twentieth Century British History* 13, no. 4 (2002): 327.

88. Interview of Thomas White, July 9, 1974, p. 14, YSU-OHP.

89. "Pickets Pass Lumber Cars," *Youngstown Vindicator,* June 12, 1937, p. 1; "Rail Men Ask Davey End 'State of Riot,'" *Youngstown Vindicator,* June 7, 1937, p. 1;

"Cut Rails after S.&T. Gets Food," *Youngstown Vindicator,* June 5, 1937, p. 1; "Warren Fight Threat Passes: Pickets, Republic Men Line Up, but Train Stops Outside Gate," *Youngstown Vindicator,* June 4, 1937, p. 1; "Railroads Sue to Bar Pickets," *Youngstown Vindicator,* June 2, 1937, p. 1; Louis Stark, "Steel Plant Siege Is Begun," *New York Times,* May 30, 1937, p. 1.

90. F. Raymond Daniell, "Railroads in Steel Area Tell Davey 'State of Riot' Threatens Wide Lay-Off," *New York Times,* June 7, 1937, p. 1.

91. Girdler, *Boot Straps,* 283–84.

92. See, for example, "Pickets Pass Lumber Cars," *Youngstown Vindicator,* June 13, 1937, p. 1.

93. See, for example, "Take Pickets by Surprise," *Youngstown Vindicator,* June 14, 1937, p. 1.

94. See, for example, LCH, 13727–28.

95. See, for example, "Warren Court Stops Pickets," *Youngstown Vindicator,* June 21, 1937, p. 1; "Blow Up Pennsylvania Main Line at Niles," *Youngstown Vindicator,* June 15, 1937, p. 1; "Rail Men Ask Davey End 'State of Riot,'" *Youngstown Vindicator,* June 7, 1937, p. 1; and "Railroads Sue to Bar Pickets," *Youngstown Vindicator,* June 2, 1937, p. 1.

96. "Penn. R.R. Dynamited at Bridge," *Western Reserve Democrat* (Warren, OH), September 17, 1937, p. 1; "Blow Up Pennsylvania Main Line at Niles," *Youngstown Vindicator,* June 15, 1937, p. 1. See also "P.R.R. Tracks Blown Up," *New York Times,* June 16, 1937, p. 8. This was not the only occasion of retaliatory sabotage. "'No General Strike' Labor Head Says," *Youngstown Vindicator,* June 14, 1937, p. 1.

97. LCH, 13654, 13671 (exhibit 5196).

98. Girdler, *Boot Straps,* 330–31; "Blast Tears Up Railroad Siding," *Canton Repository,* June 24, 1937, p. 1; "Rails Dynamited at Republic Mill," *Youngstown Vindicator,* June 18, 1937, p. 1.

99. "Strike Leader at Massillon Hurt in Morning Clash," *Canton Repository,* June 8, 1937, p. 1. See also LCH, 16195 (exhibit 7083), 16198–99.

100. "Reports of National Guardsmen to Their Commanding Officer[s]," YSSR, Box 1, Folder 9, Series 167, OHS; LCH, 16445–520 (exhibits 7243–325). See also "Dynamite Blast Rips Section of W.&L.E. Tracks," *Canton Repository,* June 25, 1937, p. 1.

101. "Two Power Lines Short Circuited in Local Strike Area," *Canton Repository,* June 2, 1937, p. 1.

102. Interview of John Johns (1 of 2), 1970, p. 8, USWA–Labor Oral History Collection, PSU-HCLA; interview of John Johns (2 of 2), March 3, 1978, p. 20, ibid.

103. Lapin, "Steel Thugs Open Fire on Pickets."

104. "Four Arrested with Dynamite," *Canton Repository,* June 21, 1937, p. 1.

105. Steuben, *Strike Strategy,* 140–41; interview of Fred A. Fortunato, January 6, 1983, pp. 22, 30–31, YSU-OHP; interview of Thomas White, July 9, 1974, pp. 2, 5, YSU-OHP; "Speeding Car Injures 3 Pickets," *Youngstown Vindicator,* June 12, 1937, p. 1; "Autos Crash Picket Lines," *Youngstown Vindicator,* June 7, 1937, p. 1.

106. *Little Steel Companies,* 218; LCH, 13139–40 (exhibits 5056F–G); "Strike Leaders Anticipate Early Timken Settlement," *Canton Repository,* June 7, 1937, p. 1.

107. Louis Stark, "Air Crashes Halt Strike Food Supply in Steel Struggle," *New York Times,* June 3, 1937, p. 1.

108. "CIO Violence Told," *New York Times,* June 20, 1937, p. 1.

109. LCH, 13634–743 (exhibit 5195); "Fracas Halts Plan to March Back to Work," *Canton Repository,* June 19, 1937, p. 1.

110. See, for example, "Text of Girdler Statement before Senate Committee," *Buffalo Evening News,* June 25, 1937, p. 4; "Girdler Denounces C.I.O. before Senate Committee; Suggests Own Peace Plan," *Canton Repository,* June 23, 1937, p. 1.

111. LCH, 13739–41 (exhibit 5197); 81 Cong. Rec. 8809–12, 8820–23 (1937).

112. 81 Cong. Rec. 8812–13 (1937).

113. 81 Cong. Rec. 8813 (1937); "Blocking Mail Charged: Postal Inspector Gets Warrants on Three Pickets," *New York Times,* June 30, 1937, p. 2.

114. See U.S. Senate, Committee on Post Offices and Post Roads, *Investigation of the Delivery or Nondelivery of Mail to Establishments Where Industrial Strife Is in Progress, Adverse Report,* Report No. 885, 75th Cong., 1st Sess. (Washington, DC: GPO, 1937); 81 Cong. Rec. 8809–23 (1937); "Assert Farley Lets C.I.O. Rule Postal System," *Chicago Daily Tribune,* June 26, 1937, p. 2; "CIO Violence Told," *New York Times,* June 20, 1937, p. 1; and "Hunts for Pickets Who Blocked Mail," *New York Times,* June 19, 1937, p. 2.

115. LCH, 13743–73 (exhibit 5198).

116. Docket of the Republic Steel Strike, May 1937, Series 5, Industrial Relations, Subseries A, Administrative Files, Strikes, Docket of Republic Steel Corporation, Container 77, Folder 31, WRHS-RSC; "Arrest Order Held Move for Peace in Strike," *Canton Repository,* June 24, 1937, p. 10; "Blocking Mail Charged," *New York Times,* June 30, 1937, p. 2; "Republic Steel Sues over Mail Ban; Farley Called to Court in Capital," *New York Times,* June 16, 1937, p. 1; "Republic Steel Tells Farley to Get Mail to Strike Mills or Face Suit," *New York Times,* June 9, 1937, p. 1.

117. Robert Bruno, *Steelworker Alley: How Class Works in Youngstown* (Ithaca, NY: Cornell University Press, 1999), 102.

118. LCH, 13544–45, 13645–754 (exhibits 5195–97).

119. Ibid., 13728 (exhibit 5197).

120. Ibid., 12841–49 (exhibits 4922–25), 12852–57 (exhibits 4930–42C), 13645–754 (exhibits 5195–97), 15487–501 (exhibits 6254–82).

121. See, for example, "Strike Areas Still in Grip of Vandalism," *Cleveland Plain Dealer,* July 21, 1937, p. 1; "Vandal Hurls Brick, Perils Aged Woman," *Cleveland Plain Dealer,* July 19, 1937, p. 1; "Fracas Halts Plan to March Back to Work," June 18, 1937, p. 1; "Labor Vandalism Hits Seven Homes," *Cleveland Plain Dealer,* July 15, 1937, p. 2; "Massillon Units of Republic Reopen as Troops Arrive," *Canton Repository,* July 2, 1937, p. 1; "Quiet Prevails in Strike Area," *Canton Repository,* June 22, 1937, p. 1; "Four Arrested with Dynamite," *Canton Repository,* June 21, 1937, p. 1; "Blast Tears Up Railroad Track," *Canton Repository,* June 18, 1937, p. 1; and "5 More Homes in City Stoned," *Canton Repository,* June 9, 1937, p. 1.

122. See, for example, "5 Men Beaten in Strike Rows," *Youngstown Vindicator,* June 18, 1937, p. 1; "Speeding Car Injures 3 Pickets," *Youngstown Vindicator,* June 12, 1937, p. 1; "Eight Arrested at Massillon," *Canton Repository,* June 11, 1937, p. 1; and "Strike Leader at Massillon Hurt in Morning Clash," *Canton Repository,* June 8, 1937, p. 1.

123. For complaints compiled by Republic, see LCH, 13645–754 (exhibits 5195–97). For arrest records, see LCH, 12841–49 (exhibits 4922–25), 12852–71 (exhibits 4930–42C), 15487–501 (exhibits 6254–82). See also "Quiet Prevails in Strike Area," *Canton Repository,* June 22, 1937, p. 1; and "Fracas Halts Plan to March Back to Work," *Canton Repository,* June 19, 1937, p. 1.

124. "We Are Going to Stick" (union handbill), n.d., in Strike Propaganda, YSSR, Box 1, Folder 1, Series 167, OHS.

125. Louis Stark, "Rail Unions to Act Over Steel Strike," *New York Times,* June 1, 1937, p. 9.

126. G3 worksheet, June 24, 1937, in "Work Sheet[s] of Ohio National Guard, June 21–July 7," YSSR, Box 1, Folder 13, Series 167, OHS; G2 worksheet, June 26, 1937, in ibid.

127. LCH, 12923 (exhibit 4985); "Grand Jury Probes Bomb Plot," *Western Reserve Democrat* (Warren, OH), July 8, 1937, p. 1; "Hunt Hall as Bomb Ringleader," *Western Reserve Democrat* (Warren, OH), July 1, 1937, p. 1; "Hunt C.I.O. Leader as Bombing Chief," *New York Times,* June 30, 1937, p. 3.

128. "C.I.O. Aide Surrenders," *New York Times,* July 2, 1937, p. 2; "Hunt C.I.O. Leader as Bomb Chief," *New York Times,* June 30, 1937, p. 3.

129. Statement of Sidney Watkins, June 30, 1937, YSSR, Box 1, Folder 12, Series 167, OHS.

130. Statement of George Bund, June 28, 1937, YSSR, Box 1, Folder 12, Series 167, OHS.

131. Statement of John Borawiec, June 27, 1937, YSSR, Box 1, Folder 12, Series 167, OHS.

132. Statement of A. C. Scott, June 27, 1937, YSSR, Box 1, Folder 12, Series 167, OHS.

133. "Ohio Authorities in Collusion with Steel Firms, C.I.O. Charges," *Daily Worker,* July 11, 1937, p. 3; "CIO Exposes Dynamite Plot Frameup," *Daily Worker,* June 30, 1937, p. 1.

134. Gus Hall, *Steel and Metal Workers—It Takes a Fight to Win!* (New York: New Outlook, 1972), 15.

135. Fred Gaboury, "Gus Hall Remembers," *People's World Weekly,* May 31, 1997.

136. Interview of Thomas White, July 9, 1974, p. 5, YSU-OHP.

137. McDonald, *Union Man,* 112–16 (quotation p. 113).

138. "Spare Burton at Airport in Pickets' Rush," *Cleveland Plain Dealer,* June 10, 1937, p. 1; "Mayor Escapes Picket Attack," *Youngstown Vindicator,* June 10, 1937, p. 4.

139. "New Deputies, Pickets Clash in E. Side Store," *Youngstown Vindicator,* June 9, 1937, p. 1; "Steel Strike Fight Starts in Store," *Cleveland Plain Dealer,* June 9, 1937, p. 1.

140. "Special Deputy Seized by Pickets," *Canton Repository,* June 19, 1937, p. 1.

141. LCH, 13673 (exhibit 5197).

142. See, for example, "Weigh Canton General Strike," *Daily Worker,* June 17, 1937, p. 1; "Strike Leaders Visit Seccombe," *Canton Repository,* June 10, 1937, p. 1; and "General Strike Threatened if Cops Use Arms," *Youngstown Vindicator,* June 10, 1937, p. 1.

143. "C.I.O. to Push Strike Drive on Republic at Buffalo Plant Today," *Cleveland Plain Dealer,* May 28, 1937, p. 1. See also "C.I.O. Leaders to Renew Picket Lines at Republic," *Buffalo Evening News,* June 5, 1937, p. 7; "Picketing Quiet at Steel Plant," *Buffalo Evening News,* June 1, 1937, p. 8; and "Few Employes *[sic]* of Local Plant Go Out on Strike," *Buffalo Evening News,* May 27, 1937, p. 1.

144. "Troops Restore Order at Warren," *Cleveland Plain Dealer,* June 24, 1937, p. 1; "Warren Threatened with Labor Holiday," *Western Reserve Democrat* (Warren, OH), June 24, 1937, p. 1; "5,000 Join Steel Sympathy Strike," *Daily Worker,* June 24, 1937, p. 1; "Girdler Denounces C.I.O. before Senate Committee; Suggests Own Peace Plan," *Canton Repository,* June 23, 1937, p. 1.

145. "'Avoid Youngstown' State Warns Trucks," *Canton Repository,* June 21, 1937, p. 3 (quotation); "Youngstown Teamsters Strike," *Daily Worker,* June 21, 1937, p. 1.

146. G3 worksheet, June 24, 1937, in "Work Sheet[s] of Ohio National Guard, June 21–July 7," YSSR, Box 1, Folder 13, Series 167, OHS.

147. Steuben, *Strike Strategy,* 149; Louis Stark, "S.W.O.C. Acts to Cut Iron Ore to Close Big Steel Mills," *New York Times,* June 4, 1937, p. 1. See also "Bloodless Interlude," *Time,* June 14, 1937, p. 15; and Spencer Fullerton, "S.W.O.C. Drives at Republic's Ore," *Cleveland Plain Dealer,* June 14, 1937, p. 1.

148. For example, early in the strike the crew of a Republic freighter prevented the ship from unloading scrap iron in Cleveland. "Two Hurt in Strike Clash," *Cleveland Plain Dealer,* June 1, 1937, p. 1. See also "Two Republic Mines Re-Open," *Youngstown Vindicator,* July 14, 1937, p. 3.

149. "17 Mines Affected," *New York Times,* June 14, 1937, p. 1; "Lewis Swats Steel with Mine Strike," *Cleveland Plain Dealer,* June 14, 1937, p. 1; "10,000 'Captive' Miners Strike," Steel Labor, June 21, 1937, p. 2; "3 Johnstown Unions Push United Fight," *Daily Worker,* June 14, 1937, p. 1.

150. "Miners a Factor in the Steel Drive," *New York Times,* February 14, 1937, p. 67; Felix Belair Jr., "25,000 Employed in 'Captive' Mines Threaten Strike," *New York Times,* January 29, 1937, p. 1.

151. "7,000 Miners Strike to Aid Steel Walkout," *Daily Worker,* June 15, 1937, p. 1.

152. Jack Metzgar, *Striking Steel: Solidarity Remembered* (Philadelphia: Temple University Press, 2000), 4; "Miners in Throngs 'Invade' Jamestown," *New York Times,* June 26, 1937, p. 3; "C.I.O. Defends Coal Strike as 'Defense in War,'" *Chicago Daily News,* June 15, 1937, p. 4; "C.I.O. Threatens to Bar All Coal to Steel Mills," *Chicago Daily News,* June 14, 1937, p. 4.

1. William Z. Foster, *The Great Steel Strike and Its Lessons* (New York: Arno, 1969), 42–44 (quotation p. 43).

2. Kenneth Warren, *Bethlehem Steel: Builder and Arsenal of America* (Pittsburgh: University of Pittsburgh Press, 2008), 112–13.

3. U.S. Senate, Committee on Education and Labor, *Violations of Free Speech and the Rights of Labor: Labor Policies of Employers' Associations; Part IV, The "Little Steel" Companies,* Report No. 151, 77th Cong., 1st Sess. (Washington, DC: GPO, 1941) (hereafter *Little Steel Companies*), 253–55; Bethlehem Steel, 14 NLRB 539 (1939); Elizabeth Fones-Wolf and Ken Fones-Wolf, "Conversion at Bethlehem: Religion and Union Building in Steel, 1930–42," *Labor History* 29, no. 4 (1998): 381; Frank Blumenthal, "Anti-Union Publicity in the Johnstown 'Little Steel' Strike of 1937," *Public Opinion Quarterly* 3, no. 4 (1939): 677–78.

4. U.S. Senate, *Hearings before the Committee on Education and Labor: Violations of Free Speech and the Rights of Labor,* 76th Cong., 1st–3rd Sess. (Washington, DC: GPO, 1937) (hereafter LCH), 8345–51.

5. Official ballot, Brotherhood of Railroad Trainmen, Brotherhood of Locomotive Firemen and Engineers, May 20, 1937, Howard Curtiss Collection, Box 5, File 36, PSU-HCLA.

6. "Strike of Railroaders in Bethlehem's Plant Starts Minus Disorder," *Johnstown Democrat,* June 11, 1937, local page; circular from David Watkins, June 11, 1937, Howard Curtiss Collection, Box 5, File 36, PSU-HCLA.

7. *Little Steel Companies,* 254–60; LCH, 8230–38; *Bethlehem Steel,* 14 NLRB at 612–13; Fones-Wolf and Fones-Wolf, "Conversion at Bethlehem," 382–83; "Steel Strike Settles on Johnstown with Total Absence of Disorder as CIO Attempts to Force Recognition," *Johnstown Democrat,* June 12, 1937, local page; "Bethlehem Steel Strike Called by CIO," *Daily Worker,* June 12, 1937, p. 4; "Cambria Mill Hit by Railway Strike," *New York Times,* June 11, 1937, p. 5.

8. LCH, 8231–32.

9. Adam Lapin, "Johnstown Vigilantes Whipped Up Race Prejudice in Strike," *Daily Worker,* July 21, 1937, p. 6.

10. LCH, 8238–39; "Strike of Railroaders in Bethlehem's Plant Starts Minus Disorder," *Johnstown Democrat,* June 11, 1937, local page.

11. *Little Steel Companies,* 263.

12. Ibid., 257–65; LCH, 8204–13, 8399–8400, 8422–24; *Bethlehem Steel,* 14 NLRB at 623–24.

13. *Little Steel Companies,* 259–68; "State Police Patrol of Picket Lines Ends Mill Gate Disorders," *Johnstown Democrat,* June 16, 1937, local page; "Police Hurl Gas to Disperse Crowd in Latest Strike Fray as Tension Increases at Mills," *Johnstown Democrat,* June 15, 1937, local page; Russell B. Porter, "Johnstown Swept by Strike Rioters throughout the Night," *New York Times,* June 15, 1937, p. 1; "Johnstown Steel Strike Reaching Crisis as Franklin Boro Disorders

Bring State Police into Territory," *Johnstown Democrat*, June 14, 1937, local page.

14. "Law and Order Must Prevail at All Times, Mayor Declares," *Johnstown Democrat*, June 14, 1937, local page.

15. "What Constitutes Lawful Picketing?" *Johnstown Democrat*, June 16, 1937, local page.

16. *Little Steel Companies*, 264–68 (quotations pp. 266–67); *Bethlehem Steel*, 14 NLRB at 617–19.

17. "We *Will* Preserve Law and Order!" (advertisement), *Johnstown Democrat*, June 16, 1937, p. 13, reprinted in *Bethlehem Steel*, 14 NLRB at 616.

18. "5,000 Reward!" (advertisement), *Johnstown Democrat*, June 17, 1937, p. 10. See also *Bethlehem Steel*, 14 NLRB at 617–24; and "*We Will* Keep Johnston Safe for Johnstowners; *We Will* Preserve Law and Order!" (advertisement), *Johnstown Democrat*, June 17, 1937, p. 15.

19. *Little Steel Companies*, 269–75 (quotation p. 269). On Shield's financial fortunes during the strike, see also LCH, 8440–41, 8648–49 (exhibits 3974–75), 8651–78 (exhibits 3977–4002).

20. *Little Steel Companies*, 275–76.

21. "Three Men Slashed in Picket Knifing at Franklin Plant," *Johnstown Democrat*, June 17, 1937, local page. See also "Bethlehem Reaffirms 'Open Shop,'" *Johnstown Democrat*," June 17, 1937, local page.

22. "Peace Returns to Strike Zone as Police Prevent Picket Line Disorders," *Johnstown Democrat*, June 18, 1937, local page.

23. "Earle Calls Upon Grace to Close Cambria Mill Before State Does," *Johnstown Democrat*, June 19, 1937, p. 1 extra.

24. LCH, 14866, (exhibit 5766); *Little Steel Companies*, 275–77; "State 'Padlocks' Bethlehem Plant," *Johnstown Democrat*, June 20, 1937, p. 1 extra; "Martial Law Declared in City; Steel Plant is Ordered Closed," *Johnstown Democrat*, June 19, 1937, p. 1 extra; "Miners' Rally Canceled as Earle Declares Martial Law," *New York Times*, June 20, 1937, p. 1; "Lewis Calls Off Mass Meeting in City," *Johnstown Democrat*, June 20, 1937, p. 1 extra.

25. *Little Steel Companies*, 276–77; LCH, 148771 (exhibits 5770A–B).

26. See Howard Curtiss Collection, Box 5, File 36, PSU-HCLA.

27. "State 'Padlocks' Bethlehem Plant," *Johnstown Democrat*, June 20, 1937, p. 1 extra; "Earle Calls Upon Grace to Close Cambria Mill Before State Does," *Johnstown Democrat*, June 19, 1937, p. 1 extra.

28. *Little Steel Companies*, 280–82.

29. "Steel Strike Closes 21 Plants of Three Large Companies; Auditorium Vote Canceled," *Canton Repository*, May 27, 1937, p. 1

30. "Union Protests Secret Ballot," *Canton Repository*, June 2, 1937, p. 1; "C. of C. Sponsors Secret Ballot of Republic Workers," *Canton Repository*, June 1, 1937, p. 1. The SWOC unsuccessfully sought to enjoin the ballot. "Action to Halt Vote Defeated," *Canton Repository*, June 4, 1937, p. 14.

31. "C. of C. Ballot Shows Men Want to Work," *Canton Repository*, June 8, 1937, p. 1.

32. *Little Steel Companies*, 220–26; LCH, 13040–118; Republic Steel, 9 NLRB 219, 326–27 (1938); "Fracas Halts Plan to March Back to Work," June 18, 1937, p. 1. See also "Canton Can Keep the Peace!" (advertisement), *Canton Repository*, July 1, 1937, p. 14; "Mayor Says He Will Keep All His Promises," *Canton Repository*, June 18, 1937, p. 1; "Worker Crowd Jams Hall to See Mayor" and "Law and Order Group Defines Its Purpose," *Canton Repository*, June 17, 1937, p. 1; "Purposes of Canton's Law and Order League" (advertisement), *Canton Repository*, June 13, 1937, p. 12; and "Citizens Form Group to Back Law and Order," *Canton Repository*, June 10, 1937, p. 1.

33. *Little Steel Companies*, 183–88; LCH, 12152–86 (exhibits 4789A–K, 4791).

34. "Tin Mill 'Back-to-Work' Meeting Is Blocked by CIO Demonstration," *Cumberland Evening Times*, June 11, 1937, p. 15.

35. *Little Steel Companies*, 209–11; LCH, 12751–81, 12792–96; "John Q. Public League Calls County Meets," *Western Reserve Democrat* (Warren, OH), June 17, 1937, p. 1; "Citizens War on Rule of CIO," *Chicago Daily Tribune*, June 13, 1937, p. 1.

36. LCH, 12801–6.

37. *Little Steel Companies*, 230–36; *Republic Steel*, 9 NLRB at 231–36, 252–69; Lois Stark, "Men Demand Jobs," *New York Times*, June 19, 1937, p. 1.

38. *Little Steel Companies*, 178–79, 207, 220–21, 291–93.

39. On the claim that some of these groups were headed by local organized crime figures, see Mary Heaton Vorse, *Labor's New Millions* (New York: Modern Age, 1938), 140.

40. *Little Steel Companies*, 183–84, 229; LCH, 16188–90 (exhibit 7076); *Republic Steel*, 9 NLRB at 268.

41. *Republic Steel*, 9 NLRB at 238–39, 245–49; Republic Steel (Beaver Falls. Pa.), 10 NLRB 868, 875, 879–82 (1938); Lapin, "Johnstown Vigilantes Whipped Up Race Prejudice in Strike"; Adam Lapin, "Vigilantes Ask Overthrow of the U.S. Government," *Daily Worker*, July 16, 1937, p. 1.

42. *Little Steel Companies*, 291–315; U.S. Senate, Committee on Education and Labor, *Violations of Free Speech and the Rights of Labor: Labor Policies of Employers' Associations; Part II, The Associated Industries of Cleveland*, Report No. 6, pt. 5, 76th Cong., 1st Sess. (Washington, DC: GPO, 1939), 134–41; U.S. Senate, Committee on Education and Labor, *Violations of Free Speech and the Rights of Labor: Labor Policies of Employers' Associations; Part III, The National Association of Manufacturers*, Report No. 6, pt. 6, 76th Cong., 1st Sess. (Washington, DC: GPO, 1939), 154–206.

43. See, for example, "Reward $500" (advertisement), *Youngstown Vindicator*, June 26, 1937, p. 14; "$1,000.00 Reward" (advertisement), *Canton Repository*, June 17, 1937, p. 14; and "Reward $500" (advertisement), *Youngstown Vindicator*, June 12, 1937, p. 13. The company also ran such advertisements in Buffalo. "$1,000 Reward" (advertisement), *Buffalo Evening News*, June 18, 1937, p. 41.

44. See, for example, "Statement of Youngstown Sheet & Tube Company" (advertisement), *Youngstown Vindicator*, June 7, 1937, p. 4.

45. "As a Citizen of Youngstown . . ." (advertisement), *Youngstown Vindicator,* June 14, 1937, p. 15.

46. "The Individual's Right in the Strike" (advertisement), *Youngstown Vindicator,* June 19, 1937, p. 3.

47. Quotations from "Issues Set Forth to Republic Men," *New York Times,* June 16, 1937, p. 8, reprinted in *Republic Steel,* 9 NLRB at 256.

48. On June 21, for example, SWOC lodges in Youngstown telegrammed exactly this warning to President Roosevelt. "Unions Appeal to White House; 4 Plants Set to Reopen at 7 A.M.," *Washington Post,* June 22, 1937, p. 1.

49. See, for example, "President Roosevelt Says: 'The Strikers Are Right'" (advertisement), *Youngstown Vindicator,* June 17, 1937, p. 8.

50. "C.I.O. Violence Told," *New York Times,* June 30, 1937, p. 1. See also F. Raymond Daniell, "Hostility to C.I.O. Spreading in Ohio," *New York Times,* July 1, 1937, p. 4; and F. Raymond Daniell, "Railroads in Steel Area Tell Davey 'State of Riot' Threatens Wide Lay-Off," *New York Times,* June 7, 1937, p. 1.

51. Porter, "Johnstown Swept by Strike Rioters throughout the Night."

52. See, for example, Daniell, "Hostility to C.I.O. Spreading in Ohio"; "Who Is Governing Us?" *Wall Street Journal,* June 23, 1937, p. 4; and "Steel Tempers," *Time,* June 21, 1937, p. 22.

53. "The Underlying Issue," *Washington Post,* June 22, 1937, p. 8 (quotation); "Violence Is No Remedy," *Washington Post,* June 1, 1937, p. 8.

54. Dean Dinwoodey, "Picket Line Has Its Legal Problems," *New York Times,* June 6, 1937, p. 73.

55. "C.I.O. and the Wagner Act," *New York Times,* June 19, 1937, p. 16.

56. "Editorial Comments on Governor Earle's Actions," *New York Times,* June 22, 1937, p. 6.

57. LCH, 8474–75.

58. Donald G. Sofchalk, "The Little Steel Strike of 1937" (PhD dissertation, Ohio State University, 1961), 120–36; Daniell, "Hostility to C.I.O. Spreading in Ohio."

59. *Gallup Poll: Public Opinion,* vol. 1, *1935–71* (New York: Random House, 1972), 31, 49, 52, 55, 62–63.

60. Sidney Fine, *Sit-Down: The General Motors Strike of 1936–37* (Ann Arbor: University of Michigan Press, 1969), ch. 10; Irving Bernstein, *The Turbulent Years: A History of the American Worker, 1933–1941* (Boston: Houghton Mifflin, 1969), 534–37, 541.

61. Edwin A. Lahey, "U.S. Watching Steel Strike Peace Moves," *Chicago Daily News,* May 28, 1937, p. 1.

62. William V. Nessly, "Roosevelt Asks Common Sense in Steel Strike," *Washington Post,* June 16, 1937, p. 2. See also "U.S. Opens Hearings to End Steel Strike," *Steel Labor,* June 21, 1937, p. 1.

63. The press actually wondered openly about the president's authority to intervene. See, for example, "Strife in Steel," *New York Times,* June 20, 1937, p. 53.

64. Walter Trohan, "Gov. Earle Adds to C.I.O. Power in Pennsylvania," *Chicago Daily Tribune,* June 23, 1937, p. 3.

65. Vorse, *Labor's New Millions*, 136.

66. "Davey to Seek Settlement of Steel Strike," *Canton Repository*, June 3, 1937, p. 1.

67. Russell B. Porter, "Deadlock Halts Davey Peace Plan," *New York Times*, June 12, 1937, p. 3; "Gov. Davey Calls Parlay to End Strike," *Western Reserve Democrat* (Warren, OH), June 10, 1937, p. 1.

68. Louis Stark, "Steel Heads Avoid New Davey Parley," *New York Times*, June 17, 1937, p. 1. See also "Purnell Delays Answer on Re-opening," *Youngstown Vindicator*, June 16, 1937, p. 1.

69. Turner Catledge, "President Steps In," *New York Times*, June 18, 1937, p. 1. For a copy of the order creating the board, which, per the statute, was issued in Perkins's name, see "Powers of Board Defined in Order," *New York Times*, June 18, 1937, p. 3.

70. William V. Nessly, "Federal Board of 3 Appointed to Speed Steel Strike Peace; Both Sides Will 'Co-operate,'" *Washington Post*, June 18, 1937, p. 1; Louis Stark, "Youngstown Asks Plants Stay Shut," *New York Times*, June 18, 1937, p. 1; Catledge, "President Steps In."

71. "Asks Curb on 'Mobs,'" *New York Times*, June 19, 1937, p. 1.

72. See, for example, "Thomas Refuses Back-to-Work Truce," *Youngstown Vindicator*, June 18, 1937, p. 1.

73. "Steel Peace Move Begun after Riots," *Washington Post*, June 21, 1937, p. 1; "Taft Calls Strike Board Tomorrow," *Cleveland Plain Dealer*, June 18, 1937, p. 1. Later, L. E. Block, chairman of Inland, would meet with the board. Louis Stark, "Mediators Fail in Peace Moves," *New York Times*, June 24, 1937, p. 1.

74. Bernstein, *Turbulent Years*, 495–96 (quotations p. 496); William V. Nessly, "Girdler Declines Roosevelt Help as Steel Strike Arbiter," *Washington Post*, June 26, 1937, p. 1; Louis Stark, "Mediators Fix Flexible Policy to Speed Work for Strike Peace," *New York Times*, June 21, 1937, p. 1.

75. Nessly, "Girdler Declines Roosevelt Help as Steel Strike Arbiter."

76. Paul Y. Anderson, "Armed Rebellion on the Right," *Nation*, August 7, 1937, pp. 146–47.

77. Report of the Federal Steel Mediation Board to Secretary of Labor Frances Perkins, pp. 1–2, Legal Department Records, Box 1, Federal Steel Mediation Board, PSU-HCLA. For a copy of this report, see LCH, 13937–41 (exhibit 5245).

78. "Parlay Is Futile," *New York Times*, June 22, 1937, p. 1; "Governor Acts to Keep Status Quo; President Joins Board's Plea," *Washington Post*, June 22, 1937, p. 1; "'Truce' Greets 3 Mediators in Steel Strike," *Washington Post*, June 19, 1937, p. 2.

79. *Little Steel Companies*, 191–93. See also "Sheet & Tube and Republic to Reopen at 7 A.M. Tuesday," *Youngstown Vindicator*, June 21, 1937, p. 1; and "Notice to Employees of Republic Steel Corporation" (advertisement), *Youngstown Vindicator*, June 21, 1937, p. 2.

80. LCH, 16174–78; Russell B. Porter, "Invaders Seized, 3,000 Turned Back," *New York Times*, June 23, 1937, p. 1; "Warren Court Stops Pickets," *Youngstown Vindicator*, June 21, 1937, p. 6.

81. Porter, "Invaders Seized, 3,000 Turned Back."

82. "City Appoints 11 to Regular Police Force," *Canton Repository,* June 22, 1937, p. 10; "Strike Leaders Ask That Quiet Continue," *Canton Repository,* June 20, 1937, p. 1; "Mayor Decides on More Police," *Canton Repository,* June 20, 1937, p. 1.

83. Hays Jones, "Inland Steel Pickets Halt 'Back-to-Scab' Movement," *Daily Worker,* June 20, 1937, p. 3.

84. "Unions Appeal to White House; 4 Plants to Reopen at 7 A.M.," *Washington Post,* June 22, 1937, p. 1.

85. *Little Steel Companies,* 194–95; LCH, 15980 (exhibit 6811).

86. "Proclamations from Gov. Davey Calling Up the National Guard," Youngstown Steel Strike Records (hereafter YSSR), Box 1, Folder 2, Series 167, OHS. See also *Little Steel Companies,* 194–95; LCH, 13012 (exhibits 5051A–B); and "Ohio Takes Action," *New York Times,* June 22, 1937, p. 1.

87. *Little Steel Companies,* 195–97; LCH, 16414 (exhibit 7206), 16418, (exhibit 7212); supplemental proclamation ordering Guard's cooperation with local authorities, in "Proclamations from Gov. Davey Calling Up the National Guard," YSSR, Box 1, Folder 2, Series 167, OHS.

88. *Little Steel Companies,* 196; LCH, 16420 (exhibit 7215).

89. LCH, 16432 (exhibit 7230), 16443 (exhibit 7240); "Machine Gun and Crew Ready as Troops Guard Steel Plant," *Youngstown Vindicator,* June 24, 1937, p. 1.

90. "'We've Won,' Unionists Shout as 4 Mills Reopen," *Washington Post,* June 23, 1937, p. 1.

91. G3 report, June 23, 1937, in "Work Sheet[s] of Ohio National Guard, June 21–July 7," YSSR, Box 1, Folder 13, Series 167, OHS; "National Guard Enforces Injunction," *Western Reserve Democrat* (Warren, OH), June 24, 1937, p. 1.

92. G3 report, June 23, 1937, in "Work Sheet[s] of Ohio National Guard, June 21–July 7," YSSR, Box 1, Folder 13, Series 167, OHS.

93. See, for example, three similar letters from Roy S. Hardeman, sheriff of Trumbull County, to Major General Gilson D. Light, June 22, 1937, in "Correspondence between Ohio Nat. Guard and Local Officials, June 21, 1937–June 29," 1937, YSSR, Box 1, Folder 3, Series 167, OHS.

94. For a copy of Earle's proclamation, see LCH, 14866 (exhibit 5766).

95. *Little Steel Companies,* 276–77. See also telegram from John L. Lewis to David Watkins, June 19, 1937, Howard Curtiss Collection, PSU-HCLA.

96. *Little Steel Companies,* 276–77; "Martial Law Declared in City; Steel Plant Is Ordered Closed," *Johnstown Democrat,* June 19, 1937, p. 1 extra.

97. "Guard Chief Acts," *New York Times,* June 20, 1937, p. 1; "Johnstown Mayor Defies Governor on Martial Law Order," *Buffalo Evening News,* June 19, 1937, p. 1.

98. Russell B. Porter, "Evacuation Begun," *New York Times,* June 21, 1937, p. 1; "Closed Bethlehem Plant Allowed 962 Workers to Maintain Needed Furnaces, Heat, Coke and Shipping," *Johnstown Democrat,* June 21, 1937, local page.

99. Sofchalk, "Little Steel Strike," 197–99; LCH, 15971 (exhibit 6799); "Purnell Protests to Davey, Says Men Have Right to Job," *Youngstown Vindicator,* June 22,

1937, p. 1; "Non-strikers Demand Davey Use Troops to Drive Out 'C.I.O. Thugs' and Open Mills," *New York Times,* June 23, 1937, p. 2.

100. Sofchalk, "Little Steel Strike," 197–99; LCH, 12161 (exhibit 4789F).

101. "The Right to Work," *Youngstown Vindicator,* June 23, 1937, p. 1; "Companies Will Do Well to Sign" (editorial), *Youngstown Vindicator,* June 13, 1937, p. 1.

102. "Evans Asks FDR, Davey to Open," *Youngstown Vindicator,* June 24, 1937, p. 1.

103. *Little Steel Companies,* 279–80; Blumenthal, "Anti-Union Publicity," 680–82. For a copy of the advertisement, see LCH, 7330 (exhibit 3787G); "We Protest!" (advertisement), *Chicago Daily Tribune,* June 24, 1937, p. 14; and "We Protest . . ." (advertisement), *Buffalo Evening News,* June 24, 1937, p. 30.

104. "Not a Strike but an Insurrection," *Chicago Daily Tribune,* June 23, 1937, p. 12; Arthur Sears Henning, "Lewis Gleeful as Government Rescues Strike," *Chicago Daily Tribune,* June 21, 1937, p. 1.

105. LCH, 14873–75 (exhibits 5770F–G, 5770I–J) (quotations pp. 14873–74). See also "Text of Grace's Wire to Earle," *Washington Post,* June 19, 1937, p. 10; and "Cambria Plant Closed by Governor Though 70% of Men Want to Work," *Iron Age,* June 24, 1937, p. 91C.

106. *Little Steel Companies,* 278–80; LCH, 7339 (exhibit 3787I), 8312, 8478–83; "Boyle Claims Inability to Request Governor's Unlocking Steel Plant," *Johnstown Democrat,* June 23, 1937, local page; "Johnstown Seeks Inquiry by Senate," *New York Times,* June 22, 1937, p. 1; "Bethlehem's Mill Closed," *Youngstown Vindicator,* June 21, 1937, p. 1; "Grace Protests Cambria Closing," *New York Times,* June 20, 1937, p. 3.

107. Report of the Federal Steel Mediation Board to Secretary of Labor Frances Perkins, pp. 6–7, Legal Department Records, Box 1, Federal Steel Mediation Board, PSU-HCLA (quotation p. 6); Stark, "Mediators Fail in Peace Moves."

108. *Little Steel Companies,* 198. For a copy of the document, see LCH, 13937–41 (exhibit 5245).

109. Report of the Federal Steel Mediation Board to Secretary of Labor Frances Perkins, p. 7, Legal Department Records, Box 1, Federal Steel Mediation Board, PSU-HCLA. Board member Edward McGrady would make one last, fruitless appeal for negotiations on June 26. "Steel Mediators in Final Gesture," *New York Times,* June 27, 1937, p. 2. The board disbanded on June 29. "Mediation Fails, Steel Board Quits," *New York Times,* June 30, 1937, p. 4.

110. "Text of Steel Companies' Joint Statement," *New York Times,* June 25, 1937, p. 4.

111. For Davey's order to reopen the mills, see "Proclamations from Gov. Davey Calling Up the National Guard," in "Correspondence between Ohio Nat. Guard and Local Officials, June 21, 1937–June 29, 1937," YSSR, Box 1, Folder 2, Series 167, OHS; LCH, 16396 (exhibit 7201); and "Right to Work Is Sacred, Uphold Law—Davey Orders," *Canton Repository,* June 25, 1937, p. 1.

112. Russell B. Porter, "Gov. Davey Orders Mills Kept Open," *New York Times,* June 25, 1937, p. 1.

113. "Johnstown Reopening Is Deferred after Earle Cancels Martial Law," *New York Times*, June 25, 1937, p. 1.

114. LCH, 12164 (exhibit 4789G).

115. Wayne Thomis, "Arrest 6 C.I.O. Mail Censors, U.S. Commands," *Chicago Daily Tribune*, June 24, 1937, p. 9. See also "Girdler Calls CIO Irresponsible: Says He Will Not Sign," *Wall Street Journal*, June 25, 1937, p. 1; "Deadlock Ends Strike Parley," *Cleveland Plain Dealer*, June 12, 1937, p. 1; and "To Meet with Davey," *Wall Street Journal*, June 10, 1937, p. 2.

116. Walter Galenson, *The CIO Challenge to the AFL: A History of the American Labor Movement, 1935–1941* (Cambridge, MA: Harvard University Press, 1960), 106; "Gov. Earle Pledges Aid to Bethlehem Strikers," *Steel Labor*, July 6, 1937, p. 1; "Gov. Earle Pledges Effort to Force Steel Election," *Cleveland Plain Dealer*, July 5, 1937, p. 1.

117. "Governor Refused," *New York Times*, June 27, 1937, p. 1.

118. "Shift by Gov. Davey Angers C.I.O.," *New York Times*, June 26, 1937, p. 2; "Davey Is No. 1 on C.I.O. 'Get' List," *Cleveland Plain Dealer*, August 15, 1937, p. 5A. Earle was barred from reelection.

119. Mayo et al. v. Davey et al., U.S. District Court for the Southern District of Ohio, No. 1218, in "Legal Documents Pertaining to Suits against the Nat'l Guard, the Governor, and the Steel Companies," YSSR, Box 1, Folder 11, Series 167, OHS; 3 "Judges Will Study CIO Suit," *Youngstown Vindicator*, July 2, 1937, p. 35; "C.I.O. Sues to Bar Use of Ohio Troops," *New York Times*, June 27, 1937, p. 4. The SWOC also sued, unsuccessfully, to have the companies' weapons seized. "Court Orders Republic Arms Records," *Youngstown Vindicator*, June 16, 1937, p. 1. See also letter from Lee Pressman to the Pennsylvania Attorney General, February 23, 1937, in SWOC, Harold Ruttenberg Papers, Box 3, Folder 11, PSU-HCLA.

120. "Strike Leaders Fear 'Massacre,' Wire Roosevelt," *New York Times*, June 28, 1937, p. 1; "Shift by Gov. Davey Angers C.I.O.," *New York Times*, June 26, 1937, p. 2.

121. "President Quotes," *New York Times*, June 30, 1937, p. 1. See also Bernstein, *Turbulent Years*, 713–14.

122. "Text of John L. Lewis's Radio Talk on C.I.O.," *New York Times*, September 4, 1937, p. 6.

123. On initial CIO anger with Roosevelt, see, for example, "Lewis Unions Lash Administration; Charge Steel Strike Rights Were Ignored," *Cleveland Plain Dealer*, July 24, 1937, p. 1. On the lasting repercussions of this conflict, see Saul Alinsky, *John L. Lewis* (New York: Vintage, 1949), 158–91; and Bernstein, *Turbulent Years*, 714–20.

124. James L. Wright, "New Deal Shows a Change of Heart," *Buffalo Evening News*, July 6, 1937, p. 1.

125. "Davey Disputes Perkins Version," *New York Times*, June 28, 1937, p. 2 (quotations); "Strike Widens Davey Breach with New Deal," *Canton Repository*, June 28, 1937, p. 1; "Governor Refused," *New York Times*, June 27, 1937, p. 1.

126. "Perkins Asked to Call 'Strike' Governors," *Youngstown Vindicator*, July 7, 1937, p. 15; "No C.I.O. Irresponsibility Shown, Miss Perkins Says; Would Force Conferences," *New York Times*, July 2, 1937, p. 1.

127. Letter from James T. Nist, sheriff of Stark County, to Brig. Gen. Wm. L. Marlin, June 25, 1937, in "Correspondence between Ohio Nat. Guard and Local Officials, June 21, 1937–June 29, 1937," YSSR, Box 1, Folder 3, Series 167, OHS.

128. "Practice What You Preach, Seccombe Tells Davey," *Canton Repository*, June 23, 1937, p. 1; "Canton Mayor Attacks Davey," *Youngstown Vindicator*, June 23, 1937, p. 8; "Canton Mayor Sharp in Letter to Davey," *New York Times*, June 24, 1937, p. 2; "Picket Killed at Plant; Order Bethlehem Shut," *Chicago Daily Tribune*, June 20, 1937, p. 1; "No Mob Rule in Ohio, Gov. Davey Warns Mayor," *Canton Repository*, June 20, 1937, p. 1.

129. Letter from Canton mayor James Seccombe to Brig. Gen. Wm. L. Marlin, June 22, 1937, in "Correspondence between Ohio Nat. Guard and Local Officials, June 21, 1937–June 29, 1937," YSSR, Box 1, Folder 3, Series 167, OHS; letter from [Massillon] mayor Henry Krier to Brig. Gen. Wm. L. Marlin, Ohio National Guard, June 26, 1937, in "Correspondence between Ohio Nat. Guard and Local Officials, June 21, 1937–June 29, 1937," YSSR, Box 1, Folder 3, Series 167, OHS.

130. *Little Steel Companies*, 227. A smaller contingent of Guardsmen had been on duty in Canton since June 23. "200 National Guardsmen in Canton for Strike Duty," *Canton Repository*, June 23, 1937, p. 1; "Orders Local Pickets to Disarm," *Massillon Evening Independent*, June 23, 1937, p. 1.

131. "Troops Arrive to Take Over 'Danger Zone'; 3 Mills Open Today," *Cleveland Plain Dealer*, July 6, 1937, p. 1; "Call on N.G. to Reopen Mills Here," *Cleveland Plain Dealer*, July 4, 1937, p. 1; "Davey Pledges Troops to Open Last of Plants," *Youngstown Vindicator*, July 4, 1937, p. 1.

132. LCH, 11499, 16397–412 (exhibits 7202–3)

133. Shirley Hurst, "First Defeat of C.I.O. Possible as Men of Steel Resume Jobs," *Washington Post*, June 27, 1937, p. 1. See also "Steel Strike Lost by C.I.O., Says Green; Another Mill Open," *New York Times*, July 9, 1937, p. 1.

134. See, for example, Wayne Thomis, "Ohio Strike Broken," *Chicago Daily Tribune*, June 26, 1937, p. 1; "Mills Here Back in Production as Bethlehem Plant Re-Opens," *Youngstown Vindicator*, June 26, 1937, p. 1; and "Mills Re-open, Workers Under Guard of State," *Youngstown Vindicator*, June 24, 1937, p. 1.

135. Vorse, *Labor's New Millions*, 147. See also Porter, "Invaders Seized, 3,000 Turned Back"; and "Troops Arriving; 5,000 Due; Troops Repel CIO Invasion," *Youngstown Vindicator*, June 22, 1937, p. 1.

136. "Reports of National Guardsmen to Their Commanding Officer[s]," YSSR, Box 1, Folder 9, Series 167, OHS; "Work Sheet[s] of Ohio National Guard, June 21–July 7," YSSR, Box 1, Folder 13, Series 167, OHS; "Police Seize Clubs, Knives, Guns and Bombs from Strike Sympathizers," *Youngstown Vindicator*, June 22, 1937, p. 1.

137. G3 worksheet, June 24, 1937, in "Work Sheet[s] of Ohio National Guard, June 21–July 7," YSSR, Box 1, Folder 13, Series 167, OHS.

138. "Workers Pour into Mills at Warren, Niles," *Youngstown Vindicator*, June 25, 1937, p. 1; "Troops Restore Order in Warren," *Cleveland Plain Dealer*, June 24,

1937, p. 1; "Troops Repulse Hostile Crowds as Workers Leave," *Youngstown Vindicator,* June 23, 1937, p. 1.

139. G3 worksheet, June 25, 1937, in "Work Sheet[s] of Ohio National Guard, June 21–July 7," YSSR, Box 1, Folder 13, Series 167, OHS.

140. "Reports of National Guardsmen to Their Commanding Officer[s]," YSSR, Box 1, Folder 9, Series 167, OHS; "Work Sheet[s] of Ohio National Guard, June 21–July 7," YSSR, Box 1, Folder 13, Series 167, OHS.

141. G2 report of 1st Lieut. Robert E. Boyd, 166th Inf., June 26–27, 1937, in "Reports of National Guardsmen to Their Commanding Officer[s]," YSSR, Box 1, Folder 9, Series 167, OHS; S2 report of Capt. E. C. Woolf, June 28, 1937, in ibid.; "Warren SWOC Sees Victory," *Youngstown Vindicator,* June 25, 1937, p. 13.

142. G2 worksheet, June 27, 1937, in "Work Sheet[s] of Ohio National Guard, June 21–July 7," YSSR, Box 1, Folder 13, Series 167, OHS (quotation); G2 worksheet, June 26, 1937, in ibid.

143. G2 worksheet, June 27, 1937, in "Work Sheet[s] of Ohio National Guard, June 21–July 7," YSSR, Box 1, Folder 13, Series 167, OHS. For larger estimates of the size of the Canton meeting, see "Strike Activities Limited to Rally and Auto Parade," *Canton Repository,* June 26, 1937, p. 1.

144. G2 worksheet, June 26, 1937, in "Work Sheet[s] of Ohio National Guard, June 21–July 7," YSSR, Box 1, Folder 13, Series 167, OHS.

145. Ibid.

146. G2 worksheet, June 27, 1937, in "Work Sheet[s] of Ohio National Guard, June 21–July 7," YSSR, Box 1, Folder 13, Series 167, OHS.

147. Chief of staff worksheet, June 28, 1937, in "Work Sheet[s] of Ohio National Guard, June 21–July 7," YSSR, Box 1, Folder 13, Series 167, OHS.

148. "What Union Says about Reopening," *Cleveland Plain Dealer,* July 6, 1937, p. 7.

149. *Little Steel Companies,* 25.

150. LCH, 13380–420, 16445–63 (exhibit 7243); "Work Sheet[s] of Ohio National Guard, June 21–July 7," YSSR, Box 1, Folder 13, Series 167, OHS; G2 worksheet, June 24, 1937, in "Work Sheet[s] of Ohio National Guard, June 21–July 7," YSSR, Box 1, Folder 13, Series 167, OHS.

151. Russell B. Porter, "C.I.O. Threatens Davey on Troops; Job Move Grows," *New York Times,* June 28, 1937, p. 1. See also Adam Lapin, "This Ohio C.I.O. Leader Knows His Labor History," *Daily Worker,* June 29, 1937, p. 7.

152. "Reports of National Guardsmen to Their Commanding Officer[s]," YSSR, Box 2, Folder 6, Series 167, OHS; "Work Sheet[s] of Ohio National Guard, June 21–July 7," YSSR, Box 1, Folder 13, Series 167, OHS.

153. "Strike Leaders Fear 'Massacre,' Wire Roosevelt," *New York Times,* June 28, 1937, p. 1.

154. G2 worksheet, June 30, 1937, in "Work Sheet[s] of Ohio National Guard, June 21–July 7," YSSR, Box 1, Folder 13, Series 167, OHS.

155. G3 worksheet, June 26, 1937, in "Work Sheet[s] of Ohio National Guard, June 21–July 7," YSSR, Box 1, Folder 13, Series 167, OHS; G2 worksheet, June 26,

1937, in ibid.; "Reports of National Guardsmen to Their Commanding Officer[s]," YSSR, Box 1, Folder 9, Series 167, OHS. Many, but not all, Ohio National Guard records cited in this chapter were gathered by the La Follette Committee and published in its hearing records. See LCH, pt. 43 passim.

156. "3,000 at Work as Quiet Reigns in Zone," *Canton Repository,* July 1, 1937, p. 1; "8 Hurt, 75 Seized in Riot at Canton," *New York Times,* July 1, 1937, p. 3; "Stone 8 Despite Troops at Steel Mills in Canton," *Chicago Daily Tribune,* July 1, 1937, p. 13; "Trouble Flares Again at Canton," *Cleveland Plain Dealer,* July 1, 1937, p. 1; "Canton Strike Siege Ends as 8000 Workers Move Into Plants with Troop Escorts," *Canton Repository,* June 30, 1937.

157. "Reporters See Guardsmen Beat Strikers," *Steel Labor,* July 7, 1937, p. 3; "3,000 at Work as Quiet Reigns in Zone," *Canton Repository,* July 1, 1937, p. 1; "Trouble Flares Again at Canton," *Cleveland Plain Dealer,* July 1, 1937, p. 1; "Troops Mobilized as 2 Mills Prepare to Reopen in Indiana," *Washington Post,* July 1, 1937, p. 1; "8 Hurt, 75 Seized in Riot at Canton," *New York Times,* July 1, 1937, p. 3. See also S2 report by Capt. William B. Higgins, June 30–July 1, 1937, in "Reports of National Guardsmen to Their Commanding Officer[s]," YSSR, Box 1, Folder 9, Series 167, OHS.

158. LCH, 16466–72 (exhibits 7247–56), 16476–79 (exhibits 7264–67), 16484–86 (exhibits 7275–79), 16513–21 (exhibits 7317–26).

159. Handwritten report, unsigned, n.d., in "Reports of National Guardsmen to Their Commanding Officer[s]," YSSR, Box 1, Folder 9, Series 167, OHS; G2 report by Capt. Joseph Parilla, 145th Inf., June 24, 1937, in ibid. See, generally, "Work Sheet[s] of Ohio National Guard, June 21–July 7," YSSR, Box 1, Folder 13, Series 167, OHS.

160. John Steuben, alias Stevenson, in "Work Sheet[s] of Ohio National Guard, June 21–July 7," YSSR, Box 1, Folder 13, Series 167, OHS.

161. S2 report of 1st Lieut. John Cianflona, 74th Brig., June 26, 1937, in "Report of Investigations Made by the Ohio National Guard," YSSR, Box 1, Folder 10, Series 167, OHS (quotations); report of 1st Lieut. Edwin Weollner, 147th Inf., June 28, 1937, in ibid.

162. Report of 1st Lieut. Robert E. Boyd, 166th Inf., June 22–24, 1937, in "Reports of National Guardsmen to Their Commanding Officer[s]," YSSR, Box 1, Folder 9, Series 167, OHS. See also G3 worksheet, June 25, 1937, in "Work Sheet[s] of Ohio National Guard, June 21–July 7," YSSR, Box 1, Folder 13, Series 167, OHS.

163. G2 report of Capt. C. M. Poston, 37th F. A. Div., June 26, 1937, in "Reports of National Guardsmen to Their Commanding Officer[s]," YSSR, Box 1, Folder 9, Series 167, OHS; G2 report by Capt. Joseph Parilla, 145th Inf., June 24, 1937, in ibid.; G2 report of Capt. [E. C.] Woolf, 37th F. A. Div., June 22–23, 1937, in ibid.

164. See, for example, report by Capt. Joseph Parilla, 37th Inf., June 20, 1937, in "Report of Investigations Made by the Ohio National Guard," YSSR, Box 1, Folder 10, Series 167, OHS.

165. Press statement on bombing, in "Press Releases from Youngstown Military Dist., June 25–June 30, 1937," YSSR, Box 1, Folder 5, Series 167, OHS; S2 report by Capt. William B. Higgins, 107th Cav., June 28–30, 1937, in "Activities of Ohio Nat. Guard in Canton Mil. Dist., June 24-July 4, 1937," YSSR, Box 2, Folder 6, Series 167, OHS; report by Capt. Joseph Parilla, 37th Inf., June 20, 1937, in "Report of Investigations Made by the Ohio National Guard," YSSR, Box 1, Folder 10, Series 167, OHS.

166. S2 report of Capt. F. G. Ruffner, 145th Inf., June 28, 1937, in "Reports of National Guardsmen to Their Commanding Officer[s]," YSSR, Box 1, Folder 9, Series 167, OHS. On sniping near Youngstown, see S2 report of 1st Lieut. Robert E. Boyd, 166th Inf., July 1–2, 1937, in ibid.; and handwritten report, June 30, 1937, in ibid.

167. S2 report of 1st Lieut. Robert E. Boyd, 166 Inf., June 23–24, 1937, in "Reports of National Guardsmen to Their Commanding Officer[s]," YSSR, Box 1, Folder 9, Series 167, OHS.

168. S2 report by 1st Lieut. Robert E. Boyd, July 1–2, June 27–28, 1937, in "Reports of National Guardsmen to Their Commanding Officer[s]," YSSR, Box 1, Folder 9, Series 167, OHS.

169. G2 worksheet, June 27, 1937, in "Work Sheet[s] of Ohio National Guard, June 21–July 7," YSSR, Box 1, Folder 13, Series 167, OHS.

170. "Bayonets Guard Workers Opening 3 Republic Plants," *Chicago Daily News*, July 6, 1937, p. 3.

171. "Johnstown Protests over Radio against Invasions by Disinterested Pickets," *Johnstown Democrat*, June 26, 1937, local page; "'Que' Pipeline Blasted," *Johnstown Democrat*, June 29, 1937, local page.

172. *Little Steel Companies*, 280–84; LCH, 8326; "Mill Workers Enter Cambria Minus Pickets," *Johnstown Democrat*, July 3, 1937, local page; "Pickets Desert Gates as Strike Strife Vanishes," *Johnstown Democrat*, July 1, 1937, local page. After a July 4 rally, SWOC leaders claimed that the strike remained effective, but this was clearly not so. "Johnstown Enters Fifth Week of Strike with CIO Banking on Labor Board," *Johnstown Democrat*, July 10, 1937, local page; "Strike Leaders Claim Cambria Not 'Normal,'" *Johnstown Democrat*, July 8, 1937, local page.

173. S2 report by 1st Lieut. Robert E. Boyd, 166 Inf., June 25–26, 1937, in "Reports of National Guardsmen to Their Commanding Officer[s]," YSSR, Box 1, Folder 9, Series 167, OHS.

174. "Use 'Flying Wedge,' Pierce Picket Line," *New York Times*, June 29, 1937, p. 4; "18,556 Resume Jobs at Youngstown," *New York Times*, June 27, 1937, p. 1; "Mills in Youngstown Open Quietly Despite C.I.O., 'Massacre' Fears," *Washington Post*, June 26, 1937, p. 1; "Mills Here Back in Production as Bethlehem Plant Re-opens," *Youngstown Vindicator*, June 26, 1937, p. 1; "Sheet & Tube and Republic Re-open at 7 A.M. Tuesday," *Youngstown Vindicator*, June 21, 1937, p. 1; "Steel Strike Broken," *Chicago Daily Tribune*, June 17, 1937, p. 14; "Little of CIO Domination Left at Steel Plant Gates," *Youngstown Vindicator*, June 26, 1937, p. 1.

1. "Plant to Reopen; Defies CIO," *Chicago Daily Tribune*, July 12, 1937, p. 1; "Indiana Harbor Plant Expected to Open Monday," *Chicago Daily Tribune*, July 10, 1937, p. 4; "3,000 More Return to Steel Mill Jobs," *New York Times*, July 7, 1937, p. 7. Sheet & Tube's nearby South Chicago mill reopened on July 3. "South Chicago Plant Reopened by Youngstown," *Chicago Daily Tribune*, July 4, 1937, p. 4.

2. U.S. Senate, *Hearings before the Committee on Education and Labor: Violations of Free Speech and the Rights of Labor*, 6th Cong., 1st–3rd Sess. (Washington, DC: GPO, 1937) (hereafter LCH), 16432 (exhibit 7230), 16438 (exhibit 7233).

3. Republic Steel, 9 NLRB 219, 241–45 (1938).

4. "Republic Plants to Stay Closed," *Massillon Evening Independent*, June 2, 1937, p. 1; "Republic Will Not Work If Plants Are Picketed Here," *Massillon Evening Independent*, May 18, 1937, p. 1. The supplies in the plants were used to board maintenance workers. *Republic Steel*, 9 NLRB at 250.

5. *Republic Steel*, 9 NLRB at 251.

6. U.S. Senate, Committee on Education and Labor, *Violations of Free Speech and the Rights of Labor: Labor Policies of Employers' Associations; Part IV, The "Little Steel" Companies*, Report No. 151, 77th Cong., 1st Sess. (Washington, DC: GPO, 1941) (hereafter *Little Steel Companies*), 231–32 (quotations p. 232); LCH, 13434–35; Stanley W. Switter, "Former Police Chief, Dies at 68," *Massillon Evening Independent*, May 12, 1971, p. 1.

7. *Little Steel Companies*, 232–33; LCH, 16195 (exhibit 7083), 16199; *Republic Steel*, 9 NLRB at 253 (quotation).

8. *Republic Steel*, 9 NLRB at 259–60.

9. *Little Steel Companies*, 233–34; *Republic Steel*, 9 NLRB at 260–61.

10. "Police Replace Guardsmen Here," *Massillon Evening Independent*, July 9, 1937, p. 1; "Units Resume Operations on 8 Hour Shifts," *Canton Repository*, July 7, 1937, p. 1; "Boost Operations at Local Mills," *Massillon Evening Independent*, July 6, 1937, p. 1; "Quiet Prevails in Strike Area," *Canton Repository*, July 4, 1937, p. 1; "Massillon Units of Republic Reopen as Troops Arrive," *Canton Repository*, July 2, 1937, p. 1; "Troops on Duty as Republic and Union Drawn Resume Operations," *Massillon Evening Independent*, July 2, 1937, p. 1.

11. *Republic Steel*, 9 NLRB at 262–63; "7,800 at Work in Two Cities, Republic Says," *Canton Repository*, July 8, 1937, p. 1.

12. *Republic Steel*, 9 NLRB at 266, 270–72, 327; LCH, 13622 (exhibit 5188).

13. *Little Steel Companies*, 235 (quotation); LCH, 13440–41 (quotation also p. 13440); *Republic Steel*, 9 NLRB at 263–66.

14. Transcript of record, respondent's witness Harry O. Curley, pp. 3379–95; Republic Steel Co. v. NLRB, 311 U.S. 7 (1940) (docket no. 14).

15. *Little Steel Companies*, 235–36; LCH, 16274, 16283 (exhibit 7104); *Republic Steel*, 9 NLRB at 264, 266–72.

16. *Little Steel Companies*, 230; LCH, 16195, 16198 (exhibit 7083); "Picketed Zones Continue Quiet," *Canton Repository*, July 10, 1937, p. 1; "Steel Strike Front

Continues Peaceful in Canton, Massillon," *Canton Repository*, July 5, 1937, p. 1; "Quiet Prevails in Strike Area," *Canton Repository*, July 4, 1937, p. 1.

17. *Republic Steel*, 9 NLRB at 275–78.

18. *Little Steel Companies*, 250; LCH, 16258–69 (exhibits 7095–102).

19. *Republic Steel*, 9 NLRB at 277–80, 312; transcript of record, respondent's witness Wilbert Coleman, pp. 3565–76, *Republic Steel Co.*, 311 U.S. 7. See also transcript of record, board's witness Martin J. Beckner, pp. 1410–11, *Republic Steel Co.*, 311 U.S. 7.

20. *Republic Steel*, 9 NLRB at 275 (quotation); transcript of record, board's witness Ora Ikes, pp. 3314–39, *Republic Steel Co.*, 311 U.S. 7.

21. LCH, 16269–84 (exhibits 7103–4) (quotation p. 16271).

22. *Little Steel Companies*, 241–42; *Republic Steel*, 9 NLRB at 280–82.

23. See *Republic Steel*, 9 NLRB at 282–87, 288–94 (quotations pp. 282, 283, 287, 288, 291, 294).

24. "2 Dead, 7 Wounded, 136 Arrested after Massillon Battle," *Canton Repository*, July 12, 1937, p. 1.

25. *Little Steel Companies*, 242–49, 333–40; *Republic Steel*, 9 NLRB at 282–310; "2 Dead, 7 Wounded, 136 Arrested after Massillon Battle," *Canton Repository*, July 12, 1937, p. 1.

26. *Republic Steel*, 9 NLRB at 313.

27. Ibid. at 294 (quotations), 313. See also *Little Steel Companies*, 250–52. Most of those arrested were taken on charges of violating the county sheriff's proclamation. LCH, 13606–7 (exhibit 5185A).

28. *Little Steel Companies*, 251–53; LCH, 13601–9 (exhibits 5182A–D, 5186); *Republic Steel*, 9 NLRB at 313–14; "More Are Freed after Quizzing," *Massillon Evening Independent*, July 14, 1937, p. 1; "Massillon Continues Probe of Strike Riot," *Canton Repository*, July 13, 1937, p. 1; "2 Dead, 7 Wounded, 136 Arrested after Massillon Battle," *Canton Repository*, July 12, 1937, p. 1.

29. LCH, 13596–601 (exhibits 5179–81).

30. See *Little Steel Companies*, 237. For the coroner's report on Drosz's death, see LCH, 16254–55 (exhibit 7093). For the NLRB's finding that three men were killed, see *Republic Steel*, 9 NLRB at 305; and transcript of record, testimony of Frank Hardesty, vol. 2, p. 1387, *Republic Steel Co.*, 311 U.S. 7.

31. LCH, 16258–84 (exhibits 7095–7104).

32. *Republic Steel*, 9 NLRB at 310.

33. *Little Steel Companies*, 252; *Republic Steel*, 9 NLRB at 315–17.

34. "'Gangway' Shout Policemen and Guards to Curious Crowds as They March Prisoners to Jail in Strike Fight Mop Up," *Massillon Evening Independent*, July 12, 1937, p. 1; "140 Strikers and Sympathizers Are Jailed in Police and Guard Lockup," *Massillon Evening Independent*, July 12, 1937, p. 1; "Mayor Krier Bans Public Meetings," *Massillon Evening Independent*, July 12, 1937, p. 1.

35. "Massillon C.I.O. Leaders to Be Arraigned Monday," *Canton Repository*, July 18, 1937, p. 10; "NLRB to Probe Local Strike Clash," *Massillon Evening Independent*, July 16, 1937, p. 1.

36. "NLRB to Probe Local Strike Clash," *Massillon Evening Independent,* July 16, 1937, p. 1; "Thomas Demands Senate Inquiry in Local Clash," *Massillon Evening Independent,* July 14, 1937, p. 1; "Thomas Visits Local Strikers; Survey Group Inspects Plants," *Canton Repository,* July 14, 1937, p. 1; "Mayor Krier Bans Public Meetings," *Massillon Evening Independent,* July 12, 1937, p. 1.

37. "Shot-Riddled CIO Headquarters after Clash," *Massillon Evening Independent,* July 12, 1937, p. 1.

38. *Little Steel Companies,* 252.

39. Earlier there had been a few relatively serious cases of violence in Cleveland, including a small riot June 15 at Republic's Upson Nut plant. See "Six Guilty in Riot at Upson," *Cleveland Plain Dealer,* July 24, 1937, p. 1.

40. "Republic Stand by Strike Policy," *Cleveland Plain Dealer,* July 15, 1937, p. 3; "First Troops Will Leave City Today," *Cleveland Plain Dealer,* July 13, 1937, p. 3; "24-Hour Crew Kept on Duty at Corrigan," *Cleveland Plain Dealer,* July 7, 1937, p. 1; "Troops Arrive to Take Over 'Danger Zones'; 3 Mills Open Today," *Cleveland Plain Dealer,* July 6, 1937, p. 1; "Ohio National Guard Rushed to Cleveland for Strikebreaking," *Daily Worker,* July 6, 1937, p. 1.

41. "Strike Is Effective in Cleveland," *Steel Labor,* July 7, 1937, p. 3. See also E. C. Greenfield, "Steel Picket Lines Tighten in Cleveland," *Daily Worker,* July 19, 1937, p. 5.

42. "61% of Strikers Back, Police Say," *Cleveland Plain Dealer,* July 17, 1937, p. 1; E. C. Greenfield, "Negroes Rally Support for Steel Strike," *Daily Worker,* July 3, 1937, p. 4.

43. See, for example, "Strike Areas Still in Grip of Vandalism," *Cleveland Plain Dealer,* July 21, 1937, p. 1; "Vandal Hurls Brick, Perils Aged Woman," *Cleveland Plain Dealer,* July 19, 1937, p. 1; and "Labor Vandalism Hits Seven Homes," *Cleveland Plain Dealer,* July 15, 1937, p. 2.

44. "Dynamiters Bomb New Suburb Home," *Cleveland Plain Dealer,* July 23, 1937, p. 1.

45. E. C. Greenfield, "Steel Striker Killed by Scab in Cleveland," *Daily Worker,* July 27, 1937, p. 1.

46. "60 Hurt in Night Steel Strike Clash," *Cleveland Plain Dealer,* July 27, 1937, p. 1; "40 Hurt in New Strike Riot," *Chicago Daily Tribune,* July 27, 1937, p. 1; "Night Clashes Follow Killing in Steel Strike," *Washington Post,* July 27, 1937, p. 1; Greenfield, "Steel Striker Killed by Scab in Cleveland"; E. C. Greenfield, "Picketing Resumed in Cleveland; Ban Lifted," *Daily Worker,* July 21, 1937, p. 1.

47. Tom Girdler, with Boyden Sparkes, *Boot Straps: The Autobiography of Tom Girdler* (New York: Scribner's, 1943), 365–66.

48. U.S. Senate, Committee on Education and Labor, *Violations of Free Speech and the Rights of Labor: Private Police Systems,* Report No. 6, pt. 2, 76th Cong., 1st Sess. (Washington, DC: GPO, 1939), 192–95, 232–35, appendix B (quotation p. 193).

49. "Night Clashes Follow Killing in Steel Strike," *Washington Post,* July 27, 1937, p. 1.

50. "Police Bring Peace to Steel Area," *Cleveland Plain Dealer,* July 28, 1937, p. 1; "Steel Co. Asks Court Order to Prevent Rioting," *Chicago Daily Tribune,*

July 28, 1937, p. 7. For a copy of Ness's proclamation and a judge's order a few days later lifting it, see LCH, 15481–83 (exhibits 6249–50).

51. "Rain Routs C.I.O. Throng at Square," *Cleveland Plain Dealer,* July 30, 1937, p. 1.

52. "Republic Rejects C.I.O. Peace Offer," *Cleveland Plain Dealer,* July 30, 1937, p. 2 (quotation); "Officials Fail to Win Truce in Republic Strike," *Canton Repository,* July 30, 1937, p. 16; "Burton Rallies Steel City Chiefs," *Cleveland Plain Dealer,* July 29, 1937, p. 1.

53. "Violence in Cleveland," *New York Times,* August 7, 1937, p. 2; "3 Hurt, 3 Held in Strike Clashes," *Cleveland Plain Dealer,* August 7, 1937, p. 1; "Hoodlums in Strike Area Stone Autos," *Cleveland Plain Dealer,* July 28, 1937, p. 1.

54. "Indiana Governor Seeks New Parlay in Strike Situation," *Canton Repository,* June 13, 1937, p. 1.

55. Telegram from Clinton Golden to James Mark, July 7, 1937, Howard Curtiss Collection, Box 5, File 36, PSU-HCLA; "Steel Truce; Inland Reopens," *Chicago Daily Tribune,* July 1, 1937, p. 1; "East Chicago Inland Plants Open Tomorrow," *Chicago Daily Tribune,* June 30, 1937, p. 3; "Blocks Indiana Steel Work," *Chicago Daily Tribune,* June 28, 1937, p. 1.

56. Edwin A. Lahey, "Inland Mills Start Work," *Chicago Daily News,* July 1, 1937, p. 1; "Steel Truce; Inland Reopens," *Chicago Daily Tribune,* July 1, 1937, p. 1; "Here Is the Text of the Inland Steel Pact," *Buffalo Evening News,* July 1, 1937, p. 8.

57. "Inland Victory Spurs CIO Drive," *Daily Worker,* July 4, 1937, p. 1; Hays Jones, "Strikers Hail Inland Steel Pact," *Daily Worker,* July 2, 1937, p. 1; "Workers Cheer 'Armistice' in Steel Strike," *Washington Post,* July 2, 1937, p. 1; "Steel Truce in Indiana, Mills Will Reopen Today;" *New York Times,* July 1, 1937, p. 1; "Celebrate All Night as Truce Reopens Inland Mill," *Chicago Daily News,* July 1, 1937, p. 36.

58. Letter from J.E. Dailey to Clifford Townsend, July 3, 1937, Youngstown Sheet & Tube 1937 Strike Records, Small Manuscript Collection, Folder 3, SMC 5143, YHCIL; letter from J.E. Dailey to Clifford Townsend, July 2, 1937, ibid.; "Decisive Moves by Youngstown Defy C.I.O. Truce," *Chicago Daily Tribune,* July 2, 1937, p. 3.

59. "South Chicago Plant Reopened by Youngstown," *Chicago Daily Tribune,* July 4, 1937, p. 4; "Youngstown Move to Reopen with Troops' Aid," *Chicago Daily Tribune,* July 3, 1937, p. 3.

60. "Demand Troops to Avert Indiana Steel Violence," *Chicago Daily Tribune,* July 5, 1937, p. 5.

61. "Indiana Harbor Plant Expected to Open Monday," *Chicago Daily Tribune,* July 10, 1937, p. 4; "Workers Told Youngstown Is to Reopen Soon," *Chicago Daily News,* July 9, 1937, p. 4; "Steel Mill Here to Reopen; Says Independent Union Head," *Chicago Daily News,* July 8, 1937, p. 8; "Governor Asks Steel Men to Delay Return Two Days," *Chicago Daily News,* July 6, 1937, p. 3.

62. "Sheet & Tube to Open in Indiana," *Cleveland Plain Dealer,* July 11, 1937, p. 1; "Republic Reopens Last Struck Unit," *New York Times,* July 8, 1937, p. 2.

63. "Sheet & Tube Opens Strike-Bound Mill at East Chicago, Ind.," *Iron Age,* July 15, 1937, p. 91; "Jubilant Crews Return to Jobs in E. Chicago Plant," *Chicago Daily Tribune,* July 14, 1937, p. 7; "Sheet & Tube to Open in Indiana," *Cleveland Plain Dealer,* July 11, 1937, p. 1; "Republic Reopens Last Struck Unit," *New York Times,* July 8, 1937, p. 2.

64. "2,500 Return to Work as Youngstown Plant Reopens," *Chicago Daily News,* July 13, 1937, p. 28 (quotation); "Steel Strikers Back on Jobs," *Chicago Daily News,* July 13, 1937, p. 1.

65. "To the Officers and Members of Lodges ... ," appended to *Steel Labor,* April 28, 1939; report of regional director, Great Lakes and Western Region, SWOC, "Reports of Officers to the Wage and Policy Convention in Pittsburgh," 1937, pp. 33, 34–36, Harold Ruttenberg Papers, Box 5, Folder 17, PSU-HCLA.

66. Meyer Bernstein, report to Mr. Philip Murray on the settlement of the Republic Steel Corporation Labor Board cases, pp. 4–5, United Steelworkers of America, Legal Department Records, Box 1, Republic Steel Corporation, PSU-HCLA; Robert R. R. Brooks, *As Steel Goes ... Unionism in a Basic Industry* (New Haven, CT: Yale University Press, 1940), 148–49.

67. "New Violence in Strike at Niles," *Western Reserve Democrat* (Warren, OH), September 30, 1937, p. 1. See also "Trouble Breaks Out Anew at Massillon," *Canton Repository,* August 8, 1937, p. 6; and "5 Machines Stoned in Strike Vicinity," *Canton Repository,* August 4, 1937, p. 1.

68. On the persistence of the strike at Republic, see "Republic Box Score," *Steel Labor,* May 26, 1939, p. 8; "Thousands Continue Republic Strike," *Steel Labor,* March 18, 1938, p. 6; "Strikers Wage Unceasing Fight for Rights at Republic Plants," *Steel Labor,* November 11, 1937, p. 2; and "Strikebreakers, Cheated by Republic Steel, Quit Plants and Return to Homes in the South," *Steel Labor,* October 15, 1937, p. 1.

CHAPTER 11: A STEEL STRIKE IS NOT A PICNIC

1. In the New Deal era, only persistent violence in coalfields around Harlan County, Kentucky, which claimed around two dozen lives between 1932 and 1937, and the multifaceted maritime strikes of 1936 and 1937, which also left about two dozen people dead, rival the Little Steel Strike. Otherwise, one has to go back to the early 1920s and a period of unrest in coal mining in and around Mingo County, West Virginia, to find a greater number of victims. Bruce Nelson, *Workers on the Waterfront: Seamen, Longshoremen, and Unionism in the 1930s* (Urbana: University of Illinois Press, 1988), 21.

2. U.S. Senate, *Hearings before the Committee on Education and Labor: Violations of Free Speech and the Rights of Labor,* 76th Cong., 1st–3rd Sess. (Washington, DC: GPO, 1937) (hereafter LCH), 7027–32 (exhibits 3612–19).

3. The death toll has long been uncertain. Union sources have tended to claim seventeen dead, but without specifying whether that number excludes Drosz,

Lopez, or Mike. See, for example, "Convention Honors Martyrs of Union," *Steel Labor*, December 31, 1937, p. 3; and "Republic Gave Guns to Massillon Cops," *Steel Labor*, August 6, 1937, p. 5. In condemning Roosevelt for betraying the CIO, John L. Lewis put the death toll at eighteen. "Text of John L. Lewis's Radio Talk on C.I.O.," *New York Times*, September, 4, 1937, p. 6. Although its case files are ambiguous, the NLRB's published decision in the case against Republic clearly includes Drosz among the victims of the Massillon riot. Republic Steel, 9 NLRB 219, 273 (1938). The La Follette Committee's report on the strike in Massillon appears to count Drosz as a victim, but its committee records seem not to. U.S. Senate, Committee on Education and Labor, *Violations of Free Speech and the Rights of Labor: Labor Policies of Employers' Associations; Part IV, The "Little Steel" Companies*, Report No. 151, 77th Cong., 1st Sess. (Washington, DC: GPO, 1941) (hereafter *Little Steel Companies*), 237; LCH, 13968–69 (exhibit 5290). Scholarly accounts of the strike also usually set the number of victims at seventeen or eighteen, but without clarifying how this tally was reached. See, for example, Robert Zieger, *The CIO, 1935–1955* (Chapel Hill: University of North Carolina Press, 1995), 62; Donald G. Sofchalk, "The Little Steel Strike of 1937" (PhD dissertation, Ohio State University, 1961), 18; and Art Preis, *Labor's Giant Step* (New York: Pathfinder, 1964), 68. One scholar cites a toll of twenty, although it is unclear how this count was reached. See Nelson Lichtenstein, *Labor's War at Home: The CIO in World War II* (New York: Cambridge University Press, 1982), 21–22.

4. "Steelworker Is Murdered in Barroom," *Massillon Evening Independent*, December 4, 1947, p. 1.

5. LCH, 13968–69 (exhibit 5250).

6. Ibid., 16055–57 (exhibit 6903).

7. U.S. Senate, *Hearings before the Committee on Education and Labor: National Labor Relations Act and Proposed Amendments*, 77th Cong., 3rd Sess. (Washington, DC: GPO, 1939) (hereafter *Senate Labor Committee Hearings*), 4200.

8. *Republic Steel*, 9 NLRB at 269–70; LCH, 8627 (exhibit 3936), 12841–49 (exhibits 4922–24), 12923–24 (exhibit 4985), 13565 (exhibit 5155), 15486–87 (exhibit 6253); "200 Indicted in Ohio Riots as Plants Reopen," *Chicago Daily Tribune*, July 7, 1937, p. 6; "Jury Indicts 200 in Steel Riot: Ex-CIO Leader Charged with Inciting Men," *Youngstown Vindicator*, July 6, 1937, p. 1.

9. Report of Legal Department, SWOC, "Reports of Officers to the Wage and Policy Convention in Pittsburgh," 1937, pp. 66–67, Harold Ruttenberg Papers, Box 3, Folder 12, PSU-HCLA.

10. "Republic Picket Convicted on Disturbance Charge," *Buffalo Evening News*, June 21, 1937, p. 6; "Eased Tension Shown at Republic Plant," *Buffalo Evening News*, June 17, 1937, p. 8; "Local C.I.O. Organizer Urges Fight for Decent Wages," *Buffalo Evening News*, June 4, 1937, p. 6; "Two Men Fined, Two Freed after Steel Plant Arrests," *Buffalo Evening News*, June 3, 1937, p. 23; "Six Arrested at Steel Plant," *Buffalo Evening News*, June 2, 1937, p. 1.

11. "8 Hurt, 75 Seized in Riot at Canton," *New York Times*, July 1, 1937, p. 3; "Stone 8 Despite Troops at Steel Mills in Canton," *Chicago Daily Tribune*, July 1,

1937, p. 13; "Trouble Flares Again at Canton," *Cleveland Plain Dealer,* July 1, 1937, p. 1; "14 Jailed, 3 Hurt in Mill Gate Clash," *Youngstown Vindicator,* June 10, 1937, p. 1.

12. *Little Steel Companies,* 228.

13. LCH, 15486–87 (exhibit 6253).

14. Russell B. Porter, "Invaders Seized, 3,000 Turned Back," *New York Times,* June 23, 1937, p. 1; "Troops Arriving; 5,000 Due; Troops Repel CIO Invasion," *Youngstown Vindicator,* June 22, 1937, p. 1.

15. LCH, 12841–49 (exhibits 4922–24).

16. "Burke of C.I.O. Is Fined," *New York Times,* October 21, 1937, p. 16; F. Raymond Daniell, "Youngstown Girds for Street Fight," *New York Times,* June 12, 1937, p. 1; Russell B. Porter, "Act in Youngstown," *New York Times,* June 11, 1937, p. 1 (quotation); "Youngstown Conviction Protested," *Daily Worker,* October 3, 1937, p. 12.

17. LCH, 12841–49 (exhibits 4922–24); "Steel Organizers Receive Suspended Sentences," *Daily Worker,* October 22, 1937, p. 3; Adam Lapin, "Steel Company's Frame-Up a Flop," *Daily Worker,* Sept. 26, 1937, p. 12; Adam Lapin, "Steuben Case Before Jury in Youngstown," *Daily Worker,* Sept. 26, 1937, p. 1; Adam Lapin, "Steel Workers Risk Jobs to Testify for CIO Organizer," *Daily Worker,* Sept. 24, 1937, p. 1.

18. LCH, 13585 (exhibit 5169), 16253 (exhibit 7092); "NLRB to Probe Local Strike Clash, *Massillon Evening Independent,*" July 16, 1937, p. 1; "Strike Leaders Under Arrest," *Canton Repository,* June 23, 1937, p. 1.

19. "C.I.O. Heads Arrested at Cumberland, Md.," *New York Times,* July 27, 1937, p. 11; "Jurist Dismisses Strikers' Plea to Void Picket-Limiting Ordinance," *Cumberland Evening Times,* July 24, 1937, p. 2; "Council Passes Ordinance to Regulate Picketing Within City," *Cumberland Evening Times,* July 19, 1937, p. 9; "Cumberland Mill May Be Abandoned," *Beckley Post-Herald* (WV), July 2, 1937, p. 7; "Strikebound Tin Mill Reopens," *Cumberland Evening Times,* July 26, 1937, p. 1.

20. LCH, 13337–46 (exhibit 5133); "Judge Graham Gives Order to Assure Safety," *Canton Repository,* June 25, 1937, p. 1; "Ten Pickets Set as Limit at Mill Gates," *Youngstown Vindicator,* June 22, 1937, p. 1; "Warren Court Stops Pickets," *Youngstown Vindicator,* June 21, 1937, p. 1; "Canton Mayor Forbids Clubs," *Youngstown Vindicator,* June 20, 1937, p. 1; "Two Cities Ban Clubs as Weapons," *Youngstown Vindicator,* June 8, 1937, p. 1; "Warren Judge Curbs Pickets," *Youngstown Vindicator,* June 5, 1937, p. 1.

21. See, for example, proclamation of Sheriff Roy S. Hardman of Trumbull County, June 22, 1937, in "Correspondence between Ohio Nat. Guard and Local Officials, June 21, 1937–June 29, 1937," Youngstown Steel Strike Records (hereafter YSSR), Box 1, Folder 3, Series 167, OHS; LCH, 12980–82 (exhibit 5026); "Barriers Fall in Strike Area as Police Act," *Canton Repository,* June 26, 1937, p. 1.

22. "Six Arrested at Steel Plant," *Buffalo Evening News,* June 2, 1937, p. 1; "Picketing Quiet at Steel Plant," *Buffalo Evening News,* June 1, 1937, p. 8; "Cleveland Police Bar Steel Pickets," *New York Times,* July 28, 1937, p. 9; "Republic Strike Situation," *Wall Street Journal,* July 28, 1937, p. 3; "Three Pickets Under Arrest," *Canton Repository,* July 26, 1937, p. 2; "Danger Zones Set Off for Mill Openings," *Cleveland Plain Dealer,* July 5, 1937, p. 1.

23. LCH, 15481–83 (exhibit 6249–50); order from Joseph T. Nist, sheriff of Stark County, June 30, 1937, in "Correspondence between Ohio Nat. Guard and Local Officials, June 21, 1937–June 29, 1937," YSSR, Box 1, Folder 3, Series 167, OHS.

24. See LCH, 15481–83 (exhibits 6249–50); "Court Bans Ness' 'No Pickets' Zone," *Cleveland Plain Dealer,* August 10, 1937, p. 1; "Nist's Status in Writ Case Delays Ruling," *Canton Repository,* July 17, 1937, p. 1; and "Seccombe and Nist Named in C.I.O. Suit," *Canton Repository,* July 16, 1937, p. 2.

25. "Strikers Set Up Picket Posts; Switter Testifies at Capital," *Canton Repository,* July 21, 1937, p. 1; "Limit on Pickets Studied by Judge after Inspection," *Canton Repository,* July 20, 1937, p. 1; "Union Granted Writ by Court," *Canton Repository,* July 19, 1937, p. 1.

26. "National Guard Enforces Injunction," *Western Reserve Democrat* (Warren, OH), June 24, 1937, p. 1; "CIO Demands That Republic Deliver Records," *Western Reserve Democrat* (Warren, OH), June 17, 1937, p. 1.

27. LCH, 6869–77 (exhibits 3526–35); F. Raymond Daniell, "900 Chicago Police Guard Strike Area as Riots Are Hinted," *New York Times,* June 2, 1937, p. 1.

28. LCH, 6940–46 (exhibit 3570A) (transcript of municipal court proceedings where guilty pleas entered); "61 Memorial Day Rioters Guilty; Fines are Small," *Chicago Daily Tribune,* December 21, 1937, p. 2.

29. LCH, 12923–24 (exhibit 4985); "Nolle Jordan Bomb Charge," *Massillon Evening Independent,* May 13, 1940, p. 1; "8 Hurt, 75 Seized in Riot at Canton," *New York Times,* July 1, 1937, p. 3; "C.I.O. Men Arrested as Warren Bombers; Strike Chief Declared Named in Confessions," *New York Times,* June 29, 1937, p. 4; "Griffith Sends Four to Pen in Bomb Plot," *Western Reserve Democrat* (Warren, OH), August 8, 1937, p. 1. See also "Last of Strike Bombers Paroled," *Western Reserve Democrat* (Warren, OH), August 12, 1937, p. 1; and "Both Sides Make Legal Moves in Republic Strike," *Canton Repository,* June 6, 1937, p. 1.

30. *Republic Steel,* 9 NLRB at 389.

31. Ibid., 389–90; "Blocking Mail Charged," *New York Times,* June 30, 1937, p2; Wayne Thomis, "Arrest 6 C.I.O. Mail Censors, U.S. Commands," *Chicago Daily Tribune,* June 24, 1937, p. 9; "Seek CIO Heads on Mail Charges," *Youngstown Vindicator,* June 15, 1937, p. 1; "Halting of Mail to be Punished, *Cleveland Plain Dealer,*" June 19, 1937, p. 1; "Both Sides Make Legal Moves in Republic Strike," *Canton Repository,* June 6, 1937, p. 1. Several of the Youngstown-area bombers were released in September 1939. "Paroles Warren Strike Bombers, *Massillon Evening Independent,*" July 21, 1939, p. 8.

32. The NLRB counted 144 convictions and guilty pleas involving strikers from Republic's Ohio plants, of which exactly half were for misdemeanor rioting. *Republic Steel,* 9 NLRB at 389–90.

33. *Senate Labor Committee Hearings,* 4200–4202

34. Records from Warren show that three Republic policemen were arrested on May 27 and charged with assault; charges were later dismissed. LCH, 12923–24 (exhibit 4985); "Violence in Cleveland," *New York Times,* August 7, 1937, p. 2.

35. Docket of the Republic Steel Strike, May 1937, Series 5, Industrial Relations, Subseries A, Administrative Files, Strikes, Docket of Republic Steel Corporation, Container 77, Folder 32, WRHS-RSC.

36. "Steel Plant Vandals Warned in Cleveland," *New York Times,* July 29, 1937, p. 10. Records from Republic's legal department describe a striker being run down and killed that day by a black man named Willie Johnson, whom the company had hired to drive two loads of workers into the plant. Johnson was supposedly hit by a brick and lost control. Although intriguing, the claim that Johnson killed a striker seems mistaken, as no other references to this event appear anywhere. In any case, Johnson was charged only with careless driving, later dismissed by a judge. Docket of the Republic Steel Strike, May 1937, Series 5, Industrial Relations, Subseries A, Administrative Files, Strikes, Docket of Republic Steel Corporation, Container 77, Folder 32, WRHS-RSC.

37. LCH, 11498–500, 11605–7 (exhibits 4670–71), 11611–33 (exhibits 4672–74).

38. Walter Galenson, *The CIO Challenge to the AFL: A History of the American Labor Movement, 1935–1941* (Cambridge, MA: Harvard University Press, 1960), 108 (table 2); W. A. Phair, "Earnings of Steel Industry in 1937 Equal 6.1% of Invested Capital," *Iron Age,* April 14, 1938, p. 54; Edwin A. Lahey, "Both Sides Dig In in Steel War; 'Back to Work' Drive Started," *Chicago Daily News,* June 4, 1937, p. 4; "Output of Steel Holds at 56 Pct. in Chicago Area," *Chicago Daily News,* June 5, 1937, p. 28.

39. *Annual Report of Bethlehem Steel Corporation, 1937* (Wilmington, DE: Bethlehem Steel Corporation, 1938), 8; *Annual Report of Inland Steel Company, 1937* (Chicago: Inland Steel Company, 1938), 4.

40. *Annual Report of Youngstown Sheet & Tube Company, 1937* (Youngstown, OH: Youngstown Sheet & Tube Company, 1938), 4.

41. Republic Steel Corporation, income statistics, n.d., Series 5, Accounting Division, General Matters, Income Statistics, 1937–79, Container 17, Folder 26, WRHS-RSC; *Annual Report of Republic Steel Corporation, 1937* (Cleveland: Republic Steel Corporation, 1938).

42. Hilton Hornaday, "Steel Business Being Shifted," *Buffalo Evening News,* June 15, 1937, p. 23.

43. *Annual Report of Republic Steel Corporation, 1937,* 7; *Annual Report of Inland Steel, 1937,* 8; *Annual Report of Youngstown Sheet & Tube, 1937,* 9; *Annual Report of Bethlehem Steel, 1937,* 13.

44. Solanics v. Republic Steel Corp. et al., 53 N.E.2d 815 (Ohio S. Ct. 1944). See also Solanics v. Republic Steel Corp., 5 Ohio Supp. 142 (1940); and "Striker Wins $20,000 Award," *Steel Labor,* December 18, 1942, p. 7.

45. When added to the $20,000 award in the jury case, this amount comes close to the $350,000 later cited by the USW as the total yield of these civil actions. Vincent D. Sweeney, *The United Steelworkers of America: The First Ten Years* (Pittsburgh: USWA, 1947), 39; "Republic Steel Pays $350,000 for Damages in 1937 Steel Strikes," *Steel Labor,* March 1945, p. 2 (*Steel Labor* changed to monthly publication in the summer of 1944).

46. Docket of the Republic Steel Strike, May 1937, Series 5, Industrial Relations, Subseries A, Administrative Files, Strikes, Docket of Republic Steel Corporation, Container 77, Folders 30–32, WRHS-RSC.

47. See, for example, "CIO Officers, Lodges Are Sued for $55,000 Damages," *Massillon Evening Independent,* Sept. 10, 1937, p. 1.

48. Complaint, in the Matter Republic Steel Corporation v. Congress of Industrial Organization [*sic*] et al., No. 19864, N.D. Ohio, May 26, 1939, United Steelworkers of America, Legal Department Records, Box 2, Republic Steel—Cure Suit, PSU-HCLA. On the company's initial lawsuit, see Louis Stark, "Unions Disturbed by Damage Suits," *New York Times,* May 28, 1939, p. 26; and "Republic Sues Lewis and CIO for 7 1/2 Million," *Washington Post,* May 24, 1939, p. 30.

49. Apex Hosiery Co. v. Leader, 310 U.S. 469 (1940).

50. Lee Pressman, "Memorandum Analyzing Stipulations Between the Steel Workers Organizing Committee and Republic Steel Corporation Covering the Ohio Plants," July 24, 1941, United Steelworkers of America, Legal Department Records, Box 2, Republic Steel Corporation, PSU-HCLA.

51. David J. McDonald, *Union Man* (New York: Dutton, 1969), 118.

52. On problems of this nature in Chicago, see June 28, 1937, SWOC Fieldworkers Notes, Calumet District, Box 1, Folder 2/3, PSU-HCLA.

53. Report of secretary-treasurer, SWOC, "Reports of Officers to the Wage and Policy Convention in Pittsburgh," 1937, pp. 25, 27–28 (quotation p. 27), Harold Ruttenberg Papers, Box 5, Folder 17, PSU-HCLA.

54. In general, access to relief was limited. James L. Baughman, "Classes and Company Towns: Legends of the 1937 Little Steel Strike," *Ohio History* 87 (1978): 190. In northeast Ohio, Trumbull (Warren and Niles) and Cuyahoga (Cleveland) Counties provided benefits, while Mahoning (Youngstown) and Stark (Canton and Massillon) did not. "Relief Will Be Given Strikers," *Western Reserve Democrat* (Warren, OH), June 10, 1937, p. 1; "No Relief Aid in Strike Cases," *Canton Repository,* June 8, 1937, p. 1. In Johnstown, workers faced unspecified difficulties getting relief, prompting SWOC people to telegram Lieutenant Governor Thomas Kennedy, a CIO official, in hopes that he might improve the situation. Telegram from James Mark to Thomas Kennedy, July 3, 1937, Howard Curtiss Collection, Box 5, File 36, PSU-HCLA; telegram from Thomas Kennedy to James Mark, July 6, 1937, ibid.

55. G2 worksheet, June 28, 1937, in "Work Sheet[s] on Ohio National Guard June 21–July 7," YSSR, Box 1, Folder 13, Series 167, OHS. On donations to strikers, see, for example, David Laurie, "Strikers at Warren Mill Patrol 11 Mile Picket Line Front," *Daily Worker,* June 2, 1937, p. 1; Adam Lapin, "Warren Business Men Donate to Steel Strike," *Daily Worker,* June 14, 1937, p. 4. On the tendency of some local businesspeople to blame the companies for the strike, see Mary Heaton Vorse, *Labor's New Millions* (New York: Modern Age, 1938), 135–36.

56. Interview of James McPhillips and Charles Shea, pp. 13–14, USWA–Labor Oral History Collection, PSU-HCLA; Edwin A. Lahey, "Landlords Fight Strike at Mills Here, Says C.I.O.," *Chicago Daily News,* July 2, 1937, p. 13.

57. F. Raymond Daniell, "Warren Divided into 2 Camps," *New York Times,* June 6, 1937, p. 2.

58. Interview of Dan Thomas, August 1, 1974, pp. 2, 9, YSU-OHP.

59. See, for example, ibid., pp. 8–9, "Finds Men Quit Strike Because They Had to Eat, *Youngstown Vindicator,*" July 19, 1937, p. 1; and "SWOC Relief Aids 15,743," *Youngstown Vindicator,* July 16, 1937, p. 1.

60. Interview of Augustine Izzo, Video Oral History Collection, at approx. min. 48–49, YHCIL.

61. George Patterson, Jesse Reese, and John Sargent, "Your Dog Don't Bark No More," in *Rank and File: Personal Histories of Working-Class Organizers,* ed. Alice Lynd and Staughton Lynd (New York: Monthly Review, 1988), 91.

62. LCH, 6756–6844 (exhibits 3424–504); "Taylor Strike Ends; Workers Report Today," *Cumberland Evening Times,* August 12, 1937, p. 13; "Taylor Plant Shut Down by CIO Campaign," *Cumberland Evening Times,* May 29, 1937, p. 17.

63. "Lewis Defeated in First Test, Green Declares," *Washington Post,* July 9, 1937, p. 7.

64. William T. Hogan, *Economic History of the Iron and Steel Industry in the United States* (Lexington, MA: Lexington Books, 1971), 1179–80. Only tin plate supplies were ever at any risk of shortage. "Steel Output Drops 1 Point to 77 Per Cent," *Chicago Daily Tribune,* June 17, 1937, p. 31.

65. "Steel Users in Chicago Area Not Yet Affected by Strikes at Mills: Expect Little Difficulty," *Wall Street Journal,* June 14, 1937, p. 2; "Steel Operations Placed at 84.3% of Capacity," *Wall Street Journal,* July 27, 1937, p. 2.

66. Galenson, *CIO,* 100. When the strike began, some signs pointed toward crisis; others did not. "Demand for Five Steel Products Sets New Record," *Chicago Daily News,* May 20, 1937, p. 27; Hilton Hornaday, "Big Steel Rush Now Subsiding," *Buffalo Evening News,* May 11, 1937, p. 31; "Steel Making Stepped up to 92 Pct. In Week," *Chicago Daily News,* May 5, 1937, p. 45; "Output of Steel to Hold Steady in Local Mills," *Chicago Daily News,* May 1, 1937, p. 23.

67. Memorandum from Harold Ruttenberg, "Drop in Rate of Operations in Steel Industry," Sept. 1, 1937, Harold Ruttenberg Papers, Box 3, Folder 12, PSU-HCLA; Harold Ruttenberg, "Outline—Business Conditions (S.W.O.C. Confidential)," November 1, 1937, Harold Ruttenberg Papers, Box 3, Folder 14, PSU-HCLA.

68. John Williamson, "Davey Must Be Defeated," PA Box 5138, OHS; Preis, *Labor's Giant Step,* 66–70; interview of Erwin Bauer, Video Oral History Collection, at approx. min. 21–28, YHCIL.

69. Memorandum from Ralph Hetzel, "Steel Strike in Ohio," September 10, 1937, Congress of Industrial Organizations Collection, Box 19, Folder 9, ACHRC.

70. Joseph M. Turrini, "The Newton Steel Strike: A Watershed in the CIO's Failure to Organize 'Little Steel,'" *Labor History* 38, nos. 2–3 (1997): 249–50; directive from Van Bittner, January 21, 1937, SWOC Fieldworkers Notes, Calumet District, Box 1, Folder 2/3, PSU-HCLA. Union officials did participate in some

antifascist events during the strike. "SWOC Leader to Speak at Peace Rally," *Daily Worker*, July 25, 1937, p. 4.

71. James C. Kollros, "Creating a Steel Workers Union in the Calumet Region, 1933–1945" (PhD dissertation, University of Illinois–Chicago, 1998), 227–29. See, for example, McDonald, *Union Man*, 113–16; and interview of Dan Thomas, August 1, 1974, p. 13, YSU-OHP.

72. For an argument that the SWOC was not ready for the strike, see Zieger, *CIO*, 61–64.

73. Benjamin Stolberg, *The Story of the CIO* (New York: Viking, 1938), 86–87.

74. Gilbert Gall, *Pursuing Justice: Lee Pressman, the New Deal, and the CIO* (Albany: SUNY Press, 1999), 78; Melvyn Dubofsky and Warren Van Tine, *John L. Lewis* (Urbana: University of Illinois Press, 1986), 230–31; Saul Alinsky, *John L. Lewis* (New York: Vintage, 1949), 149, 158.

75. Staughton Lynd, "The Possibility of Radicalism in the Early 1930s: The Case of Steel," *Radical America* 6, no. 6 (1972): 37, 57.

76. On the contours of this debate, see Ronald L. Filippelli, "The History Is Missing, Almost: Philip Murray, the Steelworkers and the Historians," in *Forging a Union of Steel*, ed. Paul F. Clark et al. (Ithaca, NY: ILR Press, 1987), 7–12; and David Brody, "The Origins of Modern Steel Unionism: The SWOC Era," in ibid., 19–24. In line with Bodnar's thesis, see also Kollros, "Creating a Steel Workers Union"; and Thomas Joseph Sabatini, "A Nation Made of Steel: The Remaking of the White Republic in Ohio's Mahoning Valley, 1915–1942" (PhD dissertation, University of Minnesota, 2006), 198–200. For an analysis in broad alignment with Lynd's thesis, see Michael Dennis, *The Memorial Day Massacre and the Movement for Industrial Democracy* (New York: Palgrave Macmillan, 2010).

77. Brody, "Origins of Modern Steel Unionism," 18.

78. Harvey O'Connor, *Steel-Dictator* (New York: John Day, 1935), 302–3.

79. Rick Fantasia, *Cultures of Solidarity: Consciousness, Action, and Contemporary American Workers* (Berkeley: University of California Press, 1988), 3–24.

80. Dennis, *Memorial Day Massacre*, 220–22; Horace Cayton, *Black Workers and the New Unions* (Chapel Hill: University of North Carolina Press, 1939), ch. 11; Bruce Nelson, *Divided We Stand: American Workers and the Struggle for Black Equality* (Princeton, NJ: Princeton University Press, 2001), 197–200; interview of Ruben Farr, p. 27, USWA–Labor Oral History Collection, PSU-HCLA; George Schuyler, "Negro Workers Lead in Great Lakes Steel Drive," *Pittsburgh Courier*, July 31, 1937, p. 1.

81. Brody, "Origins of Modern Steel Unionism," 22.

82. "Three Ousted in CIO 'Purge' by Union Head," *Youngstown Vindicator*, July 3, 1937, p. 1.

83. "Browder Reaffirms Party's Support of CIO Campaigns" *Daily Worker*, July 6, 1937, p. 1; "Steel Union Heads Deny 'Red Purge' in Ohio Strike Area," *Daily Worker*, July 5, 1937, p. 1.

84. See Gus Hall, *Steel and Metal Workers—It Takes a Fight to Win!* (New York: New Outlook, 1972), 15.

85. Dennis, *Memorial Day Massacre,* 227–28; interview of Sam Evett, pp. 5–6, USWA–Labor Oral History Collection, PSU-HCLA; SWOC Fieldworkers Notes, Calumet District, Box 1, Folders 1–4, PSU-HCLA. See also Kollros, "Creating a Steel Workers Union," 220–29.

86. Interview of John N. Grajciar (2 of 2), p. 4, USWA–Labor Oral History Collection, PSU-HCLA; interview of Sam Evett, pp. 5–11, 45, ibid.

87. Kollros, "Creating a Steel Workers Union," 227–29, 251–52; "CIO Man Hits Lawlessness," *Youngstown Vindicator,* July 5, 1937, p. 2.

88. Lizabeth Cohen, *Making a New Deal: Industrial Workers in Chicago, 1919–1939,* 2nd ed. (New York: Cambridge University Press, 2009), 299 (table 3); Max Gordon, "The Communists and the Drive to Organize Steel, 1936," *Labor History* 23, no. 2 (1982), 259; interview of Sam Evett, pp. 5–6, USWA–Labor Oral History Collection, PSU-HCLA.

89. Interview of John N. Grajciar (2 of 2), pp. 5–11, 16–17, USWA–Labor Oral History Collection, PSU-HCLA; Ruth Needleman, *Black Freedom Fighters in Steel: The Struggle for Democratic Unionism* (Ithaca, NY: Cornell University Press, 2003), 19–22, 195. See also interview of James McPhillips and Charles Shea, pp. 30–34, USWA–Labor Oral History Collection, PSU-HCLA.

90. Needleman, *Black Freedom Fighters,* 189–95.

91. Galenson, *CIO,* 110; *Proceedings of the First Constitutional Convention of the United Steelworkers of America, 1942,* vol. 1 (Cleveland: United Steelworkers of America, 1942), 42.

92. Dues reports, 1937–43, USWA District 31 Records, Box 43, Folder 3, CHS.

93. McDonald, *Union Man,* 121. See also Dubofsky and Tine, *John L. Lewis,* 204.

94. *USW Proceedings, 1942,* 42.

95. Report of secretary-treasurer, SWOC, "Reports of Officers to the Wage and Policy Convention in Pittsburgh," 1937, pp. 5–6, Harold Ruttenberg Papers, Box 5, Folder 17, PSU-HCLA; Galenson, *CIO,* 110.

96. Letter from David McDonald to financial secretaries of SWOC Lodges, September 19, 1938, David McDonald Papers, Box 197, File 4, PSU-HCLA.

97. Interview of Sam Evett, p. 13, USWA–Labor Oral History Collection, PSU-HCLA. See also field-workers' finances, SWOC Fieldworkers Notes, Calumet District, Box 1, Folders 2/3–4, PSU-HCLA.

98. McDonald, *Union Man,* 121–26; John P. Hoerr, *And the Wolf Finally Came: The Decline of the American Steel Industry* (Pittsburgh: University of Pittsburgh Press, 1988), 372.

99. Sofchalk, "Little Steel Strike," 13–14; Steven R. Scipes, "Trade Union Development and Racial Oppression in Chicago's Steel and Meatpacking Industries, 1933–1950" (PhD dissertation, University of Illinois–Chicago, 2003), 199.

100. Barbara Warne Newell, *Chicago and the Labor Movement: Metropolitan Unionism in the 1930's* (Urbana: University of Illinois Press, 1961), 144–45.

101. Dues reports, 1937–43, USWA District 31 Records, Box 43, Folder 3, CHS.

102. See USWA District 31 Records, Box 102, Folder 3, CHS; and Scipes, "Trade Union Development," 204.

CHAPTER 12: KIND OF A VICTORY

1. Memorandum, August 4, 1941, Series 5, Industrial Relations Division, Collective Bargaining, Steel & Tubes Division, Cleveland, Ohio, Container 67, Folder 20, WRHS-RSC.

2. U.S. House of Rep., *Hearing before Special Committee to Investigate the NLRB,* 76th Cong., 3rd Sess. (Washington, DC: GPO, 1940), 1919–20 (exhibit 526).

3. Louis Stark, "NLRB Region Chief Boasted of Power," *New York Times,* January 18, 1940, p. 18.

4. Christopher L. Tomlins, *The State and the Unions: Labor Relations, Law, and the Organized Labor Movement in America, 1880–1960* (New York: Cambridge University Press, 1985), 157; James A. Gross, *The Reshaping of the National Labor Relations Board* (Albany: SUNY Press, 1981), 5–23.

5. Tomlins, *State and the Unions,* 148–243.

6. National Labor Relations Act, 29 U.S.C. §10(b) (1935).

7. Gross, *Reshaping of the NLRB,* 176–78; U.S. House of Rep., *Final Report of the Special Committee to Investigate the National Labor Relations Board,* Report No. 3109, 76th Cong., 3rd Sess. (Washington, DC: GPO, 1941), 44–47; U.S. House of Rep., *Intermediate Report of the Special Committee to Investigate the National Labor Relations Board,* Report No. 1902, 76th Cong., 3rd Sess. (Washington, DC: GPO, 1940), 13–16. On Witt's relationship to Pressman, see Gilbert Gall, *Pursuing Justice: Lee Pressman, the New Deal, and the CIO* (Albany: SUNY Press, 1999), 3, 81–82.

8. Gall, *Pursuing Justice,* 81–82.

9. "Inland Hearing Resumed after Quarrel Is Settled," *Chicago Daily News,* July 6, 1937, p. 3; "Squabble Halts NLRB Hearing on Inland Steel," *Chicago Daily News,* July 3, 1937, p. 1.

10. Inland Steel, 9 NLRB 783, 797–804 (1938).

11. H.J. Heinz v. NLRB, 311 U.S. 511, 523–26 (1941); Inland Steel Co. v. NLRB, 109 F.2d (7th Cir. 1940).

12. Republic Steel, 9 NLRB 219, 222 (1938); "Strikers Set Up Picket Posts; Switter Testifies at Capital," *Canton Repository,* July 21, 1937, p. 1; "U.S. Calls Massillon Leaders; Last of Troops Leave Canton," *Canton Repository,* July 16, 1937, p. 1.

13. Gross, *Reshaping of the NLRB,* 10.

14. The board withdrew the April 8 order in order to comply with administrative procedures recently mandated by the Supreme Court. *Republic Steel,* 9 NLRB at 221–26.

15. Ibid., 273–318.

16. Gall, *Pursuing Justice*, 82–83; *Republic Steel,* 9 NLRB at 379.

17. Republic Steel v. NLRB, 107 F.2d 472, 478 (3rd Cir. 1939).

18. *Republic Steel,* 9 NLRB at 386–87, 400–404 (quotations p. 386).

19. Transcript of record, transcript of oral argument before the NLRB, vol. 1, pp. 782, 797–98, Republic Steel Co. v. NLRB, 311 U.S. 7 (1940) (docket no. 14).

20. Meyer Bernstein, report to Mr. Philip Murray on the settlement of the Republic Steel Corporation Labor Board cases, pp. 1–8, United Steelworkers of America, Legal Department Records, Box 1, Republic Steel Corporation, PSU-HCLA; Lee Pressman, memorandum analyzing stipulations between the SWOC and Republic Steel Corporation covering the Ohio Plants, pp. 2–6, ibid.

21. The outlines of this procedure can be found in the board's published opinion. *Republic Steel,* 9 NLRB at 403. For details, see Meyer Bernstein, report to Mr. Philip Murray on the settlement of the Republic Steel Corporation Labor Board cases, pp. 1–8, United Steelworkers of America, Legal Department Records, Box 1, Republic Steel Corporation, PSU-HCLA; and Lee Pressman, memorandum analyzing stipulations between the SWOC and Republic Steel Corporation covering the Ohio Plants, pp. 2–6, ibid.

22. See application for reinstatement, p. 33, United Steelworkers of America, Legal Department Records, Box 1, Republic Steel Corporation—Miscellaneous Correspondence, PSU-HCLA.

23. Meyer Bernstein, report to Mr. Philip Murray on the settlement of the Republic Steel Corporation Labor Board cases, p. 6, United Steelworkers of America, Legal Department Records, Box 1, Republic Steel Corporation, PSU-HCLA. The board petitioned the Third Circuit Court of Appeals to require vacation pay for 1937, but the court denied this request. Republic Steel v. NLRB, 114 F.2d 820 (3d Cir. 1940).

24. Republic Steel, 36 NLRB 13 (1941); Republic Steel, 34 NLRB 145 (1941); Republic Steel, 33 NLRB 1125 (1941).

25. On the procedures followed by the company and the SWOC in determining back-pay, see Meyer Bernstein, report to Mr. Philip Murray on the settlement of the Republic Steel Corporation Labor Board cases, pp. 10–11, United Steelworkers of America, Legal Department Records, Box 1, Republic Steel Corporation, PSU-HCLA. Complications also arose regarding the reinstatement of men who had been conscripted. See, for example, letter from David McDonald to all SWOC local unions, December 12, 1940, David McDonald Papers, Box 197, File 4, PSU-HCLA.

26. "Back Wages in Republic Case Are Being Paid," *Steel Labor,* November 28, 1941, p. 1; "'Little Steel' Agreement Is Goal of SWOC," *Steel Labor,* April 18, 1941, p. 1; "Scouts Back Pay Figure," *New York Times,* December 1, 1939, p. 18; Louis Stark, "Counter Suit Filed by Republic Steel against the C.I.O.," *New York Times,* May 24, 1939, p. 1.

27. Republic back-wage calculation, United Steelworkers of America Legal Department Records, Box 1, Settlement Negotiations, Republic Steel Corporation, PSU-HCLA.

28. "Back Wages in Republic Case Are Being Paid," *Steel Labor*, November 28, 1941, p. 1.

29. Vincent D. Sweeney, *The United Steelworkers of America: The First Ten Years* (Pittsburgh: USWA, 1947), 39; David J. McDonald, *Union Man* (New York: Dutton, 1969), 147–48.

30. Walter Galenson, *The CIO Challenge to the AFL: A History of the American Labor Movement, 1935–1941* (Cambridge, MA: Harvard University Press, 1960), 109; Robert Zieger, *The CIO, 1935–1955* (Chapel Hill: University of North Carolina Press, 1995), 60–65 (quotation p. 64); Irving Bernstein, *The Turbulent Years: A History of the American Worker, 1933–1941* (Boston: Houghton Mifflin, 1969), 64.

31. Meyer Bernstein, report to Mr. Philip Murray on the settlement of the Republic Steel Corporation Labor Board cases, pp. 4, 33, United Steelworkers of America, Legal Department Records, Box 1, Republic Steel Corporation, PSU-HCLA.

32. Republic Steel (Beaver Falls, Pa.), 10 NLRB 868 (1938).

33. N. & G. Taylor Company, 21 NLRB 1162 (1940).

34. Bethlehem Steel, 14 NLRB 539 (1938).

35. Youngstown Sheet & Tube, 31 NLRB 338 (1941); "Back Wages in Republic Case Are Being Paid," *Steel Labor*, November 28, 1941, p. 1; "'Little Steel' Agreement Is Goal of SWOC," *Steel Labor*, April 18, 1941, p. 1; "SWOC Rejects Offer by Sheet & Tube," *Steel Labor*, Jan. 31, 1941, p. 5.

36. Refusal to reinstate, United Steelworkers of America Legal Department Records, Box 3, Youngstown Sheet & Tube Company, PSU-HCLA ; recapitulation, ibid.

37. *Annual Report of the Youngstown Sheet & Tube Company, 1937* (Youngstown, OH: Youngstown Sheet & Tube Company, 1938), 4; *Annual Report of the Youngstown Sheet & Tube Company, 1941* (Youngstown, OH: Youngstown Sheet & Tube Company, 1942), 4.

38. Meyer Bernstein, report to Mr. Philip Murray on the settlement of the Republic Steel Corporation Labor Board cases, United Steelworkers of America, Legal Department Records, Box 1, Republic Steel Corporation, PSU-HCLA.

39. William T. Hogan, *Economic History of the Iron and Steel Industry in the United States* (Lexington, MA: Lexington Books, 1971); *Annual Report of Republic Steel Corporation, 1937* (Cleveland, OH: Republic Steel Corporation, 1938), 7; *Annual Report of Republic Steel Corporation, 1938* (Cleveland, OH: Republic Steel Corporation, 1939), 7; *Annual Report of Republic Steel Corporation, 1939* (Cleveland, OH: Republic Steel Corporation, 1940), 7; *Annual Report of Republic Steel Corporation, 1940* (Cleveland, OH: Republic Steel Corporation, 1941), 11; *Annual Report of Republic Steel Corporation, 1941* (Cleveland, OH: Republic Steel Corporation, 1942), 6.

40. United Steelworkers of America Legal Department Records, Box 1, Republic Steel—South Chicago Cases, Republic Steel—Warren Complaints, Republic Steel—Cleveland Complaints, Republic Steel—Youngstown Complaints, and Republic Steel—Monroe Plant Protests, PSU-HCLA; Meyer Bernstein Papers, Box 1, Folders 9–11, PSU-HCLA.

41. Correspondence with Mrs. Matte A. Yelich, United Steelworkers of America Legal Department Records, Box 1, Republic Steel—South Chicago Cases, PSU-HCLA.

42. Correspondence with Mrs. Joseph Hudak, United Steelworkers of America Legal Department Records, Box 1, Republic Steel—Monroe Plant Protests, PSU-HCLA.

43. "Men Who Filed Back-Pay Complaints," United Steelworkers of America Legal Department Records, Box 1, Republic Steel—Cleveland Complaints, PSU-HCLA.

44. Letter from John Mayo to Meyer Bernstein, December 29, 1941, Meyer Bernstein Papers, Box 1, Folder 9, PSU-HCLA.

45. Correspondence with John T. McCreay Jr. and correspondence with Everett V. Smith, United Steelworkers of America Legal Department Records, Box 1, Republic Steel—Youngstown Complaints, PSU-HCLA.

46. Correspondence with Everett V. Smith, United Steelworkers of America Legal Department Records, Box 1, Republic Steel—Warren Complaints, PSU-HCLA.

47. Correspondence with Tony Traficant, United Steelworkers of America Legal Department Records, Box 1, Republic Steel—Youngstown Complaints, PSU-HCLA.

48. Letter from Harold Ruttenberg to Meyer Bernstein, January 12, 1942, Meyer Bernstein Papers, Box 1, Folder 11, PSU-HCLA.

49. Interview of Dan Thomas, August 1, 1974, pp. 9–11, YSU-OHP.

50. Back pay allotment, United Steelworkers of America Legal Department Records, Box 3, Youngstown Sheet & Tube Company, PSU-HCLA.

51. Interview of Thomas White, July 9, 1974, pp. 4, 11–12, YSU-OHP.

52. John N. Grajciar (2 of 2), p. 2, USWA–Labor Oral History Collection, PSU-HCLA.

53. Consolidated Edison v. NLRB, 305 U.S. 197, 235–36 (1938).

54. *Republic Steel Co.,* 311 U.S. at 10.

55. Senator Robert Wagner confirmed the statute's basis in this concept. 78 Cong. Rec. 3678 (1934), reprinted in vol. 1 of *Legislative History of the National Labor Relations Act, 1935* (Washington, DC: GPO, 1949), 20. The courts would later affirm it. NLRB v. Insurance Agents, 361 U.S. 477 (1960); NLRB v. Brown, 380 U.S. 278 (1965).

56. On its face, Section 10(c) of the Wagner Act contemplated a broad range of remedies, as it accords the board the authority to "take such affirmative action, including reinstatement of employees with or without back-pay, as will effectuate the policies" of the act. However, the Supreme Court's invalidation of the board's attempt to order Republic to reimburse relief agencies as part of its back-pay remedy rejected such a reading. *Republic Steel Co.,* 311 U.S. at 11–13. Although problematic, this approach seems consistent with the act's legislative history. U.S. Senate, Committee on Education and Labor, *Hearings on S. 2926,* 73rd Cong., 2nd Sess., reprinted in vol. 1 of *Legislative History of the National Labor Relations Act, 1935,* 27, 60–61; S. 2926, 73rd Cong., 2nd Sess., reprinted in vol. 1 of *Legislative History of the National Labor*

Relations Act, 1935, 1070, 1072, 1076; S.J. Res. 143, 73rd Cong., 2nd Sess., reprinted in vol. 1 of *Legislative History of the National Labor Relations Act, 1935,* 1160, 1169.

57. Interview of Dan Thomas, August 1, 1974, p. 8, YSU-OHP.

58. U.S. Senate, Committee on Education and Labor, *Violations of Free Speech and the Rights of Labor: Labor Policies of Employers' Associations; Part IV, The "Little Steel" Companies,* Report No. 151, 77th Cong., 1st Sess. (Washington, DC: GPO, 1941) (hereafter *Little Steel Companies*), 301–14. For a copy of the pamphlet, see U.S. Senate, *Hearings before the Committee on Education and Labor: Violations of Free Speech and the Rights of Labor,* 76th Cong., 1st–3rd Sess. (Washington, DC: GPO, 1937) (hereafter LCH), 8031 (exhibits 3873–50).

59. See, for example, Bernstein, *Turbulent Years,* 478–79, 490–91; and Mary Heaton Vorse, *Labor's New Millions* (New York: Modern Age, 1938), 128–31, 139, 157. See also Benjamin Stolberg, *The Story of the CIO* (New York: Viking, 1938), 106; and McDonald, *Union Man,* 110.

60. James L. Baughman, "Classes and Company Towns: Legends of the 1937 Little Steel Strike," *Ohio History* 87, (1978): 188–90.

61. For example, in 1959 a federal court invalidated a similar undertaking by the governor of Minnesota, who had invoked martial law to close a meatpacking plant during a strike. Wilson & Co. v. Freeman, 179 F. Supp. 520 (D.C. Minn. 1959). On the broader aspects of this issue, see Bakery Drivers Local 802 v. Whole, 315 U.S. 769 (1942); and Carpenters Local 213 v. Ritter's Café, 315 U.S. 722 (1942).

62. Ahmed A. White, "Workers Disarmed: The Campaign against Mass Picketing and the Dilemma of Liberal Labor Rights," *Harvard Civil Rights-Civil Liberties Law Review* 49, no. 1 (2014): 59–123.

63. Transcript of record, transcript of oral argument before the NLRB, vol. 1, pp. 811–12, *Republic Steel Co.,* 311 U.S. 7.

64. This scenario came to pass in 1939 when the Supreme Court overturned the NLRB's reinstatement of sit-down strikers, rejecting the board's balancing of the strikers' culpability against the degree of employer provocation and the overriding aims of the act. Fansteel Metallurgical Corp. v. NLRB, 306 U.S. 240 (1939).

65. A key committee report on the Wagner Act disclaims that the law was intended to function as an assertion of police power in its own right. S. Rep. 573, 74th Cong., 1st Sess., p. 16, reprinted in *Legislative History of the National Labor Relations Act, 1935,* 2300, 2316.

66. James Gray Pope, "How American Workers Lost the Right to Strike, and Other Tales," *Michigan Law Review* 103, no. 3 (2004): 518, 522.

67. *Republic Steel,* 9 NLRB at 387–94. The board's position aligned with statements by Senator Wagner himself. Robert F. Wagner, "Wagner Challenges Critics of His Act," *New York Times,* July 25, 1937, p. 99. On the denial of reinstatement to Sheet & Tube strikers, see recapitulation, United Steelworkers of America Legal Department Records, Box 3, Youngstown Sheet & Tube Company, PSU-HCLA.

68. NLRB v. Republic Steel, 126 F.2d 471 (8th Cir. 1942).

69. U.S. Senate, *Hearings before the Committee on Education and Labor: National Labor Relations Act and Proposed Amendments,* 77th Cong., 3rd Sess. (Washington, DC: GPO, 1939), 4643 (statement by Philip Murray).

CHAPTER 13: UNRECONCILED

1. Kenneth Warren, *Bethlehem Steel: Builder and Arsenal of America* (Pittsburgh: University of Pittsburgh Press, 2008), 143.

2. Republic Steel Corporation, income statistics, n.d., Series 5, Accounting Division, General Matters, Income Statistics, 1937–79, Container 17, Folder 26, WRHS-RSC.

3. Gertrude G. Schroeder, *The Growth of Major Steel Companies, 1900–1950* (Baltimore: Johns Hopkins University Press, 1953), 217–25.

4. Warren, *Bethlehem Steel,* 148–49.

5. Robert Zieger, *The CIO, 1935–1955* (Chapel Hill: University of North Carolina Press, 1995), 106. See also Alan Brinkley, *The End of Reform: New Deal Liberalism in Recession and War* (New York: Vintage, 1996), 204–5.

6. James B. Atleson, *Labor and the Wartime State: Labor Relations and Law During World War II* (Urbana: University of Illinois Press, 1998), 22–24.

7. Mark McColloch, "Consolidating Industrial Citizenship: The USWA at War and Peace, 1939–1945," in *Forging a Union of Steel,* ed. Paul F. Clark et al. (Ithaca, NY: ILR Press, 1987), 46.

8. Dues reports, 1937–43, USWA District 31 Records, Box 43, Folder 3, CHS.

9. Robert R.R. Brooks, *As Steel Goes . . . Unionism in a Basic Industry* (New Haven, CT: Yale University Press, 1940), 147–48; Walter Galenson, *The CIO Challenge to the AFL: A History of the American Labor Movement, 1935–1941* (Cambridge, MA: Harvard University Press, 1960), 116–17; Vincent D. Sweeney, *The United Steelworkers of America: The First Ten Years* (Pittsburgh: USWA, 1947), 50; "SWOC Ready to Negotiate Contracts with Four 'Little Steel' Companies; Two More Bethlehem Elections Won," *Steel Labor,* August 29, 1941, p. 1; "Signed Contract to Follow Smashing Victory by SWOC at Bethlehem Steel Plant," *Steel Labor,* May 23, 1941, p. 1.

10. Little Steel Cases, 1 War Labor Reports 324, 392 (1942).

11. Letter from David McDonald to Lee Pressman, May 9, 1941, David McDonald Papers, Box 188, File 4, PSU-HCLA.

12. Telegram from Van Bittner to Eugene Grace, April 11, 1941, Howard Curtiss Collection, Box 5, Folder 38, PSU-HCLA; letter from Philip Murray to Republic Steel Corporation, March 22, 1941, David McDonald Papers, Box 188, File 4, PSU-HCLA; letter from David McDonald to Republic Steel Corporation, August 25, 1941, David McDonald Papers, Box 188, File 4, PSU-HCLA.

13. Inland Steel, 34 NLRB 1294, 1301–2 (1941).

14. Republic Steel, 35 NLRB 653 (1942); Youngstown Sheet & Tube, 35 NLRB 660 (1941); *Inland Steel,* 34 NLRB at 1301–2; *Little Steel Cases,* 1 War Labor Reports at 392–93.

15. Minutes of negotiations between SWOC and Republic Steel Corporation, David McDonald Papers, Box 188, File 3, PSU-HCLA; Thomas F. Patton, "Recollections of Some of the Highlights of the History of Republic Steel Corporation, 1930–1971," September 1, 1981, p. 39, Series 8, Public Relations Division, Container 345, Folder 9, WRHS-RSC.

16. *Little Steel Cases,* 1 War Labor Reports at 324; "'Little Steel' Signs; Union Security, Wage Raise Won," *Steel Labor,* August 28, 1942, p. 1; "USA Wins: 78-Cents-an-Hour Minimum; Union Security; Check-Off; Minimum Daily Guarantee," *Steel Labor,* July 31, 1942, p. 1. Likewise, the SWOC increasingly relied on the Walsh-Healey Act to press higher wage demands for work under government contracts. See, for example, "Republic, Bethlehem Steel Forced to Boost Wages to Rate Paid in SWOC Plants," *Steel Labor,* September 27, 1940, p. 1.

17. "Labor: Big Battle of Little Steel," *Time,* July 13, 1942, p. 75. See also "Dollar-A-Day Increase, Union Shop Are Objectives in 'Little Steel' Conferences," *Steel Labor,* January 30, 1942, p. 1.

18. *Little Steel Cases,* 1 War Labor Reports at 324.

19. Galenson, *CIO,* 117–19; "$20,000,000 Annual Wage Increase Won in 'Little Steel' through Agreements; U.S. Steel Case Goes to Labor Board," *Steel Labor,* August 28, 1942, p. 1; "'Little Steel' Gains to be Added to Pact," *Steel Labor,* July 31, 1942, p. 9.

20. Agreement between Republic Steel Corporation and the United Steelworkers of America, August 12, 1942, Series 5, Industrial Relations Division, All Divisions, Contract File, Container 49, Folder 7, WRHS-RSC; Irving Bernstein, *The Turbulent Years: A History of the American Worker, 1933–1941* (Boston: Houghton Mifflin, 1969), 731; Sweeney, *United Steelworkers of America: The First Ten Years,* 53–54. Some sources give slightly different signing dates; however, this appears to reflect some confusion between the dates on which the agreements were ratified (or presented for signing) and the dates on which they were actually signed.

21. "W. H. Lawrence, Republic Steel to Sign with C.I.O.," *New York Times,* July 16, 1941, p. 12.

22. Tom Girdler, with Boyden Sparkes, *Boot Straps: The Autobiography of Tom Girdler* (New York: Scribners,1943), 374–75. Only with these contracts in hand did the union resume in earnest its efforts to organize ARMCO and National. "ARMCO Must Pay $52,000 in Back Wages," *Steel Labor,* January 1945, p. 1; "CIO Convention Demands Action by WLB on Wage Boost," *Steel Labor,* January 1945, p. 8; "USA-CIO Scores Important Election Win at Armco Plant in Baltimore, Maryland," *Steel Labor,* November 1944, p. 9; "USA Opens Drive at Armco and Weirton," *Steel Labor,* November 17, 1942, p. 16. See also "$92,568.81 in Back Pay at Weirton Steel," *Steel Labor,* November 19, 1943, p. 12; and ARMCO, 51 NLRB 391, 392 (1943).

23. Biographic file of Tom Girdler, July 18, 1955, Series 8, Public Relations Division, Container 342, Folder 4, WRHS-RSC.

24. See, for example, "Army-Navy 'E' Award for Production, Supporting Data," 1942, p. 7, Series 8, Public Relations Division, Central Alloy District, Massillon Ohio Plant, Container 347, Folder 6, WRHS-RSC.

25. Nelson Lichtenstein, *Labor's War at Home: The CIO in World War II* (New York: Cambridge University Press, 1982), 44–45; "Union Votes Strike in Bethlehem Unit," *New York Times,* February 26, 1941, p. 1; "C.I.O. Man Warns of Steel Walkouts," *New York Times,* February 25, 1941, p. 16; "Steel Strike Vote Continues," *New York Times,* February 22, 1941, p. 9; "Tie-Up Threatened in Bethlehem Jobs," *New York Times,* February 20, 1941, p. 11.

26. Lichtenstein, *Labor's War,* 48; "OPM Offers Steel Plan," *New York Times,* February 28, 1941, p. 10; A.H. Raskin, "OPM Moves to End Bethlehem's Strike; Terms Suit Union," *New York Times,* February 28, 1941, p. 1; Louis Stark, "Concern in Capital," *New York Times,* February 27, 1941, p. 1; "Mediation Plans Are Pushed," *New York Times,* February 26, 1941, p. 13; Alfred Friendly, "Bethlehem Strike Put Off for Two Days," *Washington Post,* February 26, 1941, p. 1.

27. Art Preis, *Labor's Giant Step* (New York: Pathfinder, 1964), 108; McColloch, "Consolidating Industrial Citizenship," 48; A.H. Raskin, "Violence at Gates," *New York Times,* March 25, 1941, p. 1; "Bethlehem Union Is Set to Strike," *New York Times,* March 23, 1941, p. 32; "Board to Hold NLRB Election at Cambria," *Steel Labor,* April 18, 1941, p. 1.

28. "Strikes Peril Huge Defense Steel Output," *Washington Post,* February 25, 1941, p. 1; "Republic Cranemen Quit," *New York Times,* February 25, 1941, p. 16.

29. "Steel Strike Hits Youngstown Tube," *New York Times,* February 14, 1941, p. 10.

30. "25 Wildcat Sit Strikers Put 150 Out of Jobs," *Chicago Daily Tribune,* October 22, 1941, p. 14; "Workers Return after Sit-Down Strike at Carnegie-Illinois Plant," *Wall Street Journal,* September 17, 1941, p. 2.

31. Brody, "Origins of Modern Steel Unionism," 35. See also "Is Republic Steel 'Headed for the Rocks'?," *Steel Labor,* September 10, 1937, p. 3.

32. Lichtenstein, *Labor's War,* 16–18.

33. Chairman's report, SWOC, "Reports of Officers to the Wage and Policy Convention in Pittsburgh," 1937, p. 3, Harold Ruttenberg Papers, Box 5, Folder 17, PSU-HCLA.

34. "Is Republic Steel 'Headed for the Rocks'?," *Steel Labor,* September 10, 1937, p. 3.

35. Gilbert Gall, *Pursuing Justice: Lee Pressman, the New Deal, and the CIO* (Albany: SUNY Press, 1999), 81–84 (quotation p. 84).

36. Christopher L. Tomlins, *The State and the Unions: Labor Relations, Law, and the Organized Labor Movement in America, 1880–1960* (New York: Cambridge University Press, 1985), 188n127 (quoting Pressman's memorandum to CIO leaders).

37. See SWOC Fieldworkers Notes, Calumet District, Box 1, Folders 1–5, PSU-HCLA. See also Lichtenstein, *Labor's War,* 18–19.

38. See, for example, "Supreme Court Spurns Republic Plea; Orders Reinstatement of 5,000 with 500,000 Back Pay," *Steel Labor,* April 26, 1940, p. 1; "U.S. Court Order Republic Steel to Rehire 5,000, Pay $7,500,000; Blames Company for

1937 Strike," *Steel Labor,* November 24, 1939, p. 1; "Back-Pay Claims for 6,200 Workers in Republic Steel Filed; $7,500,000 Involved," *Steel Labor,* May 26, 1939, p. 1; and "Labor Board Again Cracks Down on Republic; Orders 5,000 Union Men Rehired," *Steel Labor,* October 28, 1938, p. 1.

39. "595 Firms Signed as SWOC Marks Anniversary by New Campaign in 'Little Steel,'" *Steel Labor,* June 23, 1939, p. 1.

40. "Court Decision in Republic Case Starts Renewed Drive," *Steel Labor,* January 26, 1940, p. 3.

41. McColloch, "Consolidating Industrial Citizenship," 45, 47.

42. Chairman's report, SWOC, "Reports of Officers to the Wage and Policy Convention in Pittsburgh," 1937, p. 144, Harold Ruttenberg Papers, Box 5, Folder 17, PSU-HCLA.

43. McColloch, "Consolidating Industrial Citizenship," 45, 80–81. See also interview of Sam Evett, pp. 40–42, USWA–Labor Oral History Collection, PSU-HCLA.

44. Lichtenstein, *Labor's War,* 158 (quotation); Zieger, *CIO,* 147.

45. Bruce Nelson, *Divided We Stand: American Workers and the Struggle for Black Equality* (Princeton, NJ: Princeton University Press, 2001), 267–68.

46. Lichtenstein, *Labor's War,* 171; Zieger, *CIO,* 167–72.

47. Tomlins, *State and the Unions,* 253–54.

48. For a summary of this point, see Brinkley, *End of Reform,* 212–13.

49. Robert S. McElvaine, *The Great Depression: America, 1929–1941* (New York: Three Rivers, 1993), 297–322; Brinkley, *End of Reform,* 140–43.

50. Brinkley, *End of Reform,* 127.

51. National Labor Relations Act, 29 U.S.C. §1 (1935).

52. See, for example, Louis Stark, "Girdler Attacks NLRB as One-Sided," *New York Times,* August 12, 1938, p. 1; "Inland Joins Attack on NLRB; Examiner 'Hostile'," *New York Times,* May 5, 1938, p. 1; "Court Orders Hearing," *Wall Street Journal,* May 4, 1938, p1; "Girdler Sees Bias in NLRB Decision; Order 'Astounding,'" *New York Times,* April 11, 1938, p. 1; and "C. of C. Blasts 'Labor Coercion,'" *Youngstown Vindicator,* June 21, 1937, p. 1.

53. Felix Belair Jr., "Washington Takes a Hand in the Steel Strike," *New York Times,* June 20, 1937, p. 55.

54. James A. Gross, *The Reshaping of the National Labor Relations Board* (Albany: SUNY Press, 1981), 74–76.

55. Ibid., 187.

56. Ibid., chs. 9–10.

57. U.S. House of Rep., *Final Report of the Special Committee to Investigate the National Labor Relations Board,* Report No. 3109, 76th Cong., 3rd Sess. (Washington, DC: GPO, 1941) (hereafter *Final Report of the Smith Committee*), 44–47, 896–927.

58. U.S. House of Rep., *Hearings before Special Committee to Investigate the National Labor Relations Board,* 76th Cong., 2nd Sess. (Washington, DC: GPO, 1939) (hereafter *Smith Committee Hearings*), 671–72, 3214–15.

59. *Final Report of the Smith Committee,* 22–24, 89–90. See also *Smith Committee Hearings,* 675, 710, 4981–85.

60. *Smith Committee Hearings,* 2512.

61. Fansteel Metallurgical Corp., 5 NLRB 930, 942–43 (1938); U.S. House of Rep., *Intermediate Report of the Special Committee to Investigate the National Labor Relations Board,* Report No. 1902, 76th Cong., 3rd Sess. (Washington, DC: GPO, 1940) (hereafter *Intermediate Report of the Smith Committee*), 1863, 1867–68, 1871.

62. NLRB v. Fansteel Metallurgical Corp., 306 U.S. 240 (1939); *Final Report of the Smith Committee,* 81–82.

63. U.S. Senate, *Hearings before the Committee on Education and Labor: National Labor Relations Act and Proposed Amendments,* 76th Cong., 1st Sess. (Washington, DC: GPO, 1939) (hereafter *Senate Labor Committee Hearings*), 1631–34, 1638–39 (quotation appears repeatedly, for example, on pp. 1631, 1632, 1633).

64. *Senate Labor Committee Hearings,* 1823–25, 2080–81; *Intermediate Report of the Smith Committee,* 21–22.

65. See, for example, Louis Stark, "NLRB Region Chief Boasted of Power," *New York Times,* January 18, 1940, p. 18; "NLRB Aide Accused of Trying to 'Trap' Company for CIO," *New York Times,* December 20, 1939, p. 1; and Willard Edwards, "CIO-NLRB Plot to Trap Inland Steel Charged," *Chicago Daily Tribune,* December 20, 1939, p. 1.

66. *Final Report of the Smith Committee,* 3–4; Gross, *Reshaping of the NLRB,* chs. 10–11.

67. Gross, *Reshaping of the NLRB,* 194–212, 222–25, 253–54.

68. U.S. House of Rep., *Report on Labor-Management Relations Act, 1947,* Report No. 245, 80th Cong., 1st Sess. (Washington, DC: GPO, 1947) (hereafter *House Majority Report on Taft-Hartley*), 318.

69. *Hearings before U.S. Senate Committee on Labor and Public Welfare, Labor Relations Program,* 80th Cong., 1st Sess. (Washington, DC: GPO, 1947) (hereafter *Senate Hearings on Taft-Hartley*), 1918–25; House Committee on Education and Labor, *Amendments to the National Labor Relations Act,* 80th Cong., 1st Sess. (Washington, DC: GPO, 1947), 3108–8, 3180–86.

70. See report of the NLRB to the Senate Labor Committee, in *Senate Hearings on Taft-Hartley,* 467, 489, 520–23.

71. *House Majority Report on Taft-Hartley,* 318, 333, 343–44, 349; U.S. House of Rep., *Conference Report on Labor-Management Relations Act of 1947,* Report No. 510, 80th Cong., 1st Sess. (Washington, DC: GPO, 1947), 542–43, 546; U.S. Senate, *Report on Labor Relations Act of 1937: Supplemental Views,* Report No. 105, 80th Cong., 1st Sess. (Washington, DC: GPO, 1947) 50; Harry A. Millis and Emily Clark Brown, *From the Wagner Act to Taft-Hartley* (Chicago: University of Chicago Press, 1950), 445–47.

72. Although the main examples of supposed abuses by the NLRB in regulating employer speech were its cases against Ford Motor and Remington Rand, the

focus could just as easily have been on the board's lead case against Republic. See *House Majority Report on Taft-Hartley,* 299, 324; *Senate Labor Committee Hearings,* 72–77, 2084–86; *Final Report of the Smith Committee,* 90–92.

73. See Los Angeles Newspaper Guild, Local 69 v. NLRB, 443 F.2d 1173 (9th Cir. 1971); and Local 456, Teamsters (Carvel Corp.), 273 NLRB 516 (1984).

74. Millis and Brown, *From the Wagner Act,* 402–20.

75. Robert Bruno, *Steelworker Alley: How Class Works in Youngstown* (Ithaca, NY: Cornell University Press, 1999), 137.

CONCLUSION: THESE THINGS THAT MEAN SO MUCH TO US

1. Larry Van Dusen in *Hard Times,* ed. Studs Terkel (New York: New Press, 1970), 105–8.

2. David Brody, "The Origins of Modern Steel Unionism: The SWOC Era," in *Forging a Union of Steel,* ed. Paul F. Clark et al. (Ithaca, NY: ILR Press, 1987), 13.

3. See Jack Metzgar, *Striking Steel: Solidarity Remembered* (Philadelphia: Temple University Press, 2000), 37n19, 40–41.

4. Ibid., 40–41.

5. Ibid., 37–39; Robert Bruno, *Steelworker Alley: How Class Works in Youngstown* (Ithaca, NY: Cornell University Press, 1999), 53–55, 72–73: Bruce Nelson, *Divided We Stand: American Workers and the Struggle for Black Equality* (Princeton, NJ: Princeton University Press, 2001), 251–63; Dennis C. Dickerson, *Out of the Crucible: Black Steelworkers in Western Pennsylvania, 1875–1980* (Albany: SUNY Press, 1986), 54, 177, 188, 242–49.

6. Interview of John Johns (1 of 2), pp. 17–18, USWA–Labor Oral History Collection, PSU-HCLA.

7. At the end of the Second World War, American mills produced nearly two-thirds of the world's steel. But by 1969, their share of global production was only 22.5 percent. Similarly, between the late 1950 and late 1960s, steel imports increased nearly sixfold, while exports remained essentially unchanged. William T. Hogan, *Economic History of the Iron and Steel Industry in the United States* (Lexington, MA: Lexington Books, 1971), 2033–35 (tables 45–1, 45–2).

8. The mini-mills use electric furnaces to render scrap into new stock. Kenneth Warren, *Bethlehem Steel: Builder and Arsenal of America* (Pittsburgh: University of Pittsburgh Press, 2008), 213–15.

9. Sherry Lee Linkon and John Russo, *Steeltown U.S.A.: Work and Memory in Youngstown* (Lawrence: University of Kansas Press, 2002), 47–49. On the effect of monetary policy on competitiveness, see John P. Hoerr, *And the Wolf Finally Came: The Decline of the American Steel Industry* (Pittsburgh: University of Pittsburgh Press, 1988), 416.

10. Hoerr, *Wolf Finally Came,* 416–19.

11. Warren, *Bethlehem Steel*, 237–38, 262; Metzgar, *Striking Steel*, 108–48.

12. Hoerr, *Wolf Finally Came*, ch. 12.

13. Ibid., 390–96, 567–88; Linkon and Russo, *Steeltown U.S.A.*

14. The Canton, Ohio-based company now called Republic Steel is a specialty steel maker, formed from remnants of its defunct namesake in the 1980s and only renamed Republic Steel in 2011.

15. Hoerr, *Wolf Finally Came*, 507–8, 589, 606; *Statistical Abstract of the United States, 2010* (Washington, DC: GPO, 2010), table 979; Iron and Steel Mills and Ferroalloy Manufacturing, BLS, www.bls.gov/oes/current/naics3_331000.htm; Steel Product Manufacturing from Purchased Steel, BJS, www.bls.gov/oes/current /naics4_331200.htm (last visited August 15, 2015).

16. Hoerr, *Wolf Finally Came*, 143–44, 333–34.

17. On changes in political economy and their effects on steel, see Judith Stein, *Pivotal Decade: How the United States Traded Factories for Finance in the Seventies* (New Haven, CT: Yale University Press, 2011).

18. Bruno, *Steelworker Alley*, ch. 7; Hoerr, *Wolf Finally Came*, 259–60, 311, 577–88.

19. Bruno, *Steelworker Alley*, 10.

20. Barry Hirsch and David Macpherson, "Union Membership, Coverage, Density and Employment by Industry," 2013, www.unionstats.com (last visited January 14, 2015).

21. Upton Sinclair, *Little Steel* (New York: Farrar and Rinehart, 1938), 149.

BIBLIOGRAPHIC NOTE

I could not have told the story of the Little Steel Strike without drawing on a great multitude of sources, including archival collections, government documents, newspapers, and quite an array of secondary publications. Rather than set forth an exhaustive list of these materials, I offer to readers who would like an overall sense of what the research for this book entailed this review of the most important sources, augmented by a few comments. Readers are urged to consult the notes for complete documentation of the materials used.

ARCHIVAL SOURCES

Foremost among the archival collections relevant to this book are the records of the United Steelworkers of America (USW) and its predecessor, the Steel Workers Organizing Committee (SWOC), at Penn State University's Historical Collections and Labor Archives (PSU-HCLA). Here repose the union's extensive Legal Department Records; transcriptions of interviews of union officials and strike participants; and a number of collections encompassing the papers of union officials, including those of Meyer Bernstein, Howard Curtiss, David McDonald, and Harold Ruttenberg. These records provide crucial information about the nature of the organizing drive and strike, including accounts of tactics, strategies, and union decision making, as well as details about key episodes in the conflict. They also document the union's involvement in numerous legal cases concerning the strike, the effects of the strike on the development of the union, and the personal experiences of rank-and-file workers and union officials alike.

Also important are the collections of several regional archives, including those of the Ohio Historical Society in Columbus (OHS) and the Youngstown Historical Center of Industry and Labor (YHCIL). The OHS houses a diversity of very important collections, including records of the Ohio governor's office, the Ohio

National Guard, and local government offices, as well as the papers of individuals involved in the strike. Many, though not all, of these records are organized within the Youngstown Steel Strike Records (YSSR). Although not as extensive, the collections at the YHCIL were also crucial, as they contain the papers of strike participants, scattered company documents, and a number of video interviews that document the recollections of rank-and-file workers. Both the OHS and the YHCIL also feature extensive photographic collections that lend great texture and realism to the story of the strike. The relevant collections at both of these institutions are focused almost entirely on aspects of the strike that occurred in Ohio. Likewise very useful were transcriptions of interviews of strike participants conducted through Youngstown State University's Oral History Project (YSU-OHP) and available online via that university's library.

The Chicago History Museum/Chicago Historical Society (CHS) also houses material relevant to the strike, especially concerning the Memorial Day Massacre and other events in the Calumet. Standouts from CHS collections include the papers of organizer George Patterson and those of Lawrence Jacques, a physician who treated many victims of the massacre. Useful, too, are union dues reports. Although focused on the Calumet, the reports are not entirely confined to that region and offer key insights about the extent of union organizing during the drive, the strike, and the years that followed. Their significance is heightened by the dearth of other records of dues payments or similar indicia of membership dynamics in the years surrounding the strike.

The collections of the Western Reserve Historical Society (WRHS) in Cleveland are likewise very valuable, as they include the records of the Republic Steel Corporation, which has been defunct for some time. Highlights include financial documents and legal files, which do much to detail the company's actions during the conflict. Also useful are internal memoranda and correspondence, which illuminate company decision making, as well as unpublished company hagiographies, which provide important information about the structure of the company, its internal politics, and its interests in the years surrounding the strike.

PUBLISHED GOVERNMENT DOCUMENTS

It would have been difficult to unfold this story without access to published government records pertaining to the strike. By far the most important of these are documents produced by the so-called La Follette Committee, a subcommittee of the U.S. Senate Committee on Education and Labor that prominently featured the strike in its contemporaneous investigations of labor conflict. The committee's publications relative to Little Steel include seven lengthy reports. The most comprehensive of these is *Labor Policies of Employers' Associations,* which is actually a well-documented narrative of most of the major episodes of the strike (U.S. Senate, Committee on Education and Labor, *Violations of Free Speech and the Rights of Labor: Labor Policies of Employers' Associations; Part IV, The "Little Steel" Companies,* Report No. 151, 77th Cong., 1st Sess. [Washington, DC: GPO, 1941], cited as *Little Steel Companies*). Also essential is the report that summarizes the committee's investigation of the Memorial Day Massacre (U.S. Senate, Committee on Education and Labor, *Violations of Free Speech and the Rights of Labor: The Chicago Memorial Day Incident,* Report No. 46, pt. 2, 75th Cong., 1st Sess. [Washington, DC: GPO, 1937], cited as *Memorial Day Incident*), as well as the committee's reports on strikebreaking practices, company police forces, and company weapons stockpiles (U.S. Senate, Committee on Education and Labor, *Violations of Free Speech and the Rights of Labor,* Report No. 6, pts. 1–3, 76th Cong., 1st Sess. [Washington, DC: GPO, 1939], the three constituent reports cited respectively as *Strikebreaking Services, Private Police,* and *Industrial Munitions*). Those inclined to pore over them may find the committee's hearing records even more useful than these reports. For the hearing records entail voluminous transcripts of testimony and reproductions of documents, including correspondence among figures involved in the strike, company and union records, reports from government officials, legal documents, photographs, maps and diagrams—in all, over fifteen thousand pages relevant to the Little Steel Strike (U.S. Senate, *Hearings before the Committee on Education and Labor: Violations of Free Speech and the Rights of Labor,* 76th Cong., 1st–3rd Sess. [Washington, DC: GPO, 1937], cited as LCH).

Also very informative are the published decisions of the National Labor Relations Board (NLRB). The agency instituted multiple prosecutions of the Little Steel companies. Besides addressing key legal issues, its decisions are characteristically replete with factual findings about the strike. Several of these cases were also appealed to the U.S. Supreme Court, which, conveniently, resulted in the development of extensive case files, complete with transcripts of administrative hearings and copies of documentary evidence pertaining to the strike. All of this is true of the most important of the NLRB's decisions, its main case against Republic Steel (9 NLRB 219 [1938]), which, like all NLRB decisions, is available in both hard copy and digitized form, including on the NLRB's website.

Not as central to the story of the strike itself, but crucial for understanding its legacy, is the work of congressional investigations undertaken after the strike. This is certainly true of the so-called Smith Committee, a House of Representatives special committee that investigated the NLRB for alleged anticompany bias and other improprieties. The most important documents in this regard are records of the committee's hearings (U.S. House of Rep., *Hearings before Special Committee to Investigate the National Labor Relations Board,* 76th Cong., 2nd Sess. [Washington, DC: GPO, 1939], cited as *Smith Committee Hearings*) and its main report

(U.S. House of Rep., *Final Report of the Special Committee to Investigate the National Labor Relations Board,* Report No. 3109, 76th Cong., 3rd Sess. [Washington, DC: GPO, 1941], cited as *Final Report of the Smith Committee*). Also useful are congressional hearings and reports that attended the 1947 enactment of the Taft-Hartley Act, including U.S. Senate, *Report on Labor Relations Act of 1947,* Report No. 105, 80th Cong., 1st Sess. (Washington, DC: GPO, 1947); U.S. House of Rep., *Report on Labor-Management Relations Act, 1947,* Report No. 245, 80th Cong., 1st Sess. (Washington, DC: GPO, 1947), cited as *House Majority Report on Taft-Hartley; Hearings before U.S. Senate Committee on Labor and Public Welfare, Labor Relations Program,* 80th Cong., 1st Sess. (Washington, DC: GPO, 1947), cited as *Senate Hearings on Taft-Hartley;* and *Hearings before the U.S. House Committee on Education and Labor: Amendments to the National Labor Relations Act,* 80th Cong., 1st Sess. (Washington, DC: GPO, 1947).

These are by no means the only congressional or other government documents relevant to the strike. Quite a number of other congressional reports are also useful in elaborating precursors of the strike and unfolding its overall context, as are several studies of working conditions in steel by the U.S. Department of Labor, published in the *Monthly Labor Review.* Although not authored by a government entity, the 1920 report of the Interchurch World Movement on the 1919 Great Steel Strike is extensive and useful in a very similar way (Interchurch World Movement, *Report on the Steel Strike of 1919* [New York: Harcourt, Brace and Howe, 1920]).

NEWSPAPERS

The story of the strike cannot be told without relying on newspaper records. National papers, including the *New York Times,* the *Chicago Daily Tribune,* and the *Washington Post,* offer vital information about the overall course of the conflict and its political fate; and their reporting from the field, including by figures like F. Raymond Daniell, Louis Stark, and Edwin Lahey, is thorough and largely reliable. Regional and local papers, including the *Cleveland Plain Dealer,* the *Chicago Daily News,* the *Buffalo Evening News,* the *Youngstown Vindicator,* the *Canton Repository,* the *Massillon* (OH) *Evening Independent,* the *Western Reserve Democrat* (Warren, OH), and the *Cumberland* (MD) *Evening Times,* provide even greater detail about the nature of the conflict. Likewise indispensable are labor and industry publications, including *Steel Labor,* published by the SWOC and the USW; the CIO's *Union News Service;* and the American Iron and Steel Institute's *Iron Age.* The Communist Party's prominence in the strike, along with the diligence of the papers' writers, makes its *Daily Worker* and *Party Organizer* important as well. In light of the critical role that blacks played in the conflict—and also because these were published in the strike zone—two papers with predominantly black audiences, the *Chicago Defender* and the *Pittsburgh Courier,* are also essential.

The published literature relevant to Little Steel falls into two categories: literature on the conflict itself; and literature concerning the social, political, and legal context of the struggle. Work on the strike itself is limited and consists disproportionately of material on the Memorial Day Massacre. Some of this scholarship is good, including Michael Dennis's recent books about the incident (*The Memorial Day Massacre and the Movement for Industrial Democracy* [New York: Palgrave Macmillan, 2010]; *Blood on Steel: Chicago Steelworkers and the Strike of 1937* [Baltimore: Johns Hopkins University Press, 2014]), as well as a recent article by Carol Quirke ("Reframing Chicago's Memorial Day Massacre, May 30, 1937," *American Quarterly* 60, no. 1 [2008]: 129–57). Among the better studies of the strike in locations other than Chicago are Joseph Turrini's article about the strike in Monroe, Michigan ("The Newton Steel Strike: A Watershed in the CIO's Failure to Organize 'Little Steel,'" *Labor History* 38, nos. 2–3 [1997]: 229–65), and James Baughman's "Classes and Company Towns: Legends of the 1937 Little Steel Strike," *Ohio History* 87 (1978): 175–92.

This book is the first comprehensive study of the strike to be published. The only previous study of any significant breadth is a 1961 doctoral dissertation by Donald Sofchalk, "The Little Steel Strike of 1937" (Ohio State University, 1961). Although very competent, Sofchalk's dissertation is largely confined to documenting the strike's constituent events, mostly ignoring its larger context and implications; and it makes limited use of archival sources. Several dissertations have since addressed the strike and are cited in the notes, but none features anything like the breadth of Sofchalk's.

Indeed, scholarship that either deals with the strike tangentially, or serves to contextualize the conflict amid broader developments in labor, is relatively abundant and well developed. Although his work features a different perspective than this book, no account of labor in this period can afford to ignore Irving Bernstein's two volumes about the history of workers in the New Deal and pre–New Deal periods: *The Turbulent Years: A History of the American Worker, 1933–1941* (1969; rev. ed., Boston: Houghton Mifflin 2010); and *The Lean Years: A History of the American Worker, 1920–1933* (Boston: Houghton Mifflin, 1960). Nor can one proceed without consulting Walter Galenson's *The CIO Challenge to the AFL: A History of the American Labor Movement, 1935–1941* (Cambridge, MA: Harvard

University Press, 1960) and Robert Zieger's *The CIO, 1935–1955* (Chapel Hill: University of North Carolina Press, 1995).

Several other books are important in addressing steel labor in the years prior to the strike and into the Depression period. Most helpful in this regard are John Andrews Fitch's classic volume, *The Steel Workers* (Pittsburgh: University of Pittsburgh Press, 1989); Robert R. R. Brooks's *As Steel Goes . . . Unionism in a Basic Industry* (New Haven, CT: Yale University Press, 1940); Horace Bancroft Davis's *Labor and Steel* (New York: International, 1933); Harvey O'Connor's *Steel-Dictator* (New York: John Day, 1935); and Mary Heaton Vorse's *Men and Steel* (New York: Boni and Liveright, 1920). Especially important for illuminating earlier struggles in steel is the work of David Brody, including his books on the Great Steel Strike (*Labor in Crisis: The Great Steel Strike of 1919* [Urbana: University of Illinois Press, 1965]) and steel unionism in the wake of Homestead (*Steelworkers in America: The Nonunion Era* [Cambridge, MA: Harvard University Press, 1960]).

Important in a different way is Brody's 1987 essay "The Origins of Modern Steel Unionism: The SWOC Era" (in *Forging a Union of Steel,* ed. Paul F. Clark et al. [Ithaca, NY: ILR Press, 1987]: 13–29), which does much to anticipate questions about the origins and character of steel unionism that are posed in this book. Deserving of a similar kind of credit for their critical (and competing) commentaries on the political underpinnings of the SWOC and the potential for a leftist alternative to that organization are Staughton Lynd's essay "The Possibility of Radicalism in the Early 1930s: The Case of Steel" in *Radical America,* no. 6 (1972): 37–64 and James Rose's *Duquesne and the Rise of Steel Unionism* (Urbana: University of Illinois Press, 2001).

Another crucial body of literature concerns the history of the steel industry. The only really competent history focused on any of the Little Steel companies is Kenneth Warren's impressive *Bethlehem Steel: Builder and Arsenal of America* (Pittsburgh: University of Pittsburgh Press, 2008). However, William T. Hogan's excellent multivolume work, *Economic History of the Iron and Steel Industry in the United States* (Lexington, MA: Lexington Books, 1971), provides an encyclopedic review of the industry that thoroughly encompasses the years surrounding the strike. Also notable are Thomas Misa's *A Nation of Steel* (Baltimore: Johns Hopkins University Press, 1995) and the immensely informative *Encyclopedia of American Business History and Biography: The Iron and Steel Industry* (New York: Facts on File, 1994).

Among the many histories of the New Deal, several are significant for their broader insights about the character of that era and the movement for industrial unionism, not least Lizabeth Cohen's study of workers in the Chicago area, *Making a New Deal: Industrial Workers in Chicago, 1919–1939,* 2nd ed. (New York: Cambridge University Press, 2009), and Robert McElvaine's *The Great Depression: America, 1929–1941*

(New York: Three Rivers, 1993), which examines the cultural underpinnings of the New Deal. Similarly important for their probing, revisionist analyses of the politics and political economy of the New Deal are Ellis Hawley's *The New Deal and the Problem of Monopoly: A Study in Economic Ambivalence* (New York: Fordham University Press, 1995) and Alan Brinkley's *The End of Reform: New Deal Liberalism in Recession and War* (New York: Vintage, 1996). No study of the strike, its origins, or its implications would be complete without a review of these works.

Any serious study of steel labor must likewise confront questions about culture and politics in the steel towns and workers' communities. Among the most useful contributions on this topic are Robert Bruno's *Steelworker Alley: How Class Works in Youngstown* (Ithaca, NY: Cornell University Press, 1999); John Bodnar's *Workers' World: Kinship, Community, and Protest in an Industrial Society, 1900–1940* (Baltimore: Johns Hopkins University Press, 1982); Sherry Lee Linkon and John Russo's *Steeltown U.S.A.: Work and Memory in Youngstown* (Lawrence: University of Kansas Press, 2002); Jack Metzgar's *Striking Steel: Solidarity Remembered* (Philadelphia: Temple University Press, 2000); and Ken Casebeer's "Aliquippa: The Company Town and Contested Power in the Construction of Law," *Buffalo Law Review* 43, no. 3 (1995): 617–87.

A study such as this one must also engage with questions about race and the position of black workers. Three relatively recent and very useful works on this topic are Bruce Nelson's *Divided We Stand: American Workers and the Struggle for Black Equality* (Princeton, NJ: Princeton University Press, 2001); Ruth Needleman's *Black Freedom Fighters in Steel: The Struggle for Democratic Unionism* (Ithaca, NY: Cornell University Press, 2003); and Dennis C. Dickerson's *Out of the Crucible: Black Steelworkers in Western Pennsylvania, 1875–1980* (Albany: SUNY Press, 1986). A classic volume that speaks to these issues and remains valuable is Horace Cayton's *Black Workers and the New Unions* (Chapel Hill: University of North Carolina Press, 1939).

Similarly, this book's concern for the vital role that representatives of the Communist Party played in the struggle at Little Steel benefits from a handful of significant publications. Especially notable in this regard are Fraser Ottanelli's *The Communist Party in the United States: From the Depression to World War II* (New Brunswick, NJ: Rutgers University Press, 1991); Judith Stepan-Norris and Maurice Zeitlin's *Left-Out: Reds and America's Industrial Unions* (New York: Cambridge University Press, 2002); Randi Storch's *Red Chicago: American Communism at its Grassroots, 1928–1935* (Urbana: University of Illinois Press, 2008); and Max Gordon's "The Communists and the Drive to Organize Steel, 1936," *Labor History* 23, no. 2 (1982): 254–65.

Attempting to understand, as this book does, the strike's legacy for labor relations in steel and elsewhere is much aided by two works that focus on labor during the war years: Nelson Lichtenstein's *Labor's War at Home: The CIO in World War II* (New York: Cambridge University Press, 1982) and James Atleson's *Labor and the Wartime State: Labor Relations and Law During World War II* (Urbana: University of Illinois Press, 1998). Beneficial for similar reasons are several works on the Wagner Act and the struggle for labor rights, notably James Pope's "Worker Lawmaking, Sit-Down Strikes, and the Shaping of American Industrial Relations, 1935–1958," *Law and History Review* 24, no. 1 (2006): 45–113; Christopher Tomlins's *The State and the Unions: Labor Relations, Law, and the Organized Labor Movement in America, 1880–1960* (New York: Cambridge University Press, 1985); and James Gross's two volumes on the development of modern labor relations law, *The Making of the National Labor Relations Board* (Albany: SUNY Press, 1974) and *The Reshaping of the National Labor Relations Board* (Albany: SUNY Press, 1981). An older book that remains very useful in this vein is Harry A. Millis and Emily Clark Brown, *From the Wagner Act to Taft-Hartley* (Chicago: University of Chicago, 1950).

INDEX

AA (Amalgamated Association of Iron, Steel, and Tin Workers): and black workers, 29, 42, 89–90; and CIO, 81–84, 310n51; dysfunctions of, 17, 25–26, 29, 50, 79–82, 85; and early steel industry, 17; and ERPs, 50; and ethnic/immigrant groups, 29–31; and Great Steel Strike, 47–48; and Homestead dispute, 14–15, 25; and Lewis, 82; membership, 45, 48–49, 80–81; origins of, 15; and strikes, 42–43, 48–49; racial and ethnic discrimination, 29–30; and SMWIU, 79; and SWOC, 82–84, 92, 96, 148, 274, 310n55. *See also* AFL (American Federation of Labor); craft unionism; SWOC (Steel Workers Organizing Committee)

Adamic, Louis, 50, 52

AFL (American Federation of Labor): and amendments to Wagner Act, 276; and black workers, 47, 89; and CIO, 76, 77, 83, 194, 240, 276; dysfunctions of, 29, 45, 47, 79, 81; and Great Steel Strike, 45, 47; and Lewis, 65, 76, 82; and Little Steel Strike, 178, 194, 240. *See also* AA (Amalgamated Association of Iron, Steel, and Tin Workers); craft unionism; SWOC (Steel Workers Organizing Committee)

AK Steel, 283, 284. *See also* ARMCO (American Rolling Mill Company)

Albert(s), Ira, 109, 160

Aliquippa Works (Jones & Laughlin Steel), 65, 102–3, 109, 230

Amalgamated Association of Iron, Steel, and Tin Workers (AA). *See* AA (Amalgamated Association of Iron, Steel, and Tin Workers)

American Federation of Labor (AFL). *See* AFL (American Federation of Labor)

American Iron and Steel Institute, 65, 66–67, 72, 93, 119, 121

American Legionnaires, 146, 150, 181, 212–14

American Liberty League, 62, 67, 121

American Rolling Mill Company (ARMCO). *See* ARMCO (American Rolling Mill Company)

American Sheet and Tin Plate Company (U.S. Steel), 43

Anderson, Hilding, 143, 237, 327n64

Anderson, Paul, 142, 196

antitrust laws, 66, 237

ArcelorMittal, 284

ARMCO (American Rolling Mill Company), 49, 59, 62, 109, 252, 278, 283, 369n22; as member of Little Steel, 20, 67; and SWOC organizing campaign, 114, 119. *See also* AK Steel

Associated Negro Press, 97

automation and mechanization, 23, 34–35, 258, 284, 296n36

back-pay liability, 256–63, 258*fig.*30, 271, 277–79, 364n25. *See also* NLRB (National Labor Relations Board); Wagner Act

steel industry, 28–32, 39, 41, 42, 45, 89–91, 314n51; and SWOC, 94–99, 110, 127, 134, 149, 162, 219–20, 245; and USW, 282

ethnic/immigrant groups, 28–32, 39, 41–42, 45, 89–91, 314n51

Fagan, Charles, 157–58
Fagan, Patrick, 83–84
Fansteel Metallurgical, 278
Fantasia, Rick, 245
Farr, Ruben, 70, 315n78
fascist groups, 307n65, 360n70
Federal Bureau of Investigation, 109
Filip, Zaki, 230
finishing mills, 15, 18–19, 22–24, 42, 51, 59
Fitch, John Andrews, 22, 24–25, 27–28, 33–34, 36, 37, 41
Fitzpatrick, John, 45
Flynn, Frank, 165–66
Fontechhio, Nick, 247
Ford hunger march, 56
Ford Motor Company, 56, 372n22
Fortunato, Fred, 232–33
Foster, William Z., 45–48, 50, 78, 80, 95, 112, 181, 246
Francisco, Leo, 143, 145, 327n64
Frick, Henry Clay, 15, 19, 22, 25, 102, 181
furnaces, 17–19, 21–23, 25, 29, 35–40

Galenson, Walter, 229, 244, 259
Gallagher, James, 86
Gallagher, Joseph, 172
Garrison, Lloyd, 195
Garvey, Marcus, 96
Gary, Elbert, 48
Gary Report (Bennett), 90
Gary Works (U.S. Steel), 38, 273
General Motors, 203; and CIO, 8, 77, 100, 115, 150, 203, 243; labor repression, 61; and SWOC, 151; strikes, 75, 100, 150, 316n80
Germano, Joe, 247
Girdler, Tom: congressional testimony, 63*fig.*3, 173; and Davey, 194; at Jones & Laughlin, 65, 102; on labor rights, 55, 63–66, 243, 244, 266; leadership of Little Steel, 63, 66, 67, 94, 195–96; and

Little Steel Strike, 119–21, 155, 169, 171, 189, 195–96, 203, 264, 287; and mediation board, 195–96; and Memorial Day Massacre, 135, 143, 146; on the New Deal, 55, 66, 68; and reopenings, 169; at Republic Steel, 62–68; and Roosevelt administration, 197, 203; and strike in Cleveland, 221; and strike in Warren and Niles, 163–64; and USW, 272–73
Girdlerism, 63, 66
Golden, Clinton "Clint," 84, 104*fig.*4, 112, 119
government relief, 53–54, 89–90, 238, 249, 259, 264, 277, 358n45, 359n54
Grace, Eugene, 22, 40, 62, 120, 186, 195, 200, 244, 269–70
Grajciar, John, 80, 86, 129, 264
Great Depression: economic and social issues, 6–7, 69–70, 78; employment statistics, 21; and labor relations, 22, 78; and labor repression, 55–57; "Roosevelt Recession," 115, 236, 241, 258; and steel industry, 50–54, 115, 241. *See also* New Deal
Great Migration, 88
Great Steel Strike, 45–48, 55, 80, 91, 109, 266
Green, William, 240
Guzman, Max, 134, 139

Halatek, Walter, 110
Halberg, Arvo Kusta. *See* Hall, Gus
Hall, Gus, 235*fig.*27; arrest and prosecution of, 176–77, 191, 234, 235*fig.* 27; background, 168–69; Burke comparison, 107; dismissal of by SWOC, 246–47; and Grajciar, 86; ideology and character of, 169; later life, 169; leadership of, 107, 168, 173–75, 178, 242, 243; Minneapolis general strike, 56; and Murray, 242; and Ohio National Guard, 208; Stolberg on, 243
Handley, Earl, 137, 142, 143, 144, 237, 327n64
Hardesty, Frank, 215
Hard Times (Terkel), 281
Harper, Harry, 135–36, 237

Kerrigan, Joe, 39
Ketchum, MacLeod & Grove, 189
Kilroy, Thomas, 135, 146
Kimbley, George, 108
King, (William Lyon) Mackenzie, 49
Knaggs, Daniel, 149–50
Koch, Kenneth, 107–8, 114
Kovach, Steve, 262–63
Krier, Henry, 203
Krzycki, Leo "Gene," 133

labor control, 13, 15, 19–20, 22–32, 35, 43,
47, 49, 54, 64, 78
Labor-Management Relations Act of 1947.
See Taft-Hartley Act
labor militancy: and AA, 82; Communist
Party, 178, 242, 246, 248; and company
propaganda, 46; and Great Depression,
69, 78; and Hall, 168–69, 242; in Little
Steel Strike, 8, 123, 127, 139, 168, 177, 181,
193, 219, 241, 246; and rank and file, 76,
77, 244; and SWOC leadership, 6, 8,
168, 177–78, 241–42, 246, 282; and
SWOC organizing campaign, 76, 98,
229, 287; and UMW, 87, 178; and
violence, 8, 193. See also mass picketing;
sabotage
labor relations: and class conflict, 278, 287;
and early steel industry, 17–19, 22; and
ethnic groups, 28–29; and Great
Depression, 54, 77–78; and legacy of
Little Steel Strike, 269–80; and New
Deal, 69–84, 276; and steel production,
16, 19–30, 33–41
labor repression, 13, 16, 26, 36, 41–48,
55–57, 59–62, 87, 100, 102, 113–16, 161,
229, 266, 271
labor rights: and black workers, 97; and
First World War, 44; limits of, 9, 276;
and Little Steel, 62, 64–65; and Little
Steel Strike, 5–6, 161, 167, 190, 251–68,
276, 286–87; and New Deal, 70–73, 78,
79; and NIRA, 57, 67, 70–73, 81;
opposition to, 276; and right to strike,
264–65, 273, 279; and Second World
War, 269–70, 271–73; and violence,
8–9, 56–57, 61, 161, 167, 190, 193; and
Wagner Act, 74–75, 251–53, 261, 264,

266–68. See also NIRA (National
Industrial Recovery Act); NLRB
(National Labor Relations Board);
Wagner Act
La Follette, Robert M., Jr., 55, 65, 138, 140,
143
La Follette Committee: back-to-work
movements and citizens' groups, 188;
Becker, Martin, 172; Berger strike
violence, 58; and company espionage,
108–9; on cost of Little Steel Strike,
235–36; and Girdler, 65, 66; influence,
115, 116; on injuries and deaths, 140–43,
230–31, 355n1; Jones, Dewey, 221; on
loyal employees, 135; and Memorial Day
Massacre, 134–35, 138, 140–43, 266;
and munitions, 60–61; on nature of
Little Steel Strike, 68, 120, 128–29, 229,
265–66; on Ohio National Guard,
206–7; and private police, 60, 153; on
public-relations firms, 191–92; purpose
of, 55–56; on relations among steel
companies, 66; and Shields, Daniel,
183–84; Stop 5 riot, 159, 160; on strike
in Johnstown, 128–29; on strike in
Massillon, 213, 217; and union violence,
174–75, 234
Lahey, Edwin, 125, 127–28, 193
Lapin, Adam, 154, 172
Law and Order League, 187–88, 189,
212–13
Lawyers Vigilance Committee, 67
Leverich (Leurich), Nicholas, 136
Levin, Meyer, 134
Lewis, John L.: and AA, 82; and AFL, 65,
76, 82; and CIO, 76–77; and
Communist Party, 86; and Girdler, 65,
195; Green on, 240; ideology and
character of, 76, 84, 101, 241, 244, 247;
Lynd on, 244; and mediation board,
195; and Memorial Day Massacre, 145;
and Murray, 243; and Republic lawsuit,
237; and Roosevelt administration,
202, 355n3; and steel industry, 77, 81;
and strike in Johnstown, 199; and
SWOC, 82–84, 87; and sympathy
strikes, 180; and Taylor, 101
Lippert, Orlando, 141, 142

McGrady, Edward, 195
McKeowan, Jack, 105
McKinney, Ernest Rice, 97
mechanization and automation, 23, 34–35, 258, 284, 296n36
mediation board, 195–96, 197, 200–201, 202–3
Mellon family, 40, 66
Memorial Day Massacre: and CIO tactics, 134, 144–45; and Communist Party, 138, 139–40, 143, 145, 146; and ethnic/immigrant groups, 144; events of, 1–2, 133–37; justifications for, 137–40, 142–43, 146; and La Follette Committee, 134–35, 138, 140–43, 266; legacy of, 3, 5, 281–82, 287; legal consequences of, 134–35, 138, 140–43, 266; media coverage of, 141–42; number and composition of demonstrators, 1, 133, 134, 138; overview, 1–3; photographs of, xii*fig*.1, 136*fig*.9; political reactions to, 145–46; strikers' reactions to, 144–46; victims of, 135–37, 143, 145, 231*fig*.26, 327n64. *See also* Chicago Police Department
Metzgar, Jack, 41
Metzgar, Johnny, 41, 52–53
Midvale Steel Company, 302n102
Mike, George, 230, 354n1
mini-mills, 282–83, 373n8
Minneapolis general strike, 56
Mitch, William, 84, 104*fig*.4
Mohawk Valley Formula, 56–57, 265–66
Montgomery, Oliver, 90
Mooney, James, 132–33, 135, 140, 146
Morgan family, 40, 66
Morton, Joe, 171, 217–18, 233
Murphy, Frank, 149–50, 151
Murray, Philip: and back-pay remedies, 262–63; and black workers, 95; and CIO leadership, 270, 274; and Communist Party, 86, 246; and ERPs, 92–93; and government interventions, 270; ideology and character of, 84, 169, 178, 244, 275; and legal actions, 246; and Lewis, 243; and mediation board, 195–96, 200; and militant tactics, 169, 177–78, 242; and Mohawk Valley

Formula, 265; and NLRB, 253; Republic lawsuit, 237; and Second World War, 270, 274–75; and SWOC leadership, 83–85, 87, 92, 103, 112, 120, 121, 124–25, 241–44, 246; and UMW, 82–84, 87, 248–49; and U.S. Steel, 103, 104*fig*.4, 120, 123–25; and Weirton Steel strike, 101

N&G Taylor Plant (Republic Steel), 167, 187, 211, 233, 260
NAACP (National Association for the Advancement of Colored People). *See* National Association for the Advancement of Colored People
NAM (National Association of Manufacturers), 56, 66, 73, 93, 121, 187, 189, 265, 276
National Association for the Advancement of Colored People (NAACP), 95
National Association of Manufacturers (NAM). *See* NAM (National Association of Manufacturers)
National Committee for Organizing Iron and Steel Workers, 45, 47, 48, 83
National Conference of Negro Organizations to Support the Steel Drive, 95
National Guard: and CIO, 207, 241–42; Indiana National Guard, 223–24; and Little Steel, 60; Michigan National Guard, 151; Pennsylvania National Guard, 186; strikebreaking role, 203, 204–10, 241, 245, 265–67; and Wagner Act, 266–67. *See also* Ohio National Guard
National Industrial Council, 94
National Industrial Information Committee, 94
National Industrial Recovery Act (NIRA). *See* NIRA (National Industrial Recovery Act)
National Labor Board (NLB), 71–72
National Labor Relations Act of 1935. *See* Wagner Act
National Labor Relations Board (first), 70–73, 71, 81, 195. *See also* NLRB (National Labor Relations Board)

National Labor Relations Board (NLRB).
See NLRB (National Labor Relations
Board)
National Lawyers Committee, 67
National Mediation Act, 195
National Metal Trades Association, 109
National Negro Congress, 95, 96
National Recovery Administration
(NRA), 72, 81. See also NIRA
(National Industrial Recovery Act)
National Steel Company, 20, 51, 52, 59, 62,
72–73, 369n22. See also Weirton Steel
National Steel Labor Relations Board, 81
National Urban League, 95
National War Labor Board (first), 44, 47,
49
National War Labor Board (WLB), 270,
271–72, 274, 275
Nelson, Bruce, 98
Nelson, Catherine, 137, 237
Ness, Eliot, 222
New Deal: Brinkley on, 7; and CIO, 180,
193–94, 202, 241, 274; and corporate
power, 7, 67–68, 181–202, 276; and
Girdler, 55, 66, 68; and industrial
capitalism, 4, 6, 7, 70; and labor rights,
70–73, 78, 79; and Little Steel, 55, 62,
66–68, 92, 121; and Little Steel Strike,
3, 5–7, 9, 121, 192–203, 274; nature and
limits of, 7, 9, 70, 78, 181; and NIRA,
57, 70, 75; opposition to, 62, 64, 94, 121,
189, 275–77, 283; and SWOC, 91–92,
100, 114–16, 193–94, 202, 241; and U.S.
Steel, 92, 101; and Wagner Act, 3,
73–75, 102, 251, 276. See also Great
Depression; Roosevelt administration;
Wagner Act
Newell, Barbara, 249
Newton Steel (Republic Steel), 128fig.8,
147–52, 151fig.11, 152fig.12
Niles plant (Republic Steel): beginning of
Little Steel Strike at, 126–27, 237;
general strike involving, 178–79;
NLRB remedies involving, 257, 259,
261; persistence of strike at, 224–25,
257, 261; reopening, 198, 204, 209; siege
of, 161–70, 173–74, 177, 178, 187, 198,
242. See also Hall, Gus; Warren Works

NIRA (National Industrial Recovery Act),
57, 67, 70, 73–75, 77, 80
NLB (National Labor Board), 71–72
NLRB (National Labor Relations Board):
and ARMCO, 252; and Bethlehem
Steel, 260, 261, 270–71, 272; and CIO,
253–54, 274, 277, 278; conservative
reforms of, 269, 276–80; creation of, 73,
81, 310n47; demands that SWOC rely
on, 191, 199; efficacy of, 7, 251, 261–68,
272; and ERPs, 100, 254, 255, 256, 260;
and espionage, 108; and Inland Steel,
114, 253–54, 260, 261, 272, 277; and
Jones & Laughlin Steel, 103; and labor
militancy, 266–68; and Little Steel, 4,
5, 6, 7, 247, 251–68, 276, 287; and Little
Steel Strike, 7, 194, 199, 200, 223, 269;
and Murray, 253; remedies, 261–68; and
Republic Steel, 113, 216, 217, 236, 255–
60, 255fig.29, 258fig.30, 261–64, 265–67,
271; and Youngstown Sheet & Tube,
114, 236, 260–61, 272; structure and
powers of, 74, 252–53; SWOC reliance
on, 8, 88, 100, 116, 274. See also back-pay
liability; NLRB v. Jones & Laughlin
Steel; Taft-Hartley Act; Wagner Act
NLRB v. Jones & Laughlin Steel, 3, 7, 67,
68, 75, 77, 102, 103, 115, 121, 251, 268
Norris-LaGuardia Act, 267
NRA (National Recovery
Administration), 72, 81. See also NIRA
(National Industrial Recovery Act)

Occhipinti, John, 39
O'Connor, Harvey, 53, 80, 244
Ohio National Guard, 176, 179, 179fig.18,
197–99, 202; in Canton, 203, 207, 208,
230, 232, 346n130; in Cleveland, 203,
218, 219fig.24; and death of striker, 207,
230; espionage of, 208–9; in greater
Youngstown, 176, 179, 179fig.18, 187–88,
197–98, 202–5, 205fig.22, 206fig.23,
207–9, 232; La Follette Committee on,
206–7; in Massillon, 203, 212–13,
216–18; strikebreaking role, 204, 206–
10, 232, 241–42; strike expenses, 235
Ohio State Police, 8
Ohio Works (U.S. Steel), 39

.